The History of the

VIRGINIA
FEDERAL CONVENTION
of
1788

The History of the
VIRGINIA
FEDERAL CONVENTION
of
1788

Hugh Blair Grigsby

Two Volumes in One

DA CAPO PRESS · NEW YORK · 1969

A Da Capo Press Reprint Edition

This Da Capo Press edition of *The History of the Virginia Federal Convention of 1788* is an unabridged republication in one volume of the two-volume first edition published in Richmond, Virginia, in 1890 as New Series, Vol. IX, of the Collections of the Virginia Historical Society.

Library of Congress Catalog Card Number 70-75319

Published by Da Capo Press
A Division of Plenum Publishing Corporation
227 West 17th Street
New York, N. Y. 10011

Printed in the United States of America

The History of the

VIRGINIA
FEDERAL CONVENTION

of

1788

THE HISTORY

OF THE

Virginia Federal Convention

OF

1788,

WITH SOME ACCOUNT OF THE EMINENT VIRGINIANS OF
THAT ERA WHO WERE MEMBERS OF THE BODY

BY

HUGH BLAIR GRIGSBY, LL.D.

WITH A

Biographical Sketch of the Author

AND

ILLUSTRATIVE NOTES

EDITED BY

R. A. BROCK,

Corresponding Secretary and Librarian of the Society.

VOL. I.

RICHMOND, VIRGINIA.
PUBLISHED BY THE SOCIETY.
MDCCCXCI.

EMENDATION.

The message referred to on p. ix, line 12, may have been one of Jefferson Davis', President of the Confederate States of America.

BIOGRAPHICAL SKETCH

OF

Hon. Hugh Blair Grigsby, LL.D.

The pure, devoted and earnest life of Hugh Blair Grigsby was a beneficent one, and signal in its incitations. Few, if any, among his contemporaries exerted a more inspiring influence in the cause of education and in behalf of virtuous resolve in Virginia than he ; not one, certainly, in glowing utterance, and in appealing picture, sounded more surely the key-note of State grandeur and the common weal.

Justly remarked the late venerable and admirable Marshall P. Wilder,[a] in his last penned effort, on his couch, in his last days—an address to be delivered before the New England Historic Genealogical Society, upon the completion of nineteen years' service as the president of that learned body, at its annual meeting in 1887 : " Recall the traditions of men ; each generation in its day bears testimony to the character of the preceding. He who worships the past believes we are connected not only with those that came before us, but with those who are to come after. What means those hieroglyphic inscriptions on the Egyptian monuments ? Says one of them : ' I speak to you who shall come a million of years after my death.' Another says, ' Grant that my words may live for hundreds and thousands of years.' The writers were evidently thinking, not only of their own time, but of the distant future of the human race, and hoped, themselves, never to be forgotten."

a Hon. Marshall Pinckney Wilder was born September 28, 1798, and died at Boston, Mass., March 16, 1886.

Hugh Blair Grigsby was born in the city of Norfolk, Virginia, November 22d, 1806, and died at his seat, "Edgehill," Charlotte county, Virginia, April 28, 1881. He was the son of Benjamin Grigsby, who was born in Orange county, September 18, 1770, and was a pupil of Rev. William Graham, at old Liberty Hall Academy, the precursor of the present Washington and Lee University. Among his fellow-students was Archibald Alexander, the subsequently eminent divine, and who was his companion when in early manhood they sought their life-work in a horseback journey to Southside Virginia. Leaving his companion in Petersburg, Grigsby, "with his sole personal possessions in a pair of saddle-bags," continued his solitary ride to Norfolk, where he located, and was the first pastor of the first Presbyterian church in that then borough. Here he married Elizabeth, daughter of Hugh and Lilias (Blair) McPherson, and providentially and faithfully labored until, as is recorded on the handsome marble obelisk erected to his memory in Trinity churchyard, Portsmouth, Virginia, "in the faithful discharge of his calling, he fell a martyr to yellow-fever on the 6th of October, 1810."[b] His widow married, secondly, January 16th,

---

[b] The paternal ancestor of Hugh Blair Grigsby is said to have emigrated from England to Virginia in 1660. His grandfather, the immediate progenitor of the Grigsbys of Rockingham county, John Grigsby, was born in Stafford county in 1720; accompanied, in 1740, Lawrence Washington in the forces of Admiral Vernon in the expedition against Carthagena; married first, in 1746, a Miss Etchison and settled on the Rapid Anne river in Culpeper county. His wife dying in 1762, he married secondly in 1764, Elizabeth, daughter of Benjamin and Ann (Campbell) Porter, of Orange county, Virginia. The issue by the first marriage was five children, the eldest of whom was James Grigsby, born November 10th, 1748. The issue of the second marriage was nine children, the youngest of whom was Captain Reuben Grigsby, born June 6th, 1780, in Rockbridge county; educated at Washington College; teacher; farmer; member of the House of Delegates of Virginia; Captain United States Army in the war of 1812; sheriff of Rockbridge county; trustee of Washington College 1830-43; died February 6th, 1863. (See obituary, *Richmond Enquirer*, February 10th, 1863). An interesting incident in the boyhood of James Grigsby has been transmitted. Whilst hunting with a pack of hounds near the Natural Bridge in 1781, he encountered the French tourist, the Marquis de Chastellux, and was his guide to the Bridge, and prevailed upon him to become the guest of his father. These attentions the Marquis records in his

1817, Dr. Nathan Colgate Whitehead[c] (born in Southampton county, Virginia, April 8th, 1792,) who, although educated as a physician, relinquished practice and was for twenty-seven years the honored president of the Farmers Bank of Virginia, in Norfolk. He died in 1856. Hon. John B. Whitehead, ex-mayor of Norfolk is the issue of this marriage. In connection with the prime service of Rev. Benjamin Grigsby as founder of the first Presbyterian church in Norfolk, it may be pleasing to add a singular exemplification of pious constancy and fealty, as recently communicated to the writer by Mr. Whitehead. He writes : " From the completion of the building of the first and only Presbyterian church in the borough of Norfolk, in 1802, to the present time, the elements for the communion service in our church have been presented by the mother and grandmother of Mr. Grigsby and the writer ; by our grandmother until 1822, and by our mother up to December, 1860 ; and by my wife to the present time, and, with the exception of three years (during the period of the late war) have been furnished from our old home (in which I reside) from the year 1808. I would also state that the Wednesday evening prayer-meetings were held in our parlors from 1808 to 1827, in which last year the late distinguished scholar and jurist, William Maxwell, LL.D. (long the effi-

---

"Travels," of which he presented a handsomely bound copy to his youthful guide and entertainer. James Grigsby married twice, first, in 1768, Frances Porter, the sister of the second wife of his father, and settled at "Fancy Hill," Rockbridge county. Their eldest son, the father of Hugh Blair Grigsby, was christened Benjamin Porter Grigsby, but appears to have omitted the use of the second name. He was a trustee of Washington College 1796-1807.

Among the descendants of John Grigsby were the following officers in the Confederate States Army :

Generals E. Frank Paxton, Albert Gallatin Jenkins and J. Warren Grigsby, Colonel Andrew Jackson Grigsby, and Major Andrew Jackson Paxton.

The editor is indebted to Miss Mary Davidson, Lexington, Va., of the Grigsby lineage, for the facts embraced in this note.

c The Whitehead is a family of early seating in Virginia. Thomas Whitehead was granted 162 acres of land in Hampton parish, York county, March 6, 1653. Book No. 3, page 9. Robert Whitehead, John Bowles and Charles Edmond were granted 3,000 acres in New Kent county, March 25, 1667. Book No. 6, page 45.

cient Corresponding Secretary and Librarian of the Virginia Historical Society), one of the elders, built for the use of the increased congregation a beautiful edifice for the purpose."

Hugh Blair Grigsby in youth was of delicate constitution, and it was feared that he would be an early victim to pulmonary disease, but prudence and systematic physical exercise on his part happily surmounted the dread tendency, and ensured to a green old age a life of abounding usefulness. He was a studious lad. Among his early tutors were Mr. William Lacy, of Prince Edward county, and the Rev. W. W. Duncan, the father of the late eloquent divine and honored president of Randolph-Macon College, Rev. James A. Duncan, D. D. He subsequently entered Yale College, remained two years, and gained creditable distinction in his studies and in versification. He took here, among other studies, the law course, with the view of making it his profession. This design he was constrained to relinquish because of an increasing infirmity—deafness—which continued through life. His bias for biography was early evinced. There is preserved by his family a volume in MS., written in his eighteenth year, giving sketches of the character, personal appearance and social traits of the distinguished of Virginian statesmen and clergy with whose careers he had become most familiar. Through special predilection, as was markedly evinced, he embarked in journalism, and became the editor and owner of the *Norfolk Beacon*, upon which he was wont often to say he did the work of two or three persons much of the time during the six years that he conducted the newspaper. His editorials were all written in a standing posture at his desk, and his daily hours of labor were often a majority of the twenty-four. Such earnest application met its reward in a comfortable competency of $60,000, with which he retired from the paper, a step, indeed, which his physical condition indicated as judicious, as his lungs seemed to be seriously threatened. He now devoted himself to athletic exercises, and acquired quite a proficiency as a boxer and a pedestrian.

It is noteworthy that he accomplished a journey on foot to Massachusetts, through several of the New England States and the lower portions of Canada, and back to Virginia.

In the midst of his arduous editorial labors, he found variation in service in the legislative halls of his State. He was a member of the House of Delegates from Norfolk in 1829 and 1830, and during the term served also as a member of that constellation of talent, the Virginia Convention of 1829-'30, succeeding in that eminent body General Robert Barraud Taylor, who resigned his seat. That his selection for this responsible representation was judicious, his subsequent manifestations gave just evidence. It is narrated of him that "an argument advanced by him, and published in the *Richmond Enquirer* under the signature of 'Virginiensis,' in reply to Sir William Harcourt in an article on international law, under the signature of 'Hortensius,' in the *London Times*, was afterwards substantially incorporated in a message of President Buchanan."

Mr. Grigsby married, November 19th, 1840, Miss Mary Venable, daughter of Colonel Clement Carrington, of "Edgehill," Charlotte county, who was the son of the distinguished jurist, Paul Carrington the elder, and a battle-scarred veteran of the Revolutionary War. Colonel Carrington, after having served first, at an early age, in several expeditions of the State line in Virginia, joined as a cadet the legion of Light-Horse Harry Lee of Greene's army. At the age of nineteen he fought bravely at the bloody battle of Eutaw, where he was struck down by a severe and dangerous wound in the thigh. He faithfully served as a just and impartial magistrate of his county for more than fifty years. He died November 28th, 1847, aged eighty-five years. From the period of his marriage until the death of Colonel Carrington, Mr. Grigsby made his home in Charlotte county. After that event he removed temporarily to Norfolk, but returned to "Edgehill," the patrimonial estate of Mr. Grigsby, upon which he henceforth resided until his death. Here, in the bosom of his loving family and in the midst of constant and admiring friends, he led a peaceful and contentful life, and yet with a marked exemplification of varied usefulness and moral and intellectual influence. The habits of systematic application, enforced and stimulated by necessity in youth, together with impelling predisposition and acute mental gifts, eminently fitted him for historical research, the results of which was an extensive mass of information which made him not only the select medium of voicing the consensus of chaste and reverential sentiment on momentous occasions, but quickened him alike in mental and physical action in the requirements of everyday life. Not only did his active being find time for an extensive correspondence with scholars of varied culture, historical students, statesmen, and the votaries of science; the frequent delivery of chaste and eloquent orations, but he found time withal to conduct with singular sagacity and providence the operations of a large plantation. As a friend and neighbor narrates[d]: "In planning and executing improvements, constructing a dyke of some three miles in length, arranging the ditches of his extensive low-grounds, so that a heavy rain fall could be easily disposed of, and bringing all into a high state of cultivation, he set an example of industry and energy which every farmer would do well to emulate. He had ample means, and we have sometimes heard his efforts characterized as fanciful or Utopian. But the result shows method, skill and industry ; the process was necessarily laborious, but the result was grand." Of his prided engineering achievements in behalf of agriculture, a venerable and revered friend has taken pleasing cognizance, as will be subsequently noted. The simplicity of character of Mr. Grigsby rendered him averse to any appearance of ostentation. He was considerate and careful in his ordinary expenditures, but amply provident in every circumstance of hospitality. His welcome was as spontaneous as his nature was genial, and his mind far-reaching and comprehensive. With the tenderest of instincts and with sympathies immediately responsive to truth, socially it was not otherwise than for him to be delightsome. His just economy gave his nobility of character ampler scope for beneficent exemplification. It allowed the means for the purchase of books and the encouragement of the arts, and thus, too, in collected treasures was afforded a warming and directing impetus towards the intellectual development of his neighbors and his kind. With heart and mind acutely sensitive to impressions of merit and conceptions of worth, his being was an expanding treasure-house of all and aught of value and virtue of which it had or might have cognizance.

Lingering reverently in the glorious walks of the past, with an instinct born of purity, and a mental grasp only possible in emulous affection, he proudly held in mirrored brightness to the contemplation of his fellows of this generation the moral worth

---

[d] Leonard Cox, Esq., editor and proprietor of *The Charlotte Gazette*, in the issue of his paper of May 12, 1881.

and glory of the past, as he conjured, to our mind's eye, in tenderness and reverence, in vivid reality, the forms of our fathers, whose deeds gave it value. Such a man, such a master-mind, systematically trained to the requirements of the present, constantly alive to enlightened progress, mental and material, could but invoke ennobling and healthful impulse—incarnation as he was of the Christian, the scholar and the patriot.

His whole being seemed a sensitive cluster of clinging tendrils, which ever sought to grasp and twine themselves about some object or action of the past to be cherished. Ennobling as he was in his warming conceptions, stimulating as he was in his glowingly pictured lessons, his being found vent also in exemplification, if less brilliant, yet scarcely less enduringly useful. "Man is a naturally acquisitive animal." Scarce one of us with an object or aim in life, it has been urged, but who is in some sense a "collector." The value of the collector is patent in the only satisfactory elucidation of the past yielded by its records, its monuments, and specially by the familiar belongings—the concomitants and appliances of every-day life—of our kind who have preceded us.

Mr. Grigsby was possessed with an insatiable fondness for and enthusiastic eagerness to possess, to hold as his own, not only the works of the great, the good, and the gifted—books, works of art, and objects of curious interest and beauty—but also souvenirs of possession, objects that had been loved and used by those worthy of his love. His library, for which he had constructed a separate building peculiarly adapted to the purpose, numbered some six thousand volumes in the varied branches of literature, in which probably the ancient classics and history and biography predominated. Many of the volumes were singularly endeared to him because they had belonged to and been lovingly conned by predecessors of worth and learning. It contained many volumes from the choice library of the erratic John Randolph, of Roanoke, to the auction sale of which Mr. Grigsby, with much self-satisfaction, liked to tell that he trudged on foot. The relics treasured by him were many and varied. Perhaps as endeared·as any, approaching the claim to a collection, was that of canes which had belonged to great men and cherished associates, or had grown in spot historic and sacred. These supporting staffs he was, with jealous impartiality to the memory of the donor or departed friend, in the habit of using in turn, thus one day he was assisted in his walks with the cane of a loved uncle, Reuben Grigsby, another with that of his revered friend, Governor Tazewell, another with a staff from the Mount of Olives, and so on through more than a score of reverential exercises.

Every available space of the walls of his dwelling and library were covered with beautiful and choice paintings, and every nook and appropriate niche was graced with a piece of statuary —busts of the great and good, or idealic creations.

He did much, if not more than any other man, to foster the genius of our lamented Virginia artist, Alexander Galt,[e] and

e His ancestry is said to have been of Norman origin, and the name originally Fitz Gaultier. They were brought with other Normans to Scotland in the twelfth century to instruct the natives in military tactics, and lands were granted them at Galston (*quasi* Galtstown) in Ayreshire. The immediate ancestor of the Galts of Tidewater Virginia was a Covenanter. Two of them were banished as Presbyterians to Virginia by the Scotch Privy Council with Lord Cardross, about 1680. One married the daughter of a wealthy planter, the other returned to Scotland after the Revolution of 1688 and was the ancestor of the well-known writer, John Galt. Alexander, the second son and fourth child of Dr. Alexander and Mary Sylvester (Jeffery) Galt, was born in Norfolk, Virginia, January 26, 1827. His talent first exhibited itself at fifteen years of age when he began to draw pencil portraits. His next advance was in carving in alabaster and conchilia, and he executed many faithful portraits in cameo. In 1848, he went to Florence, Italy, for instruction in art, and in a short time was awarded the highest prize then offered for drawing. He returned to Virginia, bringing several pieces of his work. The "Virginia" was his first ideal bust. He remained in America several years, visiting in the while the Southern States and executing a number of orders. At the State Fair held in Charleston, S. C., he received prizes for work exhibited there. He returned to Florence in 1856, with many orders, among them one from the State of Virginia for a statue of Thomas Jefferson, which preceded him on his return to Virginia in 1860, and now adorns the Library Hall of the University of Virginia. A Virginian in every pulse and instinct, he naturally tendered his service to the mother State in the rupture of the Union, and was first connected with the Engineer Corps near Norfolk in planning fortifications. Later he served on the staff of Governor Letcher. In the winter of 1862 he visited the camp of General T. J. Jackson in execution of some commission—but with the design also of studying the features of the great chieftain to prepare him for the making of a statue: He unfortunately contracted, during this visit, small-pox, from which he died in Richmond, January 19, 1863. His remains rest in

possessed a number of his choicest works, among them being
" Columbus," " Sappho," " Psyche," and " Bacchante."

The gentle, loving heart of Mr. Grigsby went out to all things
animate, and with a keen sense of the beauties of nature his admiration found grateful expression in pen and converse. " His
loving nature," as his fondly cherished wife writes, " made pets
of animals and birds," and was especially demonstrative " to
little children, whose clear infantile voices reached his impaired
hearing more distinctly than did the tones of adults." " A
scholar, and a ripe and good one," his commune with his books
was daily, with every moment to be spared from active demands
and social claims. " He was a rapid reader, and read with pen
in hand. With French and Latin authors he was in as constant
communion as with the writers of his own tongue."[f] Although
his infirmity rendered conversation with him difficult, yet his
own discourse, in its easy dignity and range of digested information, was singularly entertaining, lightened, too, as it was with
frequent ripples of playful fancy, and made piquant with a vein
of quiet humor which often found striking expression.

Mr. Grigsby was a devout and earnest Christian, and a wor-
shipper in the forms of his Presbyterian ancestors, and for years
had been in the habit of leading the regular devotions of his
household. "Although his name was not on the church book,"
he "was a punctual and large contributor to his minister's salary."
He possessed the faculty of chaste versification in a striking degree, and some of his productions are as impressive as were the
powers of his gift of oratory. His absolute trust in his Maker
is touchingly exemplified in the following :

Hollywood Cemetery. A number of his ideal works were stored in
the warehouse of a friend in Richmond, and were destroyed in the conflagration of April 3, 1865, incident on the evacuation of the city. His
meritorious works which are extant probably number two-score or
more, and include, with the statue of Jefferson, busts of eminent men
and chaste and beautiful ideal creations. Representative ancestors of
Alexander Galt in several generations have reflected lustre on the
medical profession in Virginia, and been most beneficently connected
with her asylums for the unfortunate insane. The editor is indebted to
Miss Mary Jeffery Galt, the niece and heir of the subject of this note,
for the details embodied.

f " In Memoriam," by Rev. H. C. Alexander, D. D., LL.D., Hampden-
Sydney College, Va., *Central Presbyterian*, Dec. 14, 1881.

HYMN.

Written on the morning of the 22d of November, 1877, when I entered
my seventy-second year.   H. B. G.

I.

Lord of the flaming orbs of space!
  Lord of the Ages that are gone!
Lord of the teeming years to come—
  Who sitt'st on Thy Sovereign Throne :

II.

Look down in Mercy and in Grace
  On a poor creature of a Day,
Whose mortal course is nearly run,
  Who looks to THEE, his only stay.

III.

In Thee, in Thee alone, O Lord!
  Thine aged Servant puts his Trust
Thro' the blest passion of Thy Son,
  Ere his frail frame returns to dust.

IV.

Uphold him thro' Earth's devious ways—
  Sustain him by Thy gracious Power;
And may the Glory of Thy Praise
  Break from his lips in Life's last Hour.

V.

Grant the dear Pledges of Thy Love,
  Thy mercy has vouchsaf'd to him—
PEACE in the shadow of Thine Ark—
  REST 'neath Thy shelt'ring Cherubim.

VI.

Lord, heed Thy servant's grateful praise
  For all the mercies Thou hast given :—
For Health and Friends and length of Days—
  Thy bleeding Son—a promised Heaven.

VII.

Oh! may he live in fear of Thee—
  Oh! may he rest upon Thy Love,
When he shall cross that stormy Sea
  That keeps him from his Home above.

VIII.

Oh! bless those lov'd ones of his Heart,
    While ling'ring on Earth's lonely Shore,
'Till we shall meet no more to part,
    And chant Thy Praises evermore.

What a triumphant refrain is this:

I CANNOT DIE.
John xi, 26.

BY FORTH WINTHROP. *g*

Time may glide by—
My pale wan face may show the waste of years;
My failing eyes fill with unbidden tears;—
    But I'll ne'er die!

Fierce agony,
That racks, by night and day, the mortal frame,
May leave of life aught but the empty name;
    But I'll ne'er die!

The Sea's hoarse cry
May shake the shore; and the wild toppling waves
May open wide for me their welt'ring graves—
    But I'll ne'er die!

---

g Mr. Grigsby, in reading the "Life and Letters of John Winthrop," the first Governor of Massachusetts, by the Hon. Robert C. Winthrop, LL.D., was particularly attracted by the sketch of Forth Winthrop's brief career, and has affixed his name to these verses in memoriam, and in token, it may also be taken, to the admirable friend who had piously perpetuated the memory of his young relative of so many preceding generations.

Forth Winthrop, was the third son of Governor John Winthrop. He was born on the 30th of December, 1609, at Great Stambridge, in Essex county, England, where his mother's family—the Forths—resided. He was prepared for college at the somewhat celebrated school founded by Edward VI, at Bury St. Edmunds, and entered Emanuel College, Cambridge, in 1627. After finishing his course at the University, he had engaged himself to his cousin, Ursula Sherman, and was contemplating marriage before following his father to New England. But a sudden illness terminated fatally, and the parish register at Groton records his burial on the 23d day of November, 1630. He was a young man of great promise, and his letters, while he was at school and at college, betoken him as one of the most affectionate of sons and brothers.

True Chivalry,
That bathes with patriot blood th' embattled plain,
May count my mangled corse among the slain—
But I'll ne'er die!

Around may lie,
In grassy mound, or 'neath the sculptured stone,
The dear fresh dead, and those that long have gone—
But I'll ne'er die!

Love's moisten'd eye
May watch the falling lip—the gasp for breath—
And all the sad investiture of Death—
But I'll ne'er die!

My friends may sigh,
As the house fills; and as with sable plume
The Hearse leads forth the cavalcade of gloom—
But I'll ne'er die!

All silently
Around the new-made grave my friends may crowd,
And my dear young and precious old be bow'd—
But I'll ne'er die!

As Ages ply
Their round, my shape may vanish from the land,
With those that felt the pressure of my hand—
But I'll ne'er die!

I soon must lie
Beneath the lid; and the triumphant worm
May revel on my frail and prostrate form—
But I'll ne'er die!

Full solemnly
Kind friends may place me in the narrow cell,
And in soft tones utter the last farewell—
But I'll ne'er die!

Unconsciously
My name my dearest friends will cease to call,
And the loud laugh ring in my own old hall—
But I'll ne'er die!

LIFE'S VICTORY
Is mine! I wear the CONQU'ROR'S wreath,
Thro' HIM who drew the fatal sting of Death—
How can I die?

In upper sky,
Clothed in the shining robes of Sov'reign Grace,
As 'mid Heav'n's hosts I hail my Saviour's face—
O! who can die?

That symphony,
Sounding from Earth to Heav'n responsively,
Exalts me here; "HE THAT BELIEVES IN ME
CAN NEVER DIE."

November, 1876.

Among the many of the poetic compositions of Mr. Grigsby, printed and in MS., an ode to Horace Binney, the "Nestor of the American Bar," on the completion of the ninety-third year of his age, and "Lines to my Daughter on her Fourteenth Birthday," may be noted. The latter, a pamphlet of sixteen 8vo pages, breathes a spirit of tender affection, of lofty patriotism, and of fervent piety.

Mr. Grigsby became the President of the Virginia Historical Society January 3d, 1870,[h] succeeding that profound scholar and eminent statesman, William Cabell Rives. Mr. Grigsby had for many years given essential and earnest service in support of the Society, and was, in truth, one of the vital springs of its continued existence.

He it was to first propose a hall, a safe repository of its own for the preservation of its treasures, and this hope and object he fondly cherished and fostered assiduously to his latest moment. Of his invaluable contributions to its mission, those herein listed, with others of his historical productions, are permanent memorials in the annals of American literature.

Of the inestimable value of his services in behalf of the venerable institution of learning, William and Mary College, the second in foundation in America, the action of its Board of Visitors and Governors will bear best attestation. Of this object of his fervent and constant regard, in the fullness of his heart he said: "The names of her sons have become national property, and their fame illustrates the brightest pages of our country's history."

---

h He had at a previous period been proffered the post of Corresponding Secretary and Librarian, to succeed William Maxwell, LL.D., but the demands of a large plantation and domestic claims properly forbade his acceptance of the trust.

Two features of the college to which he contributed survive in their offices for good.

He contributed, in 1870, $1,000 to the Library Fund, and in 1871 founded with a gift of a like sum the "Chancellor Scholarship."

In an address delivered by the Rev. William Stoddert, D. D.,[1] in the Chapel of William and Mary College, on the 3d of July, 1876, he made this touching mention :

" The speaker of last night gave some instances of men who had won success in spite of obstacles apparently insurmountable—he mentioned the blind professor of optics at Oxford ; Ziska, the Bohemian general, and Milton, both blind ; Prescott, nearly so ; Byron and Scott, both lame ; Beethoven, deaf ; and, continuing, said : I might, in this connection, allude to one still nearer, even within these walls, although my words do not reach him. I might speak of his style, with its exquisite attractiveness ; of his historic research, which has divined the hidden springs of human movement ; of his mind, moulded by classic models until, even in ordinary conversation, his sentences are replete with elegance and strength ; of the charm of his narration, beautified by the graces which have given immortality to Herodotus and Zenophon, to Livy and Tacitus ; whose intellect seems still to brighten as

---

[1] Rev. William Stoddert, D. D. (whose paternal name was legally changed in early manhood); born 1824; died 1886; was the son of Dr. Thomas Ewell, of Prince William County, Va., a loved and distinguished practitioner of medicine; the brother of Richard S. Ewell. Lieutenant-General C. S. Army, and of Colonel Benjamin S. Ewell, LL.D., President Emeritus of William and Mary College after quite two-score years of devoted service as instructor and President. Dr. Stoddert was graduated from Hampden-Sidney College and the Union Theological Seminary, ordained in the Presbyterian Church, and became a most successful preacher, popular lecturer, and esteemed teacher in Tennessee. William and Mary College conferred on him, on the occasion above, the degree of D. D.

After a period of suspension it is most gratifying to note that the grand old college of William and Mary has resumed its useful functions under the able and energetic presidency of the Hon. Lyon G. Tyler, son of a former Chancellor, John Tyler, President of the United States. The number of students in attendance was last reported as 120, with the prospect of increase. With its proud prestige, advantages in healthful and central location, it may be hoped that its expanding usefulness may be even greater and more influential than in any period of its glorious past.

years roll on; whose learning still increases, whose memory still improves, and who is cut off from the sweet converse of friends, so that these words can be uttered as though he were absent, before the Chancellor of William and Mary College, Doctor Hugh Blair Grigsby.''

With the studious devotion and generous spirit of Mr. Grigsby it may be inferred that membership in learned institutions was numerously and gladly conferred on him.   The writer has been informed that among such distinctions he was a member of the American Philosophical Society.   Circumstances have impelled haste in the preparation of this notice, and the writer has thus been debarred from the desired requisite reference.

Mr. Grigsby's happy and inspiring connection with the Massachusetts Historical Society is with just appreciation attested in the warm utterances of its venerated president as herewith embodied.

It is embarrassing to attempt, without accessible record, an enumeration of the literary contributions of Mr. Grigsby.   Mr. Winthrop admiringly alludes to his grace and merit as a voluminous correspondent.

In his own newspaper, in others of his native city and State, and doubtless in other sections of our Union appeared many instructive articles from his pen.

The *Virginia Historical Register*, the organ of the Virginia Historical Society, and the *Southern Literary Messenger*, were frequently contributed to.   An article in the latter may be referred to in connection with the library of Mr. Grigsby, that on "The Library of John Randolph of Roanoke." (Vol. XX, 1853, page 76).

Among his public addresses, those most often referred to are the following:

Address on the Mecklenburg Declaration of Independence, delivered in the Athenæum, Richmond, Va., in 1848.

Discourse on the Virginia Convention of 1829–30, before the Virginia Historical Society, December 15, 1853.

Discourse on the Virginia Convention of 1776, delivered before the College of William and Mary at Williamsburg, July 3, 1855.

Discourse on the Virginia Convention of 1788, before the Virginia Historical Society, February 23, 1858.

Discourse on the Character of Jefferson, at the unveiling of his statue in the library of the University of Virginia, 1860.

Address on the Life and Character of Littleton Waller Tazewell, before the bar of the city of New York, June 29, 1860.

Address before the Literary Societies of Washington and Lee University, in 1869.

Address, "Some of our Past Historic Periods bearing on the Present," delivered before the Virginia Historical Society, March 10, 1870.

Address before Hampden-Sidney College, on the centenary of its founding, June 14, 1876.

Of this, the last of such public appearances of Mr. Grigsby, it may be well that the following account should be here given :

"Mr. Grigsby, who had passed beyond the age of three-score and ten, was so pale and appeared so feeble that the audience was not surprised when he asked the indulgence of being permitted, if necessary, to sit while he delivered his address. But his strength seemed to increase as he advanced, and he remained on his feet during the whole two hours occupied in the delivery. His historical sketch displayed a familiarity with the persons and events connected with the College sixty years ago, and previously, and was clothed in language so graphic and elegant, and illustrated with anecdote and narrative so apposite, as to render the performance, in the whole, acceptable and delightful in a high degree to his hearers. The enthusiasm kindled by his theme evinced the warmth of his affection for his native State and all that belongs to her glory in the past, and gave the charm of impressive eloquence to his discourse. His plan embraced personal sketches of the six earlier presidents of the College and of the first trustees ; but he had not time nor strength to deliver all that he had prepared, and was compelled to withhold a part."

The disease which precipitated the death of Mr. Grigsby was incurred in the performance of an affectionate office. In making a visit of condolence to his cousin, Colonel John B. McPhail, who had been bereft of his wife, and who lived some distance from the home of Mr. Grigsby, the latter contracted a deep cold which developed into pneumonia. "During a protracted and painful illness of several weeks' duration, he exhibited an unfaltering patience and resignation to the will of God. When he supposed himself to be dying he summoned his immediate family to his bedside, and bade them adieu, telling them at the same time that he had made his preparation for the other world while he was in health. Three days before the final stroke, which fell April 28th, 1881, he was heard to say : " I desire to live ; yet I feel submissive to the Divine will." An offering from his friend, Mr. Winthrop, a box of exquisite white flowers, reached him in his last moments and served to decorate his grave.

His remains rest beneath a chaste and stately marble obelisk, erected by his widow, in Elmwood Cemetery, Norfolk, Va. It bears the following inscription:

Hugh Blair Grigsby, LL.D.

Born in Norfolk, Va., November 26th, 1806.

Died at "Edgehill," Charlotte county, Va.,

April 28th, 1881.

President of the Virginia Historical Society.

Member of the Virginia Convention, 1829–30.

Chancellor of the College of William and Mary.

Mr. Grigsby left issue two children : i. Hugh Carrington, born in Philadelphia, Pa., February 13, 1857. ii. Mary Blair, born in Norfolk, Va., July 9, 1861; married December 1, 1882, W. W. Galt, Paymaster United States Navy, son of Prof. W. R. Galt (an esteemed educator of Norfolk, Va.,) and nephew of Alexander Galt, the sculptor. Issue: four children: Hugh Blair Grigsby, William R., Robert Waca and Mary Carrington Galt.

At a called meeting of the Executive Committee of the Virginia Historical Society, held at one o'clock P. M. April 30th, 1881—Vice-President William Wirt Henry presiding—the following action in tribute to the late President of the Society, the Hon. Hugh Blair Grigsby, LL.D., was taken :

WHEREAS, This Committee has just learned of the death of the Hon. HUGH BLAIR GRIGSBY, LL.D., the late President of this Society, which occurred at "Edgehill," his residence, in the county of Charlotte, on Thursday the 28th instant; be it

Resolved, That we cannot too deeply deplore the heavy loss which we have sustained in the death of one whose devotion to the interests of the Society, united to his great learning and accomplishments, have been so effective in forwarding the objects for which this Society was formed.

Resolved, That the Hon. HUGH BLAIR GRIGSBY, LL.D., by his natural endowments, by his passionate devotion to learning in all its forms, by his conspicuous purity of life, and by his invaluable contributions to the literature of his native State, has deserved, as he has enjoyed, the admiration, the love, and the gratitude of his fellow-citizens, and has been recognized beyond the borders of his State as a fitting type of the men who have shed so great a lustre around the name of Virginia.

Resolved, That Dr. Charles G. Barney and George A. Barksdale, Esq., be appointed on behalf of this Society to attend the funeral obsequies of the deceased in the city of Norfolk, and that a copy of these resolutions be forwarded to his widow and children, with the assurance of our deep sympathy with them in their heavy affliction.

WILLIAM WIRT HENRY,
Chairman.

At the monthly meeting of the Massachusetts Historical Society, held in the Dowse Library, Boston, May 12th, 1881, the President, the Hon. Robert C. Winthrop, occupied the chair.   In an announcement of the deaths of members of the Society and of other distinguished men, he remarked :[j] " An absence from home of only three weeks, just ended, has been marked for us, gentlemen, by the loss of several distinguished and valued friends, at least two of whom were connected in different relations with this Society.   I had been at Washington less than a week when I was summoned as far back as Philadelphia to serve as a pall-bearer at the funeral of the revered and lamented Dr. Alexander Hamilton Vinton.   Returning to Washington from that service, I was met by a telegram announcing the death of an honorary member, who was endeared to more than one of us by long friendship and frequent correspondence—the Hon. Hugh Blair Grigsby, LL.D., of Virginia.   A day or two only had elapsed before the newspapers informed me that the venerable Dr. John Gorham Palfrey had passed away at Cambridge.   The papers of a very few days later apprised me that the excellent Charles Hudson had also been released from the burdens of the flesh.   Much more time would have been required than the few hours I have had at my command since I reached home on Thursday evening for prepar-

---

ing any adequate notice of such names; but I should not be forgiven for not dwelling for a moment on those which have had
a place on our rolls.''

After a warm tribute to the worth of Mr. Hudson, Mr. Winthrop continued : '' Of the remarkable qu ilities and accomplishments of our deceased honorary member, Mr. Grigsby, of Virginia,
I hardly dare to speak with the little preparation which it has been
in my power to make in the single day since my return home.
I trust that our friend, Dr. Deane, who knew him as well and
valued him as highly as I did, will now, or hereafter, supply all
my deficiencies, and place him on our records as he deserves to be
placed.   Indeed, he has placed himself there with no mistakable
impress.

'' No one of our. honorary members on either side of the Atlantic has ever exhibited so warm a personal interest in our proceedings, or has so often favored us with interesting letters, which
have been gladly printed in our successive serials or volumes.

'' A Virginian of the Virginians—President of their Historical
Society, and Chancellor of their oldest college ; bound to the Old
Dominion by every tie of blood and of affection ; proud of her
history, with which he was so familiar ; proud of her great men,
with so many of whom he had been personally associated in
public as well as private life ; sympathizing deeply in all of her
political views and with all her recent trials and reverses—he was
never blind to the great men and great deeds of New England,
never indifferent to our own Massachusetts history in particular ;
on the contrary, he was always eager to cultivate the regard and
friendship of our scholars and public men.   No work from our
press seemed to escape his attention.   There was no poem of
Longfellow, or Whittier, or Holmes, or Lowell, no history of
Prescott, or Bancroft, or Palfrey, or Motley, or Frothingham, or
Parkman, which he did not read with lively interest and discuss
with discrimination and candor.

'' In the little visit which he made us ten years ago, he formed
personal friendships with not a few of those whom he had known
only by their works, and they were a constant source of pleasure
and pride to him.   For myself, I look back on more than twenty
years of familiar and friendly correspondence with him—inter-
rupted by the war, but renewed with the earliest return of peace—
which was full of entertainment and instruction, and which I

shall miss greatly as the years roll on, and as the habit and art of letter-writing is more and more lost in telegraphic and telephonic and postal-card communication.

"There is hardly anything more interesting in all our seventeen volumes of Proceedings than his letter to me of March 30, 1866, beginning : 'Five years and fourteen days have elapsed since I received a letter from you'—giving a vivid description of some of his personal experiences during the Civil War—asking whether it was true that one whom he 'so much esteemed and honored as President Felton was no more,' adding : 'Is Mr. Deane living?'—and abounding in the kindest allusions to those from whom the war had so sadly separated him.

"I may not forget to mention that Horace Binney, of Philadelphia, though thirty years older than Mr. Grigsby, was a special correspondent of his, and that the last letter which Mr. Binney wrote before his death, at ninety-four, was to our lamented friend.

"Mr. Grigsby, from an early period of his life, suffered severely from imperfect hearing—an infirmity which grew upon him year by year, until knowledge at one entrance seemed quite shut out. But he bore it patiently and heroically, and his books and his pen were an unfailing source of consolation and satisfaction.

"Educated for several years at Yale, and admitted to the bar of Norfolk, with every acquisition to fit him for a distinguished career in the law and in public life, he was constrained to abandon it all and confine himself to his family, his friends and his library.

"As a very young man, however—hardly twenty-one—he had a seat in the great Constitutional Convention of Virginia in 1829–30, and was associated with all the conspicuous men of that period. Meantime, he was studying the characters and careers of the great Virginians of earlier periods, not a few of whom were still living. His 'Discourse on the Virginia Convention of 1776,' extended in print to a volume of more than two hundred pages, with its elaborate notes and appendix, is indeed as perfect a summary of the history of some of the great men of his native State—Jefferson and Madison and Patrick Henry and George Mason and others—as can easily be found ; while his discourses on the men with whom he was associated in the Convention of 1830, and on Littleton Waller Tazewell, the Senator and Governor and eminent lawyer of Virginia, are worthy supplements to that which had preceded them. Many other publications, both in prose and verse, have manifested the fertility of his mind and the extent of his culture and research, while his letters alone would have occupied more than the leisure of any common man.

"Meantime, he was devoted to agricultural pursuits, planting and hoeing and ditching with his own hands, and prouder of his dike, his 'Julius Cæsar Bridge," and his crops than of any other of his productions. His very last letter to me, dated not long before his illness, concludes by saying: 'My employments for the past two weeks have been the reading of Justin, Suetonius, Tom Moore's Diary, and the building of a rail zigzag fence, nearly a mile long, to keep my neighbors' cattle off my premises.' In a previous paragraph he said that he had just promised an invalid friend, who was anxious on the subject, to call soon and read to him 'the admirable sermon of Paley on the Recognition of Friends in Another World.' That may, perchance, have been his last neighborly office before he was called to the verification and enjoyment, as we trust, of those Christian hopes and anticipations in which he ever delighted.

"But I forbear from any further attempt to do justice, in this off-hand, *extempore* manner, to one of whom I would gladly have spoken with more deliberation and with greater fullness. He had promised to meet me and stand by my side at Yorktown next October, and I shall sorely miss his friendly counsel and assistance for that occasion should I be spared to take part in it. The son of a Presbyterian clergyman, he was to the last warmly attached to the faith and forms of the Church in which he was brought up. While tolerant toward all, 'The Westminster Confession' and 'The Shorter Catechism' were his cherished manuals of religion and theology."

Continuing with warm words of acknowledgment of the merits and services of Dr. Palfrey, Mr. Winthrop offered, with resolutions in his memory and that of Mr. Hudson, the following:

Resolved, That the Massachusetts Historical Society offer their sincere sympathy to the Historical Society of Virginia on the death of their distinguished and accomplished President, the Hon. HUGH BLAIR GRIGSBY, LL.D., whom we had long counted it a privilege to include among our own honorary members, and for whom we entertained the highest regard and respect; and that the Secretary communicate a copy of this resolution to our sister Society of Virginia.

At a Convocation of the Board of Visitors and Governors of the College of William and Mary, held the 8th of July, 1881, the following preamble and resolutions were unanimously adopted :

" Since the last meeting of the Board of the College, its officers and friends have been afflicted by the removal from their midst of HUGH BLAIR GRIGSBY, LL.D., Chancellor of the College of William and Mary. In the death of this noble man, the Board, the College, and the community at large have sustained an irreparable loss. A man of the highest character, the most uncommon cultivation, with a mind to grasp the truth, and a heart to love, defend and live it, he was among us a leader in everything true and noble, a guide in everything wise and judicious. His devotion to the College and its interests was unvarying, and by his generous, self-sacrificing spirit, by his undying faith and enthusiastic anticipation of the final success and triumph of the College that was so dear to him, he stood forth its champion in the darkest days and encouraged every fainting spirit to continue faithful in its support. The College and this Board owe him a debt of gratitude which only a loving remembrance can but partially repay, and are moved to pass as their first official act at their annual meeting. the following resolutions :

"*Resolved*, That in the death of HUGH BLAIR GRIGSBY, we mourn the loss of a friend and fellow-laborer, whose wisdom and lofty character have reflected honor on our Board, and that we feel constrained to record on our minutes this tribute of admiration and affection to his memory, which in his life-time delicacy prevented us to do, and that through coming ages the friends of this College and of all sound education will reverently recall his memory, and on the tablets of the annals of William and Mary will forever be engraved the name of HUGH BLAIR GRIGSBY—' *Clarum et venerable nomen.*'

"*Resolved*, That we tender to the family of the widowed wife and orphaned children of our deceased friend our heartfelt sympathies for the loss of one who, so lovely to his friends, must have been to his own family unspeakably dear; and we claim our share in the sorrow over his loss, as those who are proud to know that they were reckoned among his friends.

"W. H. E. MORECOCK,
"*Secretary of the Board.*"

The following is an extract from the report of Benjamin S. Ewell, LL.D., President of the College, to the Board of Visitors and Governors, made July 8th, 1881 :

"The death of HUGH BLAIR GRIGSBY, LL.D., the Chancellor and

honored Visitor, on the 28th of April, 1881, has deprived the College, the Visitors and the Faculty, of a true and constant friend.

"Mr. GRIGSBY's connection with the College began in 1855, when he delivered an address at the commencement, received the degree of Doctor of Laws, and was elected Visitor and Governor.

"He was elected Chancellor in 1871. *k* George Washington and John Tyler, Presidents of the United States, and HUGH BLAIR GRIGSBY are the only Americans who have held that office. From 1855 until the day of his death Mr. GRIGSBY was the earnest advocate of every measure tending to increase the efficiency, or promote the prosperity of the College. He was ever ready to espouse its cause with all his extraordinary powers of eloquence, logic and learning. With the exception of his kinsman, Dr. James Blair, the reverend and revered founder of the College, he was its most liberal private benefactor.

"His affectionate friendship and loving kindness are familiar to you. They extended to Visitors, Faculty and students. To the latter he never failed to say words showing interest and giving encouragement. The Faculty mourn his loss as that of their dearest official, and personal friend."

k Upon the nomination of General Henry A. Wise.

THE HISTORY

OF THE

Virginia Federal Convention

OF 1788.

CHAPTER I.

I have undertaken, at the request of the Historical Society of Virginia, to write the history of the Convention which began its sessions in the Public Buildings[1] in the town of Richmond on the second day of June, 1788, and which ratified, in the name and behalf of the good people of that Commonwealth, the present

---

[1] The Convention met the first day of its sittings in what was known as the Old Capitol, situated at the northwest corner of Cary and Fourteenth streets. It was a wooden building about fifty feet square and three stories high, with a sharply ridged roof. The Act of the Assembly for the removal of the Capital of the State from Williamsburg to Richmond was passed in May, 1779, and the "public buildings" known in later years as the "the Old Capitol," were erected in 1780 for the temporary use of the government until the permanent buildings, provided for by an act passed the same year, could be completed. About 1855, the old buildings, which had become much dilapidated and reduced in height, were torn down, and upon its site and lots adjoining on Fourteenth street several fine stores, known as the Pearl Block, were erected by Mr. Hugh W. Fry, the corner of which was occupied by himself and sons under the firm name of Hugh W. Fry & Sons, Wholesale Grocery and Commission Merchants.

Federal Constitution.[2] Our theme, both in its moral and political aspect, has a significancy which the present generation may
well heed, and which posterity will delight to contemplate. But
it receives an added grandeur at this moment when the people
of Virginia, from the Potomac to the Roanoke, and from Ohio
to the sea, have come hither on one of the most patriotic missions recorded in our annals, and under the auspices of the legislative and executive departments of their government, and in
the presence of many honorable and illustrious guests from distant States, have inaugurated, with the peaceful pageantry of war,
with the mystic rites of Masonry, with eloquence and song, and
with the august sanctions of our common Christianity, a lasting
and stately monument[3] which, with the eternal voice of sculpture,
proclaims now, and will proclaim to generations and ages to
come, that Virginia holds, and will ever hold, the names and services of all her soldiers and statesmen who aided in achieving
her independence, in grateful and affectionate veneration, and
that the spirit which inspired the Revolution still burns with
unabated fervor in the breasts of her children.

To trace those discussions of the great principles which under-
lie the social compact, to observe the modifications of those
maxims which human wisdom in a wide survey of the rights,
interests and passions of men had solemnly set apart for the
guidance of human affairs, and their application to the peculiar
necessities of a people engaged in forming a Federal Union, is an
important office, which assumes a deeper interest and a higher
dignity when we reflect that those who were engaged on that

---

[2] A discourse delivered before the Virginia Historical Society in the
Hall of the House of Delegates at Richmond, on the evening of February 23, 1858, and subsequently enlarged to the present History.

[3] The Washington Monument, inaugurated February 22d, 1858; subscriptions towards the erection of which were authorized by an Act of
Assembly passed February 22d, 1817. The sum of $13,063 was collected,
but it lay dormant until February 22d, 1828, when, by Act of Assembly, it was placed at interest. Thus it remained until 1848, when it had
accumulated to $41,833 with the aid of a new grand subscription. On
the 22d of February, the Virginia Historical Society stimulated the
Legislature to augment the fund to $100,000 for the erection of the
monument, the corner-stone of which was laid February 22d, 1850, in
the presence of General Zachary Taylor, President of the United States,
his Cabinet, and a host of other distinguished persons.

great occasion were our fathers, whose ashes repose in the soil beneath our feet, whose names we bear, whose blood yet flows in our veins, and whose glory is our richest inheritance. And the transaction is hardly less interesting from the contemplation of our fathers at such a conjunction to a minute survey of their lives and characters, of the stock from which they sprung, of their early education, of their training for the memorable events in which they were to engage, and of the general scope of their actions.

The time has gone by when the materials adequate to a full elucidation of my theme could be gathered from the living voice, and but little can be gleaned from the periodical press of the day. The last survivor of the Convention died at the advanced age of ninety-nine, twelve years ago.[4] There is no file extant of the papers published in Richmond during the session of the body. The Journal of the Convention, which, as its deliberations were held mostly in committee of the whole, consists of a few pages only, and a stenographic report of some of its debates, are its only existing records. With the exception of a memoir of Henry, which Virginia owes to the patriotism of an adopted son now no more, and which treats our subject in a cursory manner, there is no separate memoir of any one of the one hundred and seventy members who composed the House.[5] I am thrown altogether upon the sources of intelligence scattered through our whole literature, upon those letters, which, written by the actors when the contest was at the highest and instantly forgotten, have been saved in old repositories, and upon those recollections, gathered at various times during a quarter of a century past, from persons who were either members of the body, or were

---

[4] James Johnson, one of the delegates from Isle of Wight, died at his residence in that county August 16th, 1845, having survived the adjournment more than fifty-seven years.

[5] Of the younger members of the body who have lived in our times, Chief Justice Marshall has been commemorated in an admirable eulogium by Mr. Binney, and by Judge Story in the *National Portrait Gallery*. His Memoir by Mr. Flanders, in the *Lives of the Chief Justices*, has appeared since the above paragraph was written, as well as the full and most valuable life of Madison by Mr. Rives. To these may be added the chaste and eloquent oration of William Henry Rawle, LL.D. at the unveiling of the statue of Marshall at Washington, D. C., May 10, 1884, and the Memoir by A. B. Magruder in "The American Statesmen Series."

present at its deliberations, or who knew the members at a subsequent period, and which were made with no view to ulterior use. There is not living a single person who was a spectator of the scene. A boy of fifteen, who had seen Mason and Henry[6] walking arm in arm from the Swan[7] or Pendleton, as, assisted by a friend, he descended the steps of the same inn to his phæton, on their way to the Convention, would, if he were now living, have reached his eighty-fifth year. The actors and the spectators, and those who spoke and those who heard, are buried in a common grave.

Still I indulge the hope that it will not be found impracticable, out of the materials rescued from the wreck of the past, to present a picture which shall reflect in some faint degree not only the position Virginia then held among her sister States, but the personal as well as the political relations which existed between the leading actors in the Convention, and are proper to be known in order to appreciate the conduct of those who bore a conspicuous part in what we were taught from our infancy to consider the most animated parliamentary tournament of the eighteenth century, at least on this side of the Atlantic, and in those animated contests which, during twenty-five

---

[6] I learned this incident from my friend John Henry, Esq., who, though only two years old at the death of his celebrated father, is now over seventy, and resides on the patrimonial estate, Red Hill; and he heard it from the Rev. Charles Clay, a member of the Convention from Bedford, who told him that George Mason was dressed in a full suit of black, and was remarkable for the urbanity and dignity with which he received and returned the courtesies of those who passed him.

[John Henry, the youngest child of Patrick Henry that survived him, was born 14th February, 1796, and died 7th January, 1868. He was educated at Hampden-Sidney and Washington colleges. He lived the life of a planter on the "Red Hill" estate, the last homestead of his father, which he inherited, and which has descended to his son, Hon. Wm. Wirt Henry. His memory was exceptionally good, and was well stored with information concerning his father, gathered from his contemporaries, especially his mother, who lived till 14th February, 1831. Most of the information concerning Patrick Henry, contained in *Howe's Historical Collections of Virginia*, was furnished by him.—ED.]

[7] A tavern famous in former years, a long wooden building—basement, one story and attic, with wooden porch along its front, still standing, divided into small rooms, about midway of the square on the north side of Broad, between Eighth and Ninth streets.

eventful days, never flagged, and on several occasions, and especially on the Mississippi debate, were wrought to a pitch of excitement which, whether we consider the actors or the subject, was hardly exceeded by the most brilliant theatrical exhibitions. And I may venture to add that, since Death has set his seal on all the actors, and their whole lives are before us, if a more accurate and faithful delineation of their motives and actions, of their persons even—of their dress, manners, and attainments—than could have been possessed by the bulk of their contemporaries, separated by miles of forest from one another, at a time when there was not in the State a mail-coach, a post, or a press worthy of the name, and when there could be but little personal communion between individuals, be not fairly placed before the present generation, it will be owing somewhat indeed to the difficulties of the theme itself, but more to the inca·pacity or negligence of the historian who attempts to record it.

Since the adjournment of the Convention, seventy years have nearly elapsed; and in that interval two entire generations have been born, lived, and passed away. Nor has the change been felt in human life alone. This populous city, which now surrounds us with its laboratories of the arts, with its miles of railways and canals, with its immense basin and capacious docks, with its river bristling with masts and alive with those gay steamers that skirt our streams as well as those dark and statelier ones that assail the sea, with its riches collected from every clime, with its superb dwellings, with its structures reared to education, literature, and religion, with those electric wires which hold it in instantaneous rapport with Boston and New Orleans—places which, at the time of the Convention, could only be reached by weeks and even months of tedious travel—and which are destined to connect it, ere another lustrum be past, with London and Paris, with St. Petersburg and Vienna, and with its numerous lamps which diffuse, at the setting of the sun, a splendor compared with which the lights kindled by our fathers in honor of Saratoga and York, or of Bridgewater and New Orleans, would be faint and dim, was a straggling hamlet, its humble tenements scattered over the sister hills, and its muddy and ungraded streets trenched upon by the shadows of an unbroken forest.[8] This

---

[8] Morse describes Richmond in 1789, one year later, as having three hundred houses.

venerable building in which we are now assembled, which was
originally modelled after one of the most graceful temples of the
Old World, and which overlooks one of the loveliest landscapes
of the New, was yet unfinished; and the marble image of Washington, which for more than two thirds of a century has guarded
its portals, which has been recently invested with a new immortality by the genius of Hubard,[9] and which, we fondly hope, will

[9] William James Hubard (pronounced H*u*-bard), the son of an artist
of ability, was born in Warwick, England, August 20th, 1807. He early
exhibited a proclivity for art, and "pursued his studies in France, Ger-
many, and Italy."

There is evidence of the progress made by him in a testimonial preserved by his family—a silver palette which bears the inscription:
"Awarded to Master James Hubard by the admirers of his genius in
the city of Glasgow, Scotland, February 14, 1824."

He came to America in this year and was for some time a resident
of Philadelphia. Later he made Virginia his home, marrying, in 1838,
Miss Maria Mason Tabb, of Gloucester county, a lady of means and a
member of an influential family. In the same year he revisited Europe,
returning after an absence of more than three years to Virginia, and
settling finally in Richmond. His art life was an active one, as is
evinced in numerous works from his easel—original conceptions, portraits, and copies from the masters—all marked by his characteristic
boldness and beauty of color. A little while before the period of the
text (1856), he fixed his residence in the western suburbs of Richmond,
near that of an erratic brother artist, Edward Peticolas. This last
building, coming into his possession upon the death of his friend, he
converted into a foundry, specially for the reproduction in bronze of
Houdon's matchless Washington which graces the rotunda of our Capitol. There were six of these admirable casts—each a single piece of
metal—an accomplishment not often attempted. Of these, one is at
the Virginia Military Institute, Lexington, two in North Carolina—one
at Raleigh and the other at Charlotte—a fourth in Central Park, New
York city, a fifth in St. Louis, Missouri, and a sixth in the grounds of
the University of Missouri at Columbia Early in the late war between
the States, Hubard converted part of his studio into a laboratory and
engaged in the filling of shrapnel shells with a compound of his own
invention. These shells, it is said, served the famous Merrimac. Hubard's foundry is said also to have supplied light and powerful field
pieces to many of the early artillery companies of the Confederate
Army.

On the morning of the 14th of February, 1862, whilst Hubard was
engaged in filling a shell, a spark ignited the compound. The explosion inflicted fatal injuries, from which he died on the following day.

transmit to distant ages the life-like semblance of the great original, had indeed received the last touches of the chisel of Houdon, but had not been lifted to its pedestal. Our territory, though not as large as it had been, was larger than it is now. Virginia had added to the Federal Government, four years before the meeting of the Convention, her northwestern lands, which now constitute several States of the Union;[10] but still held the soil from the Atlantic to the Mississippi. For Kentucky, who, if not *matre filia pulchrior*, was worthy of the stock from which she sprung, though destined soon to leave her happy home, yet clung to the bosom of her mother.[11]

Hubard was a gifted man, and it was claimed would have attained greater distinction in modeling than in limning. An early work of his, executed at Florence, is said to have enthusiastically stirred the Sculptor Greenough—an Indian chief, with his horse in full strain, to whom a flash of lightning reveals a precipice immediately before him. This conception Hubard afterwards committed to canvass.

Nor was the pen of Hubard idle. He left in MS. a critical work on Art in America, and a novel, both of which were pronounced by competent critics productions of merit. They were unfortunately destroyed in the pillage of his residence April 3, 1865. Two children of Hubard survive—Wm. James Hubard and Mrs. Eliza Gordon, wife of Rev. John James Lloyd, Abingdon, Va. The editor is indebted to Mrs. Lloyd, through the mediation of Mann S. Valentine, Esq., of Richmond, who was an intimate friend of the lamented Hubard, for the preceding details. Mr. Valentine includes in his numerous art possessions many of the best examples of Hubard's genius.

[10] Virginia made the cession in January, 1781, but "it was not finally completed and accepted until March, 1789." *Curtis's Hist. Con.*, I, 137.

[11] As the delegates from Kentucky played an important *role* in the Convention, it may be proper to state that the District, as it was then called, was divided into seven counties, which, with their delegates, are as follows: Bourbon: Henry Lee, Notlay Conn; Fayette: Humphrey Marshall, John Fowler; Jefferson: Robert Breckenridge, Rice Bullock; Lincoln: John Logan, Henry Pawling; Madison: John Miller, Green Clay; Nelson: Matthew Walton, John Steele; Mercer: Thomas Allen, Alexander Robertson. Mann Butler, in his history of Kentucky, has fallen into one or two errors in the names of the delegates, which he probably learned from hearsay. The above list is copied from the Journal. Kentucky, soon after the adjournment of the Convention, formed a constitution for herself, and was duly admitted as one of the

The population of the State demands a deliberate notice. In spite of the numbers that had perished from disease and exposure during the war, that had been abstracted by the British,[12] that had sought the flat lands of Ohio, or that had married and settled abroad, it had, since that great day on which the people of Virginia, in convention assembled, had declared their independence of the British Crown, been steadily advancing, and from five hundred and sixty thousand at the date of the August Convention of 1774, had now reached over eight hundred thousand. Of this number, five hundred and three thousand two hundred and forty-eight were whites, twelve thousand eight hundred and eighty were free colored, and three hundred and five thousand two hundred and fifty-seven were slaves.[13] Her numbers might well inspire the respect of her sisters and the pride of her sons, and sufficiently explain the position which she held in the Confederation. Her population was over three-fourths of all that of New England. It was not far from double that of Pennsylvania. It was not far from three times that of New York. It was over three-fourths of all the population of the Southern States. It exceeded by sixty thousand that of North Carolina and what was afterwards called Tennessee, of South Carolina, and of Georgia; and it was more than a fifth of the population of the whole Union.

But the topic which claims the most serious attention, not only of the general reader but of the political economists and of the

States of the Union at the same time with Vermont—one on the 9th, the other on the 18th of February, 1791. It is to the presence of the Kentucky delegation that we owe the exciting drama of the Mississippi debate.

[12] Mr. Jefferson estimated the number of negroes taken off in a single campaign at one-fifth of the entire black population of the State, and the seaboard suffered severely throughout the war.

[13] Professor Tucker, bringing the lights of the modern census to bear upon our Colonial population, estimates that of Virginia in 1774 to have been 500,000. (*History U. S.*, I, 96.) The census of 1790 puts it down at 738,308, nearly sixty-two thousand less than the number stated in the text, which, from a careful examination made some years ago, I believe to be the true one. Indeed, the extent of Virginia at that period, which reached from the Atlantic to the Mississippi, the unsettled state of the country, the scattered population, made the taking of a correct census impossible.

statesmen, and in comparison with which the questions of the extent of our territory and the number of the population appear almost unimportant, is the condition of the commerce of Virginia when the Federal Constitution was presented for ratification. It was under her own control. Her trade was free ; the duties levied upon foreign commerce were laid by herself, and were collected by her officers. She had her own custom houses, her own marine hospitals, and her own revenue cutters bearing her own flag. Her imposts were light; because it was then deemed unwise to lay burdens upon trade, and partly from an apprehension not unfounded that a heavy duty laid upon a particular article of merchandise might direct the whole of an assorted cargo from her ports to the ports of a more liberal neighbor.[14] Yet the amount of duties collected for several years previous to the Convention constituted one of the largest items received into the treasury, and at the low rate of duty ranging from one to five per cent., represented an import trade of several millions.

Or, to speak with greater precision, the net amount of money in round numbers received into the treasury of Virginia from customs accruing during the three-quarters of the year ending the 31st of May, 1788, was sixty thousand pounds, which in our present currency are equivalent to two hundred thousand dollars.[15] The customs of the fourth quarter of the fiscal year, ending the thirty-first of August, are not given ; and, as during that interval the customs on the cargoes brought back in return for the tobacco crop carried out in the spring were received, it probably exceeded two-fold the product of either of the two preceding quarters ; but we will place it in common with the other quarters at sixty-six thousand dollars. This sum of two hundred and sixty-six thousand dollars would represent, under an average tariff of five per centum, an import trade of over five millions of dollars. And from the present value of money, five millions at that time would be nearly equal to ten millions at the present day. And farther, as credit then was comparatively

---

[14] John Randolph used to allude to the tradition that duties laid by Virginia on certain articles, which were admitted free of duty into Maryland, was the main cause of the rise of Baltimore.

[15] For the receipts from custom see the annual report of the Treasurer in the Journals of the Senate and House of Delegates of each year from 1783 to 1788.

unknown, the imports were almost wholly based upon exports, which must have reached five millions of dollars.[16] Thus the import and export trade of Virginia during the year ending the thirty-first of August, 1788, was, at the present value of money, not far from twenty millions of dollars ; an amount which it had never reached before, and which, with the exception hereinafter to be mentioned and explained, it has never reached since.

But the average rate of the tariff of 1788, instead of being five per centum as above estimated, was in fact less than two and a half per centum ;[17] and the duties collected under it would, on the grounds already stated, represent a commerce of forty millions of dollars. Enormous as this sum appears, it may be nearly reached by another process. The year 1769 was regarded an ordinary year, yet the imports of Virginia during that year are ascertained to have been over four millions and a quarter.[18] At that time our trade was almost wholly with Great Britain and possessions ; and our great and only staple which she would receive was tobacco. In the interval of nineteen years, the population had from natural increase and immigration nearly doubled, and brisk trade in all the products of the soil and the forest was prosecuted with almost every foreign power. It is not unfair to presume that a laborer in 1788 was as successful as a laborer in

---

[16] A shrewd traveller, Captain J. F. D Smyth, of the British army, who visited Virginia just before the Revolution and was present during the war, states that Virginia then exported "at least one hundred thousand hogsheads of tobacco of about one thousand pounds each, of which between ten and fifteen thousand *might be* the produce of North Carolina." He adds that Virginia exported, "besides Indian corn, provisions, skins, lumber, hemp, and some iron, large quantities of wheat and flour"; and he estimated the wheat at "five hundred thousand bushels," and the flour "at fifteen thousand barrels." *Smyth's Tour in the United States*, Vol. II, 140. In 1775, there were exported 101,828,617 pounds of tobacco, 27,623,451 pounds remaining on hand in Great Britain, and 74,205,166 pounds in other countries of Europe. *Tobacco Culture in the United States*, Tenth Census, Vol. IV ; "Succinct Account of Tobacco in Virginia—1607–1790," by R A. Brock, p. 223.

[17] I handed the Tariff Acts of Virginia, in force in 1788, to a mercantile friend, with a request that he would furnish me with a correct average of all the duties, and he made it rather under than over two per cent.

[18] $4,255,000. *Forrest's History of Norfolk, 73.*

1769, and that the imports and exports of 1788 must have nearly doubled what they were nineteen years before ; and they would thus reach over thirty millions of dollars.

Indeed, the commercial prosperity of Virginia, from the date of the treaty of peace to the meeting of the Convention, was amazing. Her accessibility by sea at all seasons, her unequalled roadstead, the safe navigation of her bays and rivers, the extent, the convenience, and the security of her great seaport, the bulk, variety and value of her agricultural produce, invited the enterprise of foreign capital. Many of the buildings of Norfolk had been burned at the beginning of the war by the British; and those that remained had been burned by the order of the Committee of Safety or of the Convention ; and in that once flourishing town, whose pleasant dwellings and capacious warehouses attracted the attention of the European visitor, and whose rental in the year preceding their destruction amounted to fifty thousand dollars,[19] not a building was allowed to remain. The whole population had been withdrawn and billeted upon families in the interior, whose claims for remuneration are strewed over our early Journals. Even the wharves, which were made of pine logs, were destroyed by the burning of the houses that rested upon them.

Nought was left of a scene once so fair but the land on which the town was built, and the noble river that laved its smouldering ruins. But in less than eight years from the date of the conflagration, and less than five from the date of the treaty of peace, new and more commodious houses, destined to be destroyed by another some years later and to rise with renovated splendor, had risen, and warehouses ample enough to hold large cargoes had been erected. We had not many merchants of our own, for the habits and prejudices of the people were in another direction ; but merchants from England, Scotland and Holland, and from the Northern States, well skilled in trade, sought our ports, settled themselves permanently among us, founded families which are still proud of the worth of their progenitors, and, it may be

---

[19] *Forrest's History of Norfolk*, 85. The burning of Norfolk by our own people was an act little short of madness. A population of six thousand men were thrown at once upon the interior to consume the provisions needful for the prosecution of the war; and Portsmouth, directly opposite, was as good a place for the military purposes of the enemy as Norfolk.

remarked, became, without exception, the most strenuous advocates of the adoption of the Federal Constitution. There were no banks in those days in Virginia, nor was there any public depository of coin, which was emptied on the upper floor of warehouses and tossed about with shovels and spades.[20] Ships of every nation filled our seaport. Their curious streamers, waving every Sabbath from the masthead and glittering in the sun, presented a scene that was long and keenly remembered by the inhabitants of Norfolk. An officer of the Revolution, who had served in the Southern army, and who visited Norfolk two years before the meeting of the present Convention, was struck at seeing ships not only crowded three or four deep at the wharves, but moored so thickly in the stream that a ferry boat passing from Norfolk to Portsmouth could advance only by cautiously working her zigzag course among them. Some of the ships at anchor awaited their chances to discharge and receive their cargoes at the wharves, while others preferred to discharge and receive their freight in those vast and gloomy lighters, that may still be seen, freighted with fuel, entering or departing from the modern city. This observing traveller happened to be present on a gala day, when the ships were dressed, and when their salutes were heard through the town, and he was reminded of that brilliant spectacle exhibited at the departure of the British men-of-war and numerous transports with flags flying, with drums beating, and amid the roar of artillery, from the harbor of Charleston on the evacuation of that city by the enemy.[21]

This trade with foreign powers was strictly legitimate. We were at peace with all nations, and the leading States of Europe were at peace with themselves. It was not the result of political regulation or of distracted times. It was not the offspring of war between the carrying nations of the globe, and certain to terminate at the close of the war ; a species of trade which some years later fell to our lot, which involved us in fruitless negotiations, perplexed us with interminable controversies, led to the impressment of our sailors and to the sequestration of our ships, dishonored our flag in our own waters, and finally brought on a

---

[20] I heard this fact from a venerable merchant of Norfolk, who is yet living (1866) ; and who saw it in his childhood.

[21] Colonel Edward Carrington.

war with one of the belligerents. The trade enjoyed by our fathers was strictly legitimate. It was stimulated by no passion, it was not the offspring of cunning or favor. It was the result of common interests. It was the exchange of commodities between nations who believed themselves benefited by the operation; and as it was the result of common interests, so it was likely to be lasting. Indeed, nothing short of war or political regulation could affect it.

Nor was this trade wholly fed by the commodities of Virginia. The waters of the Chesapeake bore to our seaport not only the product of our own countries on its shores, but the products of Maryland and Pennsylvania. New England, New York, New Jersey, North Carolina, and South Carolina contributed their aid. And although no modern facilities for the transportation of produce from the interior then existed, our own exports exceeded the anticipations of the merchants. The embarrassments which many planters had to encounter at the close of the war were numerous and severe. When they looked around on their once thrifty plantations, a scene of devastation met their eyes. Their fences had been burned by the British or by our own soldiers during a seven years' war. Most of their live stock had long disappeared. Their cattle had either been seized by our own commissaries to sustain the army in the field, and was paid for in worthless paper, or had been taken by the British and not paid for at all. A favorite measure, both of the Americans and the British, was to lay waste the country on the track which either might be required to pass. Not only were fences burned, fruit trees destroyed, houses demolished or sacked, but beasts, whether fit for use or not, were seized upon. The throats of young colts were cut by the British, lest from this source the cavalry of the Americans should thereafter be recruited. One-fifth of the black population had been carried off by the British or died on their hands; and, in the face of the treaty of Paris, few or none were returned. Money might have lessened the troubles of the planters to a certain extent, and in a desolate country to a certain extent only, but money was not to be had. The country was as bankrupt as the citizen. Debt, like a cloud, rested alike over the State Government, over the Federal Government, and over a great number of people. But, what sensibly affected many persons, debts due the British merchants, some of which had been paid into the treasury under the sanction of an Act of Assembly, were now to be paid, and to be paid in coin. Hence some heads of families, which for more than a century had commanded respect, quitted their patrimonial hearths and sought, with sad hearts, new homes in the wilderness. Others sunk down broken-hearted, and left their members in hopeless penury.

But, touching as is frequently the fate of individuals in civil convulsions, nothing is more certain that an active, industrious, and free people cannot long remain in a forlorn condition. The population, as has already been observed, had, even amid the havoc of war, been steadily increasing; and a population of eight hundred thousand, living upon fair lands and intent on retrieving bad fortune, cannot fail, in a space of time incredibly short in the eyes of superficial observers, to accomplish great and, to those who confound individual with general suffering, most unexpected results.[22] Thus it was that, in spite of innumerable obstacles to success, the country rapidly prospered. With each succeeding year the crops increased in quantity; and in five years of peace our tobacco, grain, and other productions of the soil and the forest, maintained the grandest commerce that had ever spread its wings from an Anglo-Saxon settlement in the New World towards the shores of the Old, and such as was never seen in the Colony, and such as, with the exception of a short period, has never been seen in Virginia since. It is an instructive fact, not unworthy the attention of the statesman as well as the political economist, that the period from the death of Charles the First in 1641 to the restoration of Charles the Second—a space of nineteen years[23]—and that the period between the peace of 1783 and the adoption of the Federal Constitution of 1788— a space of five years—have been the most prosperous in our history; and that of the two centuries and a half of Virginia, it was during those two periods only she enjoyed the benefits of

---

[22] The doctrine of capital reproducing itself in a very short time was first distinctly shown by Dr. Chalmers. Lord Brougham availed himself of the doctrine without stating the source from which he obtained it.

[23] *Campbell's History of Virginia*, edition of 1860, p. 242.

a trade regulated by her own authority, unrestricted and un-
taxed.[24]

It is our duty to record the mistakes of our fathers as well as
those deeds which justly entitle them to our respect and veneration.   And in no instance did they commit a greater error than
in the false estimate which the leading advocates of the Federal
Constitution had formed of the general condition and of the
commerce of Virginia, when the Federal Constitution was presented for adoption.   There were, indeed, grave and grievous
embarrassments in our domestic and in our Federal relations that
were calculated to excite apprehension in the breasts of our calmest
and wisest men.   But these embarrassments had been brought
about in a period of revolution, when all trade was suspended,
and were the result of causes which had ceased to operate, and
which could never recur.   They were the effect of time and circumstances, and were likely to be relieved by the removal of the
causes which produced them.   An old and established nation,
emerging from a long and disastrous war waged within its territory, must be viewed in a very different light from the same
nation in a long period of peace, when its resources were developed and the arts cultivated under favorable auspices.   But
more especially does this observation apply to a purely agricultural people, occupying a wide territory, and harassed during
eight years by a powerful enemy, when for the first time they
take their position in the family of nations.   And in the over-
sight of this palpable truth may be traced an error of our fathers,
the effects of which we feel to this day, and will continue to feel
for generations to come.   The wonderful increase of our population they had not the means of knowing, and did not know ;
for up to that period of the eighteenth century no census had

---

[24] I have sought in the Norfolk Custom House in vain for the full sta-
tistics of the trade and commerce of Virginia with our own and foreign
States during the interval between 1783 and 1790.   The books were
probably handed over to the new Government, and have been destroyed
in the lapse of time as rubbish.   Doubtless full reports were made to
the treasury department in Richmond, and there may be found in some
obscure place in the Capitol.   If a committee were appointed by the
Assembly to examine the public papers now on file, and publish in a
cheap form the valuable ones amongst them, the full history of that
period may yet be written.

been taken ; nor had the custom then been introduced of calling upon the treasurer and the auditor for approximating statements of the population of the State.   One of the most eloquent friends of the Constitution, who had served in Congress, and who at the time held a high office in the Commonwealth, made a mistake of 212,000 in his estimate of the people of Virginia ; or, supposing he had excluded the seven Kentucky counties, which were as much a part of Virginia as Accomac and Henrico, and are enumerated as such in the census of 1790, and which he did not exclude, his mistake would still underrate the population more than 129,000, or more than one-fifth of the whole number. And when the trade and business of the country were represented in Convention as sunk to the lowest ebb, one of the opponents of the Constitution could only affirm that several American vessels had recently doubled the Cape of Good Hope.

But there were signs of prosperity obvious to the most careless observer   The increased production of agriculture, the immense quantities of lumber which employed a heavy tonnage, the vast commerce which filled our ports and rivers, and which was growing with every year, could hardly fail to attract observation   The imposing picture of a single seaport of Virginia, which had in the space of four years risen from ashes to a prominence which it had not attained during a century and a half of colonial rule, was a living witness of developed wealth, of successful enterprise, and of good government, and afforded a cheerful omen of the future.   Such indications of prosperity, if not unheeded, were wrongly interpreted.   Eminent statesmen, forgetting what a short time before was the condition of a country in which nearly all regular agricultural labor had for a series of years been suspended, which was girt by independent States, whose interests, if not positively hostile, were, as must always be the case with independent powers not identical with its own, and which was called for the first time to arrange and settle a general policy of trade and business with commodities beyond its borders, were annoyed and perplexed by a state of things that frequently exists in the oldest country, that time and experience would insensibly adjust, and which domestic legislation might at any moment remove.   It is one of the pregnant lessons of history, that public men on the stage often overlook or slight in great emergencies the salient facts of their generation, and in the

haste of the hour take refuge from pressing difficulties in a system of measures which seem plausible at the time, which offer
the chances of a favorable change, and which posterity is left to
deplore. Overawed by those outward aspects of affairs which
assail the common eye, they do not reflect that the common eye,
even if it saw clearly, sees but a small part of a great empire;
that what it does see it sees often through a distorted medium,
and that it can embrace, at the farthest, only a few, and those
lying on the surface of those innumerable elements which com-
pose the prosperity of a Commonwealth. No people rising suddenly from a state of control which their fathers and themselves
had endured for almost two centuries into a new complicated
sphere, and capable of taking the full measure of their own
stature, or the true dimensions of their own era. Of all the
sciences which act on the business of life, the science of political economy was least studied by the statesmen of that age.
Every question of law and politics relating to men and communities, every question that pertained directly to the rights of person and property, had been critically studied by our fathers, and
were discussed with an ability that made the dialectics of the
Revolution as distinctive as the wisdom which declared independence, or the valor which achieved it. But the problems of
political economy had never engaged their deliberate attention.
That science had but recently taken its separate station in English literature, for the *Wealth of Nations* was its text-book, and
Adam Smith had not published the *Wealth of Nations* three
years before the meeting of the first Congress. Nor were the
doctrines of the new science readily received. Practical men,
then as now, viewed them with disgust, and some of the British
politicians of that day never read them at all. If, many years
later, when its theories were expounded in Parliament and from
the chairs of the schools, Charles James Fox was not ashamed
to say that he had never read the *Wealth of Nations*, it is no
reflection upon our fathers that they had not studied a science
which they had no opportunity of knowing, and which had a
slight bearing only on colonial legislation. But the science of
political economy is only the philosophy drawn from the experience of men in their commercial relations with one another;
and with some of those relations our fathers had an intimate acquaintance. It is creditable to Virginia that, though some of

her famed sons did not comprehend or disregarded the teachings of the new science, others who had for a quarter of a century, in peace and war, mainly guided her destinies, had read them wisely.

The unfortunate delusion in respect of the commerce of Virginia, which then prevailed, led to disastrous results. It kept alive in our early councils those dissensions which existed before the war began, which raged fiercely during its continuance, which, coming down to our own times, had nearly kindled the flames of civil war, but which otherwise might have ended with the eighteenth century. It led, in the vain hope of sudden improvement, to the hasty adoption of the present Federal Constitution without previous amendments, and to the surrender of the right of regulating its commerce by the greatest State of the Confederation to an authority beyond its control. It led to a state of things of which our fathers did not dream, and which, if they could behold, would make them turn in their graves. It destroyed our direct trade with foreign powers. It banished the flag of Virginia from the seas. Instead of building and manning the ships which carried the product of our labor to foreign ports, and which brought back the product of the labor of others to our own ports, as some were persuaded to believe would be the result of the change, it compelled us thenceforth to commit our produce to the ships of other States, and to receive our foreign supplies through other ports than our own. It brought about the strange result that, instead of a large part of the cost of defraying the expenses of the Government of Virginia being derived from the duties levied upon foreign commerce, those duties, though levied upon a scale unknown in that age,[25] will not suffice, in this sixty-ninth year of the new system, to pay the expenses of collection by other hands than our own.

It is due to the memory of our fathers to inquire, and it is the province of history to record, how far such a result could have been foreseen at the time; for the decision of the question has no unimportant bearing upon the reputation of the men who upheld or opposed the system from which such a revolution was

---

[25] In a manuscript letter of Edmund Pendleton, dated December 4, 1792, in my possession, that illustrious jurist says: "Five per cent. seemed to have been fixed on, as a standard of moderation, by the general consent of America." This entire letter is devoted to the subject of the tariff.

destined to proceed; and we fitly pause in our narrative to say a few words on the subject.   It is singular that, when the Federal Constitution was presented for their consideration, our fathers had already been more familiar with the theory of Federal systems than any public men of that generation.   Of the ablest men, who, more than ten years before, either aided in framing the Articles of Confederation in Congress, who discussed them in the General Assembly, who ratified them in behalf of Virginia in Congress, and who watched their operation in Congress and in the Assembly, nearly all were then living.   One of them, whose immortal name is appended to those Articles, had published his opinions on the new system.[26]   Several members of Congress were members of the present Convention.   When those Articles were maturing in Congress, and were afterwards discussed in the General Assembly, the distinctive merits of the Federal schemes recorded in history were freely canvassed.   It was soon seen that history, in its long roll of nations which have coalesced from motives of gain, ambition, or self-defense, afforded no model of a Federal alliance which was suited to the existing emergency, and that the problem was to be solved for the occasion.   It was only from general reasoning, drawn from the nature of independent States, that our fathers could arrive at their conclusions.   And that reasoning was this: The right to regulate the trade and commerce of a State is, in fact, the right to control its industry, to direct its labor, and to wield its capital at will.   It was one of those exclusive rights of sovereignty that are inseparable from its being, and that no State can commit to the discretion of another; for no State whose industry is controlled by another, can be said to be free.   To raise what products we please, to send them, in our own way, to those who are willing to take them, and to receive in exchange such commodities as we please, and those commodities to be free from all burdens, except such as we choose to put upon them, is a right which no people should voluntarily relinquish, and which no people ever relinquished but to a conquerer.   A small State may, indeed, coalesce with a larger, and on certain conditions may

---

[26] Letter of R. H. Lee to Governor Randolph, *Elliott's Debates*, Vol. I, 502, edition of 1859; objections of George Mason, *Ibid.*, 494; Edmund Randolph's letter to the Speaker of the Virginia House of Delegates, *Ibid.*, 482.

derive benefit from so intimate an alliance. The gain from an equal participation in the trade of the buyer, and a sense of security from their united strength, may be deemed a fair equivalent for the risks which it runs. But it is plain that the benefits of such a coalition depend wholly on the good faith of the stronger party ; and the rights of the weaker are enjoyed by the courtesy of the stronger. To hold the most precious rights at the discretion of another was a dangerous experiment; and experience has shown that no such union has ever been voluntarily made. No confederacy, in ancient or in modern times, was ever formed on so intimate a union of its several parts, and the unusual experience of mankind should seem to forbid it.

But if it be dangerous for a small State to form so intimate an alliance with a greater, it follows that it is equally dangerous for a large State to coalesce, not with a smaller, or a series of smaller ones, whose combined strength is inferior to its own, but with a series of States whose strength exceeds its own, whose voices can control the common counsels, and whose interests can apply the common resources at discretion. In such a case, the large State sinks its independent position, and has no more conclusive control of its own affairs than the humblest member of the association. Hence, the record of civilized States affords no instance of such an alliance. Guided by these principles, our fathers determined to form a Federal alliance more intimate, indeed, than any which has come down to us, but to reserve a conclusive control over the trade and the commerce of Virginia. They were willing to surrender the sword, but they retained the purse in their own keeping.

Of all alliances between independent States in ancient or in modern times, the Articles of Confederation presented the fairest model of a Federal system. It raised the admiration of Europe, strangely mingled with surprise. For a single province, or more provinces than one, to cast off allegiance to a distant power, was no uncommon incident in modern times. But to form a Federal alliance, which bestowed with a liberal hand upon the central executive all the powers which the general interests demanded, and yet guarded with consummate skill the integrity and independence of the component parts, was a brilliant achievement. Its reception by the people was joyous. At a later period, when its workings had been observed more closely, the

Congress which it created but echoed the general voice in pronouncing it "a glorious compact." It was destined to a short life of eight years; and its brightness has paled before the more dazzling scheme which succeeded it; but it still remains the most perfect model of a confederation which the world has ever seen. The future historian will record its worth with becoming pride, and rescue the glory of its founders from the eclipse which the ambition and passions of men have combined to darken it.

What heightened the admiration of the Federal system was the circumstances under which it was formed. It was at the darkest period of the Revolution. It was formed at a time when the greatest military and naval power which the world had ever seen was marshalling all its forces against a feeble country, and was pushing them forward with certain hopes of conquest; when some of the statesmen most active in the public councils, shrinking from the odds arrayed against them, were ready, it is alleged, to create a dictator in the State and a dictator in the Federal Government; when the punishment of treason, denounced against our fathers by a king, whose predecessor and ancestor had, within the memory of men then on the stage, converted the fields of a kingdom, whose crown he inherited, into a blackened waste, and decimated a brave though rude population, was suspended over their heads; and when every motive that could sway the bosoms of men, impelled the people of the revolted Colonies to form the strongest bulwark against the invading hosts. And it is one of the wonders of history that a State which would not surrender its purse in the midst of a crisis that invoked its existence, should, in a time of profound peace and of general prosperity, have consented to such a sacrifice.

But the deed was done, and it is our duty to inquire whether the tendency of the Federal Constitution to produce such an effect on the commerce of the State as has since been apparent, could have been foreseen at the time of its adoption. A single glance will show that it contains no provision respecting one State more than another; and that all the States stand on the same level. It is in its general scope that we must seek the cause of the commercial decline of this Commonwealth. Immemorial experience has shown that in every single and undivided political community—and such would be the States of the Union, so far as commerce is concerned, under the proposed Constitution—there must be a controlling centre of trade, of business and of money. It might not have been safe to foretell the exact spot where that centre would be, but it was very easy to foretell where it would not be. It would not be in the ports of a people whose entire capital and labor were invested in agriculture, and who had not, during the period that elapsed from the settlement at James Town to the peace of 1783, built and manned a single merchant ship of three hundred tons. But let that centre be established anywhere, and the result would not be a matter of surprise but of mathematical certainty. Its influence would be universal. It would extend to the remotest limits of the widest empire. It would be equally stringent in regulating a commercial transaction in the waters of the Bay of Fundy and at St. Mary's, which was then the southern boundary of the Union. No Southern merchant could build, equip, and load a ship, despatch her to a foreign port, and order her to return with an assorted cargo to a Virginia port, without being governed by the rates prevailing at the controlling centre of the capital and labor of the country.

Bankruptcy, immediate and irretrievable, would certainly follow the neglect of such a precaution. It would be as wild to build, load, and sail a ship in opposition to the law of trade emanating from the central power, as it would be to attempt to place a planet in the skies irrespective of the law of gravitation. The consequence would ultimately be that the money centre would increase in population and resources with an accelerated rapidity, while those parts distant from the centre, probably in some proportion to their distance from that centre, and especially those which, engaged in agriculture, were less able to change the nature of their investments, must relatively decline. It is not contended that this central power is absolutely immovable; for, as it is not the creature of law, nor derives its power from ordinary legislation, it is possible to move it at any moment; but it can only be removed by a kindred power greater than itself. We have no right to wonder that our fathers overlooked the obvious course of business and exchanges, when we see what has been done in our time by their descendants. Year after year we have denounced the Federal tariff as the cause of the commercial decline of the South, and one of the Southern States went so far in opposing it as to threaten a disruption of the Union. Yet it is plain, from what has been said, that the tariff, which, by the way, acted on the navigation of the North precisely as it acted on the navigation of the South, however odious, as laying upon the South what was deemed a high and unequal tax, had no more effect on our navigation than it had on the rise and fall of the tides, or on the course of our winds.   If the Federal revenue had been derived from direct taxation, or from the sales of the public lands ; if not a dollar from the origin of the Federal Government to the present hour had been levied upon imports ; nay, further, if not a solitary slave had existed for the last seventy years in that vast realm stretching from the Potomac to the Rio Grande; the result complained of in the South would have been essentially the same.   The evil which · the Southern States felt, and it is an existing evil, the effects of which on population, arts, and manufactures, are formidable, the acts of Congress did not cause, and the acts of Congress cannot cure.   It follows, and must follow indefinitely, from the silent operation of that organic Federal bond which makes the people of the several States, so far as commerce is concerned, one people.   It is in the various advantages resulting from the Federal compact, that we must seek a compensation for the loss of our direct trade with foreign powers.   The problem which should engage the attention of Southern statesmen is not to seek a restoration of the state of things that existed, when seventy years ago the Federal Constitution was adopted, by a dissolution of the Union, an event which would not only fail from obvious considerations to effect the desired end, but would open a hundred new questions of peace and war more perplexing and more difficult of solution than the one which now annoys us ; but acknowledging at once the binding obligation of a law of trade, which the experience of seventy years has shown our inability to resist in the absence of the right to regulate our own commerce, and adapting ourselves to the new figure of the times, to ascertain the best means of making it available in the highest degree to the prosperity of the Southern States.[27]

The basis of the Convention, a topic of so much strife in respect of the Conventions of our own times, did not much engage the attention of our fathers.   It was the basis of the House of Delegates, which was then composed of two members from each

---

[27] It will be kept in mind that this was read before the Historical Society in February, 1858, and, I may add, written a year or two before.

of the eighty-four counties, of one member from the city of Williamsburg, and of one member from the borough of Norfolk.[28] Some time was to elapse before Richmond and Petersburg were to send delegates to the Assembly. Richmond, named by Byrd after that beautiful village which looks grandly down on the waters of the Thames, and which has been commemorated by the muse of Denham, was then known in public proceedings as Richmond Town, in order to distinguish it from the county of the same name. Since the organization of the State Government in 1776—a period of twelve years—no less than twenty-eight counties had been formed ; and the naming of the new counties offered a graceful opportunity of honoring individual worth.[29] Posterity beholds in those names no uninstructive me-

---

[28] The curious eye will miss, with tender regret, the name of William and Mary College, which had sent delegates to the House of Burgesses for eighty-four years, but was disfranchised by the Convention of 1776. The delegates from this institution were always of the highest order of talents and moral worth. The amiable and excellent Blair represented the College in the Convention of 1776, its last representative.

[29] The names of the counties laid off in the interval between July, 1776, and June, 1788, were Fluvanna, Rockingham, Rockbridge, Greenbrier, Henry, Kentucky, Washington, Montgomery, Ohio, Yohoganey, Monongalia, Powhatan, Illinois, Jefferson, Fayette, Lincoln, Harrison, Greensville, Campbell, Nelson, Franklin, Randolph, Hardy, Bourbon, Russell, Mercer, Madison, and Pendleton. The reader may wish to know on which of the patriots of the Revolution the honor of having a county called by his name was conferred. Patrick Henry received that honor. He was the first Governor of the State, and the old Colonial rule of naming a county after the existing Governor was applied with peculiar propriety in his case. But, at the same session, the county of Fincastle was divided into Kentucky, Washington, and Montgomery, and the name of Fincastle dropped, as was also, at the same session, the name of Dunmore, and Shenandoah substituted in its stead. At the session of the Assembly immediately after the adjournment of the present Convention, a county was called after George Mason, and another after the gallant Woodford. Mason and Woodford counties were in the district of Kentucky, and were lost to us when the district became a State. So that at this time we have no county named after the author of the Declaration of Rights, and the General who gained the first victory of the Revolution. The present Mason county was laid off in 1804—the year after the death of Stevens Thomson Mason, a distinguished patriot, long a member of both Houses of Assembly and of the Senate of the United States ; and, I have understood, was called in honor of his name.

morial of the estimation in which the originals were held by their contemporaries. Indeed, from such materials, one skilled in the anatomy of history, might, in the absence of other sources of intelligence, reconstruct no inaccurate record of that age. Not one of those names had hitherto received any such expression of the public regard; for, up to this period, the name of no Virginian had been given to a county ; and in the number and character of the new names, it is plainly seen that some remarkable public epoch had occurred. The history of Henry, Washington, Jefferson, Harrison, Campbell, Nelson, Randolph, Hardy, Russell, Woodford, Mercer, Madison, and Pendleton, is the history of their times. The names of Montgomery, Franklin, Lincoln, and Greene, show that in the great event which had transpired, and which had called forth so many of our own citizens, we had received the succor of our sister States ; while the name of Fayette evokes the name of that chivalrous youth who, turning his back on the endearments of domestic life and the fascinations of the gayest metropolis in Europe, hastened to share with our fathers the toils and dangers of war, who attained to the rank of Major-General in the armies of the United States, and held high command in our midst, and who won on the field of York his greenest laurel ; and the name of Bourbon renews the recollection of that beneficent but unfortunate prince, without whose assistance the war of the Revolution might have lasted thirty years, and whose fleets and armies aided in gaining, in our behalf, and within the limits of this Commonwealth, one of the most glorious of those innumerable battles in which the banner of St. Louis had, during many centuries, been borne in triumph.

Near the close of Sunday, the first day of June, 1788, Richmond Town was in an unusual bustle. The day had been bright and warm, and was among the last days of a drought, which had killed nearly all the young tobacco plants in the hill uncovered by clods, and had filled the roads fetlock-deep with dust, but which fortunately made the rivers and creeks fordable on horseback. Indeed, a rainy spell at that time would have been a grave annoyance. It would have detained half of the members of the Convention on the road. It might have decided the fate of the Federal Constitution. A heavy rain at nightfall would have kept the member for Henrico, who lived on Church Hill, from taking his seat next morning in the old Capitol or in the new Academy.

Bridges were then rare; and a fresh rendered the clumsy ferry-boat of little avail. None of the appliances against the inclemency of the weather were then introduced. Oil skin and India rubber had not yet been heard of; even the umbrella, which now makes a part of the Sunday rigging of the negroes on the tobacco estates of the Staunton and the Dan, was then unknown. Rumors had reached the State that sallow men, from the remote East, might be occasionally seen on the steps of the India House, or sauntering in Piccadilly, having in their hands a curious instrument, which was used ordinarily as a cane, but which, when hoisted and held overhead, protected the body from the rays of the fiercest sun, and also from the rain, though it should descend in torrents.

People in greater numbers than had ever been known before were coming into town from every quarter. Our modes of travel are widely different from what they then were. Not only were the canal, the railway, and the steamer then unknown, but coaches were rarely seen. There were thousands of respectable men in the Commonwealth who had never seen any other four-wheeled vehicle than a wagon, and there were thousands who had never seen a wagon. Nothing shows more plainly the difference between the past and the present than the modes of conveyance used then and now. To pass from Richmond to the Valley of Virginia in a carriage and pair was seldom attempted; and, if attempted, was seldom successful. The roads, which, now winding their way gradually around the hills and mountains, make a jaunt across the Alleghany safe and pleasant, then, when there were no roads at all, sought the top the nearest way. Thirty years later, it was rare that the lowlander, who drove in his coach to the mountains, brought back the same pair of horses with which he set out on his journey. One of the pair had made his final pause in Rockfish Gap, and had been exchanged for another at the next settlement. The bones of the other had been picked by the buzzards, which, circling low and drowsily above the road of the Warm Springs mountain, had watched with listless eyes their yet breathing prey. Now the traveller may pass into the interior from the mouth of the James more than three hundred miles in canal packets, or in capacious steamers, the tonnage of one of which exceeds the combined tonnage of the fleets in which Columbus and John Smith made their first voyage to the New World, and hardly miss the comforts and quiet of home. Then, and until forty years later, when the skill of Crozet had taught the waters of the James to flow peacefully in trenches excavated by the pickaxe or blasted from the rock, the daring traveller who passed in a boat from the North river into the James, and thence through the Balcony Falls, was never tired of recounting the dangers which beset his course. The swiftness of the river was frightful ; the loudest screams of the boatman, who wielded the long oar at the helm, was lost amid the roar of the waters dashing against the rocks ; the roar of the waters smote the rugged sides of the cliffs that guarded the pass, and the sullen cliffs gave back the roar. It was Scylla and Charybdis, the whirlpool and the rock, in fearful juxtaposition. Should the long and frail boat, flying with a rapidity unknown to steam or sail, and twisted by the torrent, deviate a few feet from a tortuous channel known only to the initiated, it was shipwrecked beyond the reach of human aid. At the time of which we are treating, there was not only no mail coach running west of Richmond, but no mail coach running to Richmond itself. The planter, his legs sheathed in wrappers, his spare clothes stowed in saddle-bags, and his cloak strapped behind his saddle, left his home on his own horse.

Cavalcades of horsemen, to be traced from an elevated position by the clouds of dust that rose above them, were now seen along the highways leading into town. Just before sunset might have been observed from this hill[30] the approach of two men, whose names will be held in honor by generations to come. Though not personal enemies, they rarely thought alike on the greatest questions of that age, and they came aptly enough by different roads. One was seen advancing from the south side of the James, driving a plain and topless stick gig. He was tall, and seemed capable of enduring fatigue, but was bending forward as if worn with travel. His dress was the product of his own loom, and was covered with dust. He was to be the master-spirit of the Convention. The other approached from the north side of the river in an elegant vehicle then known as a phæton,[31]

---

[30] This was read in the hall of the House of Delegates in the Capitol.

[31] This phæton Pendleton afterwards gave to his relative, the mother of Jaquelin P. Taylor, Esq., the treasurer of the Virginia Historical Society, who distinctly remembers it.

which was driven so slowly that its occupant was seen at a glance to be pressed by age or infirmity. He had been thrown some years before from his horse and had dislocated his hip, and was never afterwards able to stand or walk without assistance. His imposing stature, the elegance of his dress, the dignity of his mien, his venerable age, bespoke no ordinary man. He was called by a unanimous vote to preside in the body. Both of these eminent men had been long distinguished in the Colony and in the Commonwealth. Both had borne a prominent part on every great occasion since the session of the House of Burgesses of 1765. Both had been intimately connected with that memorable resolution which instructed the delegates of Virginia to propose independence. One had sustained that resolution with unrivaled eloquence on the floor ; the other had drawn it with his own hand. They met on the steps of the Swan and exchanged salutations. Public expectation was at its height when it was known that Patrick Henry and Edmund Pendleton, who, for a quarter of a century, had been at the head of the two great parties of that day, were about to engage in another fierce conflict in the councils of their country.

The, occasion might well inspire the deepest interest. For more than five years the amendment of the Articles of Confederation had engaged the public attention, but within two years then past it had become an engrossing topic. On the 21st of January, 1786, Virginia, by a formal resolution of her Assembly, had invited a meeting of the States, which was ultimately held at Annapolis.[32] That body proposed the assembling of a Convention in Philadelphia on the second day of May, 1787. This resolution received the sanction of the Congress of the Confederation, and was pressed by that body on the attention of the

---

[32] For the resolution of Virginia inviting the meeting that was held at Annapolis, see the Appendix ; for the Journal of the meeting at that place, see Bioren's and Duane's edition *U. S. Laws*, I, 55; for the letter to the States sent forth by those who met, and originally prepared by Colonel Hamilton, see *Elliot's Debates*, V, 115; and for the resolution appointing delegates to the General Convention in Philadelphia, see Appendix. The resolution convoking the meeting at Annapolis, and the preamble and resolution appointing delegates to the Convention, was drawn by Mr. Madison. The preamble of the last deserves a careful perusal.

States; but even before Congress had acted upon it, the General Assembly of this Commonwealth had complied with its object, and had appointed a delegation to the proposed Convention. The number and character of the delegates selected for the service demonstrated the importance of the movement; and Virginia, when she had confided her trust to George Washington, Patrick Henry, Edmund Randolph, John Blair, James Madison, George Mason, and George Wythe, calmly awaited the result of their labors.[33]

The General Convention of the United States did not form a quorum until the twenty-fourth day of May; and, after a continuous session of four months, adjourned on the seventeenth of September following. The Constitution, the work of its hands, was duly transmitted to Congress, and was recommended by that body to the consideration of the States. Its first publication in this State gave rise to various emotions. A dark cloud evidently rested above its cradle. Most of the officers and many of the soldiers of the Revolution, swayed by the opinions of Washington, which were openly expressed in conversation, and in his letters, and charmed by the beautiful outline of a great polity presented by the instrument itself, received it with admiration and delight. But a formidable opposition was soon apparent from another quarter. The leading statesmen of Virginia, men who had sustained the resolutions of Henry against the Stamp Act, and his resolutions for embodying the militia, who had been eager for independence, and who had guided the public councils during the war and in the interval between the close of the war and the meeting of the General Convention, read the new plan with far different feelings. They saw, or thought that they saw, in its character and in its provisions, that the public liberties were seriously menaced, and that a war for independence was to be waged once more under most painful circumstances. Heretofore the people had been united in the common cause; and

---

[33] Colonel Henry declined the appointment, and R. H. Lee was appointed by the Governor in his stead; but he declined, doubtless for the same reason which induced the Assembly to pass him by, which was that he was President of Congress, which would hold its sessions simultaneously with those of the Convention. On Lee's declension, Dr. James McClurg was appointed, and took his seat at the beginning of the session.

their union, in spite of many obstacles, had carried them successfully through the late contest.   But now one portion of the people was to be arrayed against another ; and the result of the new
contest, whatever it might be, would be fraught with peril.   The
first general impression should seem to have been adverse to the
new system.   It had taken the people by surprise.   It should be
remembered that the deliberations of the General Convention
had been secret, and, that if they had been public, the facilities by
which we are now enabled to watch from its inception any measure of public policy, did not then exist.   The Constitution proposed an entirely new system of government, when the belief of
the people was universal that the powers of the General Convention were limited to an amendment of the existing system to
which they had become attached, and which they believed amply
sufficient, with certain modifications, to attain the end of its creation.   They felt at the moment that resentment which springs
from a sense of having been cajoled or deceived by those to
whom we have confided an important trust.[34]   Upon a nearer
view, they were led to believe that the new Constitution was in
opposition to the wishes of a majority of their representatives in
Convention.   It bore indeed the name most dear to the hearts of
the people, but he may have signed it as an officer, and not as

---

[34] If the reader wishes to see how far these suspicions were founded,
let him consult and compare the resolution appointing delegates to
Annapolis ; the resolution of the General Assembly of the third of
November, 1786, declaring that an act ought to pass to appoint delegates to the General Convention "with powers to devise such further
provision as shall to them appear necessary to render the Constitution
of the Federal Government adequate to the exigencies of the Union ;
and to report such an act for that purpose to the United States in Congress assembled, as, when agreed to by them, and afterwards confirmed by the *legislatures* of every State, will effectually provide for the
same" ; and especially the resolution appointing the delegates to the
Convention, which was drawn by Mr. Madison, under the instructions
of the foregoing resolution, marking the substitution of the word
"States" for legislatures ; and it will be seen that a strict and literal
amendment of the old, and not the introduction of a new one, was in
the view of the Assembly.   From the state of parties in the House of
Delegates when these resolutions were passed, it may be safely affirmed
that not thirty votes could have been obtained for any other amendment than a specific one to pass through the forms required for an
amendment to the Articles of Confederation.

an individual; but with the exception of the names of Blair and Madison, it bore no other.   Patrick Henry had declined his seat in the Convention; but neither the name of McClurg, who succeeded him, nor that of Mason, or Randolph, or Wythe were attached to its roll.   If the absence of these names meant any thing, it meant that if the vote of Virginia could have controlled the question of the adoption of the Constitution by the Convention which framed it, it would not have seen the light.   It was the work then of a minority of the delegates of Virginia in Convention, and it had the hand of bastardy on its face.   And it is certain that upon an immediate direct vote upon it by the people, it would have been rejected by an overwhelming majority.

Fortunately, there was full time for the examination of the new system.   From the adjournment of the General Convention to the time of the meeting of the Virginia Convention, which was called to discuss it, eight months would elapse ; and never were eight months spent in such animated disputation.   Essays on the new scheme filled the papers of the day, but the papers of that day were small and had but a limited circulation ; and for the first time in our recent history, the pamphlet became a frequent engine of political warfare.   Beside those essays which have come down to us in the garb of the *Federalist*, and which are still regarded with authority, there were others published throughout the States of equal popularity.   The solemn protest of George Mason, the eloquent letter of Edmund Randolph, then Governor, to the Speaker of the House of Delegates, and the statesmanlike production of Richard Henry Lee addressed to the Governor, all demonstrating the defects of the proposed plan of government, were in every hand.[35]   The bibliographer still points to the tracts of the period, bound in small volumes, as among the sybil relics of our early political literature.   But however great was the influence of the press, its influence was exceeded by oral discussions.   Public addresses were made at every gathering of the people.   The court green, the race-course, and

---

[35] Though the people in the vicinity of towns and villages could get a glance at a paper, even prominent men in the interior were not reached by the press.   Humphrey Marshall, from Kentucky, had travelled into the densely populated parts of Virginia on his way to the Convention, when he met with a number of the *Federalist* for the first time.

the muster-field, resounded with disputations. The pulpit as
well as the rostrum uttered its voice, and the saint and the sin-
ner mingled in the fierce *mêlée*.[36] An incident which occurred in
Halifax will serve to show the excitement of the times. A
preacher on a Sunday morning had pronounced from the desk a
fervent prayer for the adoption of the Federal Constitution ; but
he had no sooner ended his prayer than a clever layman ascended
the pulpit, invited the people to join a second time in the suppli-
cation, and put forth an animated petition that the new scheme
be rejected by the Convention about to assemble by an overwhelming majority.[37]

Great tact was shown by the friends of the new scheme in the
selection of candidates. The honest country gentlemen whose
fathers had been for years in the Assembly, and who had been
for years in the Assembly themselves, and who thought that they
had a prescriptive title to public honors, were gently put aside,
and the judge was taken from the bench, and the soldier, who
was reposing beneath the laurels won in many a stricken field,
was summoned from his farm to fill a seat in the approaching
Convention. Such, indeed, was the zeal with which the elections were pushed, that, for the first time in our history, personal
enmities were overlooked, and ancient political feuds, which
promised to descend for generations, were allowed to slumber.
One gentleman, who, in the beginning of the war, had been suspected of dealing with the enemy, who had been arrested and
held under heavy bonds in strict confinement, and had been
escorted by a military guard into the interior of the State, was
returned to the Convention, his friendship for the Constitution

---

[36] There was a passage at arms between the Rev. John Blair Smith,
president of Hampden-Sydney College in Prince Edward county, and
Patrick Henry, who represented that county in the Convention. Henry
had inveighed with great severity against the Constitution, and was
responded to by Dr. Smith, who pressed the question upon Henry, why
he had not taken his seat in the Convention and lent his aid in making
a good Constitution, instead of staying at home and abusing the work
of his patriotic compeers? Henry, with that magical power of acting
in which he excelled all his contemporaries, and which before a popular assembly was irresistible, replied : " I SMELT A RAT."

[37] I could "name names," if necessary, but to do so might possibly
be unpleasant to the descendants of the actors.

wiping out the sins of his earlier life. Another member, whose father had by a formal decree of one of the early Conventions been arrested, had also been placed under heavy bonds, and had been confined within certain limits, and who had himself spent the entire period of the Revolution abroad, expiated his guilt patrimonial and personal by his attachment to the new system, and took his seat by the side of men whose swords had hardly ceased to drip with the blood of the common foe. Whether we regard such results as flowing from high principles or from the impulse of eager passion, it is equally our duty to record them. Thus, when the time approached for the election of the members who were to decide the fate of the Constitution, there was not only an obvious line drawn between its friends and its enemies, but there were shrewd estimates of its ultimate fate.

The assembling of the Convention attracted attention throughout the State and throughout the Union. Few of the citizens of Virginia had ever seen a Convention of the people. The Convention of August, 1774, sate in Williamsburg, and adjourned after a session of five days. The Conventions of March, of July, and of December, 1775, sate in Richmond ; but the Convention of March was in session but seven days, the Convention of July only thirty-nine days, and that of December fifty days ; and the Richmond of 1775 differed almost as much from the Richmond of 1778, small as it was at the latter period, as the Richmond of 1788 differed from the Richmond of 1858. The Convention of 1776 sate in Williamsburg, and, as the sessions embraced sixty days, was together longer than any deliberative body in our previous annals. Still, from the emergencies of war, from the uncertainty of the times, and from the sparseness of the population, those only who lived in the vicinity of Williamsburg and Richmond had then seen any of the prominent men of that generation. Henry was the best known of our public men. He had not only been Governor twice during the last twelve years, and occasionally a member of the Assembly, which he was ever the last to reach and the first to quit, but he had frequently been called to distant counties to defend culprits which no native talents were likely to screen from the law; yet few of the men then on the stage had ever seen Henry. Pendleton, who, from his years, was more of a historical character than Henry, could for the last ten years be seen only in term time on the bench, or in his snug room at the Swan, or in vacation on his estate in Caroline. Mason, though laborious on committees and in the House of Delegates, had a horror of long sessions, and would not be persuaded to remain long beyond the smoke of "Gunston Hall." The person of Wythe was more familiar to persons from abroad ; for, since the removal of the seat of government from Williamsburg, he had taken up his abode in town,[38] and might be seen in his court or in his study, and not unfrequently of a bright frosty morning, in loose array, taking an air bath in the porch of his humble residence on Shockoe Hill. Now all these eminent men, and others who had grown into reputation during the war and since, were to be seen together. In every point of view the Convention was an imposing body. It presented as proud a galaxy of genius, worth, and public service as had ever shone in the councils of a single State. The rule of its selection had been without limit. The members were chosen without regard to the offices which they held, or to their pursuits in life. The judge, as was just observed, was called from the bench, and the soldier from his home ; while the merchant, the planter, the lawyer, the physician and the divine, made up the complement of its members. There was one feature conspicuous in the returns, and shows not only the fluctuation of the public mind at that important crisis, but the force of individual worth. Sharply drawn as were the lines of party, a county would send up one of its two members friendly to the Constitution, and the other opposed to it. As a type of the times, it may be noted that the successor of Henry in the General Convention which framed the Federal Constitution, was one of the most distinguished physicians of that age. The body was very large, and consisted, as already stated, of one hundred and seventy members, and exceeded by fifty two the number of the members who composed the Convention of 1776. It was more than four times greater than the Convention which formed the Federal Constitution when that body was full, and it exceeded it, as it ordinarily was, more than six times. It had a trait discernible in all the great Conventions of Virginia. It consisted of the public men of three generations. Some of the

---

[38] Judge Wythe's residence stood at the southeast corner of Grace and Fifth streets, on the spot where stands the residence erected by the late Abraham Warwick, and now owned and occupied by Major Legh R. Page.

eminent men who more than thirty years before had dared to assail the usurpations of ·Dinwiddie, and to dispatch to England to protest against the unconstitutional pistole tax levied by the Governor;[39] who, twenty-three years before, had voted on Henry's resolutions against the Stamp Act, and had voted thirteen years before on his resolutions for putting the Colony in a posture of defence, and had voted for the resolution proposing independence; who had distinguished themselves in the Indian wars, and who had borne a prominent part on the military and civil theatre of the Revolution.

Several of the members of that great committee, under whose wise guidance the country had passed from the Colony to the Commonwealth, with their illustrious chief at their head, were members of the body; and sitting by their side was that remarkable man, more illustrious still, who, in a time of intense excitement, had been deemed their victim.[40]

The martial aspect of the Convention would alone have attracted observation. There was hardly a battlefield, from the Monongahela and the Kanawha to the plains of Abraham, from the Great Bridge to Monmouth, and from the bloody plains of Eutaw to York, that was not illuminated by the valor of some member then present. The names of Bland, Carrington of Halifax, Samuel Jordan Cabell, Clendenin, Darke, Fleming, Grayson, Innes, Lawson, Henry Lee of the Legion, known in the Convention as Lee of Westmoreland, in distinction from his namesake and relative, Henry Lee of Bourbon, Matthews, who, when

---

[39] The conduct of the House of Burgesses on that occasion displayed great spirit. They sent Peyton Randolph, then Attorney-General, to England, who partly succeeded in his mission. His expenses were two thousand five hundred pounds, which were paid by a bill which the Governor refused to approve. The House of Burgesses then tacked the sum of two thousand five hundred pounds to the appropriation bill of twenty thousand pounds; and the Governor sent back this bill also. The House then ordered the treasurer to pay the money; which he did. Journals House of Burgesses, Nov., 1753, and *Sparks' Washington*, II, 59. *Dinwiddie Papers*, 1, 44, *et seq.*; II, 3, 57.

[40] After the adjournment of the Convention of 1776, Pendleton and Henry never met in a public body. Henry was elected Governor by that Convention; and Pendleton, after a session or two in the House of Delegates, was placed on the bench, where he remained nearly a quarter of a century. Henry was often a member of the House of Delegates in the interval between 1776 and 1788.

not engaged in the field, was a member of the House of Delegates, whose name is conspicuous in our early Journals as chairman on Committee of the Whole and Speaker of the House,
and is still borne by one of those beautiful counties that overlook our great inland sea, Mason, of Loudoun, Marshall, who had
not attained the age of thirty-three, and little dreamed that in a
few short years he was to represent the young empire at the
most renowned court in Europe, and to preside, for an entire
generation, in the judiciary of the new system which he was
about to sustain, Monroe, the junior of Marshall by three years,
his playmate at school, his colleague in camp and in college, and
destined to fill the highest offices, at home and abroad, of the
new system which he was about to oppose, McKee, Moore of
Rockbridge, George and Wilson Cary Nicholas, Read, Riddick,
Steele, Adam Stephen, Stuart of Augusta, Stuart of Greenbrier,
Zane, and others, recall alike our hardest contest with the Indians and the British. Well might Henry and George Mason
view that brilliant phalanx with doubt and fear.[41]   Pendleton, the
President of the Court of Appeals, and Wythe, a chancellor and a
member of the same court, who had been pitted against each other
in the Senate and in the forum throughout their political lives, and
were now to act in unison, were not the only representatives of
the judiciary.[42]   Bullitt had not taken his seat on the bench ; but

---

[41] A large majority of the officers of the army of the Revolution were
in favor of the new Constitution. The Cincinnati were mostly among
its warmest advocates ; and as they were organized and were, many of
them, of exalted private and public worth, and could act in concert
through all the States, their influence was foreseen and feared by its
opponents. Mason and Gerry often alluded to that influence in their
speeches in the General Convention (*Madison Papers*, II, 1208; *Elliot's
Debates*, V, 368) ; and although Judge Marshall affirms that "in Virginia certainly a large number, perhaps a majority, of the Cincinnati
were opposed to it" (meaning the *administration* of Washington),
(II, Appendix 31, second edition); yet when he enumerated the various
classes who favored a change in the Articles of Confederation, he says,
"the officers of the army threw themselves almost universally in the
same scale." *Life of Washington*, II, 77. In the present Convention
there were several who were opposed to the Constitution.

[42] These two venerable men, with George Mason and Patrick Henry,
were those first sought by the spectator, as in a convention, forty years
later, were Madison, Monroe, Marshall, and Fayette. If the reader
wishes to know the constitution of the courts in 1787, let him turn to
Mr. Minor's edition of *Wythe's Reports*, page 20 of the memoir.

Blair, Cary of Warwick, Carrington of Charlotte, Jones, and Tyler, were members of the body.   Some of the prominent members of Congress were present.   Harrison, Henry and Pendleton stood up in the Carpenters' Hall, when the eloquent Duché, then firm in his country's cause, had invoked the guidance of Heaven in the deliberations of the first Congress; while Grayson, Henry Lee of the Legion, Madison, Monroe, Edmund Randolph, and Wythe, had been or were then in the councils of the Union.   The Attorney-General of the Commonwealth, the eloquent and accomplished Innes, and the Governor, were included in that distinguished group.

Yet the eye of the aged spectator, as it ranged along those rows of heads, missed some familiar faces, which, until now, had been seen on nearly all the great civil occasions of a third of the century then past.   The venerable Richard Bland, the unerring oracle, whose responses had, for more than thirty years, been eagerly sought and rarely made in vain, and whose tall form had been so long conspicuous in the House of Burgesses and in all the previous Conventions, had fallen dead in the street in Williamsburg, twelve years before, while attending the session of the first House of Delegates, and when, as chairman of the committee, he was about to report that memorable bill, drawn by Jefferson, abolishing entails.   Benjamin Watkins, of Chesterfield, in whose character were united in noble proportions the firmness of the patriot, the charity of the philanthropist, and the wisdom of the sage, and his name, revived in the Convention that met near half a century after his death to revise the Constitution, which he assisted in framing, was invested with fresh and imperishable praise, had died three years before.[43]   The absence of the old Treasurer, Robert Carter Nicholas, that grave and venerated face, which had been seen for forty years in the House of Burgesses, and in all the Conventions, in one of which he presided, and whose presence gave to the general heart a sense of safety, was now observed for the first time in our great assemblies.   He had died, when the storm of the Revolution raged fiercest, at his

---

[43] He was the maternal grandfather of Benjamin Watkins Leigh and Judge William Leigh, who were members of the Convention of 1829-30. For further details of Mr. Watkins, consult the Watkins' genealogy, by Francis N. Watkins, Esq., page 46.

villa in Hanover, and his corpse, borne by his weeping neighbors, had been laid in its humble grave.   Archibald Cary, too,
was gone.   He had been intimately connected for the third of a
century with very great measures of our colonial policy, had, as
chairman of the Committee of the Whole, reported to the Convention of 1776 the resolution instructing our delegates in Congress to propose independence, and had been at the head of the
committee which reported the Declaration of Rights and the
Constitution.   His unconquerable spirit was an element of force
in every body of which he was a member.   Two years had
barely elapsed since his stalwart form had been committed to the
grave, at Ampthill.[44]   He had lived to behold the triumph of his
country, and to preside, until his death, in the Senate under that
Constitution at whose baptism he had been the fearless and cordial sponsor.[45]   The person of another still more beloved was
wanting.   On him the honors of every deliberative assembly of
which he was a member seemed, by common consent, to devolve.
In the warm conflict between the House of Burgesses and a royal
Governor, who sought to tax the people without the consent of
their representatives, which had occurred in his early manhood,
he had taken an honorable part, and had been sent abroad to
seek redress at the foot of the throne.   His fine person and dignified demeanor had made an impression even within the pre-
cincts of St. James.   He had filled the office of Attorney-General with acknowledged skill, and had volunteered, at a time of
danger, to march at the head of his company against the Indians.
He had presided ten years in the House of Burgesses, and had
won the affection of its members.   He was hated by those only
who hated his country.   He had presided in the August Convention of 1774, and in the Conventions of March and July,
1775, and was the first president of Congress.   He had died,

---

[44] Cary died at "Ampthill," his seat in Chesterfield county, but was
buried in the ancestral grounds at "Ceeleys," in Warwick county.—ED.

[45] In the discourse on the Convention of 1776, page 90, I allude to
Colonel Cary as rather small than large in stature, though compact and
muscular.   Subsequent investigations have led me to believe that he
was a large man of great physical strength.   His corporeal powers
have been celebrated in poetry as well as in prose.   [He was known
by the sobriquet "Old Iron."—ED.]

almost instantaneously, while attending to his duties in Congress ; but his remains had been brought to Virginia ; and persons then present remembered that melancholy morning on which the coffin of Peyton Randolph, wrapped in lead, had, twelve years before, been borne from his late residence, along the high street of Williamsburg, followed by the first General Assembly of the Commonwealth, with their speakers at their head, by the Masonic body, and by a large concourse of citizens, to the threshold of William and Mary College, the nurse of his early youth and the object of his latest care, and had been consigned, with the offices of religion and the rites of Masonry, amid the shrieks of women and the audible sobs of wise and brave men, to the ancestral vault beneath the pavement of the chapel.   Other familiar faces were also missing ; and old men shook their heads, shrugged their shoulders, and muttered that it was ill for the country that such men, at such a crisis, were in their graves ; and that public bodies were not now what they once had been.   A sounded opinion would be that, in ability and capacity for effective public service, the Convention of 1776 was surpassed by the Convention of 1788, which was in its turn surpassed by the Convention of 1829-30.[46]

[46] It is the opinion of what may be called the illustrious second growth of eminent Virginians—men who were born between 1773 and 1788— such as John Randolph, Tazewell, James Barbour, Leigh, Johnson, Philip P. Barbour, Stanard, the late President Tyler, etc., who may be said to have lived in the early shadows of the body itself, and mingled with some of the members in their old age, that the present Convention was, as a whole, the most able body which had then met in the United States.   It is creditable to the conservative character of Virginia that in all her public bodies since the passage of the Stamp Act each successive one has been largely made up from its predecessor.   Thus in the Convention of 1776 there was a large number of the leading members who voted, in 1765, on Henry's resolutions against the Stamp Act, such as Henry himself, Nicholas, Harrison, Pendleton, Wythe, Lewis, and others ; and in the present Convention there were members who had been in the House of Burgesses in 1765, as well as in the Conventions of 1774, 1775, and 1776.   And in the Convention of 1829-30, the Convention of 1776 was represented by Madison, the only surviving member, and the present Convention by Madison, Marshall and Monroe.   If we were to trace back the Journals from 1765 to 1688, the date of the British Revolution, although I have never performed that office, and state my impressions only, I believe that a continuous and con-

It has been said that the interest excited by the Convention was not confined to the Commonwealth. It was well known, as already stated, that, with the exception of Washington and Mc-Clurg, all the representatives of Virginia in the General Convention were members of the present ; and it was feared by the friends of the Constitution abroad that, as three only out of seven had signed that instrument, and one of those in an official character only, it would appear, as it were, under the protest of a majority of those to whom Virginia had committed her interests and her honor. But what enhanced the excitement beyond our borders, as well as at home, was the knowledge of the fact that, of the nine States necessary to the inauguration of the new system, eight had already ratified it, and the favorable vote of the ninth, as the result soon proved, was certain. It was also believed that Rhode Island, which was not represented in the General Convention, and North Carolina would decline to accept it.[47]

---

trolling representation of the House of Burgesses, which acknowledged allegiance to William and Mary as their lawful sovereigns, could be traced to the Burgesses of 1765, and, as I have just shown, to 1776, when that allegiance was withdrawn, to 1788, and to 1829-30, a period of nearly a century and a half. And if we go back to the first House of Burgesses held in the Colony, at James Town, July 30, 1619, a year before the May Flower left England with the Pilgrim Fathers of New England, and consisting of twenty-two members, we will find Mr. Jefferson, of Flowerdieu Hundred, represented by Mr. Jefferson, of Albemarle, in the Convention of 1776; Captain William Powell, of James City, represented in the present Convention by Colonel Levin Powell, of Loudoun ; Mr. John Jackson, of Martin's plantation, by George Jackson, of Harrison, in the same body, and Charles Jordan, of Charles City, by Colonel Samuel Jordan Cabell, of Amherst.

[47] The Convention of North Carolina met on the 21st of July, 1788, when the Constitution was lost by one hundred votes. *Wheeler's North Carolina*, II, 98. The States adopted the Constitution in the following order : Delaware, December 7, 1787 ; Pennsylvania, December 12, 1787 ; New Jersey, December 18, 1787 ; Georgia, January 2, 1788 ; Connecticut, January 9, 1788 ; Massachusetts, February 6, 1788 ; Maryland, April 28, 1788 ; South Carolina, May 23, 1788 ; New Hampshire, June 21, 1788 ; Virginia, June 26, 1788 ; North Carolina, November 21, 1789 ; Rhode Island, May 29, 1790. Hence it appears that the Constitution was accepted by nine States five days before Virginia cast her vote, a fact which, though alluded to in Convention, could not have been known positively at the time.

The vote of Virginia, which was eagerly sought by the friends of the Constitution not only as the vote of a State, but as the vote of the largest of the States, was then, if not to decide its fate, yet materially to affect its success; for, although the instrument should be ratified by New Hampshire, and the full complement of States required to the organization of the Government be attained, still there were fears that Virginia might, as was afterwards suggested by Jefferson, and attempted in the body, hold out until such amendments as she would propose as the condition of her acceptance should be ratified by the States, and become an integral part of the new system.   Nor were these apprehensions groundless.   Her western boundary was the Mississippi, and strange reports, which we know represented not less than the truth, were rife that a deliberate effort had been made by the Northern and Middle States to close the navigation of that stream by the people of the South for thirty years ; nor was it known that a scheme so fatal to the prosperity of Virginia had been abandoned.   The vote which was to decide these doubts was to be given by the Convention about to assemble.

We have said that fears for the rejection of the Constitution were not ill-founded.   At no moment from its promulgation to the meeting of the first Congress in the following year, would the new system have received more than a third of the popular vote of the State.   It was ultimately carried in a house of one hundred and seventy members by a majority of ten only, and five votes would have reversed the decision ; and it is certain that at least ten members voted, either in disobedience of the positive instructions of their constituents, or in defiance of their well-known opinions.[48]   Nor were those opinions the offspring of the

---

[48] See the proceedings of the Assembly which met three days before the adjournment of the present Convention.   Judge Marshall, who was a member of the present Convention, and probably wrote from the result of his observation in Virginia, says, "that in some of the adopting States, a majority of the people were in the opposition"; he also says, "that so small in many instances was the majority in its favor, as to afford short ground for the opinion that had *the influence of character* been removed, the intrinsic merits of the instrument would not have secured its adoption." *Life of Washington*, II, 127.   Sympathizing as I do with the views of Henry, Mason, &c., who opposed the Constitution, it might appear invidious to give the names of those who

moment.   They had been held by their ancestors and themselves
for a century and a half; and as they reflected the highest credit
upon the patriotism of our fathers and that conservative worth
which is the true safety of States, but which has fallen into dis-
repute in more recent times, it is proper to recall their modes of
thinking on political subjects, as well as to take a passing glance
at the state of parties into which the public men of that day were
divided.   A large portion of the people, even larger than at
present, were engaged in the cultivation of the earth, and were
in the main tobacco planters and slave-holders ; and a tobacco-
planting, slave-holding people are rarely eager for change.   Like
their ancestors in England, they were not anxious for the alteration of laws to which they had long been accustomed.   Even
during the contest with the mother country, no greater changes
were made than were deemed absolutely necessary to accomplish
the end in view.   The Committee of Safety, which, in the intervals of the sessions of the Conventions, administered the government until the Constitution went into effect, was but a standing
committee of the Conventions, which were the House of Burgesses under another name.   And when a declaration of independence, which was held back until it became impossible to
obtain foreign aid in men and means without such a measure,
was put forth, and a new form of government was rendered
imperative, no greater change was made in the existing system
than was required by the emergency.   The law of primogeniture, the law of entails, the Church establishment, were not
touched by the Constitution.   And when the Convention of May,

---

voted as charged in the text. As an illustration of "the influence of
character," it may be said that no four men excited more influence
in favor of the Constitution in Virginia, than George Washington,
Edmund Pendleton, George Wythe, and James Madison, and four
purer names were probably never recorded in profane history ; yet to
those who look into the secret motives that unconsciously impel the
most candid minds on great occasions, which involve the destinies of
posterity, it may be said that they were all men of wealth, or held office
by a life tenure, and that, though married, neither of them ever had a
child.   In the same spirit it may be mentioned that Mason and Henry
were men of large families, and that hundreds now living look back to
"Gunston Hall" and "Red Hill."   In the case of Henry, the cradle
began to rock in his house in his eighteenth year, and was rocking
at his death in his sixty-third.

1776, which formed the Constitution, adjourned, the polity of the Colony, with the exception of the executive department, was essentially the polity of the Commonwealth. The House of Delegates was the House of Burgesses under another name. The Senate was the Council under a different organization. It was to be chosen by the people instead of being nominated by the king, and its judicial forces, separated from its legislative, were assigned to officers who composed the new judiciary. Although the new Constitution was assailed shortly after its birth by the authority and eloquence of Jefferson, and at a later date by able men, whose talents were hardly inferior to those of Jefferson, it remained without amendment or revision for more than half a century. Our fathers were as prompt and practical as well as prudent; and when it was necessary to form a bond of union among the States, they accepted the Articles of Confederation without delay. But when so great a change in the organic law as was proposed by the Federal Constitution was presented for their approval, they were filled with distrust and suspicion. That instrument, under restrictions real or apparent, invested the new Government with the purse and the sword of the Commonwealth. Alarming as this concession appeared to the people, it was as unexpected as alarming. The colonists had brought to the new world a just appreciation of the liberties which they enjoyed in Great Britain; and the appreciation was enhanced by the representative system which was adopted here. There were times, indeed, in the previous century, as in the then existing one, when the rights and privileges of a British subject, here as well as in England, were disregarded or lost sight of for a season; but there were no times when the great bulwarks of British freedom were razed to their foundations. The governor was appointed by the king, and appeared in the Colony either by proxy or by deputy; and he had the power of proroguing the Assembly. An ancient form, which had been borrowed from England, prescribed that the member who was elected Speaker of the House of Burgesses should, before taking the chair, and before the mace was laid upon the table of the clerk, be approved by the Governor; but should the Governor refuse to approve the choice of the House, the House might proceed to elect another Speaker; and should the Governor determine to reject a second choice of the House, another election must follow, for none other than a member could occupy the chair. The assent of the king was necessary to a law ; but that assent was in extreme cases only suspended, and so rarely withheld that a law took effect on its passage ; and in the event of a refusal of the royal assent, the worst consequence was that the people were thrown on the existing laws which had been enacted by themselves. Every shilling collected from the colonists for more than a century and a half had been assessed by their own House of Burgesses, and was received and disbursed by a Treasurer, who was elected by the House, who was almost always a member of it, and was responsible to it for the performance of his duty.[49] Our fathers were always ready to give and grant their own money of their own free will, but not upon compulsion or at the dictation of another. They appropriated large sums for the Indian wars, when it was known that the hostile attacks of the savages were excited by the French, and were made upon the territory of the Colony, not from any hatred to the colonists, but because they were the subjects of the British king. During the government of Cromwell, the colonists had not only exercised the functions of a free State, but were substantially independent. They passed what laws they pleased, and carried a free trade with foreign nations. In the commercial control of the mother country, they were compelled to acquiesce ; but they denied the right of Parliament to lay a shilling in the shape of direct taxation. Hence the resistance to the Stamp Act, and the series of measures which led

---

[49] The Speaker was almost invariably appointed Treasurer until a separation of the offices was effected in 1766, on the death of Speaker Robinson, when Peyton Randolph was elected Speaker, and Robert Carter Nicholas, Treasurer. The Burgesses rarely changed their officers, John Robinson, the predecessor of Randolph, having filled the chair more than twenty years, and Randolph filled it from his first appointment to 1775, when he withdrew to attend Congress. R. C. Nicholas was re-elected Treasurer from 1766 to 1776, when he resigned because the Constitution would not allow the Treasurer to hold a seat in the Assembly. See Journal House of Delegates, November 29, 1776, where Nicholas is thanked by the House for his fidelity, and expresses his acknowledgments, closing his remarks with these words : " That he would deliver up his office to his successor, he trusted, with clean hands ; he would assure the House it would be with empty ones." These words were often quoted by our fathers when the name of Nicholas was mentioned.

slowly but surely to independence. So jealous and so careful were the people of Virginia on the subject of direct taxation that under the pressure of the war, when the Articles of Confederation were adopted, they would not part with the power of the purse, and cautiously provided in those Articles that the quota of each State in the general charge should be raised, not by taxation at the discretion of Congress, but in the form of a requisition on the State alone. This principle was so firmly planted in the general mind, that no speaker in public debate, no writer from the press, dared to assail or call it in question. And lest a delegate to Congress might prove faithless to his trust, though his term of service lasted yet a single year, and he could serve only three years out of six, he might be recalled at any moment at the bidding of the Assembly.[50] The Act of Assembly appointing delegates to the General Convention, so far from contemplating a surrender of the principle of taxation, guarded it with the greatest care, and instructed the members so appointed "to join with the delegates from other States in devising and discussing all such alterations and further provisions as may be necessary to render the Federal Constitution adequate to the exigencies of the Union, and in reporting such an act for that purpose to the United States in Congress, as, when agreed to by them, and duly confirmed by the several States, will effectually provide for the same." It was evidently an ordinary amendment to the Articles of Confederation, to take the course prescribed in that instrument in the case of amendments, and not the substitution of a different scheme of government, which they sought to obtain.[51] They dearly loved the union of the States,

---

[50] Articles of Confederation, Art. V.

[51] Nothing can be clearer than the fact stated in the text. The Articles of Confederation provide for their own amendment in these words : "unless such alterations be agreed to in a Congress of the United States, and be afterwards confirmed by the *legislatures* of every State." Art. XIII. Accordingly, when on the 3d of November, 1786, the House of Delegates, after a deliberate discussion in committee of the whole, adopted a resolution requiring a bill to be brought in appointing delegates to the General Convention, they conclude their instructions to the committee in these words : "And to report such an act for the purpose to the United States in Congress assembled, as, when agreed to by them, and afterwards confirmed by the *legislatures* of every State,

and they felt that some decided measure was necessary to sustain the public faith.   The debt of the Revolution was not only unpaid, but the money to pay the interest upon it was impracticable to obtain.   Requisitions were faithfully made by the Congress ; but, in the absence of pressure from without, and from the extraordinary difficulties which beset the States just emerging from a protracted civil war, were rarely complied with.   To amend the Articles of Confederation, therefore, was a measure required alike by our relations with our confederate States, and with the States of Europe to which we were so deeply indebted for those loans that enabled us to prosecute the war, and was demanded by every consideration of justice and of honor.

The Assembly, however, was careful and explicit in declaring that it was an amendment to the existing form that they desired, and not a change in the form itself.   With that form they were satisfied.   It had borne them through the war ; and under its

---

will effectually provide for the same." The committee so appointed consisted of Mathews, George Nicholas, Madison, Nelson, Mann Page, Bland and Corbin.   Madison drew the bill concluding with the resolution in the text, which conforms generally with the instructions, but substitutes the word "States" for *legislatures*, the word used in the Articles of Confederation, and in the resolution of the House ordering the bill to be brought in.   Now, this may have been done inadvertently ; but when we know the unpopularity of Madison in the House, which he felt so keenly that when he drew his resolution inviting the meeting at Annapolis, he had it copied by the clerk of the House, lest his handwriting should betray the authorship, and prevailed on Mr. Tyler to offer it, and which prevented him from doing any act directly with any hope of success, we hardly refrain from calling it a parliamentary manœuvre.   And this view is strengthened when we recall a similar manœuvre by which that resolution was carried through the House. It was called up on the last day of a session of more than three months' duration, when it is probable that a large number of the members had departed with the confident belief that, in their commercial Convention with Maryland, in which all the States were invited to participate, they had settled the subject of Federal relations, and was pressed through both houses in a few hours.   All these things may be legitimate in the strategy of politics, but they excite distrust and work evil.   But our present purpose is only to show that it was an amendment, in the strict sense of the word, of the Articles of Confederation, and not their entire destruction, that the Assembly had in view in sending delegates to Philadelphia.

influence, since the peace, the trade and commerce of Virginia had advanced with rapid strides.   The State and the people had been plunged, by a war of eight years, into difficulties and embarrassments, which time only could remove ; but there was every reason to believe that the time of deliverance was at hand. The duties from commerce were pouring larger and larger sums every year into the treasury of the State; and the day was not distant when, from this source alone, Virginia would be able not only to meet all the requisitions of the Federal Government, but to defray a large part of the ordinary expenses of government.

Such was the state of the public mind when the new system was proposed for the adoption of the people.   Its first appearance was calculated to excite alarm.   They beheld a total subversion of the plan of government to which they were attached, and which they had expressly instructed their delegates to amend, not to destroy.   They saw, or thought they saw, in the power of laying taxes, which the new plan gave to Congress, their most sacred privilege, which they and their fathers before them had so long enjoyed, and in defense of which they had lately concluded a fearful war, would be invaded, if not wholly alienated.   It was true that they would contribute a respectable delegation to Congress ; but, as the interests of the States were not only not identical, but antagonistic, it might well happen, nay, it would frequently happen, that a tax would be levied upon them not only without the consent of their representatives, but in spite of their opposition.   Direct taxes were unpleasant things, even when laid by their own Assembly; but when laid by men who had no common interest with those who paid them, they might be oppressive ; and when they were oppressive, the State would have no power of extending relief; for the Acts of Congress were not only to prevail over Acts of Assembly, but over the Constitution of the State.   Heretofore, even in the Colony, they had always looked to their House of Burgesses for relief, and had rarely looked in vain.   That body had ever been faithful to the rights and franchises of British freedom.   It had, ere this, deposed a royal Governor, had held him in confinement, and had transmitted him, by the first vessel from the James, to pay his respects to the King.   It had frequently sent agents to England, who were in all things but the name the ministers plenipotentiary

of the Colony.[52]   But the power of the purse and the power of
the sword were not the only invaluable rights which were to be
surrendered to the new Government.   The commerce and the
navigation of the country were to be placed under the exclusive
control of Congress.   The State had expressed a willingness to
allow a certain percentage of her revenue, derived from imports,
for the benefit of the Federal Government, and was ever willing
and ever ready to bear her full proportion in the general charge;
but she had deliberately refused, three years before,[53] when the
proposal was made in the Assembly, and was sustained by all the
authority which argument and eloquence could exert, to part
with the right to regulate the entire trade and business of the
community, and was not disposed to go farther now than she was
then willing to go.   Indeed, on this subject the people desired
no change.   Their prosperity under the existing system was as
great as could have been anticipated; nay, had surpassed their
most sanguine hopes; and, as the North was a commercial people, it was probable that, whatever the South might lose, it was
likely to gain nothing by subjecting its interests to such a super-
vision.   To sum up the whole : They thought that, however important a Federal alliance with the neighboring States would be
to the members who composed it, and however solicitous Virginia was to form such a union on the most intimate and liberal
terms, there was a price she was not disposed to pay; that such
a union was, at best, the mere machinery for conducting that
comparatively small portion of the affairs of any community
which is transacted beyond its borders more economically and
effectually than could be done by the community itself; and that,
in effecting it, to surrender the right to lay its own taxes, to regulate its own trade, to hold its own purse, and to wield its own
sword at once and forever, was a sacrifice which no large and

---

[52] Sir John Randolph was sent to England more than once.   In the
epitaph on Sir John, inscribed on the marble slab in the chapel of William and Mary College, which was destroyed by fire in 1858, it is stated
that he was frequently sent to England: "*Legati ad Anglos semel
atque iterum missi vices arduas sustinuit.*"   His sons, Peyton and John,
were also sent over, besides others.

[53] Journal of the House of Delegates, October session of 1785, pages
66–67.

prosperous Commonwealth had ever made, and which no large and prosperous Commonwealth could make without dishonor and shame.

By a people whose minds had been excited to a high pitch by fear and suspense, one aspect of the Convention, which ought not to be overlooked in the review of a great historic period, was regarded with absorbing interest. It was the peculiar relation which the members held to the State and Federal politics of the day. No error is more common than to refer the origin of the party divisions of the Commonwealth to the present Federal Constitution, and to the measures adopted by Congress under that Constitution. Long before that time, parties had been formed, not only on State topics, but on those connected with the Federal Government. From the passage of the resolutions of the House of Burgesses against the Stamp Act to the time when, eleven years later, an independent State Government was formed, there had been a palpable line drawn between the parties of the country. In that interval some prominent names might occasionally be found on either side of the line; but the line was at all times distinctly visible.[54] But, if it was visible in the Colony,

---

[54] If the critical reader will run over the names of the members of the House of Burgesses of 1765, and the names of the members of the early Conventions, he will think, with me, that a majority of the men who opposed the resolutions of Henry against the Stamp Act, opposed the resolutions of the same gentleman of March, 1775, which proposed to put the Colony into military array, and the resolution, I am inclined to think, instructing the Virginia delegates in Congress to propose independence. The same members who opposed independence, we are expressly told by Henry, in his letter to R. H. Lee, of December 8, 1777, also opposed the adoption of the Articles of Confederation. And these members were, in the main, warm advocates for the adoption of the new Federal Constitution. On the other hand, Henry, R. H. Lee, George Mason, William Cabell, and others, who sustained the measures above enumerated, were the fiercest opponents of that instrument. Heretofore the party, of which Henry was usually regarded the head, had held almost undisputed sway in the Assembly; but, though it still included a large majority of the people, the skill and tact with which the friends of the new Constitution selected their candidates among the judges, and the military men, and the old tories, who, though they opposed all the great measures of the Revolution, including the Articles of Confederation, had become strangely enamored of the new scheme, had shaken the established majority. This was one of the

it was still more boldly defined in the Commonwealth. The great office of conforming our local legislation to the genius of a republican system, would have called the two parties into life, if they had not previously existed, and presented in the daily deliberations of the Assembly innumerable themes of difference and even of discord. The abolition of the laws of primogeniture and entails; the separation of the Church from the State, which was effected only after one of the longest and most animated contests in our legislation; the expediency of religious assessments; the perpetually recurring subject of Federal requisitions for men and money; the policy of ceding to the Union that magnificent principality extending from the Ohio to the northern lakes, which, divided into four States, now sends to the House of Representatives of the United States a delegation equal to nearly two-thirds of the whole number of that House at its first session under the Federal Constitution, and a delegation to the Senate which exceeds one third of the whole number of the Senate at its first organization; the mode of conducting the war; the navigation of the Mississippi, which, even at the date of the present Convention, bounded our territory on the west; the propriety of adopting the Articles of Confederation, and, at a later date, the expediency of amending them. These, and similar topics, were of the gravest moment, and might well produce a clashing of opinions. On these questions the parties, which had taken their shape as early as 1765, usually maintained their relative positions toward each other. But, fierce as was the contention on State topics, it was mainly on questions bearing directly or indirectly on Federal politics that the greatest warmth was elicited. It is known that, from the difficulties incident to a state of war, and especially a war with a great naval force, there could be but a slight interchange of commodities with foreign countries, and no introduction of specie from abroad. The only resort was the credit of the Commonwealth. While that resource was made for a season more or less available at home, some other means of meeting Federal requisitions were indispensable.

---

causes of the public alarm at the time. The Federalists **well knew** that when such men as Edmund Pendleton, George Wythe, **John Blair**, and Paul Carrington, all of whom were on the bench, **appeared at the** hustings, nobody would vote against them.

To lay taxes, payable in gold and silver only, when there was neither gold nor silver in the State, was worse than useless. The taxes must then be laid, payable in kind, and their proceeds sold for what they would fetch in a market without outlet at home or abroad. Hence the difficulty of a prompt and full compliance with the requisitions of the Federal Government was almost insuperable. But as that Government, which was almost wholly dependent on the immediate action of the States, if not for its existence, at least for the effectual discharge of its appropriate duties, suffered severely by the default, those who were charged with its administration urged the necessity of relief upon the members of the Assembly with a warmth which the occasion justified, but which became at times embarrassing and even offensive. Nor was this state of things, the result of causes which it seemed almost impossible entirely to remove, materially changed in the years immediately succeeding the peace. There was also a strong suspicion that the members of Congress, fascinated by the allurements of a life abroad, and engaged in the consideration of questions affecting all the States, were disposed to view their own State rather as one of a confederation than as an independent sovereignty, and to regard the interests of the former as subservient to the interests of the latter. From these and other considerations equally cogent, some of the members of Congress, however honest and able, became unpopular with the majority at home, which was responsible for the conduct of the State, and were regarded with distrust. Indeed, jealousy and suspicion seem to have presided at the origin of our Federal relations, and were exhibited from the beginning partly toward the Federal Government itself, and partly toward the members of Congress, personally and collectively. The term of the service of a member of Congress originally was for one year, with the capacity of eligibility for an indefinite period. Two years later the Assembly determined, by a solemn act, to curtail the term of eligibility to the period of three successive years, when the incumbent must withdraw for a year, and, as it was alleged at the time, from party motives made the rule retroactive in its operation.[55] Richard Henry Lee, who was the first to feel the

---

[55] *Hening's Statutes at Large*, IX, 299. Mr. Jefferson drew the act and affirmed that his object was to curtail the delegation on the ground of economy.

effect of the act, complained bitterly, in a letter to Henry, that it was aimed at himself,[56] although one of the provisions of the same act fell immediately on Harrison and Braxton. It should seem that, whether from the jealousy entertained toward the Government itself, or hostility to certain members of Congress, from considerations not yet fully made public, Congress well-nigh became the slaughter-house of the popularity of the delegates who attended its sittings. Even in the days of the early Conventions the good name of Richard Bland was so blown upon that he demanded an inquisition into his conduct.[57] The popularity of Richard Henry Lee suffered for a season a total eclipse in the Assembly. From that memorable day, when in the first joint convention of both Houses of Assembly he made his eloquent defense against the charges which had led to his retirement from Congress, to the twenty-first day of January, 1786, when the resolution convoking the meeting at Annapolis was adopted, some of the warmest contentions of the Assembly were upon Federal topics. Nor to the latest hour did that body ever regard, with full faith, those who had borne a conspicuous part in the deliberations of Congress. The distrust of those who had served in that body was shown on a remarkable occasion. Madison, as an individual, was not only without fault, and one of the purest men of his times, but, in intellectual accomplishments, excelled almost all his contemporaries ; yet, when, in the House of Delegates at the October session of 1785, he sought to secure the passage of a resolution investing Congress, for a term of years, with the power to regulate commerce, and made, in its defence, a speech which, if we judge from the outlines and copious notes that have come down to us, must have been one of the ablest ever made in the House, he met with as terrible a defeat as the annals of parliament afford.[58] Heretofore, both in the Colony and in the Commonwealth, that party, which, for the want of a better name, we may style Democratic, though now and then

---

[56] Letter of R. H. Lee in the " Red Hill " papers.

[57] Journal Virginia Convention of July, 1775, page 15.

[58] For the outlines of the speech and the notes from which Madison spoke, see Mr. Rives' *History of the Life and Times of James Madison*, II, 48–51, and for the preamble and resolution, see Journal of the House of Delegates, October session of 1785, pages 66, 67, where, after his great speech, he was one of eighteen ayes to seventy-nine noes.

defeated by the ability and tact of its opponents, had been, in the main, triumphant, and had usually carried its measures by a decisive majority. And the probability was that, as the ratifying Convention was called on the basis of the House of Delegates, that party would still maintain its predominance in that body ; and it was with a full reliance on this calculation that the resolutions convoking the General as well as the State Conventions, had received the assent of the Assembly. Nor can there be a doubt that such would have been the case in ordinary times ; but the large and unexpected infusion of new members had created alarm in the breasts of the majority of the Assembly and of the people at large ; and one of the most exciting questions that engaged public attention was how far the new element would affect the balance of power. Thus, at so early a period did Federal politics rage with a violence not inferior to that which marked the close of the century.[59]

Nothwithstanding the bickerings produced by Federal politics in our councils, we should do great injustice to the men who for nearly a quarter of a century wielded the will of the Assembly, if we impute to them a want of affection for the Union. The Union was the daughter of their loins. They nursed her into action. They were the men who called the little meeting in Williamsburg in the late summer of 1774, which we honor with the title of the first Convention of Virginia, and who sent delegates to Carpenter's Hall. They were the first to advise Congress to adopt "a more intimate plan of union," and to form the Articles of Confederation ; and when those Articles were reported for the consideration of Virginia, they approved them by

---

[59] It cannot be disguised that personal and political animosities were as freely indulged in from 1776 to 1790 as from 1790 to the election of Mr. Jefferson to the Presidency. Henry, Jefferson, and Richard Henry Lee, were among the best abused. Charles Carter, of "Sabine Hall," was a gentleman, a scholar, and a patriot, and far advanced in life in 1776 ; but, in a letter of that year addressed to Washington, see what he says of Henry and Jefferson (*American Archives*, fifth series, 1776, Vol. II, pages 1304-5) ; and see the letter of Theodoric Bland, Sr., to Theodoric Bland, Jr., dated "Cawson's," January 8, 1871 (*Bland Papers*, II, 50). It is necessary to know the personal friends of the men of that era in order to judge of the weight of testimony ; but I will not touch upon them unless it is indispensable to the truth of history, and especially to the defence of private character.

a majority so overwhelming that the opponents of Union dared not to oppose them openly.[60] When the Articles on the ninth day of July, 1778, were called up from the table of Congress to be signed by the States as such, while some States signed in part only, and some not at all, the delegates of this Commonwealth, who had been recently elected by the Assembly, came forward and signed them on the spot. Throughout the war the Assembly held up the hands of Congress, and complied with its requisitions, if not to the letter, to the utmost of its ability. Since the peace, the British debts, which the definitive treaty required to be paid, excited warm feelings and produced acrimonious debates; but this was a topic on which parties divided. At the date of the Revolution, the indebtedness of individuals to England was estimated at ten millions of dollars, and the minority was far more interested in the question than the majority.[61] In fine, the cause of the Confederation was the cause of the majority. It was the work of their hands. At the May session of 1784, they assented to the amendment to the Articles of Confederation which required the whole number of free white inhabitants and three-fifths of all others to be substituted for the value of lands and their improvements as the rule of apportioning taxes, and were eager to provide Congress with such information as was needed to fix the valuation of lands and their improvements in the several States required by the existing rule of apportionment under the Articles of Confederation. At the same session they further provided that until one or the other mode of assessing taxes be ascertained, that any requisition made upon any basis by Congress on the States should be faithfully complied with. The Assembly went yet farther, and passed a resolution, said to have been drawn by Henry himself, providing that when "a fair and final settlement of the accounts subsisting between the United States and individual States" shall be made, the balance due by any State "ought to be enforced, if necessary, by such distress

---

[60] Henry to R. H. Lee, December 18, 1777. *Grigsby's Discourse on the Virginia Convention of 1776*, 142, note.

[61] To show how parties fluctuated on the subject of the payment of British debts, I refer to a note in Mr. Rives' *History of the Life and Times of Madison*, II, 538, which furnishes a remarkable instance in point, and presents with graphic spirit the effect of Henry's eloquence in a deliberative body.

on the property of the defaulting States, or of their citizens, as, by the United States, in Congress assembled, may be deemed adequate and most eligible.'' They also resolved, at the same session, to invest Congress, for the term of fifteen years, with authority to prohibit the vessels of any nation, with which no commercial treaty existed, from trading in any part of the United States ; and to prevent foreigners, unless belonging to a nation with which the States had formed a commercial treaty, from importing into the United States any merchandise not the produce or manufacture of the country of which they are citizens or subjects ; thus sanctioning a policy which would have materially impaired the prosperity of the Commonwealth.[62] When Congress determined to apply to the States for authority to levy, for the term of twenty-five years, certain specific rates of duty on certain articles, and a duty of five per cent. on all others—an application which was made as early as April, 1783, when the finances of Virginia were in great confusion, and her main dependence was upon customs—she, with that wise jealousy of Federal action, bearing directly upon the people instead of the State, declined for a time to accede to it, but ultimately was disposed to acquiesce in the measure.[63] But there was one thing the Assembly persistently refused to grant—the entire surrender of the right to regulate commerce. To regulate the trade of a country was, in their opinion, to regulate its entire industry, and control all its capital and labor, and that was a province, they honestly believed, not only without the pale of a Federal alliance, but incompatible with it. They had accordingly resisted heretofore, with all their might, every effort to extort such a concession from them ; and at the October session of 1785, when a proposition was offered to make that cession for a term of twenty-five years, and upheld by Madison and other able men, the majority of the House of Delegates, impelled by their devotion to the Union, went so far as to yield that invaluable boon for the term of thirteen years; but when a motion was made to continue the grant beyond that limit, on certain conditions, it was rejected

---

[62] For these acts, consult the Journals of the House of Delegates, May session of 1784, pages 11-12 ; and *Rives' Life and Times of Madison*, I, 563-4-5. *Tucker's History of the United States*, I, 335.

[63] *Hening's Statutes at Large*, XI, 350.

by a decisive vote, and on the following day, believing that they had gone too far in conceding the right for thirteen years, recon sidered their vote and laid the bill upon the table, to be called up no more.[64] Of that majority, Henry, when he happened to have a seat in the Assembly, was always the leader, and for near a twelvemonth later than the date of the passage of the resolution convoking the meeting at Annapolis, was regarded as the Federal champion.[65] But we have said enough to show that the majority in our councils, who were opposed to the adoption of the new Federal Constitution, had been the warm and consistent friends of a Federal alliance.

A recent   of that majority had roused the fears of the friends of the new institution. The general Federal Convention adjourned on the seventh of September, 1787, but before adjourning had adopted a resolution expressing "the opinion that the new Constitution should be submitted to the Convention of Delegates, chosen in each State by the people thereof, under the recommendation of its legislature, for their assent and ratification." The following month the General Assembly of Virginia held a session, and on the twenty-fifth of October passed a series of resolutions setting forth that the Constitution "ought to be submitted to a Convention of the people for their full and free investigation and discussion"; that "every citizen being a freeholder should be eligible to a seat in the Convention"; that "it be recommended to each county to elect two delegates, and to each city, town, or corporation, entitled, or who may be entitled, by law to representation in the legislature, to elect one delegate to the said Convention"; that "the qualifications of the electors be the same with those now established by law"; that "the elec-

---

[64] Journal House of Delegates, October session of 1785, pages 66, 67.

[65] Madison, writing to Washington, December 7, 1786, says: "Mr. Henry, who has been hitherto *the champion of the Federal party*, has become a cold advocate, and, in the event of an actual sacrifice of the Mississippi by Congress, will unquestionably go over to the other side." *Rives' Life and Times of Madison*, II, 142. When we remember that the Mississippi was the western boundary of Virginia, it would be strange indeed that Mr. Henry could approve the conduct of Congress in closing that river for thirty years, and in clothing the body with new powers to carry such a scheme into effect. The cession of that river to Spain by the Northern States has its prototype only in the partition of Poland.

tion of delegates be held at the usual place for holding elections of members of the General Assembly, and be conducted by the usual officers "; that " the election shall be held in the month of March next on the first day of the court to be held for each county, city, or corporation respectively, and that the persons so chosen shall assemble at the State House in Richmond on the fourth Monday of May next," which was afterwards changed for the first Monday in June. These resolutions should seem to have been specific enough for the purpose in view. But it was found out that they omitted an appropriation to defray the expenses of the proposed Convention ; and a bill was brought in for that object, and received the unanimous consent of both Houses. But this bill contained, likewise, a provision to defray the expenses of delegates to another general Federal Convention, should such a body be convened. If this provision meant anything, it meant that a new General Convention was possible ; and, as the Assembly rarely looked to possibilities in its legislation, that it was probable. While the lovers of union saw in this provision a determination to secure a Federal alliance on the best terms and at every hazard, those who favored the new scheme placed upon it a different interpretation.[66]

---

[66] Journal House of Delegates, October session of 1787, p. 77, and the Act in full in *Hening's Statutes at Large*, XII, 462. Bushrod Washington, then under thirty years of age, wrote to his uncle at the beginning of this session that he had met with in all his inquiries not one member opposed to the Federal Constitution except Mr. Henry, and that other members had heard of none either. When the provision for a new Convention mentioned in the bill was approved by the House of Delegates, his eyes were probably opened, for on the 7th of December, while the Assembly was still in session, he writes to his uncle as follows : " I am sorry to inform you that the Constitution has lost so considerably that it is doubted whether it has any longer a majority in its favor. From a vote that took place the other day, this would appear certain, though I cannot think it so decisive as its *enemies* consider it." Bushrod Washington to George Washington, Dec. 7, 1787, copied from the *Madison Files* by Mr. Rives, II, 537. It thus appears that the Constitution, which had not an enemy at the opening of the session, had before its close a good many, and that the scales were nearly turned against it. It is probable that a very considerable number of the delegates had not seen the Constitution at the beginning of the session. Only four days had elapsed since any body had seen it ; and when we know that intelligence at that time took sixty days to travel a distance which may

be reached in six hours at the present day ; that some of the members had to travel from three to six hundred miles on horseback to reach Richmond ; that there were no mail facilities, and no newspapers save one or two small sheets in Richmond and Norfolk, which, from the uncertainty of delivery, were rarely taken in the county, the probability is that if the members had seen the Constitution, they had not read it deliberately. But when they did read it, we know that the result was a provision to defray the expenses of a Convention to revise, etc. This matter would hardly require the attention we have given it, if inferences in favor of the early popularity of the Constitution had not been drawn from the state of things at the meeting of the Assembly. For the letter of Bushrod Washington, written at the opening of the session, see *Rives' Madison*, II, 535.

CHAPTER II.

At ten o'clock on Monday, the second day of June, 1788, the members began to assemble in the hall of the Old Capitol. It was plain that different emotions were felt by the friends and by the opponents of the Constitution. The friends of that instrument congratulated each other on the omens which they drew from the year in which their meeting was to take place. The year '88, they said, had ever been favorable to the liberties of the Anglo-Saxon race. It was in 1588, two hundred years before, when the invincible Spanish Armada, destined to subvert the liberties of Protestant England, then ruled by that virgin queen, the glory of her sex and name and race, who was the patron of Raleigh and the patron of American colonization, and from whom Virginia derived her name, was assailed by the winds of Heaven, and scattered over the face of the deep.[67] It was the recurrence of the year, the month, and almost the day, when, a century before, the cause of civil liberty and Protestant Christianity won a signal victory in the acquittal of the seven bishops whose destruction had been decreed by a false and cruel king; and when the celebrated letter inviting the Prince of Orange to make a descent on England, a letter which has been recently pronounced to be as significant a landmark in British history as Magna Charter itself, had been despatched to the Hague. Of all the kings who ever sate on the English throne, William Henry, Prince of Orange was most beloved by our fathers. Their attachment was shown in every form in which public gratitude seeks to exhibit its manifestations. The House of Burgesses called a county after the king, and called a county after the king

---

[67] See in Mr. Rush's memoranda of a residence at the Court of St. James, the opinions of modern English statesmen on the probable success of the Armada.

and his queen.[68] The metropolis of the Colony still perpetuates his name. Its great seminary, the charter of which was granted by William, and which received his fostering care, bore, as it bears still, his name and the name of his faithful consort. Incidents in his career were to be traced even in the nomenclature of the plantation. The light wherry bobbing on the waters of the York or the James, was called the Brill in honor of the gallant frigate in which the Deliverer sailed from Helvoetsluys to the harbor of Torbay. The love of the people long survived his natural life. A great county, created long after the death of William, and stretching far beyond the blue wall which now bounds it in the west to the shores of the Ohio, whether named from the colour of its soil, which is also the symbol of Protestant Christianity wherever the British race extends, or in honor of William, pleasingly recalls the name of the small principality on the banks of the Rhone, from which the Prince derived his familiar title.[69] An adjoining State has honored the name of Bertie, the first peer of the realm who joined the standard of William on the soil of Britain, and our own town of Abingdon illustrates the same event.[70] And the noble county of Halifax, though called apparently in honor of a man who filled a secretary's office in England at a later day, reminds us of that brilliant and accomplished statesman, the unfaltering enemy of the House of Bourbon of that age when the sway of that House was supreme at Whitehall; the friend of Protestant Christianity, from whose hand William received the Declaration of Right.

---

[68] Two years after the accession of William, a county was called after the Princess Anne, in honor of her claim as the successor of William and Mary, in the event of her surviving them, according to the parliamentary settlement of the crown.

[69] In the *Topographical Analysis of Virginia* for the year 1790-'1, in the Appendix of the last edition (published by J. W. Randolph, Richmond, 1853, 8vo.) of the *Notes on Virginia* left for publication by Mr. Jefferson, the county of Orange, which was cut off from Spotsylvania in 1734, almost a third of a century after the death of William, is put down without the expression of a doubt as called in honor of William.

[70] The North Carolinians may say, and justly, that Bertie county was called in commemoration of the two Berties, in whom the proprietary rights of the Earl of Clarendon vested; but as it was formed within twenty years of the death of William, I always associate it with his history.

When the intelligence of Barclay's plot against the life of the king, which had well-nigh proved successful, reached the Colony, the excitement was great. The news flew from plantation to plantation. The Burgesses instantly prepared an address in which they denounced the plotters and congratulated the king on his escape from the daggers of the Jacobite faction. Planters spurred in haste from their homes to the capital, and, bespattered with mud, hastened to the secretary's office, there to record their horror of the assassins and their joy at the safety of the king. The address, engrossed on parchment and duly incased, was despatched to London by the first packet, and was immediately placed in the hands of William. The fate of the address was peculiar. When it had been read in common with kindred memorials from all parts of the British empire, it was laid aside and forgotten. Nor was it till William had been sleeping for more than one hundred and sixty years in his ancestral tomb at the Hague, far from the dust of her on whose pure brow the diadem of Elizabeth had pressed so queenly, and to whose devoted love more than to his own consummate statesmanship he owed his emperial crown, the venerable parchment was enrolled once more, and brought to public notice by a historian whose genius has invested the dim and distant past with the freshness of current time, and who has taught how the sober events of real life may be made as fascinating as the phantoms of romance or the dreams of poetry. Even to this hour the curious eye detects in the number of William Henrys that are still seen in the advertisements of the daily press, or the sign boards of the shops, and in our political and ecclesiastical bodies, the image of that strong affection with which our ancestors regarded the name of William Henry, Prince of Orange. One of his Virginia name-sakes has already received the honors of the Presidency of the United States. Another Virginia name-sake, but for extreme illness,[71] might have reached the same exalted station. Thus it was that any omen derived from the life of William was hailed by our fathers with delight. Nor did the friends of the Constitution fail to perceive another coincidence which might well happen. Should Virginia sustain the Constitution, that instrument would certainly take effect, and the new government

---

[71] William Henry Crawford.

would be inaugurated on the fourth of March of the following
year, the centennial anniversary of the year, and almost the
month when, in the banqueting room at Whitehall, Halifax at
the head of the Lords, and Powle at the head of the Commons,
presented to William and Mary the Declaration of Right, and
when those sovereigns accepted that instrument which united for
the first time in a common bond the title of the reigning dynasty
and the liberties of the people of England.[72]

On the other hand, no cheering sign greeted the opponents of
the Constitution.   Hitherto they had ever constituted a majority
in the councils of the Commonwealth.   They now heard bruited
abroad the supposed majority by which that instrument would
be carried,[73] and the names of the individuals who would fill the
principal offices to be created by it.   Still they were sustained
by that steadfast courage which buoys up the patriot when he
wrestles in defence of his country.   They saw, indeed, in that
stern gathering of military men, who composed more than one-
fourth of the body, and of the not less formidable corps of
judges, that their hopes of triumph were faint.   They regarded
the Constitution as the offspring of usurpation.   They solemnly
believed that of all the members of the Assembly who voted for
the resolution convoking the Convention recently held in Philadelphia, not a single individual, so far as they knew, looked beyond a literal amendment of the Articles of Confederation ; and
that, if any radical change had been avowed in debate, the resolution would have been indignantly rejected.   They felt that a
great wrong had been perpetrated upon the people.   It had been
ingeniously contrived that the work of the Convention should

---

[72] I was told of these congratulations among the members by a gentleman who heard them.   The public men of the Revolution were more
intimately acquainted with the minutest details of English history than
their successors in the public councils of the present day.   One reason
may be that they had fewer books to read, and that, as colonists, it was
their interest to know critically the remarkable epochs of English history.   For an allusion to the address of the tobacco-planters of Virginia
to William on his escape from the assassin, see *Macaulay's History of
England*, IV, 478, Butler's octavo edition, 1856.

[73] " The sanguine friends of the Constitution counted on a majority
of twenty at their first meeting, which number they imagine will be
greatly increased."   Washington to Jay, June 8, 1788.   *Washington's
Writings*, IX, 374.

be referred to the action, not of the legislatures of the States, but to a convention to be called for the purpose ; while a nominal compliance with the act of Virginia was evinced by reporting the new scheme to the Congress for its recommendation to the States. This important innovation did not escape the sagacity of Richard Henry Lee, who was at the time a member of Congress, nor of the Congress as a body ; but, controlled by an extrinsic pressure, which it did not deem prudent to resist, it finally recommended the Constitution to the States, to be discussed in the mode prescribed by the Convention that framed it. Still, when the Constitution was laid before the General Assembly at its October session of 1787, victory was not wholly beyond its grasp. One of two methods of redress was yet within its reach. Either that body might refuse to receive the Constitution, and refer it back to the Congress as framed in palpable violation of the resolution of Congress, and of the resolution of Virginia instructing its delegates to the General Convention ; or, overlooking the recommendation of a special Convention for its ratification as surplusage, and regarding the Constitution as a mere amendment of the Articles of Confederation, might have rejected it forthwith ; but, unconscious of the crisis which impended over the country, or relying on its probable strength, the majority of the Assembly assented to the proposition contained in the new scheme, and called a Convention to pass upon it. The opponents of that scheme saw too late that this act was fatal. It mended all defects of form, and gave the instrument a legitimacy which it did not before possess. It not only took from the majority a weapon which, wielded by efficient hands, would have cloven down the defences of the minority, but it transferred the contest to a field in which the mighty influence of great names, heretofore the common property, would be exerted against it. That contest raged long and fiercely, and in whose favor it ultimately turned we shall presently see. But let us record the proceedings of the body in the order in which they occurred.

When the House was called to order, a motion was made that John Beckley [74] be appointed secretary to the Convention, who

---

[74] John Beckley was at various times Clerk of the House of Delegates and of the Senate of Virginia. On the organization of the House

was accordingly chosen, and took his place at the table in front
of the chair. Paul Carrington now rose, and in a short address nominated Edmund Pendleton as President.[75] A few
moments of anxious suspense followed. The opinions of Pen-

---

of Representatives of the United States, he was elected clerk, and
served from April 1, 1789, to May 15, 1797, and from December 7, 1801,
to October 26, 1807. If not born in England, he was educated at Eton,
and I have heard Governor Tazewell say that he was a classmate of
Fox.

[Beckley, or Bickley, was born in Virginia, and his full name
was John James, and he thus subscribed himself as a member of the
Phi-Beta-Kappa Society of William and Mary College, in 1776. He
was descended from the family of Bickley, or Bickleigh, anciently seated
at Bickleigh, upon the river Ex., in Devonshire. The elder branch
of this family removed into Sussex, and settled at Chidham. Other
branches settled in the counties of Cambridge, Warwick and Middlesex. Arms : Arg. a chev. embattled between three griffins' heads,
erased gules. Henry Bickley of Chidham, county Essex, born 1503;
died 1570. Joseph Bickley, seventh in descent from Henry, of Chidham, patented, 16th June, 1727, 400 acres of land in King William county,
Virginia. John James Bickley was probably the son of Sir William
Bickley, Baronet, who died in Louisa county, Virginia, March 9th, 1771.
Bickley was not only the first Clerk of the House of Representatives,
but also the first Librarian of Congress, serving from 1802 to 1807.—ED.]

[75] Neither the Journal of the Convention nor Robertson reports the
name of the member who nominated Pendleton. I heard, from a gentleman who was present at the time, that Judge Carrington made the
motion; but I am wholly at a loss for the name of the seconder, who,
I suppose, was Wythe, from the fact that he was the only member
likely to be brought out against Pendleton, and that Pendleton almost
invariably called him to the chair in Committee of the Whole. I do
not find that any of our early deliberative bodies have ever elected the
chairman of the Committee of the Whole, which was formerly the
usual practice in the House of Commons. The nomination of Pendleton was fixed upon beforehand, beyond doubt, and there can be as
little doubt that Wythe was party to it. In the Convention of 1829-30
it was arranged with the privity of Madison, and doubtless at his suggestion, that Mr. Monroe should be made president of the body, and
he was so nominated by Mr. Madison himself; but the ablest members
of the Convention were not aware of the design ; and when Mr. Madison made the nomination, those who sate near John Randolph and
observed his countenance, say that he was on the eve of rising to oppose it, not so much from hostility to Mr. Monroe as from a belief that
the honor of the presidency should first be conferred on Madison.

dleton were well known to be in favor of the Constitution; and the election of president presented a fair opportunity of testing the relative strength of parties. In the selection of their candidate, the Federalists had chosen a name which, in the pure and benevolent character of him who bore it, in his long and valuable service in the public councils, and in his venerable age, was known and honored throughout the Commonwealth, and which, with the exception of that of one who had long been his compeer in the House of Burgesses, at the bar of the General Court, in the Conventions of 1775 and 1776, in the Congress, and on the bench, may be said then to have stood almost alone in the civil service of his country.[76] But George Wythe was now known to approve the Constitution, and so far from opposing Pendleton would sustain him by his vote. Had Wythe been of the opposite party, the opponents of the Constitution would doubtless have ventured a contest. Nor is it certain that the contest would not have been successful. Wythe was, as a man, more popular than Pendleton; many of the members had been his scholars, and loved him with an affection which neither time nor distrust could weaken; and he would certainly have carried with him the votes of the smaller counties on tide, which had ever regarded him with warm attachment, and had long counted his fame among their most precious possessions. The contest, too, might have been waged without wounding the delicacy of Pendleton, who was unable to perform the duties of the presiding officer unless allowed to sit in the chair; and opposition may have taken the hue of respect for his physical infirmities. But no name was brought forward by the opponents of the Constitution, and Pendleton was elected without a division.

Twelve years which had elapsed since the adjournment of the Convention of 1776 had left their mark upon the President. He was in his sixty-seventh year, and his intellectual powers, quickened by the discussions in the court in which he had presided since its organization, were undiminished; but there was a sad

---

[76] President Pendleton, who was also president of the Court of Appeals, was now in his sixty-seventh year, but, from the breaking of a thigh-bone ten or eleven years before, which prevented him from taking exercise or moving without a crutch, looked much older than he was.

change in his outward form. Some individuals present remembered him as he was in the House of Burgesses more than a
quarter of a century past; one member had seen him in the
public councils more than the third of a century ago; and not a
few of the members could recall him as with a buoyant and
graceful step he walked from the floor of the Convention of
December, 1775, and of May, 1776, to the chair, escorted in the
former body by Paul Carrington and James Mercer, and in the
latter by the venerable Richard Bland and the inflexible Archibald Cary. It was a touching sight to behold him, his earlier
and elder compeers long laid to rest, as, with his shrunken form
upheld by crutches, he now passed between Carrington and
Wythe to the chair. He made an acknowledgment of the honor
conferred upon him in a few plain words not otherwise remarkable than as being the first ever addressed to a deliberate Assembly of Virginia from a sitting position.[77]

The Rev. Abner Waugh was, on motion of Paul Carrington,
unanimously elected chaplain, and "was ordered to attend every
morning to read prayers, immediately after the bell should be
rung for calling the Convention.[78]

When the Convention had elected the other officers of the
body,[79] had appointed a Committee of Privileges and Elections,[80]

---

[77] There was no formal resolution but rather a general understanding
that Pendleton was to sit in addressing or putting a question to the
house. It is probable that Carrington, who was his associate on the
bench of the Court of Appeals, and who knew his physical infirmities,
may have alluded to the subject in his nominating speech. Robertson,
in his Debates, thus alludes to the election of Pendleton: "He was
unanimously elected president, who being seated in the chair, thanked
the Convention for the honor conferred upon him, and strongly recommended to the members to use the utmost moderation and temper in
their deliberations on the great and important subject now before
them." Pendleton, in the sketch of his own life, mentions gratefully
that he was allowed to sit while performing the duties of the chair.

[78] The Rev. Abner Waugh, as early as 1774, had been the rector of
Saint Mary in the county of Caroline, and survived to the year 1806,
when he was chosen rector of St. George's parish, Fredericksburg,
but finding his health insufficient for the performance of his duty, he
soon resigned and died a short time after at "Hazlewood." His
valedictory to his parishioners breathes the devotion of a Christian.

[79] The other officers were William Drinkard, Sr., and William Drink-

and had chosen a printer of its proceedings, it adjourned, on the motion of George Mason to the next day at eleven, then to meet in the New Academy on Shockoe Hill.

On the morning of the next day it met in the New Academy, a large wooden structure reared by the Chevalier Quesnay, a captain in the army of the Revolution, for the promotion of the arts and literature of the rising Commonwealth. Its cornerstone had been laid two years before with great ceremony in presence of the State and town authorities ; and the scheme of the institution had received the sanction of the French Academy of Sciences in a formal report endorsed by the famous Levoisier a short time before he was led to the guillotine, and which was designed to be the fountain from which the arts and sciences in the New World would soon begin to flow, but which, like most of the schemes of foreign proprietors in a new country, was destined to a speedy dissolution. The commodious hall of this building was well adapted to the purposes of the Convention, and was now filled to overflowing.[81]

---

ard, Jr., doorkeepers; Edmund Pendleton, Jr., clerk of the Committee of Elections ; Augustine Davis, printer ; and on the following day William Pierce was elected sergeant-at-arms, and Daniel Hicks, one of the doorkeepers. Augustine Davis was the editor and proprietor of the *Virginia Gazette,* and somewhat later postmaster of Richmond. His printing office was in the basement of a house at the corner of Main and Eleventh streets, which was subsequently the office of the *Whig,* founded by John Hampden Pleasants, (who first used a press purchased from Davis) and successively of the *Enquirer,* influential organs in the past respectively of the Whig and Democratic parties.—ED.

[80] The Committee of Privileges and Elections were so distinguished a body that I annex their names, with the remark that such an array of genius, talents, and public and private worth had not been seen before, nor has it been seen since, on such a committee in Virginia : Benjamin Harrison, George Mason, His Excellency Governor Randolph, Patrick Henry, George Nicholas, John Marshall, Paul Carrington, John Tyler, Alexander White, John Blair, Theodore Bland, William Grayson, Daniel Fisher, Thomas Mathews, John Jones, George Wythe, William Cabell, James Taylor of Caroline, Gabriel Jones, Francis Corbin, James Innes, James Monroe, Henry Lee, and Cuthbert Bullitt. The committee is appointed with great liberality, the friends of the Constitution having a majority of two only.

[81] The Academy grounds included the square bounded by Broad and Marshall and Eleventh and Twelfth streets, on the lower portion of

After the transaction of some ordinary business, Benjamin
Harrison moved that all the papers relative to the Constitution

which stood the Monumental Church and the Medical College.   The
Academy stood midway in the square fronting Broad street.   "*L'Academie Des Etats—Unis De L'Amerique*" was an attempt, growing out
of the French alliance with the United States, to plant in Richmond a
kind of French Academy of the arts and sciences, with branch acad-
emies in Baltimore, Philadelphia, and New York.   The institution was
to be at once national and international.   It was to be affiliated with
the royal societies of London, Paris, Bruxelles, and other learned bodies
in Europe.   It was to be composed of a president, vice-president, six
counsellors, a treasurer-general, a secretary and a recorder, an agent
for taking European subscriptions, French professors, masters, artists-
in-chief attached to the Academy, twenty-five resident and one hundred and seventy-five non-resident associates, selected from the best
talent of the Old World and of the New.   The Academy proposed to
publish yearly from its own press in Paris, an almanac.   The Academy
was to show its zeal for science by communicating to France and other
European countries a knowledge of the natural products of North
America.   The museums and cabinets of the Old World were to be
enriched by specimens of the flora and fauna of a country as yet undis-
covered by men of science.   The proprietor of the brilliant scheme
was the Chevalier Alexander Maria Quesnay de Beaurepaire, grandson of the famous French philosopher and economist, Dr. Quesnay,
who was the court physician of Louis XV.   Chevalier Quesnay had
served as a captain in Virginia in 1777-78 in the war of the Revolution.
The idea of founding the Academy was suggested to him in 1778 by
John Page, of "Rosewell," then Lieutenant-Governor of Virginia, and
himself devoted to scientific investigation.   Quesnay succeeded in
raising by subscription the sum of 60,000 francs, the subscribers in Virginia embracing nearly one hundred prominent names.   The corner-
stone of the building, which was of wood, was laid with Masonic cere-
monies July 8th, 1786.   Having founded and organized his Academy
under the most distinguished auspices, Quesnay returned to Paris and
succeeded in enlisting in support of his plan many learned and distinguished men of France and England.   The French Revolution,
however, put an end to the scheme.   The Academy building was early
converted into a theatre, which was destroyed by fire, but a new theatre
was erected in the rear of the old.   This new building was also destroyed by fire on the night of December 26th, 1811, when seventy-two
persons perished in the flames.   The Monumental church commemo-
rates the disaster, and its portico covers the tomb and ashes of most of
its victims.   A valuable sketch of Quesnay's enlightened projection,
chiefly drawn from his curious "*Mémoire concirnant l'Academie des
Sciences et Beaux Arts des États—Unis d'Amerique, Établic à Rich-*

should be read. John Tyler observed that before any papers were read, certain rules and regulations should be established to govern the Convention in its deliberations. Edmund Randolph fully concurred in the propriety of establishing rules ; but, as this was a subject which would invoke the Convention in debate, he recommended that the rules of the House of Delegates, as far as they were applicable, should be observed. Tyler had no objection to the mode suggested by Randolph ; accordingly, the rules of the House of Delegates, as far as they were applicable, were adopted by the present, as they had been by all subsequent Conventions.

On motion, " the resolutions of Congress of the twenty-eighth of September previous,[82] together with the report of the Federal Convention, lately held in Philadelphia, the resolutions of the General Assembly of the twenty-fifth of October last, and the Act of the General Assembly, entitled an Act concerning the Convention to be held in June next," were now read, when George Mason arose to address the House. In an instant the insensible hum of the body was hushed, and the eyes of all were fixed upon him. How he appeared that day as he rose in that large assemblage, his once raven hair white as snow, his stalwart figure, attired in deep mourning, still erect, his black eyes fairly flashing forth the flame that burned in his bosom, the tones of his voice deliberate and full as when, in the first House of Delegates, he sought to sweep from the statute book those obliquities which marred the beauty of the young republic, or uttered that withering sarcasm which tinges his portrait by the hand of Jefferson, we have heard from the lips, and seen reflected from the moistened eyes of trembling age. His reputation as the author of the Declaration of Rights and of the first Constitution of a free Commonwealth; as the responsible director of some of the

---

mond," was published in *The Academy*, December, 1887, Vol. II, No. 9, pp. 403, 412, by Dr. Herbert B. Adams, of Johns-Hopkins University. A copy of Quesnay's rare " *Mémoire* " is in the library of the State of Virginia. Quesnay complains bitterly that all his letters relating to his service in the American army had been stolen from a pigeon-hole in Governor Henry's desk, and his promotion thus prevented.

[82] This resolution was merely formal, ordering the Constitution to be transmitted to the legislatures of the States. It may be seen in Fobrell's edition of the Journals of the old Congress, IX, 110.

leading measures of general legislation during the war and after its close; his position as a prominent member of the General Convention that framed the Constitution, which had been adopted under his solemn protest, and his well-known resolve to oppose the ratification with all his acknowledged abilities, were calculated to arrest attention. He was sixty-two years old, and had not been more than twelve years continuously in the public councils,[83] but from his entrance into public life he was confessedly the first man in every assembly of which he was a member, though rarely seen on the floor except on great occasions. But the interest with which he was now watched was heightened by another cause. From his lips was anxiously awaited by all parties the programme of the war which was to be waged against the new system. He rose to a matter of form. "I hope and trust," he said, "that this Convention, appointed by the people, on this great occasion, for securing, as far as possible, to the latest generations their happiness and liberty, will freely and fully investigate this important subject. For this purpose I humbly conceive the fullest and clearest investigation indispensably necessary, and that we ought not to be bound by any general rules whatsoever. The curse denounced by the Divine vengeance will be small, compared with what will justly fall on us, if from any sinister views we obstruct the fullest inquiry. This subject ought, therefore, to obtain the fullest discussion, clause by clause, before any general previous question be put, nor ought it to be precluded by any other question." Tyler then moved that the Convention should resolve itself into a Committee of the Whole to take into consideration the proposed plan of government, in order to have a fairer opportunity of examining its merits. Mason rose again, and after recapitulating his reasons urging a full discussion, clause by clause, concluded by giving his consent to the motion made by Tyler. Madison concurred with Mason in going into a full and free investigation of the subject before them, and said that he had no objection to the plan proposed. Mason then reduced to writing his motion, which was adopted by the House.

---

[83] Colonel Mason was a member of the House of Burgesses as early as 1758, with Pendleton and Wythe ; but did not adopt the favorite custom in the Colony of holding a seat for a series of years. Even during the past twelve years he was not always a member.

Tyler moved that the Convention resolve itself into a Committee of the Whole the next day to take the plan of government under consideration, but was opposed by Henry Lee, of Westmoreland, who urged the propriety of entering into the discussion at once. Mason rose to sustain the motion of Tyler, and pressed the impolicy of running precipitately into the discussion of a great measure, when the Convention was not in possession of the proper means. He was sustained by Benjamin Harrison, and the debate was closed by a rejoinder from Lee. The motion of Tyler prevailed, and it was resolved "that this Convention will to-morrow resolve itself into a committee of the whole Convention, to take into consideration the proposed Constitution of Government of the United States."[84]

But, if the motion of Mason was acceptable to his opponents, it was especially distasteful to his friends. It had been foreseen that there would be some confusion among the opponents of the Constitution in respect of the line of policy to be pursued in the outset of the campaign. Mason had been a member of the General Convention, had met in conclave with the Virginia delegation in Philadelphia, and had not offered any opposition to the resolutions which were approved by the delegation, which were proposed by Randolph to the General Convention as its basis of action, and which clearly looked to an overthrow of the existing Federal system. He could not consequently take the ground which his colleagues in opposition, Henry in particular, thought most available, of protesting against the usurpation of a body, which, charged with the office of proposing amendments to the

---

[84] It is interesting to see how often history repeats itself. The main argument of Lee for hastening a discussion, was that the General Assembly, in whose hall the Convention was sitting, would meet on the 23d of the month ; and as the Convention did not adjourn till the 27th, the two bodies were in session at the same time. The Convention of 1829-30, also ran into the meeting of the General Assembly, and the two bodies sate at the same time for a month and a half. As in both Conventions there were members who were also members of the Assembly, and, as such, were entitled to double pay, it would be curious to look over the old rolls and see who took and did not take double allowance. Of the members of the Convention of 1829-30 who were in the Assembly, though they really had double duty to perform in earnest, I do not know that more than one member received double pay, albeit it was unquestionably due.

existing government, had recommended an entirely new government in its stead.   He may, however, have deemed the Act of Assembly convoking the present Convention as a substantial endorsement of the Act of the General Convention; and with his usual sagacity may have thought it prudent, apart from any personal feeling in the case, to arrest a contest which he foresaw would result in the defeat of his friends.   At this late day, uninfluenced by the excitement of the times, we are able to appreciate the tactics of the divisions of the anti-Federal party at their proper value.   The main object of Mason was to prevent a premature committal of the House by a vote on any separate part of the Constitution; for he well knew that an approval of one part would be urged argumentatively to obtain the approval of another part, and that, if the Constitution were approved in detail, it would be approved as a whole; and so far as his motion postponed intermediate voting, it was wise and well-timed.   But in requiring the Constitution to be discussed clause by clause, he went beyond his legitimate purpose, and played into the hands of his opponents.   The Federal Constitution, to be opposed successfully, must be discussed on the ground either of its unfitness as a whole to attain the end of its creation, or on the dangerous tendency of its various provisions.   To preclude the debate on the first head, and to narrow the debate on the second to the consideration of a single clause, was almost to resign the benefits of discussion to the friends of the system.   The resolution was capable of being wielded with fatal effect, and, if enforced by a skillful and stern parliamentarian, would have effectually prevented all freedom of debate.   The anti-Federalists believed that the Constitution in its general scope was false to liberty; yet, by the resolution, they were to be strictly confined to a discussion, not of its general tendency, but of the tendency of a particular clause.   Now, it is barely possible that a single provision of a vast system, when defended at length by an able hand, cannot be made tó assume a plausible shape in the eyes of a mixed assembly.   Either its obvious meaning will be denied, or an equivocal one will be attached to its terms.   The Federalists were aware of the advantages of such a warfare, and hence the readiness with which Madison rose to accept the proposal.[85]   Indeed, it is

---

[85] Madison wrote on the 4th to Washington a letter, of which the

a topic of interest now to observe how often the dogged perti-
nacity of George Nicholas and Madison, who acted the part of
whippers-in during the discussion, was rebuked by the indignant
eloquence of Mason and Henry.[86] It is true that the timely
movement of Tyler in transferring the debate from the House to
the Committee of the Whole in some measure counteracted the
ill effects of Mason's motion ; but its evil influence was sensibly
felt by his friends throughout the session.

The opening of the session on the third day[87] was awaited by
a large assemblage. Every seat was filled, while hundreds of
respectable persons remained standing in the passages and at the
doors. Among the spectators from every part of the Commonwealth were young men of promise, eager to behold the statesmen who had long served their country with distinction, whose
names were connected with every important civil and military
event of the Revolution; and some of whom were to be seen
now for the last time in a public body, and must in the order of
nature soon pass away. It is not unworthy of remark, as an
illustration of the effects wrought by the exhibition of genius
and talents on great occasions, that some of those young men
who were so intently watching the progress of the debates, as if
touched by the inspiration of the scene, were themselves to lead
the deliberations of public bodies and to control the councils of
the State and of the Union for more than the third of a century
to come.[88]

---

following is an extract: "I found, contrary to my expectations, that
not a very full House had been made on the first day, but that it had
proceeded to the appointment of the president and other officers. Mr.
Pendleton was put into the chair without opposition. Yesterday little
more was done than settling some forms, and resolving that no question, general or particular, should be propounded till the whole plan
should be considered and debated clause by clause. This was moved
by Colonel Mason, and, *contrary to his expectations*, concurred in by
the other side." Madison to General Washington, *Writings of Washington*, IX, 370, note.

[86] *Robertson's Debates*, page 36, *et passim*. I use *Robertson's Debates*,
edition of 1805; the handsome edition of the Debates following the
entire third volume of Elliott, published in 1859 under the sanction of
Congress, not having then appeared.

[87] Wednesday, June 4, 1788.

[88] No such thing as a published speech was then known in the coun-

It was the general expectation that Henry would open the debate on the part of the opponents of the Constitution ; but those who knew the conflicting positions held by Mason and himself, and had watched him closely on the preceding day, anticipated a skirmish before the regular debate began; and in this expectation they were not disappointed. When the House had received and acted upon the reports of the Committee of Elections, the order of the day was read, and the Convention went into Committee of the Whole. Wythe was called to the chair.[89] Next to Pendleton, his fame as a jurist and a statesman had been more widely diffused at home and abroad than that of any other member. He had been longest in the public service ; had long been a member of the House of Burgesses, which he entered as early as 1758 ; had been the intimate and confidential

---

try, and the only means of forming an opinion of the powers of a public man was to hear him speak. Brief and imperfect as *Robertson's Debates* are, they present the fullest report of speeches then known in our annals. Hence, the clever young men of the State crowded to Richmond, all of them on horseback. William B. Giles was among the spectators.

[89] I have never met with an instance in our parliamentary proceedings of the election of the chairman of the Committee of the Whole by the House. In the House of Burgesses the chairman, as the name implies, literally sate in a chair, none but the Speaker, who had been approved by the Governor, and was in some sense the representative of majesty, occupying the Speaker's seat. In Committee of the Whole, the mace, which was always placed on the clerk's table in regular session, was put under the table. I confess that I have not been able to trace satisfactorily the fate of the mace of the House of Burgesses. I have been told that it was melted at some date later than 1790. There was a member of the Senate from one of the tidewater counties who made great efforts to get a mace from the Senate. The city of Norfolk still possesses its ancient silver mace presented to the corporation by Governor Gooch in 1736 or thereabouts. This mace, of which a description and a cut is given in *The Dinwiddie Papers*, Vol. I (Virginia Historical Collections, Vol. III), pp. xiv, xv, was "The gift of Hon. Robert Dinwiddie, Lieutenant-Governor of Virginia, to the corporation of Norfolk, 1753." For notice of further examples of the mace in Virginia and other British-American colonies, see the same note. The mace of the House of Burgesses, which was by purchase saved from the "smelter's pot" by Colonel William Heth, who transformed it into a drinking cup, is now in the possession of his grand nephew, Harry Heth, late Major-General C. S. Army.—ED.

friend of Fauquier and Botetourt, and the associate of all the
royal governors of Virginia who in his time had any pretensions
as gentlemen and scholars; had spoken in the great debate on the
Declaration of Independence in Congress; had voted for the
Declaration of Rights and the Constitution of Virginia; had
filled the chair of the House of Delegates, when Pendleton, suffering from his recent accident, was detained at home, and had
acquired in the performance of his various duties that knowledge of the law of parliament and those habits of a presiding
officer, which were now indispensable to an occupant of the chair.
His position in one respect was unique.   As a professor of William and Mary, he had trained some of the ablest members of
the House, who regarded him with a veneration greater than
that, great as it was, which was shared by the public at large.[90]
He had reached his sixty-second year; yet as he moved with a
brisk and graceful step from the floor to the chair, his small and
erect stature presented a pleasing image of a fresh and healthy
old man.   In a front view, as he sate in the chair, he appeared to
be bald; but his gray hair grew thick behind, and instead of
being wrapped with a ribbon, as was then and many years later
the universal custom, descended to his neck, and rose in a broad
curl   He had not yet given way to that disarrangement of his
apparel which crept upon him in extreme age, and was arrayed
in the neat and simple dress that has come down to us in the
portrait engraved by Longacre.[91]   Though never robust, he was
now more able to bear, in a physical sense, the formidable ordeal
of the chair than Pendleton.   He had been a member of the
General Convention which framed the Constitution, and had
assented to the Virginia platform presented to that body; but,
as he was absent when that instrument was subscribed by the
members, his name did not appear on its roll.   He was, however,
in favor of its ratification.

When Wythe had taken his seat, before he had ordered the
clerk to read the first clause of the Constitution, Henry was on
the floor.   It was observed that age had made itself felt in the

---

[90] Among the numerous pupils of Wythe in the Convention were
Chief Justice Marshall, President Monroe, George and Wilson Cary
Nicholas, Read, Innes, Lewis, Samuel Jordan Cabell, &c.

[91] A single-breasted coat, with a standing collar, a single-breasted
vest, and a white cravat buckled behind.

appearance of this early and constant favorite of the people. He should have been in the vigor of life, for he had just entered his fifty-third year; but he had encountered many hardships in his vagrant life as a practising attorney, and had endured much trouble as a man and as a patriot. There was a perceptible stoop in his shoulders, and he wore glasses. His hair he had lost in early life, and its place was supplied by a brown wig, the adjustment of which, when under high excitement, was, as alleged by his contemporaries, a frequent gesture.[92] He had doubtless suffered at intervals from a painful organic disease which more than any other racks the system, and which eleven years later brought him to the grave. But his voice had not yet lost its wondrous magic,[93] and his intellectual powers knew no decline. He was to display before the adjournment an ability in debate and a splendor of eloquence, which surpassed all his previous efforts, and which have rarely been exhibited in a public assembly.

Neither Mason nor Henry was skilled in the law of parliament; but it is probable that Henry, in his solitary drive from Prince Edward, had formed some outline of the course which he intended to pursue. It was generally known that the Federalists believed that they made up a majority of the House; and he well knew that if Pendleton were nominated, as he certainly would be, for the chair, he would be elected above any competitor. Such a man carried with him not only the weight of his party, but his weight as an individual. To oppose him, therefore, was to risk a signal defeat; and from a signal defeat in the onset it might not be easy to recover. The election of president was allowed accordingly to pass in silence. The next plausible

---

[92] I have heard Governor Tazewell say that he has seen Henry, in animated debate, twirl his wig round his head several times in rapid succession. Our fathers had better eyes than their descendants. Glasses were rarely worn. Colonel Thomas Lewis was the only member of the Convention that wore them habitually. Patrick Henry and Judge Wilson, of Pennsylvania, are the only two men of the Revolutionary era who are painted with glasses. Franklin wore them in the Federal Convention, but he was over eighty at that time.

[93] He told his family that he lost his voice in pleading the British Debts' cause in 1791; but that loss none who heard him speak at any time afterwards could detect.

ground of attack was to be sought in the various Acts of Assembly which had called the General Convention into existence. The most important of these acts had been plainly violated by that body, and the new scheme was the offspring of *usurpation* ; and Henry thought that, if this view was presented in all its fearful extent by his friends, the result might yet be an immediate rejection of the new government. But he had to deal with one of the wariest parliamentarians of that age. When, therefore, Henry moved, as he now proceeded to do, that the various Acts of Assembly should be read by the clerk, evidently intending to follow up the reading with a speech, Pendleton, who, foreseeing the game, was on the watch, and who feared the effect of one of Henry's speeches in the yet unfixed state of parties, was instantly helped on his crutches, and opposed the reading.[94] He did not speak more than fifteen minutes ; but the effect of his speech was conclusive. It was an occasion of all others best adapted to his talents. The discussion in his view involved no great principle to be treated at large, but the interpretation of an Act of Assembly. He occupied the ground at once on which Henry would have sought to place him by force. He boldly assumed the position that, whatever might be the meaning of the Act calling the General Convention, the Act of Assembly convoking the present Convention for the express purpose of discussing the paper on the table was paramount to all other Acts, and was the rule of action prescribed by the people. Did this speech exist as spoken by Pendleton, posterity might read in the speech itself and in its circumstances the peculiarities of his mind and character. Assign him the ground he was to occupy— plant him on the rampart of an Act of Assembly—and he was invincible. Such was the effect of his speech that Henry made no reply, and not caring to court a defeat, which he saw was inevitable, withdrew his resolution.

But, if Henry had a favorite plan, the Federalists had one of their own ; and that plan was to discuss the Constitution, clause by clause, in the House under the eye of a president to be elected by themselves ; a mode which had already been adopted on the

---

[94] The general reader may perhaps not know that the president or speaker of a House on the Committee of the Whole sits with the members in the body of the House, and is free to engage in the debates, which he cannot do when in the chair.

motion of Mason, who little dreamed that he was treading in the tracks of his foes. Fortunately for the opponents of the Constitution, Tyler, who, as Speaker of the House of Delegates, had been familiar with the tactics of deliberative bodies, and who was opposed to the new scheme, had, as if in anticipation of the purposes of the Federalists, succeeded in transferring the discussions to the Committee of the Whole.

The clerk proceeded to read the preamble of the Constitution and the two first sections of the first article. When he had read them, George Nicholas rose to explain and defend them. There was a prestige in the name of Nicholas, and in the forensic reputation of the gentleman who now bore it, which placed him in the front rank of what may be called the second growth of eminent men who attained to distinction during the Revolution, and the brightness of whose genius has been reflected even in our own times. The eldest son of the venerable patriot who so long held the keys of the treasury, and whose death, in the midst of the Revolution in which he had freely embarked his great services and a reputation that in the eyes of his compatriots approached to sanctity, had sealed his fame as a martyr in his country's cause, George Nicholas entered public life under favorable auspices. Born in the city of Williamsburg, and nurtured in that institution which has been for more than a century and a half the gem of the ancient metropolis, he early engaged in the study of the law, and soon rose to the highest distinction at the bar. Nor was his professional skill his only passport to public attention. He had entered the army at the beginning of the war, and displayed more than once a capacity for military service that received the approbation of his superiors. But it was in the House of Delegates that he gained his highest distinction. During the war, and until the meeting of the present Convention, he held a prominent place in that body, which he almost entirely controlled, now threatening with impeachment the first executive officer of the Commonwealth, now planning the laws which were to constitute the titles to land in that immense principality which reached from the Alleghany to the Mississippi.[95]   His

---

[95] Benjamin Watkins Leigh has been heard to say that George Mason drafted the first land law; but it is certain that George Nicholas exerted a greater influence in shaping the land laws than any other man.

appearance was far from prepossessing. His stature was low, ungainly, and deformed with fat. His head was bald, his nose curved ; a gray eye glanced from beneath his shaggy brows ; and his voice, though strong and clear, was without modulation. His address, which had been polished by long and intimate association in the most refined circles of the Colony, to which by birth he belonged, and of the Commonwealth; his minute acquaintance with every topic of local legislation ; his ready command of that historical knowledge within the range of a well-educated lawyer of the old *régime;* perfect self-possession, which had been acquired in many a contest at the bar and in the House of Delegates with most of the able men now opposed to him, and which enabled him to wield at will a robust logic in debate which few cared to encounter, made him one of the most promising of that group of rising statesmen who had caught their inspiration from the lips of Wythe. Without one ray of fancy gleaming throughout his discourse, without action, unless the use of his right hand and forefinger, as if he were demonstrating a proposition on a black-board, be so called, by the force of argument applied to his subject as if the sections of the Constitution were sections of an Act of Assembly, he kept that audience, the most intellectual, perhaps, ever gathered during that century under a single roof in the Colony or in the Commonwealth, anxious as it was for the appearance of the elder members in the debate, for more than two hours in rapt attention. His speech is one of the fullest reported by Robertson, and its strict and masterly examination of the two sections before the House, explains the interest which it awakened and which it sustained.[96]

Henry, who probably saw his mistake in allowing one of the

---

[96] See *Robertson's Debates of the Virginia Convention of 1788,* page 18. I have alluded to the fatness of Nicholas. As he continued a prominent politician to his death in Kentucky in 1799, and as it was hard to meet his argument, his opponents resorted to caricature, and pictured him as broad as he was long. A friend told me that he once saw Mr. Madison laugh till the tears came into his eyes at a caricature of George Nicholas, which represented him " as a plum pudding with legs to it." He was probably one of the fattest lawyers since the days of his namesake Sir Nicholas Bacon, the lord keeper, who was so blown by the mere effort of taking his seat in the court of chancery that it was understood that no lawyer should address him until he had signified the recovery of his wind by three taps of his cane on the floor.

ablest friends of the Constitution to be the first to reach the ear of the House, followed Nicholas on the debate. If Nicholas adhered to the letter of the two sections, Henry did not follow his example; nor did he allude to those sections or to the speech of Nicholas, but spoke as if his resolution had been adopted, and the desired information had been obtained by the committee. He began by saying that the public mind as well as his own was extremely weary at the proposed change of government. "Give me leave," he said, "to form one of the number of those who wish to be thoroughly acquainted with the reasons of this perilous and uneasy situation, and why we are brought hither to decide on this great national question. I consider myself as the servant of the people of this Commonwealth, as a sentinel over their rights, liberty and happiness. I represent their feelings when I say that they are exceedingly uneasy, being brought from that state of full security which they enjoyed to the present delusive appearance of things. A year ago the minds of our citizens were in perfect repose. Before the meeting of the late Federal Convention at Philadelphia, a general peace and an universal tranquility prevailed in this country ; but since that period, the people are exceedingly uneasy and disquieted. When I wished for an appointment to this Convention, my mind was extremely agitated for the situation of public affairs. I conceive the public to be in extreme danger. If our situation be thus uneasy, whence has arisen this fearful jeopardy? It arises from this fatal system. It arises from a proposal to change our government—a proposal that goes to the annihilation of the most solemn engagements of the States—a proposal of establishing nine States into a confederacy, to the eventual exclusion of four States. It goes to the annihilation of those solemn treaties we have formed with foreign nations. The present circumstances of France—the good offices rendered us by that kingdom—require our most faithful and most punctual adherence to our treaty with her. We are in alliance with the Spaniards, the Dutch, the Prussians ; those treaties bound us as thirteen States confederated together. Yet here is a proposal to sever that confederacy. Is it possible that we shall abandon all our treaties and national engagements? And for what? I expected to have heard the reasons of an event so unexpected to my mind and the minds of others. Was our civil polity or public justice endangered or sapped? Was the real existence of the country threatened, or was this preceded by a mournful progression of events? This proposal of altering the government is of a most alarming nature. Make the best of the new government—say it is composed by anything but inspiration—you ought to be extremely cautious, watchful, jealous of your liberty; for instead of securing your rights you may lose them forever. If a wrong step be now made, the republic may be lost forever. If this new government will not come up to the expectation of the people, and they should be disappointed, their liberty will be lost, and tyranny must and will arise. I repeat it again, and I beg gentlemen to consider, that a wrong step now will plunge us into misery, and our republic will be lost. It will be necessary for this Convention to have a faithful historical detail of the facts that preceded the session of the Federal Convention, and the reasons that actuated its members in proposing an entire alteration of Government, and to demonstrate the dangers that awaited us. If they were of such awful magnitude as to warrant a proposal so extremely perilous as this, I must assert that this Convention has an absolute right to a thorough discovery of every circumstance relative to this great event. And here I would make this inquiry of those worthy characters who composed a part of the late Federal Convention. I am sure they were fully impressed with the necessity of forming a great consolidated Government instead of a confederation. That this is a consolidated Government is demonstrably clear; and the danger of such a Government is to my mind very striking. I have the highest veneration for those gentlemen; but, sir, give me leave to demand what right had they to say, *We, the people?* My political curiosity, exclusive of my anxious solicitude for the public welfare, leads me to ask who authorized them to speak the language of 'We, the People' instead of 'We, the States'? *States are the characteristics and soul of a confederation.* If the States be not the agents of this compact, it must be one great consolidated Government of the people of all the States. I have the highest respect for those gentlemen who formed the Convention; and were some of them not here I would express some testimonial of esteem for them. America had, on a former occasion, put the utmost confidence in them—a confidence which was well placed—and I am sure, sir, I would give up everything to them ; I would cheerfully confide in them as my representatives.   But on this great occasion I would demand the cause of their conduct.   Even from that illustrious man, who saved us by his valor, I would have a reason for his conduct.   That liberty which he has given us by his valor tells me to ask this reason; but there are other gentlemen here who can give us this information.   The people gave them no power to use their name.   That they exceeded their power is perfectly clear.   It is not mere curiosity that actuates me.   I wish to hear the real actual existing danger, which should lead us to take those steps so dangerous in my conception.   Disorders have arisen in other parts of America, but here, sir, no dangers, no insurrection or tumult has happened ; everything has been calm and tranquil.[97]   But, notwithstanding this, we are wandering in the great ocean of human affairs.   I see no landmark to guide us.   We are running we know not whither.   Difference of opinion has gone to a degree of inflammatory resentment in different parts of the country, which has been occasioned by this perilous innovation.   *The Federal Convention ought to have amended the old system—for this purpose they were solely delegated—the object of their mission extended to no other consideration.*   You must therefore forgive the solicitation of one unwor-

---

[97] This remark is strictly true.   There was no disorder of any kind in Virginia.   While Massachusetts was rent by intestine commotions and by a formidable rebellion, Virginia was in a state of profound tranquility.   The want of profitable employment for the labor of the North, and the low state of its marine, produced by the absence of the West India trade which it enjoyed before the war, and by the abundance of foreign shipping, are two great causes of northern troubles.   Meantime our agriculture was most prosperous, and our harbors and rivers were filled with ships.   The shipping interest of Norfolk was clamorous for duties on foreign tonnage, but, as we have shown in another place, was really advancing most rapidly to a degree of success never known in the Colony.   The immediate representatives of that part and its vicinity were under the delusion that the new Government would enable them to drive foreign ships away, and to fill their places with home-built vessels—a delusion that was soon dispelled in a short season by the sad reality of ports without either foreign or domestic shipping.

thy member to know what danger could have arisen under the present confederation, and what are the causes of this proposal to change our Government."[98]

This was the first blast from the trumpet of Henry, and hardly had its echoes died on the ear, when Edmund Randolph, evidently from previous arrangement, sprang to the floor. If Nicholas lacked that exterior which commends itself to the eye, Randolph, who was his brother-in-law, was in that respect particularly fortunate. He had attained his thirty-seventh year, and was in the flower of his manhood. His portly figure; his handsome face and flowing hair; his college course in the class-room and especially in the chapel, in which, standing in the shadow of the tomb of his titled ancestor, he was wont to pour the streams of his youthful eloquence into ravished ears; his large family connections, so important to a rising politician, and so convenient to fall back upon in case of defeat; the high honors which, from his entrance on the stage in his twenty-third year, had been showered upon him by the people and by the Assembly; the eclat which he had elicited by his forensic exertions, and by the imposing part which he had borne in the deliberations of the Convention at Philadelphia; his liberal acquaintance with English literature; his stately periods, fashioned in imitation of that celebrated orator who, in the earlier part of the century, had sought to conceal, under the forms of exquisite drapery, the tenets of a dangerous philosophy, and set off by a voice finely modulated, the tones of which rolled grandly through the hall and were reverberated from the gallery, constituted some of the titles to the distinction universally accorded him of being the most accomplished statesman of his age in the Commonwealth. An incident which occurred in his early life, and which could not be recalled by him at any time without painful emotions, tended

---

[98] This speech, imperfect as it is reported, will give the reader some notion of the topics of the speakers; but he must supply from his imagination the influence which the voice, the action, and the character of Henry, imparted to everything he said. Mr. Madison, in his latter days, told Governor Coles that when he had made a most conclusive argument in favor of the Constitution, Henry would rise to reply to him, and by some significant action, such as a pause, a shake of the head, or a striking gesture, before he uttered a word, would undo all that Madison had been trying to do for an hour before.

ultimately to his advantage. His father, who had been at the beginning of the Revolution Attorney General of the Colony, had adhered to the standard of England. The son, undaunted by the conduct of his father, who is said to have disinherited him for refusing to follow his example, and impelled by that spirit of chivalry which has ever been the heir-loom of his race, hastened to the army then encamped on the heights of Boston, that he might win an escutcheon of his own, undebased by the act of his sire.[99] On his return to Virginia the most flattering honors awaited him—honors the more valuable from the prejudices which distrusted the shoulders of youth. He was returned to the Convention of May, 1776, by the city of Williamsburg which had ever selected the ablest men of the Colony as its representatives. In that Convention he was placed on the committee which reported the resolution instructing the delegates of Virginia in Congress to propose independence, the Declaration of Rights, and a plan of government. He was elected by the body Attorney-General of the new Commonwealth—an honor which his grandfather, his uncle, and his father, in the meridian of their fame, had been proud to possess. Three years later he was elected by the General Assembly a member of Congress, and was successively re-elected for the usual term. In 1786 he was deputed one of the seven members dispatched from Virginia to the meeting of Annapolis; and in 1787 he was sent to the General Convention which framed the Federal Constitution. He was now Governor of the Commonwealth.

But with all his advantages, he was involved at this critical juncture in one of those distressing dilemmas into which impulsive politicians are prone to fall, and which tend to unnerve the strongest minds. The title of renegade, however falsely applied, is apt to blast the fairest flowers of rhetoric, and to impair or render unavailing the greatest powers of logic ; and by this title he well knew he was regarded in the estimation of a large and influential number of the members whom he was now to address. In the Philadelphia Convention he had exerted great influence in giving to the Constitution its main outline ; but, differing on

---

[99] He passed through Philadelphia on his way to Boston, and was strongly commended to Washington by a remarkable letter, for a copy of which I am indebted to Mr. Connarroe, of the former city.

some important points from his three colleagues, who had approved that instrument, he, sustained by Mason and Gerry alone, declined to vote in its favor.   Nor did his opposition to the new scheme halt at this stage of the proceeding.   In a letter which he addressed to the Speaker of the House of Delegates,[100] which was designed for publication, and which was published far and wide, he expressed his opinions at length, and led the opponents of the Constitution to believe that they would receive the aid of his talents and those of his family connection in their favorite plan of withholding the assent of Virginia to its ratification until certain amendments, designed to remedy the defects enumerated by him, should become an integral part of the new system.   The change of his views, which, though it took place some time previous to the meeting of the Convention, was not universally known until that body assembled, and was received at a time when the public excitement was intense, and when a single vote, or the influence of a single name, might decide the great question at issue, by his former opponents with warm approbation, and by his former friends with indignant scorn.   How far he was justified in the course which he pursued, will be discussed elsewhere, our present purpose being only to explain the relation in which he stood when he rose to address the House.[101]

Conscious of the delicacy of his position, and not indisposed to throw off a weight that pressed heavily upon him ; or, perhaps, willing to deprive his opponents of the benefit likely to accrue to them from that formal and fearful arraignment which

---

[100] *Elliot's Debates*, I, 482.

[101] The letter which he prepared for the Assembly in the winter of 1787-'88, but which he did not transmit, and which was afterwards published, was the first conclusive indication that he would vote for the ratification of the Constitution with or without amendments.   The letter may be found in *Carey's Museum*, III, 61.   Madison, writing to Jefferson as late as April 22, 1788, forty days before the meeting of the present Convention, and in intimate correspondence with Randolph, reports Randolph as " so temperate in his opposition, and goes so far with the friends of the Constitution, that he cannot be properly classed with its enemies."   If Madison could not speak confidently on the subject, no other person well could.

he knew would, sooner or later, inevitably follow, he resolved to
introduce the unpleasant topic at once.   After a graceful allusion
to the philosophy of the passions which were apt to rage most
fiercely on those occasions which required the calmest deliberation, but excepting the members of the Convention from such
an influence, he continued : " Pardon me, sir, if I am particularly
sanguine in my expectations from the chair ; it well knows *what
is order, how to command obedience*,[102] and that political opinions
may be as honest on one side as the other.   Before I pass into
the body of the argument, I must take the liberty of mentioning
the part I have already borne in this great question; but let me
not here be misunderstood.   I come not to apologize to any member within these walls, to the Convention as a body, or even to
my fellow citizens at large.   Having obeyed the impulse of duty ;
having satisfied my conscience, and, I trust, my God, I shall
appeal to no other tribunal ; nor do I become a candidate for
popularity ; my manner of life has never yet betrayed such a
desire.   The highest honors and emoluments of the Commonwealth are a poor compensation for the surrender of personal
independence.   The history of England from the revolution (of
1688), and that of Virginia for more than twenty years past,
show the vanity of a hope that general favor should ever follow
the man, who without partiality or prejudice praises or disap-
proves the opinions of friends or of foes ; nay, I might enlarge
the field, and declare, from the great volume of human nature
itself, that to be moderate in politics forbids an ascent to the
summit of political fame.   But I come hither regardless of
allurements, to continue as I have begun, to repeat my earnest
endeavors for a firm, energetic government, to enforce my objections to the Constitution, and to concur in any practical scheme
of amendments; but I will never assent to any scheme that will
operate a dissolution of the Union, or any measure which may
lead to it.   This conduct may probably be uphanded as injurious
to my own views ; if it be so, it is at least the natural offspring
of my judgment.   I refused to sign, and if the same were to

---

[102] This very pointed intimation to Wythe to keep the discussion from
wandering from the sections under debate, shows very plainly the programme of the Federalists.   If such was their policy in committee of
the whole, we can well judge what they designed it to be in the House.

return, again would I refuse. Wholly to adopt or wholly to
reject, as proposed by the Convention, seemed too hard an
alternative to the citizens of America, whose servants we were,
and whose pretensions amply to discuss the means of their happiness were undeniable. Even if adopted under the tenor of
impending anarchy, the government must have been without
that safest bulwark, the hearts of the people; and if rejected
because the chance of amendments was cut off, the Union would
have been irredeemably lost. This seems to have been verified
by the event in Massachusetts; but our Assembly have removed
these inconveniences by propounding the Constitution to our
full and free inquiry. When I withheld my supscription, I had
not even the glimpse of the genius of America relative to the
principles of the new Constitution. Who, arguing from the
preceding history of Virginia, could have divined that she was
prepared for the important change? In former times, indeed,
she transcended every Colony in professions and practices of
loyalty; but she opened a perilous war under a democracy almost
as pure as representation would admit. She supported it under
a Constitution which subjects all rule, authority, and power to
the legislature. Every attempt to alter it had been baffled ; the
increase of Congressional power had always excited alarm. I
therefore would not bind myself to uphold the new Constitution
before I had tried it by the true touchstone; especially, too,
when I foresaw that even the members of the General Convention might be instructed by the comments of those without doors.
But, moreover, I had objections to the Constitution, the most
material of which, too lengthy in detail, I have as yet barely
stated to the public, but will explain when we arrive at the proper
points. Amendments were consequently my wish ; these were
the grounds of my repugnance to subscribe, and were perfectly
reconcilable with my unalterable resolution to be regulated by
the spirit of America, if after our best efforts for amendments,
they could not be removed. I freely indulge those who may
think this declaration too candid in believing that I hereby depart from the concealment belonging to the character of a statesman. Their censure would be more reasonable were it not for
an unquestionable fact, that the spirit of America depends upon
a combination of circumstances which no individual can control,
and arises not from the prospect of advantages which may be

gained by the acts of negotiation, but from deeper and more honest causes. As with me the only question has ever been between previous and subsequent amendments, so I will express my apprehensions, that the postponement of this Convention to so late a day has extinguished the probability of the former without inevitable ruin to the Union ; and the Union is the anchor of our political salvation ; and I will assent to the lopping of this limb (meaning his arm) before I assent to the dissolutiou of the Union." Then, turning to Henry, he said : " I shall now follow the honorable gentleman in his inquiry. Before the meeting of the Federal Convention," says the honorable gentleman, " we rested in peace. A miracle it was that we were so ; miraculous must it appear to those who consider the distresses of the war, and the no less afflicting calamities which we suffered in the succeeding peace. Be so good as to recollect how we fared under the Confederation. I am ready to pour forth sentiments of the fullest gratitude to those gentlemen who framed that system.. I believe they had the most enlightened heads in this western hemisphere. Notwithstanding their intelligence and earnest solicitude for the good of their country, this system has proved totally inadequate to the purpose for which it was devised ; but, sir, it was no disgrace to them. The subject of confederations was then new, and the necessity of speedily forming some government for the States to defend them against the passing dangers prevented, perhaps, those able statesmen from making the system as perfect as more leisure and deliberation would have enabled them to do. I cannot otherwise conceive how they would have formed a system that provided no means of enforcing the powers which were nominally given to it. Was it not a political farce to pretend to vest powers without accompanying them with the means of putting them into execution.[103] This

---

[103] The wonder is, not as Mr. Randolph thinks, that the Congress made such a confederation, but that they succeeded in making any confederation at all. Among other evidences in my possession of the difficulties which environed the subject, I quote the annexed extract from a letter of Edward Rutledge, a member of Congress, which I received from an esteemed friend at the North, dated August, 1776, and which will show that the work was nearly given up in despair: " We have nothing with the confederation for some days, and it is of little consequence if we never see again ; for we have made such a

want of energy was not a greater solecism than the blending together and vesting in one body all the branches of government. The utter inefficacy of this system was discovered the moment the danger was over by the introduction of peace. The accumulated public misfortunes that resulted from its inefficacy rendered an alteration necessary. This necessity was obvious to all America. Attempts have accordingly been made for this purpose. I have been a witness to this business from its earliest beginning. I was honored with a seat in the small Convention held at Annapolis. The members of that Convention thought unanimously that the control of commerce should be given to Congress and recommended to their States to extend the improvement to the whole system. The members of the General Convention were particularly deputed to meliorate the Confederation. On a thorough contemplation of the subject, they found it impossible to amend that system : what was to be done? The dangers of America, which will be shown at another time by particular enumeration, suggested the expedient of forming a new plan. The Confederation has done a great deal for us we all allow; but it was the danger of a powerful enemy, and the spirit of America, sir, and not any energy in that system, that carried us through that perilous war; for what were its best aims? The greatest exertions were made when the danger was most imminent. This system was not signed till March, 1781, Maryland not having acceded to it before; yet the military achievements and other exertions of America, previous to that period, were as brilliant, effectual, and successful as they could have been under the most energetic government. This clearly shows that our perilous situation was the cement of our Union. How different the scene when this peril vanished and peace was restored! The demands of Congress were treated with neglect. One State complained that another had not completed its quotas as well as itself; public credit gone, for, I believe, were it not for the private credit of individuals, we should have been ruined

---

(devil) of it already that the Colonies can never agree to it. If my opinion was likely to be taken, I would propose that the States should appoint a special Congress to be composed of new members for this purpose; and that no person should disclose any part of the present plan. If that was done, we might then stand some chance of a Confederation; at present we stand none at all."

long before that time ; commerce languishing ; produce falling
in value ; and justice trampled under foot. We became contemptible in the eyes of foreign nations ; they discarded us as
little wanton bees who had played for liberty, but had no sufficient solidity or wisdom to secure it on a permanent basis, and
were therefore unworthy of their regard. It was found that
Congress could not even enforce the observance of treaties. The
treaty under which we enjoy our present tranquility was disregarded. Making no difference between the justice of paying
debts due to people here, and that of paying those due to people on the other side of the Atlantic, I wished to see the treaty
complied with, by the payment of the British debts, but have not
been able to know why it has been neglected. What was the
reply to the demands and requisites of Congress ? You are too
contemptible ; we will despise and disregard you.

" I shall endeavor to satisfy the gentleman's political curiosity.
Did not our compliance with any demand of Congress depend
on our own free will ? If we refused, I know of no coercive
power to compel a compliance.[104]   After meeting in Convention,
the deputies from the States communicated their information to
one another.   On a review of our critical situation, and of the
impossibility of introducing any degree of improvement into the
old system, what ought they to have done?   Would it not have
been treason to return without proposing some scheme to relieve
their distressed country ?   The honorable gentleman asks why
we should adopt a system that shall annihilate and destroy our
treaties with France and other nations.   I think the misfortune
is that these treaties are violated already under the honorable
gentleman's favorite system.   I conceive that our engagements
with foreign nations are not at all affected by this system ; for
the sixth article expressly provides that ' all debts contracted,
and engagements entered into, before the adoption of this Constitution, shall be as valid against the United States under this
Constitution as under the Confederation.'   Does this system,
then, cancel debts due to or from the continent ?   Is it not a well

---

[104] The two first sentences of this paragraph have a personal bearing
upon Henry. The allusion is to Henry's proposition that the delinquent States should be compelled by force to make full payment of
their quotas. This is only important to show that Randolph is the ag-
gressor in the furious quarrel that was soon to take place.

known maxim that no change of situation can alter an obligation once rightly entered into? He also objects because nine States are sufficient to put the Government in motion. What number of States ought we to have said? Ought we to have required the concurrence of all the thirteen? Rhode Island—in rebellion against integrity—Rhode Island plundered all the world by her paper money; and, notorious for her uniform opposition to every Federal duty, would then have it in her power to defeat the Union; and may we not judge with absolute certainty, from her past conduct, that she would do so? Therefore, to have required the ratification of all the thirteen States would have been tantamount to returning without having done anything. What other number would have been proper? Twelve? The same spirit that has actuated me in the whole progress of the business, would have prevented me from leaving it in the power of any one State to dissolve the Union; for would it not be lamentable that nothing could be done for the defection of one State? A majority of the whole would have been too few. Nine States, therefore, seem to be a most proper number.

"The gentleman then proceeds, and inquired why we assumed the language of 'We, the people.' I ask, why not? The Government is for the people; and the misfortune was that the people had no agency in the Government before. The Congress had power to make peace and war under the old Confederation. Granting passports, by the law of nations, is annexed to this power; yet Congress was reduced to the humiliating condition of being obliged to send deputies to Virginia to solicit a passport. Notwithstanding the exclusive power of war was given to Congress, the second Article of the Confederation was interpreted to forbid that body to grant a passport for tobacco, which, during the war, and in pursuance of engagements made at Little York, was to have been sent into New York. What harm is there in consulting the people on the construction of a Government by which they are to be bound? Is it unfair? Is it unjust? If the Government is to be binding upon the people, are not the people the proper persons to examine its merits or defects? I take this to be one of the least and most trivial objections that will be made to the Constitution. In the whole of this business I have acted in the strictest obedience to the dictates of my conscience in discharging what I conceive to be my duty to my country. I refused my signature, and if the same reasons operated on my mind, I would still refuse ; but as I think that those eight States, which have adopted the Constitution, will not recede, I am a friend to the Union.''

This speech, the report of which is meagre and evidently disconnected, had considerable effect on the body. It placed the speaker at once in the party of the Federalists, and put an end to the favorable expectations in which the opponents of the Constitution had indulged. The bold and sarcastic tone in which he answered the inquiries of Henry told that, instead of dreading, he defied the attacks of the orator of the people. At this day we can see the ingenious sophisms with which the speech abounds; and it is obvious that Randolph did not fully see, or purposely made light of, the most significant interrogatory of Henry.

He was followed by Mason, whose words were now watched with an interest hardly exceeded by that which existed when he first rose to address the House ; for he, too, had been a member of the General Convention, and had declared in that body that, on certain conditions, none of which included the words of the preamble, he would approve the Constitution ; but, though no parliamentarian, he saw the snare into which his opponents were anxious that he should fall, and adroitly avoided it by taking ground which placed him in instant communion with Henry. He began by saying that, whether the Constitution be good or bad, the present clause demonstrated that it is a national Government, and no longer a confederation ;[105] that popular governments could only exist in small territories ; that what would be a proper tax in one State would not be a proper tax in another ; that the mode of levying taxes was of the utmost consequence ; that the subject of taxation differed in three-fourths of the States ; that, if the national Government was enabled to raise what is necessary, that was sufficient; but, he said, why yield this dangerous power of unlimited taxation? He objected to the

---

[105] The clause to which he alludes is as follows : " Representatives and direct taxes shall be apportioned among the several States, which may be included within this Union, according to their respective numbers, which shall be determined by adding to the whole number of free persons, including those bound to service for a term of years, and excluding Indians not taxed, three-fifths of all other persons."

rule apportioning the number of representatives—"the number of representatives," the Constitution said, "shall not exceed one for every thirty thousand ;" now, will not this be complied with, although the present number should never be increased? "When we come to the judiciary," he said, "we shall be more convinced that this Government will terminate in the annihilation of the State Government. The question then will be, whether a consolidated Government can preserve the freedom and secure the great rights of the people. If such amendments be introduced as shall exclude danger, I shall most gladly put my hand to this Constitution. When such amendments as shall secure the great essential rights of the people be agreed to by gentlemen, I shall most heartily make the greatest concessions, and concur in any reasonable measure to obtain the desirable end of conciliation and unanimity ; but an indispensable amendment is that Congress shall not exercise the power of raising direct taxes till the States shall have refused to comply with the requisitions of Congress. On this condition it may be granted ; but I see no reason to grant it unconditionally ; as the States can raise the taxes with more ease, and lay them on the inhabitants with more propriety than it is possible for the general Government to do. If Congress hath this power without control, the taxes will be laid by those who have no fellow feeling or acquaintance with the people. This is my objection to the article under consideration. It is a very great and important one. I beg, gentlemen, seriously to consider it. Should this power be restrained, I shall withdraw my objections to this part of the Constitution ; but, as it stands, it is an objection so strong in my mind that its amendment is with me a *sine qua non* of its adoption. I wish for such amendments, and such only, as are necessary to secure the dearest rights of the people."

Madison, who had kept himself in reserve to answer Mason, then took the floor. We must not confound the Madison who presided in the Federal Government, and who appeared in extreme old age in the Convention of 1829, with the Madison who now in his thirty-eighth year rose to address the House. Twelve years before he had entered the Convention of 1776, a small, frail youth, who, though he had reached his twenty-fifth year, looked as if he had not attained his majority. Diffident as he was on that his first appearance in public life, his merits did not even

then pass unobserved ; and he was placed on the grand committee of that body which reported the resolution instructing
the delegates of Virginia in Congress to propose independence,
and which reported the declaration of rights and the Constitution.   After serving in the first House of Delegates to the close
of its session,[106] he was soon after chosen a member of the Council, and was in due time transferred thence to Congress, when his
talents were first exerted in debate, and of which body he was at
that time a member.   He had at an early day foreseen the necessity of an amendment of the Articles of Confederation ; had
been a member of the meeting at Annapolis ; and was, perhaps,
more instrumental in the call of the General Convention than
any other of his distinguised contemporaries.   In that body he
had performed a leading part ; and in addition to his ordinary
duties as a member, he undertook the task of reporting the sub-
stance of the debates, and thus preserved for posterity the only
full record of its deliberations that we possess.   His services in

---

[106] As Mr. Madison was a member of the May Convention of 1776,
and also a member of the first House of Delegates, it is reasonable to
suppose that he had been elected on two distinct occasions by the people ; but as such was not the fact, and as both Mr. Jefferson and Mr.
Madison have made statements in some measure derogatory from the
true nature of our early Convention, it may be worth while to say that,
after the subsidence of the House of Burgesses in the Revolution, the
members who were returned by the people on the basis of that House,
acted on the sovereign capacity of conventions, as we now understand
the word   The conventions, like the House of Burgesses, were elected
for a given term ; and the members of the Convention of May, 1776,
after framing the Constitution, having been elected to serve one year,
did not adjourn *sine die*, but being on the identical basis of the House
of Delegates under the new Constitution, held over, and became the
first House of Delegates of the General Assembly, the Senate of which
had been elected by the people.   Hence, Mr. Madison and Mr. Jefferson have frequently affirmed that the first Constitution of Virginia was
made by an ordinary legislature ; overlooking the facts stated above,
and failing to recognize the two remarkable precedents afforded by
English history in the Convention Parliament of 1660, which restored
Charles the Second, and the Convention Parliament of 1688, which
settled the British crown on William and Mary ; both of which bodies,
when their conventional duties were finished, became the ordinary
House of Commons until the expiration of the term for which the
members had been elected.

this respect were invaluable.[107] From his entrance into Congress
he was compelled to engage in public speaking; and as all his
intellectual powers had for years been trained to discussion, when
he took his seat in the present Convention he was probably one
of the most thorough debaters of that age. His figure had
during the last twelve years become more manly, and though
below the middle stature, was muscular and well-proportioned.
His manners and address were sensibly improved by the refined
society in which he had appeared during that interval, and his
complexion, formerly pale, had become ruddy. He was a bach-
elor, and was handsomely arrayed in blue and buff. His coat
was single-breasted, with a straight collar doubled, such as the
Methodists wore thirty years ago; and at the wrist and on his
breast he wore ruffles. His hair, which was combed low on his
forehead to conceal a baldness which appeared in early life, was
dressed with powder, and ended in a long queue, the arrangement of which was the chief trouble of the toilet of our fathers.
The moustache, then seen only on some foreign lip, was held in
abhorrence, and served to recall the carnage of Blackbeard, who
had been slain in the early part of the century, in the waters of
Carolina, by the gallant Maynard, and whose name made the
burden of the song with which Mason and Wythe had been
scared to sleep in their cradles. Even the modest whisker was
rarely worn by eminent public men ; and neither the moustache

---

[107] Mr. Madison told Governor Edward Coles that the labor of writing out the debates, added to the confinement to which his attendance
in Convention subjected him, almost killed him ; but that having
undertaken the task, he was determined to accomplish it. It is not
improbable that other members made memoranda ; but as yet we have
nothing more than a very respectable record from Chief Justice Robert
Yates, of New York, who, however, withdrew at an early period of the
session. I attempted to sketch the debates in the Convention of 1829,
and have saved a few things which occurred in the legislative committee ; but gave the matter up when I saw the full and accurate reports made under the auspices of Mr. Ritchie. My slight experience
convinced me that the task would be incompatible with any participation in society. It enhances our opinion of the talents of Madison,
when we reflect that in addition to his formidable labor in reporting
and writing out the proceedings of the Convention, he was able to bear
a principal part in its deliberations.

nor the whisker was ever seen on the face of Madison, Monroe, Jefferson or Washington. He walked with a bouncing step, which he adopted with a view of adding to his height, or had unconsciously caught during his residence at the North, and which was apparent to any one who saw him, forty years later, enter the parlor at Montpellier. But what was far more important than any mere physical quality, he not only possessed, as before observed, the faculty of debate in such a degree that he may be said to exhaust every subject which he discussed and to leave nothing for his successors to say, but a self-possession, acquired partly by conflict with able men, partly by the consciousness of his strength, without which, in the body in which he was now to act, the finest powers would have been of little avail, and a critical knowledge of the rules of deliberative assemblies. He was fortunate in another particular of hardly less importance than the possession of great powers; he had an intimate knowledge of the men to whom he was opposed, and whose eloquence and authority would be apt to silence an opponent when felt for the first time. He had known Grayson in Congress, and had heard Henry in the Convention of 1776, and had encountered him in the House of Delegates on several grave questions that arose during the Revolution and subsequently. With Mason also he had served the same apprenticeship, and had recently acted with him in the General Convention; and he knew as well as any man living wherein the secret of the strength of these formidable opponents lay. But with all these advantages of knowledge and experience, of which he availed himself during the session to the greatest extent and with consummate tact, he had the physical qualities of an orator in a less degree than any of his great contemporaries. His low stature made it difficult for him to be seen from all parts of the house; his voice was rarely loud enough to be heard throughout the hall; and this want of size and weakness of voice were the more apparent from the contrast with the appearance of Henry, and Innes, and Randolph, who were large men, and whose clarion notes were no contemptible sources of their power. He always rose to speak as if with a view of expressing some thought that had casually occurred to him, with his hat in his hand, and with his notes in his hat; and the warmest excitement of debate was visible in him only by a more or less rapid and forward see-saw motion of his body.[108] Yet such was the force of his genius that one of his warmest opponents in the Convention declared, years after the adjournment, that he listened with more delight to his clear and cunning argumentation than to the eloquent and startling appeals of Henry; and he established a reputation in this body which was diffused throughout the State, and which was the ground-work of his subsequent popularity. One quality which was perceptible in all the great occasions of his life, occurring on the floor or in the cabinet, and which can never be commended too highly, was the courtesy and the respect with which he regarded the motives and treated the arguments of the humblest as well as the ablest of his opponents, and which placed him on a noble vantage ground when he was personally assailed by others.[109] He viewed an argument in debate, not in respect of the worth or want of worth of him who urged it, but in respect of

---

[108] I have often heard of Mr. Madison's mode of speaking from members of the Assembly of 1799. One of those members, some years ago, wrote a capital sketch of his manner, which appeared in the *Richmond Enquirer*. I am sorry that I have mislaid the reference to it. When the *Euquirer* was first published it always contained an index at the close of the year, and that index was a great help to the memory. The style of Mr. Madison's speaking was well adapted to the old Congress and the General Convention, which were small bodies; but he never could have been heard at any time in the hall of the House of Delegates. In the Convention of 1829 he spoke once or twice, but he was inaudible by the members who crowded about him. On one occasion I remember John Randolph rising and advancing several steps to hear him, and holding his hand to his ear for a minute or two, and then dropping his hand with a look of despair.

[109] The sternest judge, before the merits of Madison as a speaker, could pass in review — one who was the Ajax Telamon of the opposite party — was the late Chief-Justice Marshall; yet, towards the close of his life, being asked which of the various public speakers he had heard — and he had heard all the great orators, parliamentary and forensic, of America — he considered the most eloquent, replied: "Eloquence has been defined to be the art of persuasion. If it includes persuasion by convincing, Mr. Madison was the most eloquent man I ever heard." *Rives' Madison*, II, 612, note. As an instance of the courtesy of Mr. Madison, while conversing on a very irritating theme with the late Lord Jeffery, who visited the United States in 1813, see *Lord Cockburn's Life of Jeffery*, I, 179.

its own intrinsic worth.   The same sense of propriety which led
him to respect the feelings and motives of others, impelled him
to resent with stern severity any attack upon his own ; and on
two occasions during the session, when he thought a reflection
was cast upon him, he demanded reparation in a tone that menaced an immediate call to the field.   On the present occasion he
saw that the utmost discretion was indispensable, if any conclusive and really valuable conquest was to be won by the friends of
the Constitution.   He could not know that the Constitution
would be carried at all ; and he knew that, if it was, it would be
carried in opposition to the wishes of some of the ablest and
wisest men of that age—men to whom, for more than twenty
years, Virginia had looked for guidance in war and in peace, and
who, if they were not sustained by a large majority of the people, held in their keeping the keys of the General Assembly.   He
saw that, if a triumph worth enjoying was to be attained by his
friends, it was to be accomplished by conciliation and forbear-
ance, not by intimidation or by obloquy ; and instead of imitating his friend Randolph, who could not repress a spirit of sarcasm and defiance in answering the purely political interroga-
tories of Henry, he addressed himself to the arguments of Mason
with the blandness with which one friend in private life would
seek to remove the objections of another.   He said "it would
give him great pleasure to concur with his honorable colleague
on any conciliating plan.   The clause to which he alludes is only
explanatory of the proportion which representation and taxation
shall respectively bear to one another.   The power of laying direct taxes will be more properly discussed when we come to that
part of the Constitution which rests that power in Congress.   At
present I must endeavor to reconcile our proceedings to the
resolution we have taken by postponing the examination of this
power till we come properly to it.   With respect to converting
the Confederation to a complete consolidation, I think no such
consequence will follow from the Constitution ; and that with
more attention the gentleman will see that he is mistaken ; and,
with respect to the number of representatives, I reconcile it to
my mind, when I consider it may be increased to the **proportion**
fixed ; and that, as it may be so increased, *it shall*, **because it is**
the interest of those who alone can prevent it, who **are our rep-**
resentatives, and who depend on their good **behavior for re-elec-**

tion. Let me observe also that, as far as the number of representatives may seem to be inadequate to discharge their duty, they will have sufficient information from the laws of particular States, from the State legislatures, from their own experience, and from a great number of individuals; and as to our security against them, I conceive that the general limitation of their powers, and the general watchfulness of the States, will be a sufficient guard. As it is now late, I shall defer any further investigation till a more convenient time."

When he ended, the House rose, and Madison hastened to his solitary room at the Swan, and wrote to Washington that Randolph had thrown himself fully in the Federal scale; that Henry and Mason had made a lame figure, and appeared to take different and awkward grounds; that the Federalists were elated at their present prospects; that he could not speak certainly of the result; that Kentucky was extremely tainted, and was supposed to be adverse; and that every kind of address was going on privately to work on the local interests and prejudices of that and other quarters.[110]

---

[110] Madison to Washington, June 4, 1788, *Writings of Washington*, IX, 370, note. Washington received the earliest intelligence of the proceedings of the Convention from his friends in the body, and communicated freely his advices to his distant correspondents. As a specimen of his *reporting* at second hand, I annex his letter to John Jay, dated June 8, 1788 (*Ibid.*, 373), in which he gives the proceedings to the close of this day's session: "On the day appointed for the meeting of the Convention, a large proportion of the members assembled, and unanimously placed Mr. Pendleton in the chair. Having on that and the subsequent day chosen the rest of the officers, and fixed upon the mode of conducting the business, it was moved by some one of those opposed to the Constitution to debate the whole by paragraphs, without taking any question until the investigation should be completed. This was as unexpected as acceptable to the Federalists, and their hearty acquiescence seems to have somewhat startled the opposite party, for fear they had committed themselves.

"Mr. Nicholas opened the business by very ably advocating the system of representation. Mr. Henry, in answer, went more vaguely into the discussion of the Constitution, intimating that the Federal Convention had exceeded its powers, and that we had been and might be happy under the old Confederation with a few alterations. This called up Governor Randolph, who is reported to have spoken with great pathos in reply, and who declared that, since so many of the States had

Nor was Madison the only correspondent of Washington in the Convention. There was a young man, who had just reached his thirtieth year, who had been educated at William and Mary, had made a short tour in the Revolution, and, going to Phila delphia, had studied law under Wilson ; and who, having settled in Richmond, devoted himself to his profession, and published two volumes of reports, which still preserve his name in association with his native State. He was destined to distinction in after life. He was the nephew of Washington, bore that honored name, became the heir of Mount Vernon, and for nearly the third of a century after his illustrious uncle had descended to the tomb held a seat in the Supreme Court created by the Constitution, the fate of which he was about to decide. It was from this young man, from Madison, and from other friends, that Washington received as regular reports of the proceedings of the Convention as the postal facilities of that day would convey ; and he was thus enabled to keep his friends in other States well instructed in the progress of that great debate, which he re-

adopted the proposed Constitution, he considered the sense of America to be already taken, and that he should give his vote in favor of it without insisting previously upon amendments. Mr. Mason rose in opposition, and Mr. Madison reserved himself to obviate the objections of Mr. Henry and Colonel Mason the next day. Thus the matter rested when the last accounts gave way.

"Upon the whole, the following inferences seem to have been drawn : That Mr. Randolph's declaration will have considerable effect with those who had hitherto been wavering ; that Mr. Henry and Colonel Mason took different and awkward ground, and by no means equaled the public expectations in their speeches; that the former has receded somewhat from his violent measures to coalesce with the latter ; and that the leaders of the opposition appear rather chagrined, and hardly to be decided as to their mode of opposition.

"The sanguine friends of the Constitution counted upon a majority of twenty at their first meeting, which number, they imagine, will be greatly increased; while those equally strong in their wishes, but more temperate in their habits of thinking, speak less confidently of the greatness of the majority, and express apprehension of the acts that may yet be practiced to excite alarms with the members from the Western District (Kentucky)." It is much to be regretted that Mr. Sparks did not publish all the letters received by Washington during the session of the Convention. In the absence of the newspapers, which seem to have been all lost, they would have been important in many respects.

garded with an interest not less intense than that with which he had watched the tide of battle or the issue of a campaign.

The morning of Thursday, the fifth day of June, witnessed a dense crowd in the New Academy. It was expected that Madison would reply to Henry and Mason; and that Henry and Mason, unrestrained by the order of discussion, would review the Constitution at large. Some business appertaining to contested elections was soon despatched; and Pendleton, having called Wythe to the chair, was helped to a seat in the body of the house. There was a pause, for the courtesies of parliament were strictly observed, and Madison was entitled to the floor. But he was nowhere to be seen. It was whispered that he had been taken suddenly ill, and was confined to his room. Every eye was then turned to Henry and Mason, when, to the amazement of all, Pendleton was seen to make an effort to rise, and, supported on crutches, addressed the chair. Those who forty years later, in the Convention of 1829 beheld Mr. Madison, in the midst of an excited discussion rise from his seat, and proceed to make a speech, and can recall the confusion produced by the members hastening from their seats to gather around him, or leaping on the benches in the hope of seeing, if they could not hear, what was passing before them, may form some conception of the interest so suddenly excited by the appearance of Pendleton on the floor with a view of making a regular speech. He had been for the third of a century eminent for skill in debate, and his fame had become a matter of history; and he had never before been in a body the discussions of which were better adapted to the display of his extraordinary talents ; but he was so far advanced in life, so crippled by his hurt, and so long absent from public bodies and unused to debate, it was not expected that he would be able to do more than to speak to some point of order or to give his vote. He soon, however, gave a remarkable proof that fine powers kept in full employment do not sensibly decay with time, and that he only wanted physical strength to take the lead out of the hands of the promising statesmen who had been born and had grown up since he first entered a deliberative assembly. It is said that some of the oldest members,[111] as they looked at the feeble old man on his

---

[111] In the Convention of 1829, when Mr. Monroe was conducted to the chair by Mr. Madison and Chief Justice Marshall, several members

feet, and at his ancient compeer Wythe leaning forward in the chair to catch the tones of a voice which for the past thirty years he had heard with various emotions, were affected to tears. But there was no snivelling or passion in Pendleton himself. He had resolved to refute the arguments urged by Henry the day before, and he performed his task as thoroughly and as deliberately, and very much in the same way, as he would deliver an opinion upon the bench. On its face the speech seems conclusive ; for, as like Nicholas, he was purely argumentative, and, as he dealt only with special objections, his words are reported with a force and connection which are altogether wanting in the speeches of Henry and Randolph.

He met the objection of Henry, that the General Convention had exceeded its powers in substituting an entirely new system in the place of the Confederation which they were required to amend, in the following manner : " But the power of the Convention is doubted. What is the power ? To propose, and not to determine. This power of proposing is very broad ; it extended to remove all defects in government. The members of that Convention were to consider all the defects in our general government ; they were not confined to any particular plan. Were they deceived ? This is the proper question here. Suppose the paper on your table dropped from one of the planets ; the people found it, and sent us here to consider whether it is proper for their adoption. Must we not obey them ? Then the question must be between this Government and the Confederation. The latter is no government at all. It has been said that it carried us through a dangerous war to a happy issue. Not

---

were seen to weep. There are several points of resemblance in the incidents of the two bodies. Pendleton, speaking on his crutches, recalls William B. Giles, who had broken a leg by a similar accident, [his descendants say that he was disabled by rheumatism—ED.] and was only a year or two younger than Pendleton. The change in the opinions of Edmund Randolph has its counterpart in the change attributed to Chapman Johnson ; and the collision between Patrick Henry and Edmund Randolph was repeated in that between Chapman Johnson and John Randolph. The election of Pendleton instead of Wythe, who was the more popular of the two, is reflected in the election of Monroe instead of Madison, who was universally fixed upon both in and out of the Convention as its presiding officer, and who alone could have defeated his election, which he did by instantly rising when the body was called to order and nominating Mr. Monroe.

that Confederation, but common danger and the spirit of America were the bonds of our union. Union and unanimity, and not that insignificant paper, carried us through that dangerous war. 'United we stand; divided we fall,' echoed and re-echoed through America, from Congress to the drunken carpenter, was effectual, and procured the end of our wishes, though now forgot by gentlemen, if such there be, who incline to let go this strong hold to catch at feathers—for such all substituted projects may prove.''

He also met the objection of Henry, to the words in the preamble of the Constitution, " We, the people," in this wise : "An objection is made to the form. The expression, ' We, the people,' is thought improper. Permit me to ask the gentleman who made this objection, who but the people can delegate powers ? Who but the people have a right to form government ? The expression is a common one, and a favorite one with me. The representatives of the people, by their authority, is a mode wholly inessential. If the objection be that the union ought to be not of the people, but of the State Governments, then I think the choice of the former very happy and proper. What have the State Governments to do with it ? Were they to determine, the people would not, in that case, be the judges upon what terms it was adopted.''

In allusion to the fears expressed by Henry, of the loss of liberty under a particular form of Government, he thus expressed his views of the nature of Government, and the mode of relief in the event of maladministration: " Happiness and security cannot be attained without Government. What was it that brought us from a state of nature to society but to secure happiness ? Personify Government ; apply to it as to a friend to assist you, and it will grant your request. This is the only Government founded on real compact. There is no quarrel between Government and Liberty ; the former is the shield and protector of the latter. The war is between Government and licentiousness, faction, turbulence, and other violations of the rule of society to preserve liberty. Where is the cause of alarm ? We, the people, possessing all power, form a Government such as we think will secure happiness ; and suppose in adopting this plan we shall be mistaken in the end, where is the cause of alarm on that quarter ? In the same plan we point out an easy and quiet method of reforming what may be found amiss. No; but say, gentlemen, we have put the introduction of that method in the hands of our servants, who will interrupt it from motives of self-interest. What then? We will resist, did my friend say, conveying an idea of force? Who shall dare to resist the people? No; *we will assemble in Convention, wholly recall our delegated powers*,[112] or reform them so as to prevent such an abuse; and punish those servants who have perverted powers designed for our happiness to their own emolument. We should be extremely cautious not to be drawn into dispute with regular Government by faction and turbulence, its natural enemies. Here, then, there is no cause of alarm on this side; but on the other side, rejecting of Government and dissolving of the Union, produce confusion and despotism."

Before taking his seat, he said he was of no party, nor actuated by any influence but the true interest and real happiness of those whom he represented; that his age and situation, he trusted, would sufficiently demonstrate the truth of his assertion, and that he was perfectly satisfied with this part of the system.

This was a characteristic effort of the venerable President. Meagre as the report is, we know from the report itself, as well as from tradition, that it was able and effective; and it displays not only the skill of the lawyer, but that familiarity with public bodies which places a speaker abreast of his audience, and enables a wary debater to strike the level of the general mind. As far as Pendleton saw—and on strictly legal questions he saw all the way—no man saw more clearly; but his range of political vision was limited; and his speech is the speech rather of a great lawyer than of a great statesman. While he affirmed in the strongest manner the right of the people of Virginia, in Conven-

---

[112] This opinion, which at that day was deemed a truism, let it be remembered, was uttered by an old man verging to seventy, who had been the leader of the conservative party of the Colony and of the Commonwealth for forty yea If such a man so thought, what might be expected from the younger members, three-fourths of whom had actually drawn the sword, and one-fourth of whom had held the highest civil offices, in the great Rebellion of 1776? When Henry touched upon this point in his reply to Pendleton, he admitted it, of course, urged with that sound, practical sense which was his polar star in politics, that, if the power of the purse and the sword were surrendered, the State would have no power to enforce its action.

tion assembled, to recall their delegated powers at will, he did
not see, or failed to recognize, the distinction between the people
of the United States and the States so pointedly drawn by Henry,
and the bounden duty of representatives charged with a public
trust of performing it according to the letter of their instructions
and the obvious wishes of their constituents.   He did not see
that the example of such a body as the General Federal Convention, at so early a period in the history of free systems, if
unchecked and uncondemned, would take away from posterity
all hope of a limited Convention, and that, when a Convention is
called to amend a specific system, it may destroy that system entirely, and introduce even a monarchy in its stead, and be free
from the blame or censure of those whom they have betrayed.
It is not enough to say that the people may adopt or reject the
new scheme at pleasure.   That scheme, ushered under the sanction of able and honorable men, and sustained by august names
and an extrinsic authority, is a power in itself; and it is unjust
to impose upon the people the risk of a battle which they did
not seek, and which, by the intrigues, of a wealthy and unscru-
pulous minority, they may lose.

We may well imagine the feelings with which Henry listened
to this sophistical, though apparently conclusive, answer to his
speech of the previous day.   In all the great conjunctures of our
history, in which he had borne a conspicuous part, he had been
opposed by Pendleton.   In the House of Burgesses, in the debate on his own resolutions against the Stamp Act; and on the
bill separating the office of treasurer from that of the speaker,
the success of which had been hailed as a triumph by the people ; on the resolutions of the March Convention of 1775, putting the Colony into a posture of defence ; and on nearly all the
dividing questions in the Conventions and in the House of Dele-
getes, that old man, then in the meridian of his strength, and
now in his decline, had opposed him with untiring zeal, and
made victory itself little more than a drawn battle.   There were
other recollections which might have flashed across the mind of
the husband and the father.   When, young and poorly clad, and
ruined in fortune, with a wife and children looking to him for
daily bread, he had ventured, under the unconscious impulse,
perhaps, of that genius which was in a few short years to invest
his humble name and the name of his country with unfading lus-

tro, as a last resort to seek a license to practice law, with the hope of gathering, in the suburbs of a proud profession, a scanty support for his family, he had applied to Pendleton for his signature, and had been denied so humble a boon—a boon which, though refused by a man who, like himself, had sprung from the people, was promptly granted by the generous Randolphs, whose blood could be traced in the veins of men whose career in British annals was to be measured by centuries.

Therefore, the cause which Henry had upheld was successful. Was his star to decline now when he believed that he was engaged in a cause in comparison with which his other contests seemed unimportant, and when the liberties of his country were at stake ? Some such thoughts may have occurred to him as he rose to make one of the greatest exhibitions of his genius which his compeers had ever witnessed, and which, though in a mutilated form, has come down to us in the pages of Robertson.

He was anticipated, however, by Henry Lee, who, rising near the chairman, caught his eye, and proceeded to address the House. This remarkable young man, now in his thirty-second year, was excelled by none of his contemporaries, with the exception of Hamilton, who was his junior by a single year, if indeed excelled by him, in the display from the beginning to the close of the war of the highest qualities in the field, and in his subsequent position in the legislature of his native State and in the Congress.[113] His brilliant achievements in war had conferred upon a patronymic known for more than a hundred years in the councils of the Colony a fresh and peculiar honor, the splendor of which was rather enhanced than diminished by the exhibition of those eminent endowments which his kinsmen during the Revolution had exerted in civil life. He had taken his degree in the college of New Jersey in 1773, when he had reached his seventeenth year, entering that institution as Madison was about to leave it, and received the instruction of Witherspoon, whose distinctive praise it was not only to have signed with his own hand the Declaration of Independence, but to have trained a band of young men who nobly sustained that instru-

---

[113] It may be worth noting that our fathers always spoke of *the* Congress as we speak of the Congress of Verona, or Vienna, a fact not without political significance.

ment in the field and in the cabinet, and whose genius ruled in
the deliberations of the Union from the end of the war until
nearly the middle of the present century.   In 1776, he was
elected an ensign in one of the Virginia regiments, and was soon
promoted by Governor Henry to a troop of horse ; and having
soon been transferred to the North, developed qualities which
attracted the commander-in-chief, who in due time despatched
him with a separate command to the South.   The skill, gallantry
and success with which he led his corps amid the complicated
embarrassments of a long and predatory war in a sickly and
inhospitable country, have not only made his own name immortal, but invested the name of his legion with the dignity of a
household word of the Revolution.   His soldiers were hailed
with the most flattering name.   The legion was called the right
hand of Greene.   It was the eye of the army of the South.   On
that great occasion, when, on the evacuation of Charleston by
the British, whose outstretched canvas, spread upon innumerable
spars, was seen in the distant offing seeking the Atlantic, Lee,
at the head of his gallant corps, constituting, as a mark of valor,
the van of the army of Greene, was the first to enter the lovely
city of the South.[114]   His reputation, which had culminated
during his Southern campaigns, was regarded as the property of
Georgia, South Carolina and North Carolina, as well as of Virginia; and each of those States would have been proud to offer
him, in common with his illustrious commander, a home within
her territory.   Returning to his patrimonial estate, he entered
the General Assembly, and in 1785 he was elected a member of
the Congress of the Confederation, and was present during the
discussion of the most momentous Southern question that occurred in that body.   Of his course on that occasion we shall
treat in another place.   His delight, however, was in arms ; and
when the French Revolution broke out, and France, our old
ally, was beset by the combined powers of Europe, he wished to
offer his sword to the young republic, but was dissuaded from
his purpose by his friends.   As a soldier, he enjoyed the unlim-
ted confidence, respect and esteem of Washington, and he recip-
rocated the attachment with an affection which was perceptible
in his entire political career.   When the death of his illustrious

---

[114] Written in 1857.   1866—alas !

friend was announced to Congress, the resolutions which were adopted by the body, though offered by the hand of another, were from his pen ; and in the presence of both houses he pronounced the funeral oration of the man whom he justly called "first in war, first in peace, and first in the hearts of his fellow-citizens." Ten years later he won a victory, not achieved in the field over prostrate foes, but in the closet—the fairest and most unfading of all his honors—in recording with uncommon grace the events of the war in the South. Writing in the shadows of a prison, within the bounds of which he had been committed for debt, oppressed with pecuniary responsibilities which he was unable to meet, anxious to provide for approaching old age, and distant from those records without which an accurate and full history could not be written,[115] we know what his indomitable spirit achieved ; but what he would have done in the enjoyment of honorable repose, surrounded by admiring friends, in close communion with his surviving compeers, whose recollections might have corrected and refreshed his own, and with the affectionate and approving eye of the South watching and cheering him in the progress of the history of the war of her deliverance, what animated scenes he would have portrayed, now vanished forever, how many heroic deeds he would have recorded, never to be heard of more, we can only deplore that now we can never know. The deep gloom of his latter life was in sad contrast with the splendor of its dawn. The brutal treatment which he received in the city of Baltimore from a ruthless banditti on an occasion which involved no personal interest of his own, but into which he was led by the generous impulse of friendship, while it inflicted bodily wounds, from the effects of which he never recovered, was yet more revolting to the sensibilities of a gentleman, a scholar, a soldier, and a patriot; and after a brief sojourn in the West Indies, whither he had gone in the vain hope of restoring his shattered system, calling at the residence of his old commander in the Southern war, who had departed before him, but whose hospitable mansion was yet renowned for the cordiality of that welcome which his daughter extended to the friends of her honored sire, he there breathed his last. A

---

[115] If he could have consulted Washington's letters and papers, and especially his own letters in the cabinet of Mount Vernon, he would have been saved from some great mistakes.

gleam of that military pageantry so familiar to his early years shone at his grave. His pall, borne by six officers of the army and navy along the line of soldiers and sailors who were then engaged in the public service at St. Mary's, was conveyed to the place of interment, and was buried with the honors of war.[116]

But when he now rose in the vigor of manhood to reply to Henry, the spectator would easily believe that the highest honors of the new system, in the event of its adoption, would be within his reach. From his childhood a noble ambition animated his bosom. He knew that his ancestors had time immemorial filled many prominent posts in the Colony, and had heard the tradition that the house which sheltered him in his infancy, and which, abounding in historic associations, is still to be seen by the traveller as he winds his solitary way through the county of Westmoreland, had been reared by the munificence of a British queen. He had already secured an honorable fame in the field; and in the Congress of the Confederation he had gained some experience in civil affairs. Looking forward with the prophetic cast of genius, he clearly saw that there were questions in our civil affairs which in a few years must be decided, if decided at all, by the sword, and that a vigorous and self-sustaining government, by whatever name it might be called, was an element almost indispensable to complete success. It was impossible that a large and warlike population of savages, hovering like vultures on three sides of the Confederacy, daily excited by the aggressive progress of the white settler, and fostered by the wiles

---

[116] General Lee died at Dungeness House, the property of the daughter of General Nathaniel Greene, on the evening of the 25th of March, 1818. When he arrived there from the West Indies, he brought with him a number of papers in barrels, and it was thought that he was engaged in writing a history of the United States. If these papers could be found, they might throw light on several subjects of the war of the Revolution. See in the Appendix an extract from an interesting letter of a lady giving an account of the funeral of the General, at which she was present. There is no separate memoir of Lee that I know of; but the reader will find in the latest edition of the letter of his son Henry on Mr. Jefferson's books some authentic details, as also in a memoir prefixed to an edition of *Lee's Memoirs*, which was written by his son Charles C. Lee, Esq. [There is a "*Life of General Henry Lee*" prefixed to the third edition of his *Memoirs of the War*, 8vo, 1870. Edited ostensibly by his illustrious son, Robert E. Lee—ED.]

of a great military nation which held our frontier posts in the face of a solemn treaty, could long be kept down, and that he might gather new laurels in a familiar sphere.[117]   And if peace, contrary to present appearances, should prevail, there were prospects of a civil career under the new system such as the old Confederation, however modified, was not likely to afford.   A long and prosperous course seemed to lie before him ; and, as he was a scholar as well as a politician, there was a vision of a serene and honored old age, in which he might imitate Xenophon an Cæsar, and record his history for the eye of future ages.

His external appearance was in unison with his intellectual character.   His stature approached six feet ; the expression of his handsome face was bland and captivating ; his voice, which had been trained in war, and had often been heard in battle amid the clangor of charging horsemen, was full and clear, and evidently modulated in the closet, made a most favorable impression upon his audiences.   But he was a partisan in the Senate as well as in the camp ; and, as he knew the result of a panic among soldiers in the beginning of a fight, and saw the effect of Henry's first speech on the House, he sought to rally the members by a bold attack upon his most formidable opponent.   With this view he assailed Henry with a vehemence which few of his seniors would have dared to use : " I feel every power of my mind," he said, " moved by the language of the honorable gentleman yesterday.   The eclät and brilliancy which have distinguished that gentleman, the honors by which he has been dignified, and the talents which he has so often displayed, have attracted my respect and attention.   On so important an occasion, and before so respectable a body, I expected a new display of his powers of oratory ; but, instead of proceeding to investigate the merits of the new plan of government, the worthy character informed us of horrors which he felt, of apprehensions in his mind, which made him tremblingly fearful of the fate of the Commonwealth.   Was it proper, Mr. Chairman, to appea to the fear of this House ?   I trust that he is come to judge, and not to alarm.   I trust that he, and every other gentleman in this

---

[117] The fear of Indian hostilities controlled the vote of the Valley of Virginia in favor of the Constitution ; and the fate of Harman and St. Clair, and the battles of Wayne, very soon justified these apprehensions.

house, comes with a firm resolution coolly and calmly to examine, and fairly and impartially to determine. He was pleased to pass an eulogium on that character who is the pride of peace and the support of war, and declared that, even from him, he would require the reason of proposing such a system. I cannot see the propriety of mentioning that illustrious character on this occasion; we must all be fully impressed with a conviction of his extreme rectitude of conduct. But, sir, this system is to be examined on its own merits. He then adverted to the style of the government, and asked what authority they had to use the expression 'We, the people' instead of 'We, the States.' This expression was introduced into that paper with great propriety; this system is submitted to the people for their consideration, because on them it is to operate if adopted. It is not binding upon the people until it becomes their act. It is now submitted to the people of Virginia. If we do not adopt it, it will always be null and void to us. Suppose it was found proper for our adoption, in becoming the government of the people of Virginia, by what style should it be done? Ought we not to make use of the name of the people? No other style would be proper." He then spoke of the characters of the men who framed the Constitution, and continued: "This question was inapplicable, strange, and unexpected; it was a more proper inquiry whether such evils existed as rendered necessary a change of government. This necessity is evidenced by the concurrent testimony of almost all America. The legislative acts of different States avow it. It is acknowledged by the acts of this State; under such an act we are here now assembled. If reference to the Acts of Assembly will not sufficiently convince him of this necessity, let him go to our seaports—let him see our commerce languishing—not an American bottom to be seen. Let him ask the price of land and of produce in different parts of the country; to what shall we ascribe the very low prices of these? To what cause are we to attribute the decrease of population and industry?[118] and the impossibility of employing our tradesmen

---

[118] It is to be regretted that the speaker did not specify some fact in proof of his assertions. Even Edmund Randolph spoke of the population flowing into Virginia. The truth is that Lee represented the landed interest of a particular section which had lost slaves, carried off by the enemy, and all its investments in bonds and securities, which

and mechanics? To what cause will the gentleman impute these and a thousand other misfortunes our people labor under? These, sir, are owing to the imbecility of the Confederation—to that defective system which never can make us happy at home nor respectable abroad. The gentleman sate down as he began, leaving us to ruminate on the horrors which he opened with. Although I could trust to the argument of the gentlemen who spoke yesterday in favor of the plan, permit me to make one observation on the weight of our representatives in the Government. If the House of Commons in England, possessing less power, are now able to withstand the power of the Crown; if that House of Commons, which has been undermined by corruption in every age, with far less power than our representatives posses, is still able to contend with the executive of that country, what danger have we to fear that our representatives cannot successfully oppose the encroachments of the other branches of the Government? Let it be remembered that in the year 1782 the East India bill was brought into the House of Commons. Although the members of that House are only elected in part by the landed interest, that bill was carried in the House by a majority of one hundred and thirty, and the king was obliged to dissolve the Parliament to prevent its effect. If, then, the House of Commons was so powerful, no danger can be apprehended that our House of Representatives is not amply able to protect our liberties. I trust that this representation is sufficient to secure our happiness, and that we may fairly congratulate ourselves on the superiority of our Government to that I just referred to.''

---

had been paid off in depreciated currency during the war. As for the price of lands, those in Westmoreland and that section had been cultivated for more than a century without domestic or foreign manures, and all the lands of the Piedmont country, to say nothing of Kentucky, could be purchased on moderate terms, at a time when the money flowing in from abroad, to fill the vacuum made by the Revolution, had only begun to diffuse itself through the ordinary channels of trade. The lands in Westmoreland, even, would have brought as good prices at that time as they would have done when the new government had been in operation half a century. The great and innumerable facts of a prosperous period gradually succeeding a state of depression pass unheeded by a common observer; while some specific grievance, which, when properly explained, is no grievance at all, looms in gigantic proportions.

Henry, who was always placable, and showed through a long life an indisposition to engage in personal controversies, and who was well aware that clever young men, speaking under the excitement of the floor, were prone to utter what in their calmer moments they would be the first to condemn, now rose, and after a slight recognition of the compliment which Lee paid to his genius, passed at once to the discussion of his subject: "I am not free from suspicion," he said; "I am apt to entertain doubts. I rose yesterday to ask a question which arose in my mind. When I asked that question, I thought the meaning of my inter-rogation obvious; the fate of this question and America may depend on this. Have they said, ' We, the States ' ? Have they made a proposal of a compact between States? If they had, this would be a confederation. It is otherwise most clearly a consolidated government. The question turns, sir, on that poor little thing—the expression, ' We, the people,' instead of the States of America. I need not take much pains to show that the principles of this system are extremely pernicious, impolitic, and dangerous. Is this a monarchy like England—a compact between prince and people, with checks on the former to secure the liberty of the latter? Is this a confederacy like Holland, an association of a number of independent States, each of which retains its individual sovereignty? It is not a democracy, wherein the people retain all their rights securely. Had these principles been adhered to, we should not have been brought to this alarming transition from a confederacy to a consolidated government. We have no detail of those great considerations, which, in my opinion, ought to have abounded, before we should recur to a government of this kind. Here is a resolution as radical as that which separated us from Great Britain. It is as radical, if in this transition our rights and privileges are endan-gered and the sovereignty of the States be relinquished ; and cannot we see that this is actually the case? The rights of con-science, trial by jury, liberty of the press, all your immunities and franchises, all pretensions to human rights and privileges, are rendered insecure, if not lost, by this change so loudly talked of by some, and inconsiderately by others. Is this tame relin-quishment of right worthy of freemen? Is it worthy of that manly fortitude that ought to characterize republicans?

"It is said that eight States have adopted this plan. I declare that, if twelve States and a half had adopted it, I would with manly firmness, and in spite of an erring world, reject it. You are not to inquire how your trade may be increased, nor how you are to become a great and powerful people; but how your liberties can be secured, for liberty ought to be the direct end of your government. Having premised these things, I shall, with the aid of my judgment and information, which, I confess, are not extensive, go into the discussion of this system more minutely. Is it necessary for your liberty that you should abandon those great rights by the adoption of this system? Is the relinquishment of trial by jury and the liberty of the press necessary for your liberty? Will the abandonment of your most sacred rights tend to the security of your liberty? Liberty—the greatest of all earthly blessings—give us that precious jewel, and you may take everything else. But I am fearful that I have lived long enough to become an old-fashioned fellow. Perhaps an invincible attachment to the dearest rights of man may in these refined and enlightened days be deemed *old-fashioned;* if so, I am contented to be so. I say the time has been when every pulse of my heart beat for American liberty, and which, I believe, had a counter-part in the breast of every American. But suspicions have gone forth—suspicions of my integrity—publicly reputed that my professions are not real.[119] Twenty-three years ago, was I supposed to be a traitor to my country? I was then said to be a bane of sedition, because I supported the rights of my country."

" We have come hither to preserve the poor Commonwealth of Virginia, if it can possibly be done ; something must be done to preserve your liberty and mine. The Confederation—this same despised government—merits in my opinion the highest encomium. It carried us through a long and dangerous war. It

---

[119] Even Madison, in a letter to Edmund Randolph, dated New York, January 10, 1788, talks of Henry's "real designs"; and Washington, in the heat of the moment, wrote about Henry and Mason—the Gamaliels at whose feet he sate for twenty years—in a manner that betrayed more passion than judgment. Great as were the merits of Washington and Madison, and none rejoices in them more than I do, it is simply stating a historical fact in saying that in 1788 neither of them stood in the estimation of the Virginia of that day on the same platform with Patrick Henry and George Mason as a statesman.

rendered us victorious in that bloody conflict with a powerful nation. It has secured us a territory greater than any European monarch possesses. And shall a government which has been thus strong and vigorous be accused of imbecility and abandoned for want of energy ? Consider what you are about to do before you part with this government. Take longer time in reckoning things. Revolutions like this have happened in almost every country in Europe ; similar examples are to be found in ancient Greece and ancient Rome ; instances of the people losing their liberty by their own carelessness and the ambition of a few.''

After animadverting at length on the inadequate representation in the House of Representatives, he then aimed his attacks at the system in general. "In some parts of the plan before you," he said, "the great rights of freemen are endangered; in other parts absolutely taken away. How does your trial by jury stand? In civil cases gone—not sufficiently secured in criminal—this best privilege is gone ! But we are told that we need not fear, because those in power, being our representatives, will not abuse the powers we put into their hands. I am not well versed in history, but I will submit to your recollection whether liberty has been destroyed most often by the licentiousness of the people or by the tyranny of rulers ? I imagine, sir, that you will find the balance on the side of tyranny. Happy will you be, if you miss the fate of those nations, who, omitting to resist their oppressors, or negligently suffering their liberty to be wrested from them, have groaned under intolerable despotism. Most of the human race are now in this deplorable condition. And those nations which have gone in search of grandeur, power, and splendor, they have also fallen a sacrifice, and been the victims of their own folly. While they acquired these visionary blessings, they lost their freedom.''

" The honorable gentleman who presides (Pendleton) told us that to prevent abuses in our government, we will assemble in Convention, recall our delegated powers, and punish our servants for abusing the trust reposed in them. O ! sir, we should have fine times indeed, if to punish tyrants it were only sufficient to assemble the people. Your arms wherewith you could defend yourselves are gone ! You have no longer an aristocratical, no longer a democratical spirit. Did you ever read of any revolution in any nation brought about by the punishment of those in power inflicted by those who have no power at all?"

He then contrasts the security of the State government founded on the Declaration of Rights with the various provisions of the Federal Constitution, and opposes the policy of direct taxation. "The voice of tradition," he said, "will, I trust, inform posterity of our struggles for freedom. If our descendants be worthy of the name of Americans, they will preserve and hand down to the latest posterity the transactions of the present time ; and although my exclamations are not worthy the hearing, they will see that I have done my utmost to preserve their liberty. For I will never give up the power of direct taxation but for a scourge. I am willing to give it conditionally, that is, after a non-compliance with requisitions. I will do more, sir, and what I hope will convince the most skeptical man that I am a lover of the American Union ; that, in case Virginia shall not make punctual payment, the control of our custom-houses and the whole regulation of our trade shall be given to Congress, and that Virginia shall depend upon Congress even for passports, till Virginia shall have paid the last farthing, and furnished the last soldier. Nay, sir, there is another alternative to which I would consent ; even that they should strike us out of the Union, and take away from us all Federal privileges, till we comply with Federal requisitions ; but let it depend on our own pleasure to pay our money in the most easy manner for our people. Were all the States, more terrible than the mother country, to join against us, I hope Virginia could defend herself; but, sir, the dissolution of the Union is most abhorrent to my mind. The first thing I have at heart is American liberty ; the second thing is American union." He then proceeded to show the incompatibility of direct taxation at the same time by the Federal and State governments, drawing a vivid picture of the malfeasance of the State sheriffs who acted under the eye of the Assembly, and of the utter ruin of the people by the combined array of Federal and State collectors, and closing the part of his speech with a declaration that "on this subject he should be an infidel till the day of his death."

When he had rallied for a moment, he continued his general examination of the new plan, opening with that description of

the Constitution which has been repeated so often since by the
school-boy and the statesman, "This Constitution is said to have
beautiful features ; but when I come to examine these features,
sir, they appear to me horribly frightful.   Among other de-
formities it has an awful squinting—it squints towards monarchy.
And does not this raise indignation in the breast of every true
American?   Your President may easily become king.   Your
Senate is so imperfectly constituted that your dearest rights may
be sacrificed by what may be a small minority, and a very small
minority may continue forever unchangeably this Government
although horribly defective.   Where are your checks in this
Government?   Your strongholds will be in the hands of your
enemies.   If your American chief be a man of ambition and
abilities, how easy it is for him to render himself absolute !
The army is in his hands, and if he be a man of address, it will
be attached to him ; and it will be a subject of long meditation
with him to seize the first auspicious moment to accomplish his
designs.   And, sir, will the American spirit solely relieve you
when this happens?   I would rather infinitely, and I am sure
most of this Convention are of the same opinion, have a king,
lords, and commons, than a government so replete with insupportable evils.   If we make a king, we may prescribe the rules
by which he shall rule his people, and interpose such checks as
shall prevent him from infringing them ; but the President in
the field at the head of his army can prescribe the terms on
which he shall reign master so far that it will puzzle any American to get his neck from under the galling yoke.   I cannot with
patience think of this idea.   If ever he violates the laws, one of
two things will happen : he will come at the head of his army to
carry every thing before him, or he will give bail to do what
Mr. Chief Justice will order him.[120]   If he be guilty, will not the
recollection of his crimes teach him to make one bold push for
the American throne?   Will not the immense difference between
being master of everything, and being ignominiously tried and
punished, powerfully excite him to make this bold push?   But,
sir, where is the existing force to punish him?   Can he not at

---

[120] This was uttered in the presence of gentlemen, two of whom
afterwards became President of the United States, one of whom became Chief Justice, and another of whom became a Justice of the
Supreme Court.

the head of his army beat down every opposition? Away with your President; we shall have a king. The army will salute him monarch; your militia will leave you and assist in making him king, and fight against you. And what have you to oppose this force? What will then become of you and your rights? Will not absolute despotism ensue?" (Here, says the reporter, Mr. Henry strongly and pathetically expatiated on the probability of the President's enslaving America, and the horrid consequences that must result).

He then passed on to the subject of the elections under the Constitution, which he discussed at length; and when he had examined the argument of Lee, derived from the composition of the House of Commons, apologized for the time he had consumed and for his departure from the order adopted by the Convention, and indulged the hope that the House would allow him the privilege of again addressing it, ending with the prayer, " may you be fully apprized of the dangers of the new plan of government, not by fatal experience, but by some abler advocate than I."

The speech of Henry lasted more than three hours, and was not only the longest he ever made, but the most eloquent ever pronounced in public bodies.[121] Two well-authenticated instances of its effect have come down to us. General Thomas Posey was an officer of distinction in the army of the Revolution, was subsequently second in command under Wayne in the successful

---

[121] I am inclined to think that this was the longest speech made by Henry during 'the session. Judge Curtis (*History of the Constitution*, &c., II, 558, note) reports a newspaper rumor that Henry spoke on some one occasion seven hours, and thinks it was when this speech was delivered. Pendleton and Lee, the only speakers that day, did not consume much of the morning before Henry began and spoke till the adjournment. We know that the speech of Randolph, delivered in reply the following day consumed two hours and a half, and that Madison and George Nicholas made long and elaborate speeches after him. In the debates, the speech of Randolph occupies more space than the speech of Henry, but in the case of the latter, we have the confession of the reporter that he could not follow him in his pathetic appeals. Tradition affirms that if Henry had offered at the close of his speech a motion of indefinite postponement of the Constitution, it would have succeeded by a considerable majority. The testimony of General Posey would lead us to think so.

Indian campaigns of that general, and was warmly in favor of the adoption of the Constitution ; yet he declared to a friend that he was so overpowered by the eloquence of Henry on this occasion as to believe that the Constitution would, if adopted, be the ruin of our liberties as certainly as he believed in his own existence ; that subsequent reflection reassured his judgment, and his well considered opinion resumed its place.[122]   Mr. Best, an intelligent gentleman of Nansemond, who heard the fervid description which Henry gave of the slavery of the people wrought by a Federal executive at the head of his armed hosts, declared that so thrilling was the delineation of the scene, " he involuntarily felt his wrists to assure himself that the fetters were not already pressing his flesh ; and that the gallery on which he was sitting seemed to become as dark as a dungeon."[123]

An incident occurred while Henry was speaking which shows that the feelings of the husband and father were not wholly lost in those of the patriot.   As his eye ranged over the house, when in the height of his argument, he caught the face of his son, whom he had left a few days before in Prince Edward as the protector of his family during his absence, and he knew that some important domestic event had brought him to Richmond.   He hesitated for a moment, stooped down, and with a full heart whispered to a friend who was sitting before him : " Dawson, I see my son in the hall ; take him out."   Dawson instantly withdrew with young Henry, and soon returned with the grateful intelligence that Mrs. Henry had been safely delivered of a son, and that mother and child were doing well.   That new-born babe, called from a maternal ancestor Spotswood, lived to become familiar with the features of his father's face, and to enjoy his splendid fame ; and in the quiet burial-ground of Red Hill, at the mature age of sixty-five, was laid by his side.[134]

---

[122] *Life of Dr. A. Alexander* by his son, page 190.

[123] Letter of Joseph B. Whitehead, Esq., to the author.   To save repetition, the reader will regard all letters, when the name of the person to whom they are written is not stated, as addressed to the author. One evidence of the effect of the speech was seen in the fact that the following day three of the strongest federalists, Randolph, Madison, and George Nicholas, the last the most powerful man of the three in debate at a great crisis, occupied the whole of the session.

[124] Henry, on his return home, told this fact to his wife, who told it to her son John, who told it to me.

When Henry finished his speech Edmund Randolph rose to deprecate the irregular mode of debate and the departure from the order of the House. He said that if the House proceeded in that irregular manner, contrary to its resolution, instead of three or six weeks, it would take six months to decide the question. He should endeavor to make the committee sensible of the necessity of establishing a national Government, and the inefficacy of the Confederation. He should take the first opportunity of doing so; and he mentioned the fact merely to show that he had not answered the gentleman fully, nor in a general way, yesterday. The House then adjourned.

CHAPTER III.

The effect of Henry's speech both in and out of the House had been great. It startled the friends of the new system from that sense of security in which the more sanguine had indulged ; and they saw that unless prompt measures were adopted to counteract the present feeling all hopes of a successful issue would be vain. Accordingly, on Friday, the sixth day of June, and the fifth of the session, the federalists summoned to the field the most able array of talents, which, abounding as they did in able men, their ranks afforded. It was feared that Henry might rise to deepen the impression which he had already made ; for Randolph in his few remarks the previous day had not secured the floor, and every effort must be exerted to prevent such an untoward movement. It was evidently arranged that Randolph should discuss the whole subject in an elaborate speech ; that Madison, who had been ill, should be on the alert to succeed him ; and should his feeble health prevent him from consuming the entire day, that George Nicholas, who was more familiar with large public bodies than either Randolph or Madison, should exhaust the remainder of the sitting.

When the President called the Convention to order, a debate arose on the returns of an election case, which was soon dispatched, and the House resolved itself into committee—Wythe in the chair. As soon as he was fairly seated, Edmund Randolph rose to reply to the speech delivered by Henry. In an exordium of rare beauty, in which he called himself a child of the Revolution, he alluded to the early manifestations of affection to him by Virginia at a time when, from peculiar circumstances well known to the House, he needed it most, and to the honors which had been bestowed upon him ; and in which he declared that it should be the unwearied study of his life to pro-

mote her happiness, and that in a twelvemonth he should withdraw from all public employments. Then launching into his
subject, "We are told," he said, "that the report of dangers is
false. The cry of peace, sir, is false; it is but a sudden calm.
The tempest growls over you. Look around: wheresoever you
look you see danger. When there are so many witnesses in
many parts of America that justice is suffocated, shall peace and
happiness still be said to reign? Candor requires an undis-
guised representation of our situation. Candor demands a
faithful exposition of facts. Many citizens have found justice
strangled and trampled under foot through the course of juris-
prudence in this country. Are those who have debts due them
satisfied with your Government? Are not creditors wearied
with the tedious procrastination of your legal process?—a process obscured by legislative mists. Cast your eyes to your seaports—see how commerce languishes. This country, so blessed
by nature with every advantage that can render commerce
profitable, through defective legislation is deprived of all the
benefits and emoluments which she might otherwise reap from
it. We hear many complaints of located lands—a variety of
competitors claiming the same lands under legislative acts;[125]
public faith prostrated, and private confidence destroyed. I
ask you if your laws are reverenced? In every well-regulated
community the laws command respect. Are yours entitled to
reverence? We not only see violations of the Constitution, but
of national principles, in repeated instances.

"How is the fact? The history of the violations of the Consti-
tion from the year 1776 to this present time—violations made by
formal acts of the Legislature. Everything has been drawn
within the legislative vortex. There is one example of this violation in Virginia of a most striking and shocking nature—an
example so horrid that if I conceived my country would passively permit a repetition of it, dear as it is to me, I would seek
means of expatriating myself from it. A man who was then a
citizen was deprived of his life in the following manner: From
mere reliance on general reports, a gentleman in the House of
Delegates informed that body that a certain man (Josiah Philips)
had committed several crimes, and was running at large perpe-

---

[125] A hit at George Mason, who drew the first land law.

trating other crimes.   He therefore moved for leave to attaint him.   He obtained that leave instantly.   No sooner did he obtain it than he drew from his pocket a bill ready written for that effect.   It was read three times in one day, and carried to the Senate.   I will not say that it passed the same day through the Senate ; but he was attainted very speedily and precipitately, without any proof better than vague reports.   Without being confronted with his accusers and witnesses, without the privilege of calling for evidence in his behalf, he was sentenced to death, and was afterwards actually executed.   Was this arbitrary deprivation of life, the dearest gift of God to man, consistent with the genius of a republican government ?   Is this compatible with the spirit of freedom ?   *This, sir, has made the deepest impression on my heart, and I cannot contemplate it without horror.*[126]

[126] The reader must keep in mind that this severe tirade against the legislation of Virginia was designed by the speaker to reflect partly on Mason, but especially on Henry, who, throughout the war and until the session of the Convention, bore a leading part either in the executive or legislative department of the State.   But never was an orator more unfortunate than Randolph in his selection of an instance of tyranny. The case of Philips was presented to the Assembly, not by a member, but by the Governor (Henry), who enclosed the letter of Colonel Wilson, of Norfolk county, detailing the enormities perpetrated on unoffending and helpless women and children in the county of Princess Anne by that infamous outlaw.   The message of the Governor was referred to a committee of the whole, which reported a resolution attainting Philips.   A bill was brought in accordingly, was read on three several days as usual, was passed and sent to the Senate, which adopted it without amendment.   Nor was Philips executed in consequence of the act of attainder.   On the contrary, having been apprehended, he was indicted for highway robbery by Randolph himself, who was Attorney General at the time, an after a fair trial by a jury was condemned and executed.   Possibly, as Randolph was clerk of the House of Delegates (as well as Attorney-General) at the time, he may have remembered that Harrison was speaker of the body at the time, and that Tyler was one of the committe which brought in the bill, both of whom were members of the present Convention, and were warmly opposed to the new Constitution.   But granting for the sake of argument that at the most trying period of the Revolution the people of Princess Anne, instead of hanging a desperate outlaw to the first tree, sought to attain their end by an act of attainder, and that the wretch had suffered accordingly, what does it prove?   Simply that there were occasional errors in the legislation of the State at a difficult crisis—errors that

There are still a multiplicity of complaints of the debility of the laws. Justice in many cases is so unattainable that commerce may be said in fact to be stopped entirely. There is no peace, sir, in this land. Can peace exist with injustice, licentiousness, insecurity and oppression? These considerations, independent of many others which I have not yet enumerated, would be a sufficient reason for the adoption of this Constitution, because it secures the liberty of the citizen, his person and property, and will invigorate and restore commerce and industry.''

He argued at length to prove that the excessive licentiousness which has resulted from the relaxation of the laws 'would be checked by the new system ; that the danger and impolicy of waiting for subsequent amendments were extreme ; that jury trial was safe or would readily be made safe ; that the position and the connections of the Swiss Cantons were so diverse from ours that no argument drawn from them was applicable to the present case ; that the extent of a country was not an insuperable objection to a national government; that the union was necessary to Virginia from her accessibility by sea, from her proximity to Maryland and Pennsylvania, which had adopted the Constitution, from the number of savages on her borders, and from the presence of the black population. " The day may come," he said, " when that population may make an impression upon us. Gentlemen who have long been accustomed to the contemplation of the subject, think there is cause of alarm in this case. The number of those people, compared to that of the whites, is in an immense proportion. Their number amounts to two hundred and thirty-six thousand; that of the whites only to three hundred and fifty-two thousand.[127] Will the American

---

might have occurred under any form of government, and that might argue an amendment of the State Government, and not of a Confederation. It may not be amiss to say that Randolph was a warm advocate of a Convention to amend the Constitution of the State.

[127] By the census of 1790, the number of whites in Virginia, including the district of Kentucky, was 442,115 ; the number of blacks, 293,427 ; and the whole population, including all other persons, was 748,308. Either the figures of Randolph are far below the actual population of the State in 1788, or the census taken two years later indicates a wonderful increase ; and it is known that the census of 1790 underated our numbers.

spirit so much spoken of, repel an invading enemy or enable you to obtain an advantageous peace? Manufactures and military stores may afford relief to a country exposed. Have we these at present? If we shall be separated from the Union, shall our chance of having these be greater, or will not the want of these be the more deplorable?

He spoke of the debts due to foreign nations—to France, Spain, England, and Holland—and the ability of those powers to close our ports on our failure to comply with their demands. "Suppose," he said, "the American spirit in fullest vigor in Virginia, what military preparations and exertions is she capable of making? The other States have upwards of three hundred and thirty thousand men capable of bearing arms. Our militia amounts to fifty thousand, or say sixty thousand. In case of an attack, what defence can we make? The militia of our country will be wanted for agriculture. Some also will be necessary for manufactures and those mechanic arts which are necessary for the aid of the farmer and the planter. If we had men sufficient in number to defend ourselves, it could not avail without other requisites. We must have a navy, to be supported in time of peace as well as in war, to guard our coasts and defend us against invasion. The maintaining a navy will require money ; and where can we get money for this and other purposes? How shall we raise it? Review the enormity of the debts due by this country. The amount of debt we owe to the continent for bills of credit, rating at forty to one, will amount to between six and seven hundred thousand pounds.[128] There is also due the continent the balance of requisitions due by us ; and in addition to this proportion of the old continental debt, there are the foreign, domestic, State-military, and loan-office debts ; to which, when you add the British debt, where is the possibility of finding money to raise an army or navy? Review your real ability. Shall we recur to loans? Nothing can be more impolitic; they impoverish a nation. We, sir, have nothing to repay them ; nor can we procure them. If the imposts and duties in Virginia, even on the present footing, be very unproductive and not equal to our necessity, what would it be if we were separated from the Union? From the first of September to the first of June, the

---

[128] Virginia currency; the pound at $3.33⅓.

amount put into the treasury is only fifty-nine thousand pounds, or a little more.[129] But if smuggling be introduced in consequence of high duties, or otherwise, and the Potomac should be lost, what hope of getting money from these? Our commerce will not be kindly received by foreigners if transacted solely by ourselves. It is the spirit of commercial nations to engross as much as possible the carrying trade. This makes it necessary to defend our commerce ; but how shall we compass this end ? England has arisen to the greatest height in modern times by her navigation act and other excellent regulations. The same means would produce the same effect. We have inland navigation. Our last exports did not exceed one millions of pounds value. Our export trade is entirely in the hands of foreigners. I beg, gentlemen, to consider these two things : our inability to raise and man a navy, and the dreadful consequences of a dissolution of the Union.''

He next adverts to an argument used by Henry. ''It is

---

[129] The exact amount from November 30th, 1787 to November, 1788, derived from customs, was *seventy four thousand pounds ;* and as the average of the tariff was very low, not exceeding two per cent., we can readily see the amount of the imports during that period. The whole receipts in that interval, including customs. reached £417,498 9s 8½d, collected from a people as industrious and quiet as existed on the face of the globe. This immense commerce, it must be remembered, sprang from nothing to its present amount in about four years and a little more ; and proves that the talk about our commerce gone forever and our languishing industry, was only the talk of politicians. Even Randolph admits that our population was increasing ; but he did not appreciate the enormous accessions that had been made and were daily making from abroad, *and especially from the Northern States.* As for what Randolph denounces as want of justice and violations of the Constitution of the State by the General Assembly, they were mere matters of opinion among public men, and unknown to the mass of the people. Let the reader consult the report of the Committee of the House of Delegates on the Treasury, made on the 19th of December, 1788, (*Journal House of Delegates*, 106) and note the amount of back taxes which were gradually coming in from the poorer counties, and the various items of receipts, and the sum of money paid down, and he will see an exhibit honorable to any country. It was in the society in which Randolph moved, men formerly of princely wealth, who had suffered seriously by the war, as such classes always do, that the talk about declining agriculture and vanishing commerce was heard.

insinuated," he said, "by the honorable gentleman that we want to be a grand, splendid and magnificent people. We wish not to become so. The magnificence of a royal court is not our object. We want government, sir ; a government that will have stability and give us security ; for our present Government is des-stitute of the one and incapable of producing the other. It cannot with propriety be denominated a government, being void of that energy requisite to enforce sanctions. I wish my country not to be contemptible in the eyes of foreign nations. A well regulated community is always respected. It is the internal situation, the defects of government, that attracts foreign contempt. That contempt, sir, is too often followed by subjugation."

"The object of a federal government," he said, "is to remedy and strengthen the weakness of its individual branches, whether that weakness arises from situation or from any external cause. With respect to the first, is it not a miracle that the confederation carried us through the war ? It was our unanimity that carried us through it. That system was not ultimately concluded till the year 1781. Although the greatest exertions were made before that time, when came requisitions for men and money, its defects then were immediately discovered. The quotas of men were readily sent ; not so those of money. One State feigned inability ; another would not comply till the rest did ; and various excuses were offered, so that no money was sent into the treasury —not a requisition was fully complied with. Loans were the next measure fallen upon. Upwards of eighty millions of dollars were wanting, beside the emissions of dollars forty for one. These things show the impossibility of relying on requisitions."

"Without adequate powers vested in Congress, America cannot be respectable in the eyes of other nations. Congress ought to be fully vested with power to support the Union; protect the interests of the United States; maintain their commerce and defend them from external invasions and insults and internal insurrections ; to maintain justice and promote harmony and public tranquility among the States. A government not vested with these powers will ever be found unable to make us happy or respectable. How the Confederation is different from such a government is known to all America. What are the powers of Congress ? They have full authority to recommend what they please; this recommendatory power reduces them to the condition of poor supplicants.

Consider the dignified language of the members of the American
Congress. May it please your high mightiness of Virginia to
pay your just proportionate quota of our national debt; we
humbly supplicate that it may please you to comply with your
federal duties. Their operations are of no validity when counteracted by the States. Their authority to recommend is a mere
mockery of government. But the amendability of the Confederation seems to have great weight on the minds of some gentlemen. To what points will the amendments go? What part
makes the most important figure? What part deserves to be
retained? In it one body has the legislative, executive and judicial powers; but the want of efficient powers has prevented the
dangers naturally consequent on the union of these. Is this
union consistent with an augmentation of their powers? Will
you, then, amend it by taking away one of these three powers?
Suppose, for instance, you only vested it with the legislative and
executive powers without any control on the judiciary, what must
be the result? Are we not taught by reason, experience and
governmental history that tyranny is the natural and certain consequence of uniting these two powers, or the legislative and
judicial powers exclusively, in the same body? Whenever any
two of these three powers are vested in one single body, they
must at one time or other terminate in the destruction of liberty.
In the most important cases the assent of nine States is necessary
to pass a law. This is too great a restriction, and whatever good
consequences it may in some cases produce, yet it will prevent
energy in many other cases. It will prevent energy which is
most necessary in some emergencies, even in cases wherein the
existence of the community depends on vigor and expedition.
It is incompatible with that secrecy which is the life of execution
and despatch. Did ever thirty or forty men retain a secret?
Without secrecy no government can carry on its operations on
great occasions; this is what gives that superiority in action to
the government of one. If anything were wanting to complete
this farce, it would be that a resolution of the Assembly of Virginia and the other legislatures should be necessary to confirm
and render of any validity the congressional acts; this would
openly discover the debility of the general Government to all the
world. An act of the Assembly of Virginia, controverting a
resolution of Congress, would certainly prevail. I therefore con-

clude that the Confederation is too defective to deserve correction. Let us take farewell of it with reverential respect as an old benefactor. It is gone whether this House says so or not. It is gone, sir, by its own weakness."

He thus concluded : " I intended to show the nature of the powers which ought to have been given to the general Government, and the reason of investing it with the power of taxation ; but this would require more time than my strength or the patience of the committee would now admit of. I shall conclude with a few objections which come from my heart. I have labored for the continuance of the Union—the rock of our salvation. I believe that, as sure as there is a God in Heaven, our safety, our political happiness and existence, depend on the union of the States ; and that without this union the people of this and the other States will undergo the unspeakable calamities which discord, faction, turbulence, war and bloodshed, have produced in other countries. The American spirit ought to be mixed with American pride to see the Union magnificently triumphant. Let that glorious pride, which once defied the British thunder, reanimate you again. Let it not be recorded of America that, after having performed the most gallant exploits, after having overcome the most astonishing difficulties, and after having gained the admiration of the world by their incomparable valor and policy, they lose their acquired reputation, their national consequence and happiness, by their own indiscretion. Let no future historian inform posterity that they wanted wisdom and virtue to concur in any regular efficient government. Catch the present moment—seize it with avidity and eagerness—for it may be lost, never to be regained. If the Union be now lost, I fear it will remain so forever. I believe gentlemen are sincere in their opposition, and actuated by pure motives ; but when I maturely weigh the advantages of the Union and the dreadful consequences of dissolution; when I see safety on my right and destruction on my left ; when I behold respectability and happiness acquired by the one, but annihilated by the other, I cannot hesitate to decide in favor of the former. I hope my weakness for speaking so long will apologize for my leaving this subject in so mutilated a condition. If a further explanation be desired, I shall take the liberty to enter into it more fully another time."

This able, eloquent, and patriotic speech, which consumed two hours and a half in the delivery, was received with warm applause by the friends of the speaker, and with the admiration which genius and talents always inspire in the breasts of honorable opponents. Before his manly form had disappeared in the mass of the house, and the tones of his sonorous voice had ceased to fill that crowded hall, Madison, diminutive in stature and weak from recent illness, rose to address the Assembly. Nought but a sense of public duty, upheld by a proud consciousness of superior worth, would have impelled him at that moment to such a serious undertaking. His few first sentences were wholly inaudible. When his voice was more assured he was understood to say that he would not attempt to make impressions by ardent professions of zeal for the public welfare; that the principles of every man will be, and ought to be, judged, not by his professions and declarations, but by his conduct; by that criterion he wished, in common with every other member, to be judged; and should it prove unfavorable to his reputation, yet it was a criterion from which he would by no means depart. He said the occasion demanded proofs . and demonstration, not opinion and assertion. "It gives me pain," he said, "to hear gentlemen continually distorting the natural construction of language; for it is sufficient if any human production can stand a fair discussion. Before I proceed to make some additions to the reasons which have been adduced by my honorable friend over the way (Randolph), I must take the liberty to make some observations on what was said by another gentleman (Henry). He told us this Constitution ought to rejected because it endangered the public liberty. Give me leave to make one answer to that observation : let the dangers which this system is supposed to be replete with be clearly pointed out ; if any dangerous and unnecessary powers be given to the general legislature, let them be plainly demonstrated ; if powers be necessary, apparent danger is not a sufficient reason against conceding them. He has suggested that licentiousness has seldom produced the loss of liberty; but that the tyranny of rulers has almost always effected it. Since the general civilization of mankind, I believe there are more instances of the abridgement of the freedom of the people by gradual and silent encroachments of those in power, than by violent and sudden usurpations. On a candid examination of history we shall find that turbulence, violence, and abuse of power, by the majority trampling on the rights of the minority, have produced factions and commotions, which, in republics, have more frequently than any other cause produced despotism. If we go over the whole history of ancient and modern republics, we shall find their destruction to have generally resulted from those causes. If we consider the peculiar situation of the United States, and what are the sources of that diversity of sentiment which pervades their inhabitants, we shall find great danger to fear that the same causes may terminate here in the same fatal effects which they produced in those republics. This danger ought to be wisely guarded against. Perhaps in the progress of this discussion it may appear that the only possible remedy for those evils, and the means of preserving and protecting the principles of republicanism, will be found in that very system which is now exclaimed against as the parent of oppression."

He next reverts to Henry's observation that the people were at peace until the new system was put upon them : "I wish sincerely, sir, this were true. If this be their happy situation, why has every State acknowledged the contrary ? Why were deputies from all the States sent to the General Convention? Why have complaints of national and individual distresses been echoed and re-echoed throughout the continent ? Why has our general government been so shamefully disgraced and our Constitution violated? Wherefore have laws been made to authorize a change, and wherefore are we now assembled here ?"[130] After

---

[130] This argument, when used by Mr. Madison, was hardly fair. He knew that the Annapolis resolution had brought about the present state of things, and that he had offered that resolution when Virginia had settled upon a plan to arrange her commercial relations with Maryland, Pennsylvania, and other States. That arrangement was completed by the Assembly by the selection of five delegates, consisting of St. George Tucker, William Ronald, Robert Townsend Hooe, Thomas Pleasants, and Francis Corbin, on the 25th of November, 1786, and it was believed that our Federal relations were at an end for the session, and a large number of the members had probably left for their homes ; when, on the 30th of the same month, or five days later, *and on the last day of the session,* Mr. Madison caused the Annapolis resolution to be called up, to be hurried through the House, and sent to the Senate, which body passed it within an hour after receiving it. But two members in the House opposed the resolution. It was plain that the sequel

replying to Henry's arguments on the majority of three-fourths, on the exclusive legislation of Congress in the federal district, on the provision concerning the militia, and on the tendency of power once transferred never to be voluntarily renounced, he discussed the objection that the raising and supporting of armies

---

of the resolution was mainly a matter of course, and afforded no legitimate argument to Mr. Madison, who was privy to the whole game. Nor was it quite fair for Mr. Madison to talk of the Constitution of the State as having been violated. These so-called violations were by acts of the Assembly, not by violence; and on Madison's own principles the Legislature might be authorized to take what liberties they pleased with that instrument; for he contended in his speech on the Convention question in the House of Delegates, at the May session of 1784, that the Convention of May, 1776, which framed the Constitution, was "without due power from the people;" that it was framed in consequence of the recommendation of Congress of the 15th of May (which is a great mistake, as the Virginia resolution of absolute independence was adopted on that very day, and a resolution to report a plan of government for an independent State also, while the resolution of the 15th of May [or rather the 10th, see Folwell's edition of the Journals of Congress, II, 158], which was only a re-enactment of the resolution of Congress of the previous year, advising the colonies to form such a plan of government "as would most effectually secure good order in the province *during the present dispute between Great Britain and the colonies*," was a temporizing measure only), which was prior to the Declaration of Independence; that the Convention that framed the Constitution did not "pretend" that they had received "any power from the people" for that purpose; that they passed other ordinances during the same session that were deemed "alterable;" that they made themselves a branch of the Legislature under the Constitution which they had framed; that the Constitution, *if it be so called*, etc., etc. (*Rives' Madison*, I, 559.) It is thus evident that in Madison's deliberate judgment the Constitution of Virginia had no higher dignity than other ordinances of the Convention, which all admit were alterable; and that it was competent for the legislature, in Mr. Madison's opinion, to alter the instrument at pleasure. It was then a little prudish to blame the Assembly for doing what they had a right to do, or to apply any other test than that of expediency to their action. We have shown in a previous note our views upon this subject, and will merely add that Mr. Randolph's views were quite as capricious as those of Mr. Madison, as that gentleman alleged in the course of one of his speeches in Convention that the Declaration of Rights was no part of the Constitution, and, of course, of no obligation whatever. It is necessary to know what ideas these gentlemen had of the Constitution before we can estimate what they call "violations" of it.

was a dangerous element in the Constitution. With apparent candor he declared that he wished there was no necessity of vesting this power in the general Government. '' But,'' he said, ''suppose a foreign nation to declare war against the United States ; must not the general legislature have the power of defending the United States ? Ought it to be known to foreign nations that the general Government of the United States of America has no power to raise and support an army, even in the utmost danger, when attacked by external enemies ? Would not their knowledge of such a circumstance stimulate them to fall upon us ? If, sir, Congress be not invested with this power, any powerful nation, prompted by ambition or avarice, will be invited by our weakness to attack us ; and such an attack by disciplined veterans would certainly be attended with success when only opposed by irregular, undisciplined militia. Whoever considers the peculiar situation of this country, the multiplicity of its excellent inlets and harbors, and the uncommon facility of attacking it—however he may regret the necessity of such a power—cannot hesitate a moment in granting it. One fact may elucidate this argument. In the course of the late war, when the weak parts of the Union were exposed, and many States were in the most deplorable condition by the enemies ravages, the assistance of foreign nations was thought so urgently necessary for our protection that the relinquishment of territorial advantages was not deemed too great a sacrifice for the acquisition of one ally. This expedient was admitted with great reluctance, even by those States who expected advantages from it. The crisis, however, at length arrived, when it was judged necessary for the salvation of this country to make certain cessions to Spain, whether wisely or otherwise is not for me to say ; but the fact was that instructions were sent to our representative at the court of Spain to empower him to enter into negotiations for that purpose. How it terminated is well known. This fact shows the extremities to which nations will go in cases of imminent danger, and demonstrates the necessity of making ourselves more respectable. The necessity of making dangerous cessions, and of applying to foreign aid, ought to be excluded.''

When he had replied to the argument derived from the policy of the Swiss Cantons in their confederate alliance, and stated his impression that uniformity of religion, which he thought ineligible, would not necessarily flow from uniformity of government, and that the government had no jurisdiction over religion, he adverted to the policy of previous amendments, contending that if amendments are to be proposed by one State, other States have the same right, and will also propose alterations, which would be dissimilar and opposite in their nature. "I beg leave," he said, "to remark that the governments of the different States are in many respects dissimilar in their structure; their legislative bodies are not similar; their executive are more different. In several of the States the first magistrate is elected by the people at large; in others by joint ballot of the members of both branches of the legislature; and in others in a different mode still. This dissimilarity has occasioned a diversity of opinion on the theory of government, which will, without many reciprocal concessions, render a concurrence impossible. Although the appointment of an executive magistrate has not been thought destructive to the principles of democracy in many of the States, yet, in the course of the debate, we find objections to the federal executive. It is argued that the President will degenerate into a tyrant. I intended, in compliance with the call of the honorable member, to explain the reasons of proposing this Constitution and develop its principles; but I shall postpone my remarks till we hear the supplement, which, he has informed us, he intends to add to what he has already said."

He next investigated the nature of the government, and whether it was a consolidated system as had been urged by Henry. On this subject, he said, "there are a number of opinions; but the principal question is whether it be a federal or consolidated government. In order to judge properly of the question before us, we must consider it minutely in its principal parts. I conceive myself that it is of a mixed nature; it is in a manner unprecedented. We cannot find one express example in the experience of the world. It stands by itself. In some respects it is a government of a federal nature; in others it is of a consolidated nature. Even if we attend to the manner in which the Constitution is investigated, ratified, and made the act of the people of America, I can say, notwithstanding what the honorable gentleman has alleged, that this Government is not completely consolidated, nor is it entirely federal. Who are parties to it? The people—but not the people as composing one great body ; but the people as composing thirteen sovereignties. Were it, as the gentleman asserts, a consolidated government, the assent of the majority of the people would be sufficient for its establishment ; and as a majority has adopted it already, the remaining States would be bound by the act of the majority, even if they unanimously reprobated it. Were it such a government as suggested, it would now be binding upon the people of this State, without their having had the privilege of deliberating upon it.[131] But, sir, no State is bound by it, as it is without its own consent. Should all the States adopt it, it will then be a government established by the thirteen States of America, not through the intervention of the legislature, but by the people at large. In this particular respect the distinction between the existing and proposed governments is very material. The existing system has been derived from the dependent derivative authority of the legislatures of the States ; whereas this is derived from the superior power of the people. If we look at the manner in which alterations are to be made in it, the same idea is in some degree attended to. By the new system a majority of the States cannot introduce amendments; nor are all the States required for that purpose. Three-fourths of them must concur in alterations; in this there is a departure from the federal idea. The members to the national House of Representatives are to be chosen by the people at large, in proportion to the numbers in the respective districts. When we come to the Senate, its members are elected by the States in their equal and political capacity. But had the Government been *completely consolidated*, the Senate would have been chosen by the people in their individual capacity, in the same manner as the members of the other house. Thus it is of a complicated nature, and this complication will, I trust, be found to exclude the evils of absolute consolidation, as well as of a mere confederacy. If Virginia was separated from all the States, her power and authority would extend to all cases ; in like manner, were all powers vested in the general Government it would be a consolidated government; but the powers of the Federal Government are enumerated ; it can

---

[131] This is an obvious sophism. Each State is called upon *in the usual mode* to say whether a particular system, be that system what it may, shall be henceforth its plan of government. Its mode of assent or dissent from the scheme cannot be called a part of the scheme itself.

only operate in certain cases ; it has legislative powers on defined and limited objects, beyond which it cannot extend its jurisdiction.''

This reasoning of Madison, in seeking to establish the nature of a government from the mode of conducting elections prescribed by the rule creating it, is sophistical and unjust, and wars at once with sound philosophy and simple truth. Had William the Third been elected under the declaration of right by the people of Great Britain, assembled at the polls, instead of a convention of both houses of Parliament, the nature of the government which he was invited to administer would not have been altered by the change. He would still have been the King of England, the occupant of a hereditary throne, bound to rule according to the instrument which contained his right to the crown. Nor is the case altered by the frequent recurrence of elections under a particular system. The mode of electing the agents of that system cannot affect the nature of the system itself, which is fixed and unalterable except in the way agreed upon by its framers. It is evident that Madison believed the new government to be a consolidated system. The favorite term of a complete consolidation is a mere play upon words. A government must be either integral or federal. In can no more be both than an individual can—like the fabulous centaur of antiquity, be at one and the same time half a man and half a brute. If he is human at all he is human all over ; if he is a brute at all he is a brute all over. So with a collection of human beings united in a political system. If that system is integral at all it is wholly integral ; if federal at all it is wholly federal. Details may complicate and disguise, but cannot alter the nature of the thing.

Thus the new constitution was the chart of a strictly federal system. Had not Madison been swayed by early prepossessions, his admirable powers of analysis and his unrivalled stores of historic lore would have enabled him to furnish a conclusive answer to the arguments of Mason and of Henry, and to force those able men from their strongest ground to a contest on the mere details of the constitution—a ground peculiarly his own. Ten years later the true argument would instantly have risen to his lips. He would have said that compacts between States, like compacts between private persons, might be as various as the necessities or interests of the parties should require ; that a compact which should embrace an infinite variety of details bearing directly or indirectly on persons and things, however voluminous, was as strictly a federal alliance as an ordinary treaty of a few sections. Under the Confederation, he might have said, the legislative, judicial and executive powers were vested in a single body which might exercise them in the manner most conducive to the public welfare ; that revenue was obtained by requisitions on the States; and that all control over the customs was denied to Congress; that the same parties which made these arrangements could abolish them and substitute others in their place ; might decree that the legislative, judicial and executive powers should be exercised by separate bodies under certain limitations ; that money should be obtained by levying a tax on persons and things in any given mode ; that the entire revenue accruing from customs should be appropriated by the central agency ; that these and other changes might be made, and that the nature of the federal alliance, however changed in outward form, would be no more changed in reality than an individual would be changed by throwing off the clothing of one season and putting on the clothing of another.

When Madison had concluded his review of the nature of the proposed Government, he adverted to the argument of Henry against the large powers which had been conferred by the Constitution on Congress. "I conceive," he said, "that the first question on this subject is whether these powers be necessary ; if they be, we are reduced to the dilemma of either submitting to the inconvenience or of losing the Union. Let us consider the most important of these reprobated powers ; that of direct taxation is most generally objected to. With respect to the exigencies of government, there is no question but the most easy mode for providing for them will be adopted. When, therefore, direct taxes are not necessary they will not be recurred to. It can be of little advantage to those in power to raise money in a manner oppressive to the people. To consult the conveniences of the people will cost them nothing, and in many respects will be advantageous to them. Direct taxes will only be recurred to for great purposes. What has brought on other nations those immense debts, under the pressure of which many of them labor ? Not the expenses of their governments, but war. If this country should be engaged in war—and I conceive we ought to provide for the possibility of such a case—how would it be carried on? By the usual means provided from year to year? As our imports will be necessary for the expenses of government and other common exigencies, how are we to carry on the means of defense? How is it possible a war could be supported without money or credit? And would it be possible for a government to have credit without having the power of raising money? No; it would be impossible for any government in such a case to defend itself. Then, I say, sir, that it is necessary to establish funds for extraordinary exigencies, and to give this power to the general Government; for the utter inutility of previous requisitions upon the States is too well known. Would it be possible for those countries, whose finances and revenues are carried to the highest perfection, to carry on the operations of government on great emergencies, such as the maintenance of a war, without an uncontrolled power of raising money? Has it not been necessary for Great Britain, notwithstanding the facility of the collection of her taxes, to have recourse very often to this and other extraordinary methods of procuring money? Would not her public credit have been ruined if it was known that her power to raise money was limited? Has not France been obliged on great occasions to use unusual means to raise funds? It has been the case in many countries, and no government can exist unless its powers extend to make provisions for every contingency. If we were actually attacked by a powerful nation, and our general Government had not the power of raising money, but depended solely on requisitions, our condition would be truly deplorable; if the revenue of this Commonwealth were to depend on twenty distinct authorities, it would be impossible for it to carry on its operations. This must be obvious to every member here; I think, therefore, that it is necessary, for the preservation of the Union, that this power shall be given to the general Government.''

It had been urged by Henry and Mason that the consolidated nature of the Government, combined with the power of direct taxation, would eventually destroy all subordinate authority, and result in the absorption of the State governments. Madison thought that this would not be the case. "If the general Government," he said, "were wholly independent of the governments of the particular States, then indeed, usurpation might be expected to the fullest extent. But, sir, on whom does this general Government depend? It derives its authority from these governments, and from the same sources from which their authority is derived. The members of the Federal Government are taken from the same men from whom those of the State legislatures are taken. If we consider the mode in which the federal representatives will be chosen, we shall be convinced that the general will never destroy the individual governments; and this conviction must be strengthened by an attention to the construction of the Senate. The representatives will be chosen probably under the influence of the members of the State legislatures; but there is not the least probability that the election of the latter will be influenced by the former. One hundred and sixty members represent this Commonwealth in one branch of the legislature, are drawn from the people at large, and must ever possess more influence than the few men who will be elected to the general legislature."

He concluded by showing that the members of Congress would depend for their election on the popular men in the different counties, and the members of the Senate, appointed by the legislatures, would not be likely to forget or defy the source of their existence; that the biennial exclusion of one-third of the number of Federal senators would lessen the facility of combinations; that the members of Congress had hitherto "signalized themselves by their attachment to their seats," and were not likely to neglect the interests of their constituents : closing this remarkable speech in these words: "I wish this Government may answer the expectation of its friends, and foil the apprehensions of its enemies. I hope the patriotism of the people will continue, and be a sufficient guard to their liberties. I believe its tendency will be that the State governments will counteract the general interest and ultimately prevail. The number of representatives is yet sufficient for our safety and will gradually increase; and if we consider their different sources of information, the number will not appear too small."

It must ever be a source of regret to the student of history that a more extended report of this speech, revised by its author, has not been preserved. With all the faithful care of Robertson the existing report is hardly more than an outline of the original. The beautiful philosophy with which he illustrated the various causes which led to the loss of liberty among the nations of the earth wholly escaped the reporter ; and when, forty years later, an opportunity was presented on the republication of the debates to fill the void, a refined sense of delicacy, which we may admire while we deplore the result, impelled him to decline it.

But, however attractive and eloquent was the performance of Randolph ; however rich in the philosophy of history and in its application to the subject in hand, and in its wonderful display of the probable working of the new system, was the effort of Madison ; the speech which was now to be made, was, in logical vigor and practical sense, and in its present force on a popular body, perhaps more effective than either of its predecessors of this remarkable day.

George Nicholas succeeded Madison in the debate.   Of all the friends of the Constitution he was the most formidable to Henry.   His perfect acquaintance with all the local and domestic topics of State policy, and especially of the whole system of legislation, in which he was a prominent actor since the dawn of the Commonwealth; his connections by descent and affinity with the old aristocratic families ; his physical qualities, which made him equally fearless in the House and out of the House, were evinced by his civil and military career since manhood ; his great powers of minute and sustained argumentation, so minute and so sustained that posterity in perusing the debates of the Convention will hesitate in awarding the palm of superiority to Madison ; his expositions of the Constitution more elaborate in their details than those of Madison, added to his character of a thorough and unflinching representative of the patrimonial feuds and preju- dices with which from his early life Henry had been continually battling, made his opposition not only unwelcome but galling to the opponents of the new system.   It was alike difficult to evade and repel his attacks.   Henry would neutralize the speeches of Madison by the thunders of his oratory, and he could throw Randolph from his balance by a covert sarcasm discernible only by the person who felt its sting ; but neither oratory nor sarcasm availed in a contest with Nicholas, who was as potent in the war of wit as he was irresistible by the force of his logic.   Not that Nicholas possessed or coveted wit in its higher manifestations ; but his knowledge of his opponents had supplied him with such an array of facts bearing on their past history, that, by a mar-

shalling of their absurdities and inconsistencies, he could produce in the way of argument an effect similar to that wrought by
a faculty which he did not possess, and of which in his busy and
speculating life he never felt the want. He now rose to address
himself specially to Henry, and analyzed his arguments with a
severity of discrimination that neither Madison, who never forgot
the statesman in the debates, nor Randolph, who, under the
pressure of the interminable topics crowding upon him, was
compelled to pass over many, and to touch lightly upon others,
could not well imitate. On this occasion, as on others, Nicholas
was fortunate in his reporter. He discussed a single topic at a
time ; his style of argument was clear and was within the reach
of the stenographer, who, by the aid of his recollections and by
his own skill in argument, could impart a completeness to a speech
of Nicholas, which is almost wholly wanting to the speeches of
Henry and Randolph, and even of Madison.

He began by saying that if the resolution taken by the House
of going regularly through the system, clause by clause, had
been followed, he could have confined himself to one particular
paragraph ; but as, to his surprise, the debates have taken a different turn, he would follow the train of the argument of the
gentleman in opposition. Then, addressing himself to Henry,
"the worthy gentleman," he said, " entertained us very largely on
the impropriety and dangers of the powers given by this plan
to the general Government ; but his argument appears to me inconclusive and inaccurate. It amounts to this : that the powers
given to any government ought to be small ; a new idea in politics. Powers being given for some certain purpose ought to be
proportionate to that purpose, or else the end for which they
were delegated will not be assured. If a due medium be not
observed in the delegation of such powers, one of two things
must happen : if they be too small, the Government must moulder
and decay away ; if too extensive, the people must be oppressed.
As there can be no liberty without government, it must be as
dangerous to make powers too limited as too great. He objects
to the expression ' We, the people,' and demands the reason
why they had not said, ' We, the United States of America.' In
my opinion, the expression is highly proper : it is submitted to
the people, because on them it is to operate ; till adopted, it is but
a dead letter, and not binding on any one ; when adopted, it

becomes binding on the people who adopted it.   It is proper on
another account.   We are under great obligations to the Federal
Convention for securing to the people the source of all power."
He then animadverts on the difficulties apprehended from two
sets of collectors, from direct taxes, from a reduction of the
number of representatives, from being taxed without our consent, from the suspension of the writ of *habeas corpus*, and from
the want of responsibility, discussing each topic with syllogistic
force, and following Henry step by step throughout his speech.
One argument on the subject of Northern influence has an interest at this day.   " The influence," he observed, "of New England and the other Northern States is dreaded; there are apprehensions of their combining against us.   Not to advert to the
improbability and illiterality of this idea, it must be supposed
that our population will in a short period exceed theirs, as their
country is well settled, and we have very extensive uncultivated
tracts.   We shall soon outnumber them in as great a degree as
they do us at this time; therefore, this Government, which, I
trust, will last to the remotest ages, will be very shortly in our
favor."   His answer to the argument on the want of responsibility in the representatives of the new Constitution shows the
summary manner in which he dealt with the objections of Henry.
" We are told," he said, "that there is wanting in this Government that responsibility which has been the salvation of
Great Britain, although one-half of the House of Commons purchase their seats.   It has already been shown that we have much
greater security from our federal representatives than the people
in England can boast.   But the worthy member has found out a
way of solving our difficulties.   He tells us that we have nothing
to fear if separated from the adopting States ; but to send on our
money and men to Congress.   In that case, can we receive the
benefits of the union ?   If we furnish money at all, it will be our
proportionate share.   The consequence will be that we shall pay
our share without the privilege of being represented.   So that,
to avoid the inconvenience of not having a sufficient number of
representatives, he would advise us to relinquish the number we
are entitled to, *and have none at all.*"   This speech would have
been received in such a body as the House of Commons with
heartier applause than either the speech of Randolph or the
speech of Madison.   It is, however, the speech rather of a wily

logician whose paramount object is to overthrow his opponent, than of a politician who embraces in his view the interests of a remote posterity. It is the speech of an emissary of Westminster Hall entering St. Stephen's on a special retainer, and instructed to answer Burke's speeeh on American conciliation.

At the close of the speech of Nicholas, the House rose and cordial greetings were exchanged by the friends of the Constitution. Even their opponents could not deny that three such speeches as had been delivered at that sitting had never before been heard in a single day in a deliberative assembly of Virginia. A contemporaneous account has come down to us. Immediately on the adjournment, Bushrod Washington wrote to his uncle that Governor Randolph made an able and elegant harangue of two hours and a half; that Madison followed with such force of reasoning and a display of such irresistible truths that opposition seemed to have quitted the field, and that Nicholas concluded the day with a very powerful speech inferior to none that had been made before as to close and connected argument. Washington went so far as to say that Madison's speech had made several converts to the Constitution.[132]

On the following day (Saturday, the seventh of June), as soon as some election details were disposed of, Wythe was called to the chair of the committee, the first and second sections of the Constitution still under consideration. While the expectation of the public was eager to hear the reply of Henry to the three powerful opponents who had spent the whole of the previous day in answering his objections to the Constitution, a young man whose person was unknown to the elder spectators, rose and proceeded to address the House in defence of the new plan. Francis Corbin[133] was descended from an ancestor who, near the middle

---

[132] B. Washington to G. Washington, June 6, 1788.—*Writings of Washington.* IX, 378, note. When Nicholas made this speech he was thirty-two; Madison and Randolph, both of whom were born in 1751, were thirty-seven.

[133] Of the lineage of Robert Corbion or Corbin, who gave lands to the Abbey of Talesworth in 1154 and 1161. Francis Corbin was third in descent from Henry Corbin (and his wife, Alice Eltonhead), born 1629; came to Virginia 1654; member of the House of Burgesses for old Lancaster county, 1658-9 and of the Council from 1663 to his death, January 8, 1675; acquired a great landed estate, his seat being " Buck-

of the seventeenth century, had emigrated to the Colony, who
had acquired great wealth, and who had risen to distinction in
the public councils.   From the date of the arrival of the ancestor
to that of the Revolution the family which he founded had enjoyed high consideration, and in the public acts and in the civil
and religious proceedings relative to the county of Middlesex the
name of Corbin always appears with honor.[134] Inheriting from
the patriarch of his race a reverence for kingly government, the
representative of the family at the Revolution, then advanced in
life, had been suspected of co-operating with some of his rela-
tives who had taken sides with the Bristish, and had been placed
under surveillance by the Convention of 1775.   Francis, then a
mere lad, was sent over to England and had spent the entire
period of the war of the Revolution in attendance on British
schools and at the University.   On his return, he soon entered
the Assembly, where his fine person, his polished manners, his
talents in debate, his knowledge of foreign affairs, aided by the
prestige of an ancient name, were observed and applauded.   He
was not far from thirty and had opposed the passage of the resolution convoking the meeting of Annapolis ;[135] but, fascinated
by its supposed beauties, had given in his adhesion to the new
system.   The speech which he made sustains the reputation
which he had acquired in the House of Delegates and fully
evinces the zeal and success with which, amid the allurements of
a fashionable residence abroad, he had cultivated the powers of
his mind and the strict observation with which he had surveyed
the political systems of that age.   He made a neat apology for
engaging in a debate in which so many older and abler men had
taken part and replied in detail to the arguments of Henry.   His

---

ingham House," in Middlesex county. He was born in 1760; sent to
England at an early age and educated at Canterbury school, Cambridge,
and at the Inner Temple ; returned to Virginia about 1783 and resided at
" Buckingham House," and subsequently at "The Reeds," Caroline
county ; member of the House of Delegates from Middlesex county
1787-1793 and other years, and of the Convention of 1788; died June
15, 1821 ; married Anne Munford, of " Blandfield," Essex county,
Virginia.—ED.

[134] Bishop Meade's *Old Churches, &c.*, I, 357.

[135] Mr. Madison states that Meriwether Smith and Corbin were the
only persons who spoke against the Annapolis resolution.   Madison to
Monroe, January 22, 1786.   See the letter in *Rives' Madison*, II, 65.

definition of the new system was ingenious. "There are controversies," he observed, "about the name of this Government. It is denominated by some, federal; by others, a consolidated government. The definition given of it by my honorable friend (Mr. Madison) is, in my opinion, accurate. Let me, however, call it by another name—a representative federal republic—as contradistinguished from a confederacy. The former is more wisely constructed than the latter. It places the remedy in the hands which *feel* the disorder ; the other places the remedy in those hands which *cause* the disorder." Another view of this young statesman displayed a perspicuity which was not so fully apparent among his more prominent coadjutors and deserves to be recorded. The hostility manifested by the opponents of the Constitution was founded very much upon the belief that the ordinary revenues of the new Government would be drawn from that source ; and had such been the result, it is hardly probable that the new system would have survived the last century. Corbin saw the danger to which the Constitution was exposed from such a quarter, and having examined with uncommon pains and research all the records and other sources of intelligence within his reach, showed that "the probable annual amount of duties on imported articles throughout the continent, including West India produce, would, from the best calculation he could procure, exceed the annual expenses of the administration of the general Government, including the civil list, contingent charges, and the interest of the foreign and domestic debts, by eighty or ninety thousand pounds ; which would enable the United States to discharge in a few years the principal debts due to foreign nations ; and that in thirty years that surplus would enable the United States to perform the most splendid enterprises." He then concluded that no danger was to be apprehended from the power of direct taxation "since there was every reason to believe that it would be very seldom used "—a prediction which, but for two special exceptions of short duration, would have almost been strictly verified.[136]

---

[136] Written in 1857. Corbin, in describing Henry's style, speaks of "the elegance of his periods," and he was familiar with the best models of that age. He also alludes to a motion made in the House of Delegates in 1789, which Henry approved, of vesting in Congress

He spoke nearly an hour, and, on taking his seat was warmly congratulated on his chaste and statesmanlike effort. Henry then rose and expressed a wish that Randolph should continue his observations left unfinished the day before, and that he would now give him, as he had already done, a most patient hearing, as he wished to be informed of everything that gentlemen could urge in defence of that system which appeared to him so defective. Randolph resumed his remarks, and spoke at great length and, perhaps, with even greater ability than he had yet done, reviewing what had been said by his opponents, pointing out in detail the defects of the Confederation, and stating some of the defects of the proposed system which had led him to withhold his signature from it in the General Convention. He gave way to Madison, who made, perhaps, the most elaborate and the most profound speech delivered during the entire session of the Convention, in which he exhibited with the skill of a political philosopher the nature and defects of the Amphyctionic and Achaian leagues of the Germanic body of the Swiss Confederation, and of the confederate government of Holland, not overlooking the ancient union of the colonies of Massachusetts, Bristol, Connecticut, and New Hampshire, quoting his authorities in full, and concluding with an application of all the facts and reasons of his grand argument to the case in hand. Henry rose in reply. He spoke of the value of maxims, which have attracted the admiration of the virtuous and the wise in all nations, and have stood the shock of ages—that the bill of rights of 'Virginia contains those admirable maxims dear to every friend of liberty, of virtue and manhood ; that their observance was essential to our security; that it was impiously inviting the avenging hand of Heaven, when a people, who are in the full enjoyment of freedom, launch out in the wide ocean of human affairs, and desert those maxims which alone can preserve liberty. "Now, sir," he said, "let us consider whether the picture given of American affairs ought to drive us from those beloved maxims. The honorable gentleman (Randolph) has said it is too late in the day for us to reject this new plan. That system which was once execrated by the honorable member must now be adopted, let its defects be ever

the power of forcing delinquent States to pay their respective quotas, without, however, alluding to Henry's course on that occasion.

so glaring. That honorable member will not accuse me of want of candor, when I cast in my mind what he has given the public,[137] and compare it with what has happened since. It seems to me very strange and unaccountable that that which was the object of his execration should now receive his encomiums. Something extraordinary must have operated so great a change in his opinion. It is too late in the day! I never can believe, sir, that it is too late to save all that is precious. At present, we have our liberties and privileges in our own hands. Let us not adopt this system till we see them secure. There is some small possibility that should we follow the conduct of Massachusetts, amendments might be obtained. There is a small possibility of amending any government; but, sir, shall we abandon our most inestimable rights, and rest their security on a mere possibility? If it be amended every State will accede to it; but by an imprudent adoption in its defective and dangerous state, a schism must inevitably be the consequence. I can never, therefore, consent to hazard our most inalienable rights on an absolute uncertainty. You are told that there is no peace, although you fondly flatter yourselves that all is peace; no peace—a general cry and alarm in the country—commerce, riches and wealth vanished—citizens going to seek comfort in other parts of the world—laws insulted—many instances of tyrannical legislation. These things are new to me. The gentleman has made the discovery. As to the administration of justice, I believe that failure in commerce cannot be attributed to it. My age enables me to recollect its progress under the old government. I can justify it by saying that it continues in the same manner in this State as it did under the former government. As to other parts of the continent, I refer that to other gentlemen. As to the ability of those who administer our Government, I believe that they could not suffer by a comparison with those who administered it under the royal authority. Where is the cause of complaint that the wealthy go away? Is this, added to the other circumstances, of such enormity, and does it bring such danger over this Commonwealth as to warrant so important and so awful a change in so precipitate a

---

[137] Governor Randolph's letter to the Speaker of the House of Delegates of Virginia, heretofore alluded to, which may be seen in Elliot's Debates, I, 482.

manner? As to insults offered to the laws, I know of none. In this respect, I believe this Commonwealth would not suffer by a comparison with the former government. The laws are as well executed and as patiently acquiesced in as they were under the royal administration. Compare the situation of the country—compare that of our citizens to what it was then—and decide whether persons and property are not as safe and secure as they were at that time. Is there a man in this Commonwealth whose person can be insulted with impunity? Cannot redress be had here for personal insults or injuries, as well as in any part of the world?—as well as in those countries where aristocrats and monarchs triumph and reign? Is not the protection of property in full operation here? The contrary cannot with truth be charged on this Commonwealth. Those severe charges which are exhibited against it appear to be *totally groundless*. On a fair investigation we shall be found to be surrounded with no real dangers."

He adverted to the case of Josiah Philips, which Randolph had introduced, and, overlooking the fact that he had been tried on an indictment for highway robbery and not under the act of attainder, justified his execution on the ground of his being an outlaw and enemy of the human race. He insisted that the middle and lower ranks of the people were not discontented; that if there were discontents, they existed among politicians whose microscopic vision could see defects in old systems, and whose illuminated imaginations discovered the necessity of a change. He urged that by the confederation the rights of territory were secured; that under the new system, you will most infallibly lose the Mississippi. He declared that we might be confederated with the adopting States without ratifying this system. "You will find no reductions of the public burdens by this system. The splendid maintenance of the President, and of the members of both houses, and the salaries and fees of the swarm of officers and dependents of the Government, will cost the continent immense sums. Double sets of collectors will double the expenses; to those are to be added oppressive excise men and custom-house officers. The people have an hereditary hatred of custom-house officers. The experience of the mother country leads me to detest them."[138]

---

[138] The hostility to tax gatherers of all kinds, which Henry here expressed, as on several other occasions during the session, reminds us

An incident in the delivery of this speech should be noted, not so much on its own account, as tending to show the temper of Randolph and Henry toward each other, which resulted the following day in one of the most celebrated parliamentary explosions in our annals. In the course of his remarks Henry had animadverted upon the words "We, the people," as designed to appeal to the prejudices of the people. "The words," he contended, "were introduced to recommend it to the people at large—to those citizens who are to be levelled and degraded to a *herd*, and who, by the operation of this *blessed* system, are to be transformed from respectable independent citizens to abject dependent subjects or slaves. The honorable gentleman (Randolph) has anticipated what we are to be reduced to by degradingly assimilating us to a *herd*." Here Randolph rose and said that he did not use that word to excite any odium, but merely to convey an idea of a multitude. Henry replied that the word had made a deep impression on his mind, and that he verily believed that system would operate as he had said. He then said : " I will exchange that abominable word for requisitions—requisitions which gentlemen affect to despise, have nothing degrading in them. On this depends our political prosperity. I will never give up that darling word requisitions. My country may give it up. A majority may wrest it from me ; but I will never give it up till my grave. Requisitions are attended with one singular advantage. They are attended by deliberation."

When Henry concluded his remarks the House rose. Thus closed the first week of the Convention, during which we have seen that Henry stood alone in opposition to a phalanx of the ablest men of that era ; for, with the exception of a speech from Mason, he had received no assistance from his friends. It was easy, however, to perceive, from his last effort as well as from the tone of his opponents, that, instead of losing ground, he was evidently advancing ; that his arguments were more compact and guarded ; that his sarcasm, though within the limits of the strictest decorum, wore a keener edge, and that he would either

---

of Dr. Johnson's definition of the word excise—"a hateful tax levied upon commodities, and adjudged, not by the common judges of property, but wretches hired by those to whom excise is paid."—Johnson's Folio Dictionary, Ed. 1765.

ultimately triumph or make the victory of his opponents hardly
worth the wearing.[139]

---

[139] It was often remarked by the contemporaries of Henry that his
best school of preparation on any great question was listening to the
speeches of those who engaged in the debate. A friend informs me
that he "spent several days with the late James Marshall, of Fauquier,
a brother of the Chief Justice, a gentleman of almost as high intellect
as the Judge, and of more various accomplishments, who told him that
Henry's opponents in debate, to contrast their knowledge with his
want of it, would often display ostentatiously all they knew respecting
the subject under discussion, and that, consequently, when they were
done speaking Mr. Henry knew as much of the subject in hand as they
did. Then the superiority of his intellect would show itself in the perfect mastery which he would evince over the whole subject. 'And if,'
said Mr. Marshall, 'he spoke three times on the same subject, which
he sometimes did, his last view of it would be the clearest and most
striking that could be conceived.'" C. C. Lee, Esq., letter dated December 6, 1856.

CHAPTER IV.

On Monday, the ninth of June, the combatants, refreshed by the rest of the Sabbath, returned with new vigor to the field. The House had now gone through with the election details which had heretofore consumed the first half hour of the morning, and immediately went into committee. The first and second sections of the first article of the Constitution were still the nominal order of the day; but the debate from the first had comprehended the entire scope of that instrument. The rumors of great debates had spread over the neighboring counties, and the crowd that pressed the hall and the galleries seemed rather to increase than diminish. Henry and Mason, who had, according to their usual habit, walked arm in arm from the Swan, were seen to pause a few moments at the steps of the Academy, evidently engaged in consultation, and with difficulty made their way to their seats in the house.[140]

Wythe had just taken the chair, when Henry rose to conclude his unfinished speech of Saturday. His first sentences were short and broken, as if uttered to assure himself of his voice and position. He then introduced a topic which had long been dreaded by his opponents, but which startled them like a clap of thunder in a clear sky. "There is one thing," he said, "that I must mention. There is a dispute between us and the Spaniards about the right of navigating the Mississippi. This dispute has sprung from the Federal Government. I wish a great deal may be said upon the subject. In my opinion, the preservation of that river calls for our most serious consideration. It has been agitated in Congress. Seven States have

---

[140] On the authority of the Rev. Mr. Clay, of Bedford, who was a member of the Convention.

voted so, as that it is known to the Spaniards, that under our
existing system the Mississippi shall be taken from them. Seven
States wished to relinquish this river to them. The six Southern
States opposed it. Seven States not being sufficient to convey
it away, it remains ours. If I am wrong, there is a member on
this floor who can contradict the facts ; I will readily retract.
This new government, I conceive, will enable those States who
have already discovered their inclination that way to give
away this river. Will the honorable gentleman (Randolph)
advise us to relinquish this inestimable navigation, and to place
formidable enemies on our backs ? I hope this will be explained.
I was not in Congress at the time these transactions took place.
I may not have stated every fact. Let us hear how the great
and important right of navigating that river has been attended
to, and whether I am mistaken that Federal measures will lose it
to us forever. If a bare majority of Congress can make laws, the
situation of our Western citizens is dreadful.''

Of the connection of the Mississippi with the interests of Virginia we will treat at length when the memorable discussion of
the subject took place a few days later ; at present it is only
necessary to say that Kentucky, whose western boundary
impinged on that river, was then a part of Virginia, and was represented in the Convention by twelve members, whose votes
might decide the fate of the new plan.

Henry then proceeded to reply to the arguments of Randolph,
Madison, and Corbin in detail, with a force of logic and with a
fullness of illustration which he had not before evinced in his
speeches. He reviewed the dangers likely to flow from the non-
payment of the debt due to France, bestowing an elegant compliment on Mr. Jefferson, whom he called '' an illustrious citizen,
who, at a great distance from us, remembers and studies our
happiness ; who was well acquainted with the policy of European
nations, and who, amid the splendor and dissipation of courts,
yet thinks of bills of rights and those despised little things
called maxims ;'' and speaking of Louis the Sixteenth as '' that
great friend of America.'' He reviewed our relations with Spain
and with Holland, and showed with great plausibility that we had
nothing to fear from them. He then examined the arguments of
Randolph, drawn from our position in respect of the neighboring
States, and gave his reasons for concluding that neither Mary-

land nor Pennsylvania would give us serious trouble. He reviewed our Indian relations, and showed that there was no cause for alarm in that quarter, closing this branch of this subject in these words: " You will *sip sorrow*, to use a vulgar phrase, if you want any other security than the laws of Virginia."

He adduced the authority of several eminent citizens to prove the consolidating tenderness of the new plan, and asked " if any one who heard him could restrain his indignation at a system which takes from the State legislatures the care and the preservation of the interests of the people. One hundred and eighty representatives, the choice of the people of Virginia, not to be trusted with their interests! They are a mobbish, suspected *herd*. So degrading an indignity, so flagrant an outrage on the States, so vile a suspicion, is humiliating to my mind, and to the minds of many others." He ridiculed the notion that a change of government could pay the debts of the people. " At present," he said, " you buy too much, and make too little to pay. The evils that attend us lie in extravagance and want of industry, and can only be removed by assiduity and economy. Perhaps we shall be told by gentlemen that these things will happen, because the administration is to be taken from us and placed in the hands of the luminous few, who will pay different attention, and be more studiously careful than we can be supposed to be."

With respect to the economical operation of the new government, he urged that the national expenses would be increased by it tenfold. " I might tell you," he said, " of a standing army, of a great powerful navy, of a long and rapacious train of officers and dependents, independent of the president, senators, and representatives, whose compensations are without limitation. How are our debts to be discharged when the expenses of government are so greatly augmented? The defects of this system are so numerous and palpable, and so many States object to it, no union can be expected unless it be amended. Let us take a review of the facts." He then examined the condition of the different States at length, ending his remarks on this topic with these words : " Without a radical alteration of this plan, sir, the States will never be embraced in one federal pale. If you attempt to force it down men's throats and call it union dreadful consequences must follow."

He now urged upon Randolph the inconsistency of his course

in relation to the adoption of the Constitution. "The gentleman has said a great deal of disunion and the dangers that are to arise from it. When we are on the subject of union and dangers, let me ask him how will his present doctrine hold with what has happened? Is it consistent with that noble and disinterested conduct which he displayed on a former occasion? Did he not tell us that he withheld his signature? Where then were the dangers which now appear to him so formidable? He saw all America eagerly confiding that the result of their deliberations would remove our distresses. He saw all America acting under the impulses of hope, expectation, and anxiety arising from our situation, and our partiality for the members of that Convention; yet, his enlightened mind, knowing that system to be defective, magnanimously and nobly refused to approve it. He was not led by the illumined, the illustrious few. He was actuated by the dictates of his own judgment, and a better judgment than I can form. He did not stand out of the way of information. He must have been possessed of every intelligence. What alterations have a few months brought about? The internal difference between right and wrong does not fluctuate. It is immutable. I ask this question as a public man, and out of no particular view. I wish, as such, to consult every source of information, to form my judgment on so awful a question. I had the highest respect for the honorable gentleman's abilities. I considered his opinion as a great authority. He taught me, sir, in despite of the approbation of that great Federal Convention, to doubt of the propriety of that system. When I found my honorable friend in the number of those who doubted, I began to doubt also. I coincided with him in opinion. I shall be a staunch and faithful disciple of his. I applaud that magnanimity which led him to withhold his signature. If he thinks now differently, he is as free as I am. Such is my situation, that, as a poor individual, I look for information everywhere." He continued: "This Government is so new it wants a name. I wish its other novelties were as harmless as this. The gentleman told us that we had an American dictator in the year 1781—we never had an American *President*. In making a dictator, we followed the example of the most glorious, magnanimous, and skillful nations. In great dangers this power has been given. Rome had furnished us with an illustrious example. America

found a person worthy of that trust ; she looked to Virginia for
him.   We gave a dictatorial power to hands that used it glori-
ously ; and which were rendered more glorious by surrendering
it up.   Where is there a breed of such dictators ?   Shall we find
a set of American presidents of such a breed ?   Will the American President come and lay prostrate at the feet of Congress his
laurels ?   I fear there are few men who can be trusted on that
head.   The glorious republic of Holland has erected monuments
of her warlike intrepidity and valor, yet she is now totally ruined
by a Stadt-holder—a Dutch president.''   He then drew some
seemingly apposite illustrations from the policy of the Dutch in
favor of his views.   He touched one of the arguments of Corbin,
in passing which that gentleman drew from the domestic legislation of Virginia.   '' Why,'' he said, ''did it please the gentleman to bestow such epithets on our country ?   Have the worms
taken possession of the wood, that our strong vessel—our political vessel has sprung a leak ?   He may know better than I, but
I consider such epithets to be most illiberal and unwarrantable
aspersions on our laws.   The system of laws under which we
live has been tried and found to suit our genius.   I trust we shall
not change this happy system.''   Then, turning to Corbin, he
said : '' Till I see that gentleman following after and pursuing
other objects than those which prevent the great objects of
human legislation, pardon me if I withhold my assent.''

When he had discoursed on the subject of forming new codes
of law, of the nature of the various checks which were regarded
as sufficient to prevent federal usurpation, of the abuses of implied powers, of the complicated union of State and Federal
collectors, he argued with great earnestness in opposition to that
part of the Constitution which gives to Congress jurisdiction
over forts and arsenals in the State.   '' Congress,'' he said, ''you
sell to Congress such places as are proper for these, within your
State, you will not be consistent after adoption.   It results, therefore, clearly that you are to give into their hands all such places
as are fit for strongholds.   When you have those fortifications
and garrisons within your State, your State legislature will
have no power over them, though they see the most dangerous
insults offered to the people daily.   They are also to have magazines in each State.   These depositories for arms, though within
the States, will be free from the control of its legislature.   Are

we at last brought to such a humiliating and debasing degrada-
tion, that we cannot be trusted with arms for our own defence?
If *our* defence be the *real* object of having those arms, in whose
hands can they be trusted with more propriety or equal safety to
us, as in our own hands? If our legislature be unworthy of
legislating for every foot of land in this State, they are unworthy
of saying another word."

He showed that by the power of taxation and by the right to
raise armies, Congress would possess the power of the purse and
the power of the sword, and sought to prove that, without a
miracle, no nation could retain its liberty, after the loss of the
purse and the sword. He contended that requisitions were the
proper means of collecting money from the States, and appealed
to Randolph, as he said " he was *a child* of the Revolution,"[141]
whether he did not recollect with gratitude the glorious effects
of requisitions throughout the war.

He thus animadverted upon the definition which Madison had
given of the new plan : " We are told," he said, " that this new
government, collectively taken, is without an example; that it is
national in this part and federal in that part, &c. We may be
amused, if we please, by a treatise of political anatomy. In the
brain it is national; the stamina are federal—some limbs are federal, some national. The senators are to be voted for by the
State legislatures ; so far it is federal. Individuals choose the
members of the first branch ; here it is national. It is federal in
conferring general powers; but national in retaining them. It is
not to be supported by the States—the pockets of individuals
are to be searched for its maintenance. What signifies it to me
that you have the most curious anatomical description of it on its
creation ? To all the common purposes of legislation it is a great
CONSOLIDATION of government. You are not to have the right
to legislate in any but trivial cases. You are not to touch private
contracts. You are not to have the rights of having arms on
your own defences. You cannot be trusted with dealing out
justice between man and man. What shall the States have to

---

[141] Randolph opened his speech to which Henry was replying with
the words: "I am a child of the Revolution." The reader must keep
in mind Henry's inimitable powers of acting, and his ability by a mere
accent on a word or a look to raise the laughter of both friends and
foes.

do? Take care of the poor, repair and make highways, erect bridges, and so on, and so on. Abolish the State legislatures at once. What purposes should they be continued for? Our Legislature will indeed be a ludicrous spectacle. One hundred and eighty men marching in solemn farcical procession, exhibiting a mournful proof of the lost liberty of their country, without the power of restoring it. But, sir, we have the consolation that it is a *mixed* government; that is, it may work sorely on your neck; but you will have some comfort by saying that it was a federal government on its origin!"[142]

"I am constrained," he added, "to make a few remarks on the absurdity of adopting this system, and relying on the chance of getting it amended afterwards. When it is confessed to be replete with defects, is it not offering to insult your understandings to attempt to reason you out of the propriety of rejecting it till it be amended? Does it not insult your judgments to tell you adopt first and then amend? Is your rage for novelty so great that you are first to sign and seal and then to retract? Is it possible to conceive a greater solecism? I am at a loss what to say. You agree to bind yourselves hand and foot—for the sake of what? Of being unbound. You go into a dungeon—for what? To get out. Is there no danger when you go in that the bolts of federal authority shall shut you in? Human nature will never part from power." After illustrating his position by facts drawn from the history of Europe, and paying a compliment to the younger Pitt on account of his opinions favorable to reform in the British Constitution, he closed his argument on this point

---

[142] I have heard that this passage, of which we have but a condensed report, and which blended irony and pathos in a remarkable degree, was delivered with transcendant effect. On one of the occasions which the reporter passes over with some such remark as, " Here Mr. Henry declaimed with great pathos on the loss of our liberties," I was told by a person on the floor of the Convention at the time, that when Henry had painted in the most vivid colors the dangers likely to result to the black population from the unlimited power of the general government, wielded by men who had little or no interest in that species of property, and had filled his audience with fear, he suddenly broke out with the homely exclamation: " *They'll free your niggers!*" The audience passed instantly from fear to wayward laughter; and my informant said that it was most ludicrous to see men who a moment before were half frightened to death, with a broad grin on their faces.

with the inquiry: "I ask you again, where is the example that a government was amended by those who instituted it? Where is the instance of the errors of a government rectified by those who adopted them?"

He closed the most brilliant argument which he had then ever made with this affecting and patriotic peroration: "Perhaps I shall be told that I have gone through the regions of fancy— that I deal in noisy exclamations and mighty professions of patriotism. Gentlemen may retain their opinions; but *I look on that paper as the most fatal plan that could possibly be conceived to enslave a free people.* If such be your rage for novelty, take it and welcome, but you never shall have my consent. My sentiments may appear extravagant; but I can tell you that a number of my fellow-citizens have kindred sentiments. And I am anxious, that if my country should come into the hands of tyranny, to exculpate myself from being in any degree the cause; and to exert my faculties to the utmost to extricate her. Whether I am gratified or not in my beloved form of government, I consider that the more she is plunged into distress the more it is my duty to relieve her. Whatever may be the result, I shall wait with patience till the day may come when an opportunity shall offer to exert myself in her cause."

Before the pathetic tones of Henry's voice had died away, and when every eye was fixed on Randolph, who could not conceal his emotions under Henry's frequent and pointed assaults, Henry Lee obtained possession of the floor. In conducting a campaign, whether in the field or in a deliberative assembly, no member of the body had a keener sense of the policy to be pursued in a great conjuncture than this daring young man; and it was observed by those who knew him well that, if his attention had been as early and as ardently devoted to civil as to military employments, he would not have fallen behind the most distinguished of his contemporaries. He now felt that no majority, however large, could long withstand the glowing appeals of Henry, and that it was of vital importance to the cause which he embraced to break that spell which for the last three hours had been cast by his eloquence over the house. He also knew that if argument could accomplish such a result, the admirable speeches of Pendleton, of Madison, and of Nicholas, would have left nothing to be desired. He accordingly, as on a former occasion, adopted a different mode of tactics. He said that, when he was up before, he had called upon that gentlemen (Henry) to give his *reasons* for his opposition in a systematic manner ; and he had done so from respect to the character of that gentleman. He had also taken the liberty to tell him that the subject belonged to the *judgments* of the members of the committee, and not to their *passions.* He felt obliged to him for his politeness in the committee; "but," he added, "as the honorable gentleman seems to have discarded in a great measure solid argument and strong reasoning, and has established a new system of throwing those bolts which he has so peculiar a dexterity in discharging, I trust I shall not incur the displeasure of the committe by answering the honorable gentleman in the desultory manner in .which he has treated the subject. I shall touch a few of those *luminous* points he has entertained us with. He told us the other day that the enemies of the Constitution were firm supporters of liberty, and implied that its friends were not republicans. I conceive that I may say with truth that the friends of that paper are true republicans, and by no means less attached to liberty than their opponents. Much is said by gentlemen out of doors. They ought to urge all their objections here. In all the rage of the gentleman for democracy, how often does he express his admiration of the king and parliament over the Atlantic? But we republicans are contemned and despised.

Here, sir, I conceive that *implication* might operate against himself. He tells us that he is a staunch republican, and adores liberty. I believe him, and when I do I wonder that he should say that a kingly government is superior to that system which we admire. He tells you that it cherishes a standing army, and that militia alone ought to be depended upon for the defence of every free country. There is not a gentlemen in this house— there is no man without these walls—not even the gentleman himself, who admires the militia more than I do. Without vanity I may say that I have had different experience of their service from that of the honorable gentleman. It was my fortune to be a soldier of my country. In the discharge of my duty I knew the worth of militia. I have seen them perform feats that would do do honor to the first veterans, and submitting to what would daunt German soldiers. I saw what the honorable gentleman did *not* see—our men fighting with the troops of that king which he so much admires. I have seen proofs of the wisdom of that paper on your table. I have seen incontrovertible evidence that militia cannot always be relied on. I could enumerate many instances, but one will suffice. Let the gentleman recollect the action of Guilford. The American troops behaved there with gallant intrepidity. What did the militia do? The greatest numbers of them fled. The abandonment of the regulars occasioned the loss of the field. Had the line been supported that day, Cornwallis, instead of surrendering at York, would have laid down his arms at Guilford.''[143]

In replying to the argument of Henry, that the States would be left without arms, he said he could not understand the implication of the gentleman that, because Congress may arm the militia, the States cannot do it. The States are, by no part of the plan before you, precluded from arming and disciplining the militia should Congress neglect it. He rebuked Henry for his seemingly exclusive attachment to Virginia, and uttered the following manly sentiment: "In the course of Saturday, and in previous harangues, from the terms in which some of the Northern States were spoken of, one would have thought that the love of an *American* was in some degree criminal, as being incompatible with a proper degree of affection for a Virginian. The people of America, sir, are one people. I love the people of the North, not because they have adopted the Constitution, but because I fought with them as my countrymen, and because I consider them as such. Does it follow from hence that I have forgotten my attachment to my native State? In all local matters I shall be a Virginian. In those of a general nature I shall never forget that I am an American.'' In referring to the proposed surrender of the navigation of the Mississippi, he said that he

---

[143] The reader familiar with our early history will discover several covert allusions to Henry's military character in the above-cited passage. The military officers of the United States were sometimes inclined to assume rather too much authority in the States at particular times. The correspondence between Colonel Edward Carrington and Henry (when Governor) shows this very plainly. The ultimate result was the triumph of the civilians in putting down the Cincinnati Society, and the triumph of the military in effecting a ratification of the Federal Constitution, especially by Virginia, where it was opposed by our ablest and wisest statesmen, and probably by three-fourths of the people.

"was in Congress at the time, and that there was not a member of the body who had an idea of such a surrender. They thought of the best mode of securing that river, some thinking one way, some another. There was no desire to conceal any of the trans- actions on that important question. Let the gentleman write to the President of Congress for information. He will be gratified fully." He then reviewed the opinions of the States on the sub- ject of ratification. "The gentleman says Rhode Island and New Hampshire have refused to ratify. Is that a *fact?* It is *not* a fact. He says that New York and North Carolina will reject it. Here is another of his *facts*. As he dislikes *the veil of secrecy*, I beg that he would tell us the high authority from which he gets this fact. Have the executives of those States in- formed him? I believe not. I hold his unsupported authority in *contempt*." He thus closed his survey of the arguments of Henry: "I contend for myself and the friends of the Constitution that we are as great friends to liberty as he or any other person, and that we will not be behind him in exertions in its defence when it is invaded. For my part I trust, young as I am, I will be trusted in the support of freedom as far as the honorable gentleman. I feel that indignation and contempt with respect to his previous amendments which he expresses against posterior amendments. I can see no danger from a previous ratification. I see infinite dangers from previous amendments. I shall give my suffrage for the former, because I think the happiness of my country depends upon it. To maintain and secure that happiness, the first object of my wishes, I shall brave all storms and politi- cal dangers."[144]

---

[144] The bold and unsparing severity of Lee's speech was silently rel- ished by his friends, but its tone towards Henry cannot be justified. Now that Henry and Lee are dead and their whole lives are before us, it is worth knowing that Lee, in a year or two after the adoption of the Constitution, was elected Governor of Virginia. and that when a va- cancy occurred in the Senate of the United States which he was re- quested to fill, his first act was to make out a commission for Henry, which I have seen, and to despatch it by express to him in Prince Ed- ward. Their personal relations subsequently were most intimate and cordial. It is said that Lee, in aiding Henry to exchange his Dismal Swamp lands for some valuable Saura Town lands, greatly improved the fortunes of his friend. It is also worth noting that Henry made no reply to Lee.

We now come to the only severe personal quarrel to which the discussions of the Convention gave birth, which made a strong sensation at the time, and the details of which will be eagerly read by posterity. As soon as Lee took his seat, Edmund Randolph with evident emotion rose to reply to Henry. He began by saying that having consumed so much of the time of the committee, he did not intend to trouble it so soon; "but," he said, "I find myself attacked in the most illiberal manner by the honorable gentleman (Henry). I disdain his aspersions and his insinuations. His asperity is warranted by no principle of parliamentary decency, nor compatible with the least shadow of friendship. And if our friendship must fall, *let it fall like Lucifer, never to rise again.* Let him remember that it is not to answer him, but to satisfy this respectable audience, that I now get up. He has accused me of inconsistency in this very respectable assembly. Sir, if I do not stand on the bottom of integrity, and pure love for Virginia, as much as those who can be most clamorous, I wish to resign my existence. Consistency consists in actions, and not in empty specious words. Ever since the first entrance into that Federal business, I have been invariably governed by an invincible attachment to the happiness of the people of America. Federal measures had been before that time repudiated. The augmentation of Congressional powers was dreaded. The imbecility of the confederation was proved and acknowledged. When I had the honor of being deputed to the Federal Convention to revise the existing system, I was impressed with the necessity of a more energetic government, and thoroughly persuaded that the salvation of the people of America depended on an intimate and firm union. The honorable gentlemen there [145] can say that when I went thither, no man was a stronger friend to such an union than myself. I informed you why I refused to sign. I understand not him who wishes to give full scope to licentiousness and dissipation, and who would advise me to reject the proposed plan, and plunge us into anarchy."

(Here His Excellency read the conclusion of his public letter,[146]

---

[145] Meaning Mason, Wythe, Madison and John Blair, his colleagues in the general Federal Convention, and also members of the present Convention.

[146] Addressed to the Speaker of the House of Delegates.

wherein he says that notwithstanding his objections to the Constitution, he would adopt it rather than lose the Union), and proceeded to prove the consistency of his present opinion with his former conduct, when Henry rose and declared that he had no personal intention of offending anyone; that he did his duty, but that he did not mean to wound the feelings of any gentleman; that he was sorry if he offended the honorable gentleman without intending it; and that every gentleman had a right to maintain his opinion. Randolph then said that he was relieved by what the honorable gentleman had said; that were it not for the concession of that gentleman, he would have made some men's hair stand on end by the disclosure of certain facts. Henry then requested that if he had anything to say against him to disclose it. Randolph continued, that as there were some gentlemen there who might not be satisfied with the recantation of the honorable gentleman, without being informed, he should give them some information on the subject; that his ambition had ever been to promote the Union; that he was no more attached to it now than he ever had been; and that he could in some degree prove it by the paper which he held in his hand, which was a letter which he had written to his constituents. After some further explanation of his course, he threw down the letter on the clerk's table, and declared that it might lie there *for the inspection of the curious and the malicious.*

With those who look impartially at this passage of arms between these two eminent and accomplished statesmen, there cannot well be at this day but one opinion, and that opinion wholly adverse to the conduct of Randolph. In no respect had Henry overleaped the strictest rules of parliamentary decorum. He had exhibited what he regarded as inconsistency in the course of a public man, who had been charged by the Commonwealth with an important trust, and in the arguments which he had used on the subject of the adoption of the Constitution. There was not the slightest personal reflection or allusion in anything that he had said. And when Randolph recited his charge against Henry, it was mainly that he had accused him of inconsistency before that very respectable assembly. Now there is not in the whole armory of forensic warfare a more legitimate weapon than that which is used to demonstrate the inconsistency of the arguments of an opponent with each other, or with other arguments urged by him in different stages of the same case. This process is sometimes very unpleasant to the person whose character is at stake, and not a little annoying ; but the only honorable mode of defence is a proper exposition of the alleged inconsistency, and a similar retaliation on the offending party. Indignation, hard names, and downright insult have here no more place than in any other mode of logical refutation. Henry had also used the word "herd" in a different sense from that in which Randolph had used it, but upon an explanation of the meaning passed to another topic. He had also quoted the remark of Randolph that "he was a child of the Revolution," and had used it argumentatively ; but such a quotation was neither inappropriate nor indecorous. Indeed, the only shadow of unfairness, if in truth it be as palpable as a shadow, was the use of the word "herd" on a single occasion after the explanation of Randolph, and when Henry may be supposed to have used it in its ordinary meaning ; but if the use of this word afforded ground for animadversion, it was the least possible, and when regarded as a ground whereon to fasten a mortal quarrel upon an opponent, it was utterly contemptible. It is honorable to the temper of Henry that he did not interrupt Randolph in the harsh, unjust, and ungenerous remarks with which he began his speech ; and above all, it is honorable to his character that, in despite of such grievous provocation, he subsequently rose, disavowed in the strongest terms any personal allusion, and expressed his sorrow that he had unintentionally given offence to Randolph. He had thus made all the reparation which one gentleman can well receive from another. His course was in the highest degree magnanimous, and ought to have been in the highest degree satisfactory. Randolph, on the other hand, accepted the explanation of Henry, but in one and the same breath insulted Henry, not by showing any discrepancy in his arguments, not by attacking the inconsistencies of his public career, not by referring to any topic or incident that had occurred in any deliberative assembly of which Henry had been a member, but by uttering a threat to the effect that if the gentleman had not *recanted*—Henry having recanted nothing, having merely explained his original meaning—he would have made revelations which would not have merely affected him as a member of a public body, but would have blasted his reputation as a gentle-

man and as a man.   If anything could have enhanced this most
wanton, this most unparliamentary, and wholly unjustifiable
threat, it was the withholding from the instant demand of Henry
those charges which would involve his character in infamy, and
which he professed to be able to make, and which he would have
made but for the explanation.   Nor did Randolph cease to fling
insult upon Henry with what he had thus far done.   He gave a
new, uncalled for, and most aggravated insult to Henry when,
throwing down his own public letter on the table of the clerk, he
declared that it should lie there *for the inspection of the curious
and the malicious.*   This taunting and somewhat theatrical
remark could apply only to Henry, who now saw that the dispute had passed beyond the walls of the House.   He saw that
he was involved in an unpleasant predicament ; but he felt that
he had been placed there by no fault of his own.   His entire life
had been free from personal quarrels.   He was declining in the
vale of life.   He had passed his fifty-second year, had a young
and dependent family, and was poor.   Randolph was in the vigor
of manhood, not having reached his thirty-seventh year, and had
also a young family ; and, if not poor, his life, even in a pecuniary view, was of the last importance to his family.   A hostile
meeting between two such men, whose lives were wrapped up in
so many endearing domestic ties, whose distinguished talents,
as they were the common property, so they were the pride of
their country, and who had lived up to that time in the relations
of friendship, would have appalled the public mind ; and accordingly when on Tuesday morning it was known that Col. William
Cabell had the evening before, as the friend of Henry, waited
on Randolph ; that the unpleasant affair had been settled without a resort to the field, and that a reconciliation between the
parties had been effected,[147] both the great divisions in the House
were sensibly relieved.

---

[147] The most direct personal charge of inconsistency that I have ever
seen in a public body was that made in the Convention of 1829-30 by
Colonel John B. George, of Tazewell, against General William F. Gordon, of Albemarle.   Colonel George rose directly from his seat to
make the charge, made it in as few and as forcible words as he could
utter, and instantly sate down.   General Gordon, who saw at once
what the occasion required, defended his course with eminent grace
and skill, and gained eclät by the affair.   When John Randolph, in the

When the personal altercation was past, Randolph, as if relieved from a weight that hung heavily upon him, spoke with great freedom in defence of the Constitution, analyzed in detail the objections of Henry, and made one of the longest, most learned, and, at the same time, one of the most brilliant speeches of his life.[148]

He was followed by a member in the opposition, who had not yet engaged in the discussion, who was as yet a very young man, almost wholly unknown to many of the leading members of the House ; who had none of those outward advantages which stand in the stead of a letter of introduction ; but whose name, indissolubly connected with the great events of the first third of a century of that government, the adoption of which he now rose to resist, is destined to survive the names of some whose fair reputations were then in full leaf, and to become a household word to succeeding generations.   It was not in the roll of a re-mote ancestry, or in the splendor of patrimonial wealth, or even in the fostering care of those who enjoyed such advantages, that the youthful speaker looked for his titles to success in the world, and to the approbation of his country.   So far from hav-

---

same body, marshalled what he deemed the inconsistencies of Chapman Johnson in thick array against him, that great and good man took the first opportunity of replying ; but no friend of Johnson dreamed that the affair ought to have been transferred elsewhere.

[148] In a note on the preceding page I alluded to the subsequent connections of Lee and Henry. Those between Randolph and Henry were not so intimate. Randolph became the first Attorney-General under the new plan, and succeeded Mr. Jefferson as Secretary of State in the Cabinet of Washington. Henry went into opposition, as, indeed, in a certain sense, was Randolph himself. Both were eager to obtain amendments, and were equally disappointed in their efforts. Randolph soon withdrew from the State department under the most painful circumstances, and went into full opposition. Henry, who had warmly opposed the British Treaty, became alarmed at what he deemed the rash measures of his old opponents in the Convention, who had assumed the name of republicans, and rallied in support of the administration of Washington. And it happened singularly enough that when Randolph withdrew from the Cabinet, Henry was invited to take his seat. These topics will be discussed more at length when I come to treat of the general course of Henry and Randolph, as well as the nature of the charges which Randolph threatened to throw at the head of Henry.

ing been born in that elevated position in which he now stood—
side by side with the most illustrious men to whom the State had
given birth—he was the son of a Scotchman, or of Scotch descent,
a carpenter, wno had settled in Westmoreland, and who was enabled by his industry to gratify an honorable passion of the
Scotch by affording to his son all the advantages of education
within his reach.   And in this praiseworthy purpose he was
aided to the fullest extent by his son.

From the first, whether in the old-field school-house, in the
camp, in the college, which in his case instead of preceding succeeded the camp, or in the council, or when, as it sometimes,
though rarely, happened, he was in neither the one nor the
other, James Monroe never lost an advantage. He had attended
a country school with John Marshall, in company with whom
he was to travel, in war and in peace, the trail of a long and
honored career, and had spent a term in William and Mary ;
but his elementary stock of knowledge was exceedingly small,
and his real education was on the stage of busy life.   In his
eighteenth year he entered the army as a cadet, became in due
time a lieutenant and captain, and alternately an aid to a general
officer.   From the beginning of the war to nearly its close he
was in active service, and he numbered among the battles in
which he was engaged those of Harlem Heights and White
Plains, of Princeton and Trenton, in which last he was wounded
in the shoulder, of Brandywine, Germantown and Monmouth.
As a military commissioner of Virginia he visited the Southern
army under De Kalb, and in 1782 he was returned from King
George to the House of Delegates.   At the age of twenty-four
he was deputed to Congress, having been the youngest member
which the Assembly had ever elected to that body, in which, as
in the House of Delegates, and in many other high appointments,
in the course of a long life, he had been preceded by Madison.
He plunged at once into affairs, and displayed that firm purpose,
that moral hardihood, which, attributed by Sydney Smith to
Lord John Russell, would lead the English statesman, though
ignorant of seamanship, to take command of the Channel fleet,
which is one of the greatest qualities of a public man, and which
even impelled Monroe to meet rather than avoid difficult topics,
and to push them to a practical conclusion ; and which, we may
add, is more nearly allied to wisdom than to folly, inasmuch as

in the affairs of a nation the prompt settlement of a disputed
question, however dangerous to the propects of the individual,
is not unfrequently of far greater importance to the general welfare than the particular mode by which that settlement was
effected.   He was now thirty; he was tall and erect in person;
his face with its high cheek bones betokening his Caledonian
descent, and not uncomely; his manners kind and affectionate,
which had not yet lost their martial stiffness, and which, even in
the midst of courts and cabinets, at home and abroad, never
attained the easy freedom of a well-bred man.   His demeanor
was marked by a gravity, another trait of his Scotch extraction,
which is not uncommon with those on whom the heavy responsibilities of life are early cast, and which concealed from the common observer a warm and generous heart.   These qualities were
not more perceptible to the public than his intense application
to business, the entire concentration of all his faculties to the
case in hand, his sincerity of purpose, his truthfulness, his utter
want of those accomplishments which amuse, instruct and adorn
the social sphere, and perhaps his incapacity of appreciating
them in another, his slowness in comprehending a subject,
equalled only by the soundness of the conclusions which he ultimately reached,[149] his faculties invigorated by the exercise to
which they had been subjected, but neither very large nor very
bright, nor highly cultivated by art, nor much enriched by learning drawn from books, yet vigorous and eminently practical,
were recognized by those who knew him well.   Yet, in this
unfriended, not half-educated, unpolished youth the elements of
political success were mingled in an amazing degree.   Inferior
to Randolph in genius, in eloquence, in literature, and in that
social position which made the wealth, the talents, and the influence of a vast family connection ancillary to his views; to Madison in the early culture of the faculties under the most favorable
auspices, in acquirements, and in universality of intellectual
power; to Henry Lee in the extent and caste of domestic relationship, in early and thorough instruction in military talents as
well as in martial fame, and in a ready and striking elocution;
to Marshall in unbounded vigor of mind as well as in the knowl-

---

[149] Patrick Henry always thought well of Monroe, and used to say of
him " that he was slow, but give him time and he was sure."

edge of the law to which they had served an apprenticeship together, as they had done in the Northern army ; to Innes, another colleague in the Northern army, in classical literature, in general learning, and, above all, in a splendid eloquence ; to Grayson, another compatriot of the Northern army, in fascinating manners, in humor, in wit, in a perfect mastery of the science of political economy, in an almost unrivalled play of the intellectual powers, and in that exquisite taste in letters, which imparts even to consummate statesmanship an attractive and ever living grace ; to George Nicholas in those subtle faculties and in that profound acquaintance with the law which enabled him to pass instantly from an opinion on a land warrant shingled three deep to the discussion of the most intricate questions in government and in the laws of nations ; to Corbin in habits of public speaking, in political research, and in elegant learning ; to Ralph Wormeley in a critical knowledge of the entire compass of English literature as in that honorable lineage which as early as King Charles' time held the keys of the public treasure ; [150] inferior to these, and not to these only of that galaxy of genius and worth which then appeared on the Virginia horizon, and which our later statesmen, themselves now passed away, were wont to point at and to dwell upon with conscious pride, this remarkable young man succeeded in winning and wearing at his pleasure every honor which public office at home or abroad could bestow, from

---

[150] The Wormeley family can be traced to 1312, when they were seated in Yorkshire, England. The first in Virginia was Captain Christopher Wormeley, Governor of Tortuga in 1632-5 ; was granted 1.420 acres of land in Charles River (York) county January 27, 1638 ; member of the Council ; married, and had issue : Captain Ralph Wormeley of York county, member of the Council in 1640 ; patented land, and settled at "Rosegill," Middlesex county ; died before 1669, leaving issue : Ralph. His widow Agatha married secondly Sir Henry Chicheley, Governor of Virginia. Ralph Wormeley, second of the name, died 1700, leaving issue : John Wormeley, of "Rosegill," and Judith, married Colonel Mann Page, of "Rosewell." Of the issue of John was Ralph Wormeley, of "Rosegill," married, 1736, Sarah Berkeley of "Barn Elms"; Burgess for Middlesex county 1748-1758 ; member of the Council 1756-1761. Of their issue was Ralph Wormeley, Jr., of the text, a scholar who possessed one of the choicest libraries in Virginia ; married Eleanor Tayloe, sister of Colonel John Tayloe, of "Mount Airy" ; died January 19, 1806, in the 62nd year of his age.—ED.

that of Governor of the Commonwealth and Senator of the United States, from repeated missions to the most distinguished courts of Europe, from a seat in the Department of War and in the Department of State, to that most exalted of all the honors to which an American citizen can aspire, the Presidency itself; while of his early compatriots, as well as those who had already reached a high position as those who, like himself, were pluming their wings for the new scene soon to open upon them, some dropped almost immediately out of sight, or, enamoured of rural life, clung to the domestic hearth and declined public trusts, or devoted their time to State affairs, or were lost in the haze of a local celebrity, or soared for a time only in the fresh azure of a Federal sky, upborne on untiring wings, or voluntarily to descend after a season to the perch from which they had risen, or, stricken by the hostile arrow, to be precipitated with a disastrous fall, and others who were content to accept from his hands those offices which they not only did not aspire to bestow, but were thankful to receive; three only of that entire number running continuously with him the long race of fifty years with equal though various distinction; and of those three one only attaining to the first office of the nation.[151]

The secret of this unparalleled success is difficult to find only because it lies on the surface. Industry, integrity, personal intrepidity, whether it was to be exhibited amid the clashing of swords or the more fearful clashing of tongues, a satisfaction with small things, which kept him within the range of affairs till great things were ready, one by one, to fall into his lap, so that, though sometimes not in office, he may be said, in a certain sense, never to have been out of office—the great office of his life, strong common sense, which, though more than once begrimed by the fallacies and passion of interested partisans, enabled him at last to see things as they were, and to recover himself ere it was too late, and a firmness of purpose and a constancy of pursuit which kept the great object of his ambition steadily before his eyes. These were the means on which he relied, and in which he was not deceived. Nor was his career unmarked by fluctuations which even at this distance of time appear formidable. His recall from the French mission by Washington, was one of those

---

[151] Bushrod Washington, John Marshall, and James Madison.

ominous incidents in his history which would have proved fatal
to the ambition of a less-determined spirit than his own.   And
at a later day, when, on his return from the court of St. James,
he found himself almost unconsciously at the head of a small but
influential faction which had stolen off rather than broke off from
the great party to which he had devoted his life, and which sought
to put him forward for the succession.   In ordinary times no eye
would have detected sooner than his own the specious snare
which was spread for his destruction; but his long absence from
home, which had precluded him from a correct knowledge of
affairs, the noise made by his advocates in public bodies, and
especially in the social circles of Virginia, which he now made
his residence, and some private griefs which, if they had been
left alone, would have soon healed without a scar, but which, by
the chirurgery of his new allies, were made to inflame and fester,
obscured for a season his better judgment, and he lent for a while
a not unwilling ear to the tempter.   From the predicament, the
most dangerous in his whole career, in which he was now placed,
and which was regarded with unfeigned delight by his old enemies and with mortification by his old friends, he was rescued by
one of those trivial incidents which are usually thought beneath
the dignity of history, but which sometimes explain results otherwise beyond the keenest vision.   But even here, in this fortunate
reconciliation with his late and successful rival in the game of
presidential honors, it was the distinctive peculiarity of his character and the honesty of his nature which effected his deliverance.[152]

Our view of the character of Monroe would be incomplete, so
far as our present theme is concerned, if it did not embrace his
qualities as a public speaker.   He had acquired the habit of debate in the House of Delegates and in the Congress of the Confederation, but he had never studied the art of speech.   Pronunciation, emphasis, gesture, in their full significancy, never crossed
his mind as things deserving a moment's consideration ; and, as
he did not value them himself, so he set a very slight value upon
them in the speaking of others.   Like a workman who, in
choosing from the forest a shaft for his present purpose, heeds

[152] I do not feel altogether at liberty to state the circumst nces which
led to the reconciliation between Mr. Madison and Colonel Monroe,
but it will be known in due time.

not the elevation and grandeur of the tree which he is about to fell, or the magnificent sweep of those branches which have wrestled with the tempests of ages, or in the shadow of which, ere the foot of the Anglo-Saxon had touched the shores of the New World, the Indian hero had wooed his dusky mate, or the tremulous glory of its leaf, he disregarded that splendid illustration which invests the speeches of an Everett with the dignity of an epic, and looked to the staple of a speech as the only object that could justify a rational creature in expending his own breath and the time of other people. Hence there is hardly a perceptible change, certainly no improvement, in his oratorical powers from the beginning to the end of his parliamentary course. As he spoke now, so he spoke forty years later, when, in the midst of an august assembly whose passions were roused by a prolonged discussion of the most exciting topics, he most unexpectedly rose to present his views of the subject under debate. Now, as then, his manner, if indeed he may be said to have had any manner at all, was to the last degree awkward, warring at once with the common laws of motion and the established rules of pronunciation ; while in both instances his matter was sterling, his purposes were manifestly sincere, and his aims were those of a statesman who had reflected profoundly upon his theme. What seemed at the first view to be a defect, really contributed no little to his success in public bodies. The temper of mind which made him overlook the mere drapery of rhetoric rendered him ever ready to take the floor. He had no idea of the *mollia tempora fandi*. He could not conceive why a man who had anything to say could not say it at one time as well as another. The same temper rendered him invulnerable to the gibes of wit and to the sword of sarcasm ; and, free from nervous palpitations, and unhurt in the wildest storm of party missiles, he was an invaluable leader in times of trouble.

It is not an unworthy office to hold up the example of Monroe for the imitation of the young, and especially of the friendless young, who are entering on the public stage. It is a beacon, the light of which may not necessarily, in the shifting changes of the world, conduct to ultimate triumph in politics, but will lead to personal improvement, certainly to distinction, and as certainly to the esteem and love of mankind. And even this view of the subject appears low when we look abroad and embrace within the scope of our vision those grand arrangements of Providence which control the operation of human affairs, which so frequently confound the schemes of a vain imagination and even of brilliant genius, and which stamp the moral virtues with a far deeper impress of approval than those more alluring and more dazzling qualities which men are so eager to cultivate and rely upon as the foundation of success in the business of life.

We have said that the training of Monroe was effected mainly by his commerce with the world; and to him the scene now shifting its many-colored hues around him was the best of schools. Before he entered the Convention he had studied the new plan carefully, aided by the lights which, from both sides, had been cast upon it ; and during the present discussion he had listened attentively, making notes of the arguments and referring to the cited authorities ; and his speech is a wonderful proof of the success with which he prosecuted his labors.   Viewed apart from the discussions of the period, both in and out of the House, both on the rostrum and from the press, it evinces not only a thorough acquaintance with the instrument itself, perfect logical consistency, and no little familiarity with the more abstruse illustrations drawn from ancient and modern history, with which it was sustained or opposed, but such a comprehensive grasp of his subject as to lead to the conviction that he had demonstrated the true cause of the existing troubles of the country, that he was ready to apply an immediate, safe, and effective remedy.   His introduction was modest and appropriate : "I cannot avoid expressing," he said, "the great anxiety which I feel upon the present occasion—an anxiety that proceeds not only from a high sense of the importance of the subject, but from a profound respect for this august and venerable assembly.   When we contemplate the fate that has befallen other nations, whether we cast our eyes back into the remotest ages of antiquity, or derive instruction from those examples which modern times have presented to our view, and observe how prone all human institutions have been to decay ; how subject the best formed and wisely organized governments have been to lose their checks and totally dissolve ; how difficult it has been for mankind, in all ages and countries, to preserve their dearest rights and best privileges, impelled, as it were, by an irresistible fate to despotism ; if we look forward to those prospects that sooner or later await our country, unless we shall be exempted from the fate of other nations, even to a mind the most sanguine and benevolent, some gloomy apprehensions must necessarily crowd upon it. This consideration is sufficient to teach us the limited capacity of the human mind—how subject the wisest men have been to error. For my own part, sir, I come forward here, not as the partisan of this or that side of the question, but to commend where the subject appears to me to deserve commendation, to suggest my doubts where I have any, to hear with candor the explication of others, and, in the ultimate result, to act as shall appear for the best advantage of our common country.''

He called attention to the spectacle of a people about to frame a new plan of government as in striking contrast with the history of Europe for the last twelve centuries ; pointed out the distinctive elements of our colonial settlement, and the change effected by the Revolution, which put the government into the hands of one class only—not of nobles and freemen as in other systems, but of freemen only ; that the success of the American polity could only be sustained by the union of the States, and that this union was dearly cherished by all the States except Rhode Island,[153] and that the question now was on what principles the union should be constructed. With a view of reaching a correct result, he reviewed the Federal alliances of ancient and modern times, and especially the construction of the Amphyctionic Council, and showed the causes of its downfall ; he next adverted to the Achaian league, and pointed out its closer analogy with the Articles of Confederation, arguing with seeming force from that resemblance that our Confederation was not as weak as was contended by the friends of the new plan, and seeking to sustain his argument by quotations from Polybius, which he read to the House. He successively reviewed in detail the constitution of the Germanic body, of the Swiss Cantons, of the United Netherlands, and of the New England Confederacy, and inferred that as the destruction or inadequacy of the foreign federal associations arose from a dissimilarity of structure in the individual members, the facility of foreign interference, and the recurrence

---

[153] The conduct of Rhode Island during the Revolution and subsequently, met with no quarter from either side of the House throughout the debates.

to foreign aid, which were not applicable to us, there was no propriety in rejecting a federal system and in accepting a consolidated government in its stead. This view was enforced at great
length, and with an intimate knowledge of the circumstances of
the country. He then discussed the question, " What are the
powers which the Federal Government ought to possess?"
arguing from various considerations that the entire control of
commerce ought to be given to the new plan, and that the power
of direct taxation, from its inexpediency, from the impracticability
of its use, and from its peculiarity, should be withheld from it,
demonstrated that the present pressure on the Confederation was
from obvious causes not likely to occur again, but temporary,
and would soon pass away ; and that the means of relief, in addition to the control of commerce and the imposts which at five
per cent. it was estimated would exceed a million of dollars,
would be found in the sale of public lands which were rapidly
settling, in loans, which would be readily negotiated at a low
rate under the auspices of a large and certain revenue, and in
the last resort to requisitions upon the States. These topics
were argued deliberately and with great tact. He then proceeded to analyze the new scheme of government, and concluded
that it was dangerous ; that a bill of rights was necessary; that
the doctrine that all powers not ceded were retained might prove
utterly delusive, as by an evasion the Congress, under the clause
which gives power to pass all laws necessary for carrying the
plan into effect, might pass what laws they pleased, and might
destroy trial by jury, and the liberty of the press, and other
precious rights. He considered the alleged probability of harmony between the General Government and the States, concluding that, as history did not afford a single instance of the concurrent exercise of powers by two parties without producing a
struggle between them, such would certainly be the case with us.
He then objected to the construction of the executive department as violating the correct idea of a legislative power, and of
other parts of the new plan, ending in these words, " upon reviewing this government, I must say, under my present impression,
I think it a dangerous government and calculated to secure
neither the interests nor the rights of our countrymen. Under
such an one I shall be averse to embark the best hopes and
prospects of a free people. We have struggled long to bring

about this Revolution by which we enjoy our present freedom and security. Why then this haste, this wild precipitation?''

Monroe was immediately succeeded on the floor by a tall young man, slovenly dressed in loose summer apparel, with piercing black eyes, that would lead the observer to believe that their possessor was more destined to toy with the Muses than to worship at the sterner shrine of Themis, his senior by three years ; who had been his colleague in the old-field school, in the army of the North through a long and perilous war, in the college, and at the bar; who, as on the present occasion, differed with him in opinion, as on all others, during their continuous race of half a century, and who was destined, like him, to fill the mission to France when one of the greatest political maelstroms of modern times was in full whirl, and to preside in the Department of War and in the Department of State under the Federal Constitution. But when one of them withdrew from the House of Representatives and the other from the Senate of the United States, their paths diverged, the elder devoting himself entirely to politics, the younger to law, each with such success that the pen which traces the history of James Monroe as the head of the Federal Executive, will record on the same page the history of John Marshall as the head of the Federal Judiciary. Marshall was in his thirty-third year, and from the close of the war to the meeting of the Convention, had applied himself, with the exception of an occasional session in the House of Delegates, to the practice of the law. His manners, like those of Monroe, were in strange contrast with those of Edmund Randolph or of Grayson, and had been formed in the tutelage of the camp, without, however, a tinge of that martinet address which derides the rule of Hogarth, and consists in making a stiff vertebral column the line of beauty and of grace ; his habits were convivial almost to excess ; and he regarded as matters beneath his notice those appliances of dress and demeanor which are commonly considered not unimportant to advancement in a public profession. Nor should those personal qualities which cement friendships and gain the affections of men, and which he possessed in an eminent degree, be passed over in a likeness of this young man—qualities as prominently marked in the decline of his honored life, when his robe had for a third of a century been fringed with ermine, as when, in the heyday of youth, dressed in a light roundabout, he won his way to every heart.   Nor, as it is our duty as well as our plea- sure to dwell on the domestic relations of our subjects, should we fail to say that he had married, some years before, a charming woman, whose loveliness was the least of her perfections ; who was the guardian angel of his earlier years, beckoning him from the snares which thickly beset his amiable temper and social pro- pensities ; who was the delight of his long life ; whom, when laid for years upon that bed from which she was never to rise, he tended with the watchfulness of early love ; and whom, when taken from him after an union of near half a century, he commemorated, on the first anniversary of her death, in a tri- bute which never saw the light till he was no more, written with such exquisite pathos as to touch the sternest heart, and which, in a mere literary point of view, excels the productions, not only of his own pen, but the pen of almost all his illustrious contem- poraries.[154]

His speech now delivered has the peculiar marks which were visible in his subsequent speeches in the House of Delegates, and especially in that most celebrated of all his speeches—the speech delivered in the case of Jonathan Robbins in the House of Representatives, of which Gallatin, when pressed by a leading politician to answer it, said in his then broken English : " An- swer it yourself ; for my part I think it unanswerable."   It will afford in after times a worthy theme to those who are curious in watching the development of a great mind in the several stages of its progress.   Nothing could be more directly to the point than its exordium.   " I conceive," he said " that the object of the discussion now before us is whether democracy or despotism be most eligible.   I am sure that those who framed the system submitted to our investigation, and those who now support it, intend the establishment and security of the former.   The sup-

---

[154] The maiden name of Mrs. Marshall was Mary Ambler, who was married to the Judge on the 3d of January, 1783, and died on the 25th day of December, 1831.   The paper alluded to was written on the 25th of December, 1832, and may be found in Bishop Meade's "Old Churches," Etc., II, 222.   The letter of Mr. Jefferson to John Adams is another specimen of tender affection, and shows, in connection with the paper in question, that long and almost exclusive attention to pub- lic affairs does not always deaden the kindlier feelings of the heart.

porters of the Constitution claim the title of being firm friends of liberty and of the rights of mankind. They say that they consider it as the best means of protecting liberty. We, sir, idolize democracy. Those who oppose it have bestowed eulo- giums on monarchy. We prefer this system to any monarchy, because we are convinced that it has a greater tendency to se- cure our liberty and promote our happiness. We admire it, because we think it a well-regulated democracy. It is recom- mended to the good people of this country; they are, through us, to declare whether it be such a plan of government as will establish and secure their freedom. Permit me to attend to what the honorable gentleman (Henry) has said. He has expatiated on the necessity of a due attention to certain maxims, to certain fundamental principles from which a free people ought never to depart. I concur with him in the propriety of the observance of such maxims. They are necessary in any government, but more essential to a democracy than to any other. What are the favorite maxims of democracy? A strict observance of justice and public faith, and a steady adherence to virtue. These, sir, are the principles of a good government. No mischief—no mis- fortune ought to deter us from a strict observance of justice and public faith. Would to heaven that these principles had been observed under the present government! Had this been the case, the friends of liberty would not be so willing now to part with it. Can we boast that our government is founded on these maxims? Can we pretend to the enjoyment of political freedom or security, when we are told that a man has been, by an Act of Assembly, struck out of existence without a trial by jury, without examination, without being affronted by his accusers and witnesses, without the benefits of the law of the land? Where is our safety, when we are told that this act was justifi- able, because the person was not a Socrates?[155]   What has be- come of the worthy member's maxims? Is this one of them?

---

[155] Nothing shows more plainly the desire of the friends of the Con- stitution to undermine the influence of Henry than the repetition of this charge, which is not only false in every respect, but which, if true, would only prove mal-administration in the State government, which the new plan, if adopted, could neither punish nor prevent a repetition of. The belief at the time was, though wholly wrong, that Henry, as Governor, had recommended the measure.

Shall it be a maxim that a man shall be deprived of his life without the benefit of law? Shall such a deprecation of life be justified by answering that the man's life was not taken *secundum artem*, because he was a bad man? Shall it be a maxim that government ought not to be empowered to protect virtue?''

His purpose was to follow in the track of Henry; and proceeded to controvert the views of that gentleman on the Mississippi question; on the relative expediency of previous and subsequent amendments, and on the propriety of vesting the power of direct taxation in Congress, which he discussed at considerable length. He agreed with Henry that a government should rest on the affections of the people, and that the Constitution, founded upon their authority, and resting upon them, deserved and would receive their cordial support; showed that the argument derived from the union of the purse and the sword in the same hands would apply to every government as well as the one under consideration; that the objection urged against the Constitution from the construction of the British government, which requires war to be declared by the executive and the resources for carrying it on to be provided by Parliament, was inapplicable, and that in fact the new plan gave a far greater and more reliable security to the people; and closed with an able and critical comparison of the British Constitution with the plan under discussion, which last, he contended, was superior in every respect to the British, and peculiarly adapted to the wants and to the genius of the people of America.

When we look to the subsequent career of Monroe and Marshall, their speeches delivered successively in the same debate have an interest which might not attach to them in an abstract view. The speech of Marshall is direct and conclusive, never departing a hair's breadth from the line of his argument. The objection which he wishes to overcome is stated fairly and fully, and he proceeds forthwith to remove it, using when possible the concessions of his antagonist for his purposes, and sometimes with such effect that an honest antagonist, confiding in his own maxims, feels inclined to accept the hostile commentary in place of his own. But his speech on this occasion, though in passing judgment the circumstances of its delivery must be kept in view, is plainly rather that of a lawyer than a statesman. He demonstrates with apparent conclusiveness the propriety of adopting the Constitution, but he seeks to effect his object not so much by arguments derived from the state of affairs, or from an examination of the different Federal systems analogous to our own, or from a statesmanlike survey of the instrument itself, but mainly from the weakness of the arguments urged against it by its opponents, a mode of argumentation as applicable to the defence of the worst as well as the wisest political system.

In drawing the auguries of subsequent success from these speeches of the young debaters, while it is evident that each, as an intellectual effort, exhibited abilities likely to attain distinction in any sphere of public employment, the speech of Marshall indicates those qualities which become rather the bar and the bench than the Senate and the cabinet, while the opposite conclusion would probably be drawn from the speech of Monroe. It will be observed that these speeches, although following consecutively in the same debate, have no relation to each other, each speaker having arranged his line of argument before he entered the House.

Those who have come upon the stage since this illustrious man has descended to his grave, have a right to inquire into his habits of public speaking. Of his intellectual powers, the speeches, few indeed, but signally representative, which he has left behind him,[156] his celebrated letter to Adet, and his diplomatic correspondence, his arguments in the Virginia reported cases, and above all, his judicial opinions, which from the first abounding in strength, became more elaborate and more elegant as he advanced in life, afford imperishable materials for the formation of a critical judgment. But not only have his equals and rivals, who heard his finest speeches at the bar and in public assemblies, passed away with him, but nearly all of that brilliant second growth of eminent men who took their places at the bar, and on whose ears the echoes of his speeches were almost as distinct as the original sounds which gave them birth, now rest beneath the sod. There is not more than one man living in Virginia, himself distinguished, who heard his speeches in the House of Delegates during Washington's administration, nor, perhaps,

---

[156] I regret to say that with the exception of his speech in the present Convention, in the case of Jonathan Robbins, and those in the Convention of 1829–30, I fear all are lost; but even in this respect he is more fortunate than most of his compeers.

with the exception of an eminent citizen of Massachusetts, who, in extreme old age but with unimpaired faculties, appeared to honor a literary festival recently held in his native State,[157] who heard the speech of Marshall in the case of Jonathan Robbins. Yet, we are rejoiced to say that so prolonged was his life, so prominent was his position as the head of the Federal Judiciary and the presiding judge of his circuit for the first third of the present century, so accessible by the young as well as the old, by the poor as well as the rich, by the fair sex as well as the manlier, the former of which he treated with a true and a high chivalrous courtesy, which Bayard could not have surpassed—a courtesy the more sincere, as it was but the reflection of his own guileless bosom—that there are hundreds yet living who can recall with delight the modest and the deep thoughtful lines of his benignant face, those piercing black eyes which never let the image of a friend any more than the semblance of an argument escape his vision, and his lofty figure clothed in the plainest dress of an ordinary citizen, and mingling constantly and kindly with his fellow-men in the street, in the market, on the quoit-ground, or reverently bent in the humblest posture at the Throne of Grace.   But, intimate as was his knowledge of the human heart, gathered from a long experience in the camp and at the bar, those fruitful schools of human nature, it was not by appeals to the interests and to the passions of men that he sought to lay the stress of his public efforts.   Indeed, so utterly did he disregard all such appeals, that he launched in the opposite extreme, and as if conscious of the true sources of his power, he avoided everything that might influence the mind through the eye.   Indeed, like his friend Monroe, he had no manner at all as a public speaker, if by manner we mean something deliberate and studied in action; and he might be as readily expected to speak in a court-room with his hands on a chair, or with one of his legs over its back, or within two feet of a presiding officer in a public body, as in any other way.   We have heard in early life from those who knew him at the bar, that his manner did not differ

---

[157] The Hon. Josiah Quincey, who said in his speech on the occasion alluded to that he was the only living member of Congress of the last century. Governor Tazewell entered the House of Representatives in 1800 to fill Judge Marshall's unexpired term.

essentially from what it was when, forty years later than our present period, in the Convention of 1829–30, at several important conjunctures, under a sense of deep responsibility, and pressed by powerful opponents, he engaged in discussion. In the common parts of his discourse he spoke with a serious earnestness and with an occasional swing of his right arm, but when he became animated, as we once beheld him, by the delivery of his theme, which was the true import of certain words of the Federal Constitution relating to the Judiciary, and by the presence of several of the most astute men of that age who were opposed to him in debate, and who were watching him to his destruction, he rose to the highest pitch of pathetic declamation thoroughly blended with argument, the most powerful of all declamation ; and he might have been seen leaning forward with both arms outstretched towards the chair, as if in the act of calling down vengeance on his opponents, or of deprecating some enormous evil which was about to befall his country; while the tones of his voice, exalted above his usual habit, were in plaintive unison with his action. The report of this remarkable debate may be found elsewhere.[158] The triumph of Marshall's eloquence was heightened by the almost unequalled talents which were arrayed against him—by the subtle and terrible strength of Tazewell, by the severe and sustained logic of Barbour, by the versatile and brilliant but vigorous sallies of Randolph, whose fame as the chairman of the Judiciary committee of 1802, which reported the bill of repeal of the law passed by the Federalists altering the judiciary system to the House of Representatives, was at stake, and by the extraordinary skill and blasting sarcasm of Giles, heightened and stimulated by the recollections of ancient feuds which still burned brightly in the breast of his antagonist and in his own, and from a sense of personal reputation which was involved in the passage of the act of repeal in the House of Representatives, which he mainly carried through that body. Of all the scenes which occurred in the Convention of 1829–30, varied, animated, and intellectual as they were, whether we respect the exciting nature of the topic in debate, the zeal, the abilities, the public services, the venerable

---

[158] In the Debates of the Virginia Convention of 1829-30.

age, and the historical reputation of those who engaged in the
discussion—all enhanced in interest by the unequal division of
the combatants in the field, this was, perhaps, the most striking
which occurred in that body.   And we feel the solemnity of this
scene the more, when we recall the fact that in less than five
years from the date of this eloquent exhibition of their faculties,
every member who participated in the discussion, with the exception of one who is yet living, was consigned to the grave.

Now on such an occasion, opposed as we were to his views,
and familiar with the topic as we then were—a topic which had
been so thoroughly discussed in Congress as to be incapable of
novelty—we could but accord the palm of eloquence to Marshall ; and as that eloquence did not consist in the strength of
his argument— for we thought his opponents had the better of the
argument, or at least the right side of the question—it was the
triumph of his action, at once unexpected to his audience,
unpremeditated by himself, and affording an unequivocal proof
of what he was capable of accomplishing on a proper occasion
and in the prime of his powers.

As soon as Marshall had resumed his seat, and while the
members were exchanging opinions respecting the relative merits
of the two young men who had just appeared for the first time
on the floor, there arose a large and venerable old man, elegantly
arrayed in a rich suit of blue and buff, a long queue tied with
a black ribbon dangling from his full locks of snow, and his long,
black boots encroaching on his knees, who proceeded, evidently
under high excitement, to address the House. He had been
so long a member of the public councils that even Wythe and
Pendleton could not easily recall the time when he had not been
a member of the House of Burgesses.   His ancestors had landed
in the Colony before the first House of Burgesses had assembled
in the church on the banks of the James, and had invoked in
the presence of Governor Yeardley the blessing of heaven on
the great enterprise of founding an Anglo-Saxon colony on the
continent of America.   One of his ancestors had been governor
of Somer's Islands, when those islands were a part of Virginia.
Others had been members and presidents of the Council of Virginia from the beginning of the seventeenth century to that
memorable day in August, 1774, when the first Virginia Conven-

tion met in Williamsburg, and appointed the first delegation to the American Congress.[159] Of that delegation, whose names are familiar to our school-boys, and will be more familiar to the youth of future generations, this venerable man had been a member, had hastened to Philadelphia, and had declared to John Adams that, if there had been no other means of reaching the city, he would have taken up his bed and walked. But this was not his first engagement in the public service. Educated at William and Mary, when that institution was under the guardianship of Commissary Blair, he entered at an early age the House of Burgesses, and in the session of 1764 was a member of the committee which drafted the memorials to the king, the lords, and the commons of Great Britain against the passage of the Stamp Act. During the following session of the House of Burgesses, in 1765, he opposed the resolutions of Henry, not from any want of a cordial appreciation of the doctrines asserted by them, but on the ground that the House had not received an answer to the memorials which he had assisted in drawing the year before, which were daily expected to arrive. In the patriotic associations of those times his name was always among the first on the roll. He was a member of all the Conventions until the inauguration of the Commonwealth, and in the first House of Delegates gave a hearty co-operation in accommodating the ancient polity of the Colony to the requisitions of a republican system. But his most arduous services were rendered in the Congress, and as a representative of Virginia in that body he signed the Declaration of American Independence. While in Congress he had presided on the most important committees, especially on those relating to military affairs, and on the Committee of the Whole during the animated discussions on the formation of the Articles of Confederation, and had been repeatedly deputed by Congress on various missions at critical periods to the army and to the States. On his return home he had been regularly a member of the House of Delegates, of which he was almost invariably the Speaker while he had a seat in the Assembly. He was in the

---

[159] That delegation consisted of Peyton Randolph, George Washington, Benjamin Harrison, Edmund Pendleton, Patrick Henry, and Richard Bland.

chair of the House when, in 1777, the bill attainting Philips had
been passed, and he knew that the bill had been drawn by Jefferson, his old colleague in the House of Burgesses, in the Conventions, and in Congress, in whose judgment and patriotism he had
unlimited confidence.   He remembered what a dark cloud was
resting upon his country when the miscreant Philips with his
band was plundering and murdering the wives and daughters of
the patriotic citizens of Norfolk and Princess Anne, who were
engaged elsewhere in defending the Commonwealth, attacking
them in the dead of night, burning their habitations, perpetrating
the vilest outrages, and then retreating at daybreak into the
recesses of the swamp; and that all the Assembly had done
under such provocation was to provide that, if the wretch did
not appear within a certain time and be tried by the laws of the
Commonwealth for the crimes with which he was charged, he
should be deemed an outlaw; and he felt indignant that such a
patriotic measure, designed to protect the lives and property of
the people, should be wrested from its true meaning by the quib-
bles of attorneys, and receive such severe condemnation.   Before
he took his seat he declared his opposition to the Constitution,
little dreaming that the half-grown boy whom he had left at
Berkeley blazing away at the cat-birds in the cherry-trees, or
angling from a canoe for perch in the river that flowed by his
farm, would one day wield the powers of that executive which
he now pronounced so kingly.

When Benjamin Harrison had pronounced the accusation of
the General Assembly in respect to Josiah Philips, unjust, he
declared that it had been uniformly lenient and moderate in its
measures, and that, as the debates would probably be published,
he thought it very unwarrantable in gentlemen to utter expressions here which might induce the world to believe that the
Assembly of Virginia had perpetrated murder.   He reviewed in
a succinct manner the proposed plan of government, declared
that it would infringe the rights and liberties of the people; that
he was amazed that facts should be so distorted with a view of
effecting the adoption of the Constitution, and that he trusted
they would not ratify it as it then stood.   This aged patriot did
not engage in debate during the subsequent proceedings of the
Convention.   He felt that his time of departure was near, and in
less than three years after the adjournment of the Convention, at

Berkeley his patrimonial seat on the James, he was gathered to his fathers.[160]

George Nicholas replied to Harrison that in the case of Philips, the turpitude of a man's character was not a sufficient reason to deprive him of his life without a trial—that such a doctrine was a subversion of every shadow of freedom. He then passed to an examination of the various arguments which had been urged by Henry in his last speech, taking them up one by one, and sought to demonstrate that they were either unsound in them-

---

[160] I have represented Harrison as a large man, over six feet ; but the reader will not confound him with his namesake and relative, Benjamin Harrison, who removed to Georgia, where he died in 1818, aged forty-five, and who measured seven feet two inches and a-half in his stockings I frequently allude to the stature of our early statesmen, not only because their physical qualities are proper subjects for remark, but because of the theory of the French philosopher about the dwindling of the human race on this side of the Atlantic was a playful subject with our fathers. Every member of the first deputation to Congress reached six feet or over. Randolph. Washington, Henry, Pendleton, R. H. Lee, Bland, and Harrison were six feet—their average height being over six feet, and their average weight would have been two hundred.

In another place I have spoken of Herman Harrison as one of the early governors of Virginia ; I should have said of the Somer's Islands. By the way, it was during the term of Herman Harrison that tobacco worms and rats became popular on our plantations, as will be seen by the tract of Captain John Smith on the "Confusion of Rats," Vol. II, 141. From copies of records in the British State Paper Office, made by my friend Conway Robinson, Esq., I perceive that the Harrisons were among the earlier settlers. I ought to allude to the harsh comments on Colonel Harrison, which appear in the diary of John Adams, recently published in the edition of his works by his son. It was evidently a hasty entry, made under some casual provocation, and never revised. There could be, however, but little congeniality between the two men. from their tastes and prejudices. and their modes of life, but it is known that there was something like a feud in the Virginia delegation at the time the entry was made, and Adams sided warmly with Richard Henry Lee and against Harrison. Perhaps this notice is all the entry requires and deserves. Harrison corresponded with Washington during the war, and in one of his letters commended Edmund Randolph to him as a promising young man, when that young man, in 1775, visited Cambridge with a view of entering the army. A copy of this letter, which is too racy for publication, I have in my collection, and am indebted for it to George M. Conarroe, Esq., of Philadelphia.

selves or inapplicable to the plan under consideration.   On the conclusion of the speech of Nicholas, the House adjourned.

On Wednesday, the eleventh of June, the first and second sections still nominally the order of the day, and Wythe in the chair, Madison took the floor and discussed the subject of direct taxation in all its bearings, replying by the way to the arguments of Henry against the expediency of vesting that power in the Constitution, and delivered the most elaborate speech of his whole life.   It will ever afford an admirable commentary on that part of the Constitution which it was designed to expound.   But our limits will allow us only to refer to a topic he touched upon, which has a singular interest in connection with his subsequent career in the administration of the Federal Government.   When he had showed the importance of a certain and adequate revenue to a State in order to guard against foreign aggression, he said : " I do not want to frighten the members of this Convention into a concession of this power, but to bring to their minds those considerations which demonstrate its necessity.   If we were secured from the possibility or the probability of danger, it might be unnecessary.   I shall not review that concourse of dangers which may probably arise at remote periods of maturity, nor all those which we have immediately to apprehend ; for this would lead me beyond the bounds which I have prescribed myself.   But I will mention one single consideration drawn from the fact itself.   By the treaty between the United States and his most Christian majesty, among other things it is stipulated that the great principle on which the armed neutrality in Europe was founded, should prevail in case of future wars.   The principle is this, that free ships shall make free goods, and that vessels and goods both shall be free from condemnation.   Great Britain did not recognize it.   While all Europe was against her, she held out without acceding to it.   It has been considered for some time past that the flames of war already kindled would spread, and that France and England were likely to draw those swords which were so recently put up.   This is judged probable.   We should not be surprised in a short time to consider ourselves a neutral nation ; France on one side and Great Britain on the other. What is the situation of America ?   She is remote from Europe and ought not to engage in her politics or wars.   The American vessels, if they can do it with advantage, may carry on the com-

merce of the contending nations. It is a source of wealth
which we ought not to deny to our citizens. But, sir, is there
not infinite danger, that in spite of all our caution we may be
drawn into the war? If American vessels have French property on board, Great Britain will seize them. By this means we
shall be obliged to relinquish the advantage of a neutral nation,
or be engaged in a war. A neutral nation ought to be respectable, or else it will be insulted or attacked. America in her
present impotent situation would run the risk of being drawn in
as a party in the war, and lose the advantage of being neutral.
Should it happen that the British fleet should be superior, have
we not reason to conclude, from the spirit displayed by that
nation to us and to all the world, that we should be insulted in
our own ports, and our vessels seized? But if we be in a respectable situation, if it be known that our government can command
the whole resources of the nation, we shall be suffered to enjoy
the great advantages of carrying on the commerce of the nations
at war, for none of them would be anxious to add us to the number of their enemies. I shall say no more on this point, there
being others which merit your consideration.''

The future historian, when he peruses the speech from which
we have made an extract, will pause in silent wonder, and will
hesitate whether most to admire the thorough knowledge of the
operations of a government yet untried which it displays, the
vigor of its reasoning, now close, now wide, as the particular
topic in hand required, or the profound sagacity of its author.

Madison was succeeded by George Mason. It has been
remarked by one of the most celebrated orators of the present
age, that it is an advantage to a speaker of the first order of
ability, and to such only, to succeed the delivery of a first-rate
speech, that the attention of the audience is fixed firmly on the
subject in debate, and that there is a craving for a reply.[161] In
this respect, Mason could not have been more fortunate, and in
another not less so ; for the speech which had just been delivered
was addressed to the reason and not to the passions of the
House, and the eminent perfection of Mason rested on his logical power, in his knowledge of the British polity, and in his
experience as a statesman. Hitherto Henry had stood alone—

---

[161] *Lord Brougham's Miscellanies*, I, 184, note.

alone, but unsubdued—exposed to the severest fire which up to
this moment in our parliamentary history had ever been levelled
against a single speaker. The maxims drawn by Henry from
the British Constitution, and so long accepted as undeniable
truths, the examples cited by him from ancient and modern history, the practical doctrines and lessons drawn from our own
institutions, which he had from time to time reiterated in the
House, had been examined in detail by the able debaters who
had successively appeared on the floor, and had almost been
frittered away, and in the comparatively brief space of time
allowed for a reply amid the innumerable arguments against the
new plan with which his mind was teeming, as the discussion
advanced, and as the fate of the Constitution was drawing nigh,
it was impossible for him to reply in detail. Hence the service
of such a coadjutor as Mason at that time was as appropriate as
it was welcome.

After some observations on the propriety of arguing at large
instead of confining the debate to a particular clause in the
present condition of the House, he reverted to an argument of
Nicholas', borrowed from Dr. Price, on the subject of the representation of the British people in the House of Commons, and
showed that the remark could only apply to a single political
system—a government *totus teres alque rotundus*—that as it was
admitted by Nicholas that five hundred and fifty members could
be bribed, then it was as much easier to bribe sixty-five, the
number of the new House of Representatives, as sixty five was
less five hundred and fifty ; that the bribery of the House of
Commons was effected mainly by the distribution of places,
offices and posts, and that Congress was authorized to create
these at its discretion, and, as he sought to show, without any
practical restraint. He proceeded to prove that the unlimited
power of taxation vested in the Constitution would ultimately
result in the oppression of the people ; that the concurrent
power of taxation by two governments would necessarily clash ;
that the mode of requisitions, while it would promote economy
in the administration of the Federal Government, would prevent
any unpleasant collision between the parties, and that he was
willing to yield the power of taxation as a resource where requisitions failed. He showed what would be the subject of taxation
under the new plan, establishing his point by a quotation from a

letter of Robert Morris, the financier of the government, denounced the poll-tax, as well as the other taxes proposed in that
letter, as peculiarly severe upon the slave-holding States, and
invoking a certain conflict between the governments.   He
denied that Congress would possess the proper information for
the assessment of direct taxes, especially as it was said that the
body would be composed of the *well-born*—that aristocratic
idol, that flattering idea, that *exotic* plant, which has been lately
imported from Great Britain and planted in the luxuriant soil of
this country.[162]   He established the position of Henry about the
difficulty of getting back powers once given away, and showed
that out of a thousand instances where the people precipitately
and unguardedly relinquished power, there has not yet been one
solitary instance of a voluntary surrender of it back by rulers,
and defied the production of a single case to the contrary.
Following the line of argument pursued by Randolph, he expressed his love of the union and his opinion on another topic
not devoid of interest at the present time.   "The gentleman
(Randolph) dwelt largely on the necessity of the union.   A
great many others have enlarged upon this subject.   Foreigners
would suppose, from the declamation about union, that there
was a great dislike in America to any general American government.   I have never in my whole life heard one single man
deny the necessity and propriety of the union.   This necessity
is deeply impressed upon every American mind.   There can be
no danger of any object being lost when the mind of every man
in the country is strongly attached to it.   But I hope it is not to
the name, but to the blessings of union that we are attached.
Those gentlemen who are the loudest in their praises of the
name are not more attached to the reality than I am.   The
security of our liberty and happiness is the object we ought to
have in view in wishing to establish the union.   If, instead of
securing these we endanger them, the name of union will be but
a trivial consolation.   If the objections be removed—if those
parts which are clearly subversive of our rights be altered—no
man will go further than I will to advance the union.   We are
told in strong language of the dangers to which we will be ex-

---

[162] The term " well-born " had dropped in conversation from a friend
of the Constitution.

posed unless we adopt this Constitution. Among the rest, domestic safety is said to be endangered. This government does not attend to our domestic safety. It authorizes the importation of slaves for twenty-odd years, and thus continues upon us that nefarious trade. Instead of securing and protecting us, the continuation of this trade adds daily to our weakness. Though this evil is increasing, there is no clause in the Constitution that will prevent the Northern and Eastern States from meddling with our whole property of that kind. There is a clause to prohibit the importation of slaves after twenty years; but there is no provision made for securing to the Southern States those they now possess. It is far from being a desirable property. But it will involve us in great difficulty and infelicity to be now deprived of them. There ought to be a clause in the Constitution to secure us that property, which we have acquired under our former laws, and the loss of which would bring ruin on a great many people."

When Mason had replied to most of the arguments of Randolph, maintaining his opinions from authorities, which he read on the floor, he discussed the objection of the difficulties that might result from delay, and referred to the inconsistency of the course of that gentleman : " My honorable colleague in the late Convention seems to raise phantoms, and to show a singular skill in exorcisms, to terrify and compel us to take the new government with all its sins and dangers. *I know he once saw as great danger in it as I do.* What has happened since to alter his opinion? If anything, I know it not. But the Virginia Assembly has occasioned it by postponing the matter! The Convention has met in June, instead of March or April! The liberty or misery of millions yet unborn are deeply concerned in our decision. When this is the case, I cannot imagine that the short period between the last of September and the first of June ought to make any difference. The union between England and Scotland has been strongly instanced by the honorable gentleman to prove the necessity of acceding to this new government. He must know that the act of union secured the rights of the Scotch nation. The rights and privileges of the people of Scotland are expressly secured. We wish only our rights to be secured. We must have such amendments as will secure the liberty and happiness of the people on a plain, simple construction, not on

a doubtful ground. We wish to give the Government sufficient
energy on real republican principles ; but we wish to withhold
such powers as are not absolutely necessary in themselves, but
are extremely dangerous. We wish to shut the door against
corruption in that place where it is most dangerous—to secure
against the corruption of our own representatives.[163] We ask
such amendments as will point out what powers are reserved to
the State governments, and clearly discriminate between them
and those that are given to the General Government, so as to
prevent future disputes and clashing of interests. Grant us
amendments like these, and we will cheerfully with our hands
and hearts unite with those who advocate it, and we will do everything we can to support and carry it into execution. But in its
present form we can never accede to it. Our duty to God and
to our posterity forbids it. We acknowledge the defects of the
Confederation, and the necessity of a reform. We ardently wish
for an union with our sister States on terms of security. This, I
am bold to declare, is the desire of most of the people. On
these terms we will most cheerfully join with the warmest friends
of this Constitution. On another occasion I shall point out the
great dangers of this Constitution, and the amendments which
are necessary. I will likewise endeavor to show that amendments, after ratification, are delusive and fallacious—perhaps
utterly impracticable.''

There is one passage in this speech which, in a historical view,
should not be omitted. We have more than once observed that
the ratification of the Federal Constitution by Virginia was
effected mainly by the military officers of the Revolution and by
the judiciary of the State, in opposition to the wishes of a large
majority of the ablest and wisest statesmen who had engaged in
the theatre of that contest, and we readily conceive the reasons
which impelled them to desire a more energetic government than
could well exist under the Articles of Confederation. Soldiers
and judges are rarely safe statesmen in great civil conjunctures ;
but in the present instance their purity of purpose and their

---

[163] The disclosures made at a late session of Congress show that the
evil apprehended by Mason is not imaginary. In fact, most of the
leading opponents of the Constitution in Convention went down to
their graves in the full belief that they had witnessed for themselves a
remarkable case of corruption in Congress.

patriotism were unquestionable. There was, however, another class of men friendly to the Federal Constitution, who had manifested from the dawn of the contest with Great Britain a decided reluctance to a change of dynasty, but who, with the object of securing their estates from confiscation, determined to take sides with the people. These disaffected, on all trying occasions, hung on the rear of the friends of freedom, and sought to obstruct their progress when they could effect their object safely and without suspicion. They opposed the resolution of independence in the Convention of 1776, and the Constitution of the Commonwealth, and, disinclined to widen the rupture with Great Britain, zealously opposed the ratification of the Articles of Confederation by the Virginia Assembly.[164] When the independence of the United States was recognized by Britain, and a return to the rule of the mother country became impracticable, guided by that distrust of the people which led them to obstruct the several capital stages of the Revolution, they were eager to establish a government as nearly allied in form to that which had been overthrown as they could succeed in accomplishing. As these persons were possessed of high position, wide family connections, and abilities, their influence was sensibly felt by those able and patriotic men who believed that the Constitution, however wisely intended by its framers, would ultimately result in impairing the liberties of the people. Yet it was a most delicate and difficult task to assail them. It was this aspect of the case which Mason had the courage to denounce, when he said : " I have some acquaintance with a great many characters who favor this Government, their connections, their conduct, their political principles, and a number of other circumstances. There are a great many wise and good men among them. But when I look around the number of my acquaintance in Virginia, the country wherein I was born, and have lived so many years, and observe *who* are the warmest and most zealous friends to this new government, it makes me think of the story of the cat transformed into a fine lady—forgetting her transformation, and happening to see a rat, she could not restrain herself, but sprung upon it out of the chair."

---

[164] Letter of George Mason to R. H. Lee, May 18, 1776, in the archives of the Virginia Historical Society; and Patrick Henry to R. H. Lee, December 18, 1777, in the " Red Hill " papers.

Henry Lee, ever mindful of the tactics of his profession, and thinking he saw an opening for a charge upon the enemy, sprang to the floor, and demurred to Mason's illustration of the cat and the fine lady. "The gentleman," he said, "has endeavored to draw our attention from the merits of the question by jocose observations and by satirical allusions. Does he imagine that he who can raise the loudest laugh is the soundest reasoner? Sir, the judgments and not the risibility of men are to be consulted. Had the gentleman followed that rule which he himself proposed, he would not have shown the letter of a private gentleman, who, in times of difficulty, had offered his opinion respecting the mode in which it would be most expedient to raise the public funds. Does it follow that since a private individual proposed such a scheme of taxation, the new Government will adopt it? But the same principle also governs the gentleman, when he mentions the expressions of another private gentleman—*the well-born*—that our representatives are to be chosen from the higher orders of the people—*from the well-born*. Is there a single expression like this in the Constitution? This insinuation is totally unwarrantable. Is it proper that the Constitution should be thus attacked with the opinions of every private gentleman? I hope we shall hear no more of such groundless aspersions. Raising a laugh, sir, will not prove the merits nor expose the defects of this system."[165]

When Lee had exhausted his fire, there appeared on the floor for the first time one of those eminent men, the immediate growth of the Commonwealth, who blended in his character the qualities of the soldier and the statesman, and whose fame, won in various fields and in contact with his most distinguished contemporaries, though obscured by the mists which have so long gathered over the memory of our early statesmen, may fitly fill

---

[165] It is evident from Lee's speech that the cat and the fine lady was not the only piece of fun with which Mason relieved one of his ablest arguments; but there is not a shadow of humor in any other part of the reported speech. I may say here that it is almost impossible in a short synopsis to present fairly the arguments of a speech ranging over the entire Constitution, and recurring time and again to the same topics. Under such a process all the speeches lose what little savour is left by the original reporter, but especially those of Henry, Mason, and Grayson, the three great champions of the opposition.

one of the brightest pages in our annals.   His military career, beginning with the dawn of the Revolution, and pursued for the most part under the eye of Washington—with whom in early life he had hunted foxes over the moors of Westmoreland, and whose respect and esteem he enjoyed to the end of his life—continued nearly to its close, and was marked by enterprise, by intrepidity, and by success.   But the military services of William Grayson, prominent as they were, were lost sight of in the blaze which his civic accomplishments kindled about his name. It is hard to say whether he was more fortunate in his natural genius, or in those advantages which enabled him to discipline and develop it.   Educated at Oxford,[166] to which he early repaired, he not only acquired a correct knowledge of the Latin and Greek tongues and of the sciences, but cultivated so assiduously the purer literature of England, especially in the department of British history, that in his splendid conversational debates, and in his speeches at the bar and in public bodies, his excellence in this respect was universally confessed. The time of his abode in England was opportune.   There was indeed a momentary pause in the productions of English genius. The wits of Queen Anne's time had disappeared, but the glory of the Georgian era was yet in its dawn.   The Johnsonian galaxy yet shone with a moderate lustre.   Burke, who was known as the author of "a very pretty treatise on the sublime," was yet to make his magnificent speeches in the House of Commons, and Gibbon, who was spoken of in a small circle as the author of a clever tract in refutation of one of the ingenious theories which Warburton had ventured upon in his *Divine Legation*, had not yet put forth the first volume of the *Decline and Fall*.   Even Johnson had not published the most elegant of his prose compositions, the *Lives of the British Poets*.   But in the sister kingdom of the north there appeared in rapid succession a series of literary works which reminded the world that Scotland was the home of Buchanan, of Boethius, and of Napier, and was now the abode of Hume, of Ferguson, of Kames, of Robertson, and of Adam Smith.   Grayson, smitten with a love of learning, eagerly perused the works of these authors as they

---

[166] Grayson's name does not appear in the *Alumni Oxienses* of the eminent antiquary and genealogist, Joseph Foster.—ED.

appeared ; but it was to the *Wealth of Nations* that he devoted all the energies of his intellect, and so thoroughly did he master the problems of the new philosophy, that in conversation and in debate he was proud to declare his allegiance to Adam Smith as the founder, or if not the founder, the great modern expositor of the science of political economy.[167]

After serving his terms in the Temple, with a mind richly imbued alike with the learning of the law and with the living literature of the age, and panting for honorable distinction, he returned to Virginia at a time when the opposition to British rule, begun in the House of Burgesses, had passed to the people, and when Associations were regarded by the colonists as the surest means of defending their rights. A rapid and striking panorama then passed before his eyes. The Conventions soon began to assemble; the royal governor soon fled from his palace; the House of Burgesses soon went down to rise no more; and the Virginia regiments, fully equipped, were to be seen drawn up in the square at Williamsburg, or lounging in the shade of Waller's grove. Grayson instantly enrolled his name in one of the Associations, and became a candidate for the majority in the new corps, but was defeated by Alexander Spotswood.[168] In the

---

[167] A gentleman who knew Grayson intimately, told me that the *Wealth of Nations* had long been his favorite book, and that a favorite expression with him in the House of Delegates, when Virginia regulated her own commerce, and in Congress, was, "Let commerce alone ; it will take care of itself"—a version of the answer of the French merchants to Colbert.

[168] Journal Convention of July, 1775, page 19. The first public act of Grayson was his participation in the Westmoreland meeting, which adopted the rules of association on the 27th day of February, 1766. *Va. Hist. Reg.*, II, 17. I regret that I cannot ascertain his age, which is unknown to most of his descendants. As he was buried in a vault, we have no tombstone to refer to. and his coffin had no inscription upon it, as I learn from one who examined it. I have reason to believe that he was in England as late as 1765. One of his descendants states that he was educated at Edinburg ; another, equally intelligent and devoted to his memory, insists that he was educated at Oxford. Professor Tucker says he certainly studied law in the Temple. I have decided, from all the facts within my reach, that Oxford was the true place of his education. His combined classical and scientific acquirements, and especially his skill in Latin prosody, betoken an English training. My belief is that he was in his forty eighth year when he took his seat in

following year he was appointed colonel of the first battalion of infantry raised for the internal security and defence of the State. His spirit and intelligence early attracted the attention of Washington, who invited him to become a member of his military family. With the affairs at Valley Forge his name is intimately connected, and was associated with that of Hamilton in the discharge of several important trusts.[169]   He was at the battles of Long Island and White Plains, of Brandywine and Germantown, and at Monmouth he is believed to have commanded the first brigade in the order of attack.[170]   He had been appointed colonel of a regiment to be raised in Virginia in January, 1777, and it was probably in the command of this regiment that he was engaged at Monmouth.[171]   In 1779 his regiment was blended with Nathaniel Gist's, and, having become a supernumerary, he accepted the office of a Commissioner of the Board of War, which he had previously declined when a prospect of active service was before him, and in December of that year he took his seat at that Board, which he ultimately resigned on the 10th of September, 1781.[172]   In closing this allusion to the military

the present Convention, as in the year 1775 he was a candidate for the office of major, along with such men as Thomas Marshall, the father of the Chief Justice, and in the following year was elected a full colonel (Journal House of Delegates, 1776, p. 104), while Henry Lee and Theodoric Bland were satisfied with captaincies. Colonel Clement Carrington told me that when he saw Grayson attending Congress in New York, in 1786, he thought he was about fifty, but it is well known that very young men are prone to overestimate the age of their seniors. The age of an individual may seem unimportant, but in a body of men made up of two or three generations, a knowledge of the relative ages of the members is indispensable to a correct representation of their characters, and of their relative positions towards each other.

[169] *Writings of Washington.* V, 272.   He was officially announced as aid to Washington in a general order dated " Headquarters at New York, 24th August, 1776."

[170] Morse, in a school history of the United States, is the authority of this statement.

[171] Journals of the Old Congress, Vol. II, pp. 19, 60, 300.   His lieutenant colonel was Levin Powell, also a member of the present Convention; born in 1738, in Loudoun county; representative in Congress, 1799-1801 ; died at Bedford, Pa., in August, 1810.—Ed.

[172] Journals of Congress, IV, 505, 524; V, 335; VII, 144.

offices which Colonel Grayson held during the war, one marked instance of his intrepidity, taken from the lips of the late and ever venerable Bishop White, deserves a record : " I was sitting in this house during the war," he said to a friend in conversation with him at his residence on Fifth street, Philadelphia, a short time before his death, "when a most furious mob of several hundred persons assembled on the opposite side of the street, and a few doors above this house, and I saw Colonel Grayson with some fifteen men, with fixed bayonets, hastily pass.   My apprehension was that they would be torn to pieces ; but Colonel Grayson instantly entered the house of the rioters at the head of his small force, and in a few minutes the ringleaders were secured and the mob was dispersed."[173]

On his return to Virginia, Grayson continued the practice of the law until 1784, when he was deputed to Congress, and in March of the following year he took his seat in that body.   To such a man opportunity was alone wanting to become an expert debater; and, although the deliberations of Congress were secret, we know that he soon acquired distinction on the floor.   During his term of service some of the most serious questions that sprung up under the Confederation were disposed of.   Among the number was the Connecticut cession of western lands with the Reserve, which he warmly opposed, and the passage of the Northwestern Ordinance, which he as warmly sustained.[174]   But, to pass over his Congressional career, to which we shall revert hereafter, although firmly attached to the Government prescribed by the Articles of Confederation, he was candid enough to declare as early as 1785 that new and extensive powers ought to be engrafted upon it, and that the ninth article should be amended

---

[173] On the authority of a letter from Peter G Washington, Esq., dated August 24, 1856.   Mr. Washington heard the Bishop narrate the incident in the text.   Mr. Washington is the grandson of the Rev. Spence Grayson, the brother of the Colonel.   I must confess my obligations to Mr. Washington for the information contained in his letters to me, which are the more valuable from their reference to the proper authorities.

[174] I regret that I cannot put my finger on the short note of Grayson addressed to a friend in Virginia announcing the passage of the Ordinance.   One ground of his satisfaction was, that the Northwestern States would not be able to make tobacco.   The letter was published in the papers in 1845.

and extended,[175] and he was equally explicit in declaring what these new powers ought to be, and with what limitations they should be granted.   Still there was a barrier in the way of his approval of the new Constitution which it was impossible to remove.   It involved, in his opinion, a total change of polity; and for this change he felt that he was able to prove that there was no real necessity.

But before we proceed to develop his views of the new plan, we must speak of him as he now was, in the meridian of his fame as the most elegant gentleman as well as the most accomplished debater of his age.   In this respect he had some qualities which were possessed in no ordinary degree by his great contemporaries; but there were other qualities which he alone possessed, and which he possessed in an eminent degree.   In massive logical power he had his equals; but his distinctive superiority in this respect was marked by the mode of argumentation which he pursued, and which was peculiar to himself. Thoroughly comprehending his theme in all its parts, as if it were a problem in pure mathematics, and conscious of his strength, he would play with his subject most wantonly, calling to his aid arguments and illustrations the full bearing of which he saw, and which he knew he could manage, but which to ordinary hearers were as fraught with danger as they were easy of misrepresentation.   He was equally wanton in his manner of treating the arguments of his adversaries, pushing them to the greatest extremes, and, as he worked his way without the slightest intermixture of passion, often producing an effect upon his audience most worrying to his opponents, and near akin to the exhibition of humor itself.   One practical effect was, that men laughed as heartily during his most profound arguments at the display of the wit of reason, as they are wont to do at the display of the wit which in other speakers ordinarily flows from the imagination.   But there was one result which sometimes followed this sport of dialectics which was embarrassing in itself, and which was likely to lead to a loss of the game.   He was liable to be misunderstood by those who were either unable or unwilling to follow him in the course of his flight, and he was

---

[175] *Writings of Washington.*   Washington to Grayson, August 22, 1785, IX, 125.

further liable to the wilful misrepresentations of those whose arguments he had handled with so little reserve. It exposed him also to the suspicion and distrust of a class of men, who, though they never engaged in debate, exercised no little influence in and out of the House, and who had learned to confound gravity with logic, and thought that a man could no more reason than he could tell the truth with a smile, and who, if they had lived at the time of the invention of gunpowder, would have denied to the last that a man could be as effectually killed by a bullet or a round shot as by a bow and arrow ; or in the time of the Holy Wars, that a head could be as completely severed from the neck by the scimiter of Saladin as by the sword of Richard.

But his uncommon versatility of logical power, which made every speech a specimen in dialectics, was only one of his accomplishments as a debater.   In the more refined departments of learning we have already said he was a proficient ; but in a minute acquaintance with the affairs of Congress since the war, when the defects of the Confederation had been fully developed, in a knowledge of all questions of commerce and political economy, and of the politics of England and of the continental States, which had been his favorite study abroad, and in a sound common sense, which he did not suffer to be dazzled by his own speculations any more than by the speculations of others, or deterred by the cumulative terrors of a present crisis, if he may be said to have had an equal in the House, he certainly had no superior in or out of it.   Even these abundant stores of information, applied by an unimpassioned intellect to the case in hand, sometimes failed to produce their effects upon common minds ; for, as was observed of a celebrated English statesman, he was inclined to view questions requiring an immediate solution, not as they appeared, clogged with the interests and the passions of the moment, but as they would appear in the eyes of the next generation—a trait, which, though favorable to a reputation with posterity, is in ordinary cases fatal to a reputation for practical affairs, but which was peculiarly adapted to the investigation of a new plan of government.[176]

---

[176] One of the most perfect exhibitions in recent times of powers kindred with those of Grayson was the speech delivered by Governor Tazewell in the House of Delegates on the Convention bill of 1816. I heard in conversation with Mr. Tazewell the general outline of his

His powers of humor, wit, sarcasm, ridicule, prolonged and sustained by argument and declamation, were unrivalled. The speech which he now rose to deliver abounds in passages of humor and sarcasm, not put forth to excite mirth, but to advance his argument, and to annoy his adversaries. Nor did he confine himself to those illustrations which, reflected from the classics, have a lustre not to be questioned, though sometimes hard to perceive, but drew his images from the common life around him. When, in proving that the dangers from the neighboring States, which had been marshalled by the friends of the Constitution in dread array as likely to overwhelm Virginia in the event of the rejection of that instrument, were imaginary, he ridiculed such apprehensions of alarm, and, turning to South Carolina, described the citizens of that gallant State as rushing to invade us, mounted, not on the noble Arabian which poetry as well as history had clothed with beauty and with terror— not with the cavalry of civilized nations—but upon alligators, suddenly summoned from the swamp and bridled and saddled for the nonce—a cavalry worthy of such a cause—that of crushing a sister Commonwealth—his sally was received with roars

---

argument twelve years after it was delivered, with a pleasure which I have rarely received since from any public effort. The late Philip Doddridge, who took a part in the debate, told me that it was not only the most extraordinary exhibition of logical power which he had ever witnessed in debate, but which he believed was ever delivered in any public body in America. There, too, the speech was subjected to the misrepresentation of opponents, who fell upon the words "many-headed monster," which Mr Tazewell used in animadverting on the word "people," which was contained in the bill, and which he contended included men, women and children, white, black, and mulatto, and every other description and complexion known among men. Twenty years afterwards I heard these words, which had been carried to the counties and brought back again to Richmond, where they had been forgotten, quoted to show that Mr. Tazewell had spoken disrespectfully of the people, of whom he and his large family were a part, and whose rights, at a severe pecuniary loss to himself, he had been elected without his knowledge to maintain on this very question. To have made such an objection in debate would have been to raise loud laughter.

The great speech of Upshur on the basis of representation in the Virginia Convention of 1829-30, was another splendid example of Grayson's mode of debate.

of laughter from both sides of the House. A Latin scholar, skilled in prosody, he ever showed a reluctance to let a slip in a quotation pass unreproved; and when a friend of the Constitution, in using the words "*spolia opima*," made the penult of the last word short, Grayson whispered in a tone that reached the ear of the orator: "*Opīma*, if you please"; and when another friend of the Constitution sought to derive the word contract from *con* and *tracto*, Grayson, with a lengthened twirl of the lips, trolled out in an undertone that was heard by the learned gentleman in possession of the floor: "*Tra-ho*." And the laugh in this case, as in the preceding, passed like a wave from the spot where it was raised gradually to the remote parts of the house. He was not surprised, he is reported to have said, that men who were, in his opinion, about to vote away the freedom of a living people, should take such liberties with a dead tongue.

The physical qualities of Grayson were quite as distinctive as the intellectual. He was considered, as we have already said, the handsomest man in the Convention. He had a most comely and imposing person—his stature exceeded six feet, and though his weight exceeded two hundred and fifty pounds, such was the symmetry of his figure, the beholder was struck more with its height than its magnitude. His head was very large, but its outline was good; his forehead unusually broad and high, and in its resemblance to that of Chalmer's indicating a predilection for the abstract sciences; his eyes were black and deep-seated; his nose large and curved; his lips well-formed, disclosing teeth white and regular, which retained their beauty to the last; a fine complexion gave animation to the whole. When he was walking, his head leaned slightly forward as if he were lost in thought. Lest our sketch may seem to be overdrawn, although no person who, as an adult, had known Grayson, with one exception, is now alive, we have fortunately a singular proof of the fidelity of the portrait which we have delineated. When Grayson had lain forty-six years in his coffin its lid was lifted, and there his majestic form lay as if it had been recently wrapped in the shroud. The face was uncovered by the hand of a descendant, and its noble features, which had frowned in battle, which had sparkled in debate, and on which the eyes long closed of tender affection had loved to dwell, were fresh and full. The towering forehead; the long black hair—the growth of the grave; the black eye, glazed and slightly sunken, yet eloquent of its ancient fire ; the large Roman nose; the finely wrought lip; the perfect teeth, which bespoke a temperate life ended too soon ; the wide expanded chest ; the long and sinewy limbs terminating in those small and delicate hands that rested on his breast, and in those small feet that had been motionless so long ; the grand and graceful outline of the form as it was when laid away to its final rest, told touchingly with what faithfulness tradition had retained the image of the beloved original.[177]

The address of Grayson was winning and courteous. His manners, formed abroad at a time when the young American was apt to be taken for a young savage, and improved by a large experience with the world, were highly polished. He was

---

[177] One of the descendants of Colonel Grayson represents him as over six feet, another quite six, and another, a lady who in her childhood knew him, as very tall. A friend, now dead, who knew Grayson, thought him over six feet.

I derive the particulars of the appearance of Colonel Grayson in his coffin from Robert Grayson Carter, Esq , of Grayson, Carter county, Kentucky, who uncovered the face of Grayson, and examined the body. He particularly alludes to the size of the head, and of the smallness of hands and feet, the hair, the features, and the teeth. I am indebted to Mr. Carter for his efforts to obtain information respecting his illustrious grandfather. The father of Colonel Grayson was named Benjamin ; was, it is believed by some of my correspondents, a Scotchman, and married a lady whose maiden name was Monroe ; and it is thought that Grayson and James Monroe were first or second cousins. Grayson himself married Eleanor, sister of General William Smallwood.

[It is a suggestive coincidence that the christian name of the father of James Monroe and of a brother of Colonel Grayson was Spence—in such use an uncommon name.—ED.]

I shall trace the career of Grayson more particularly when I come to speak of the members at large. Grayson was buried in the vault of Belle Air, then the seat of the Rev. Spence Grayson, near Dumfries.

I must also acknowledge my indebtedness to John M. Orr. Esq., another connection of Grayson's, for an interesting letter about Colonel Grayson. Mr. Orr thinks that the Graysons are English, and were residents of the Colony for several generations before the Revolution. He also says that Grayson was educated at Edinburg ; but as Mr. P. G. Washington, whose grandfather, Spence Grayson, was a brother of Colonel William, and was abroad with him at the same time, may be supposed to have heard or learned from authentic sources where his grandfather was educated, and affirms that it was at Oxford, I lean to his side of the question.

fond of society, and whether he appeared at the fireside of the man of one hogshead,[178] or in the aristocratic circles of the Colony, he was ever a welcome and honored guest.   His conversation, playful, sparkling, or profound, as the time or topic required, or the mood prompted, was not only admired by his contemporaries, but has left its impress upon our own times; and it was in conversation that he appeared with a lustre hardly inferior to that which adorned his forensic disputations.   His humor was inexhaustible, and the young and the old, grave statesmen as well as young men who are ever ready to show their charity by honoring the jests of middle-aged people, were alike captivated by it.   We are told by a friend who, in 1786, walked from the hall of Congress, then sitting in New York, in company with Grayson, Colonel Edward Carrington, and Judge St. George Tucker on their way to their boarding-house, that Grayson became lively, and threw out jests with such an effect that the gentlemen were so convulsed with laughter as hardly to be able to walk erect through the streets, he quite serious the while, *gravitate incolumi.*[179]   And in an humbler sphere his loving nature and pleasant talk were so relished by the family of a worthy woman at whose house, in visiting his mills on Opequon creek, he usually stopped, that, when his death was announced, all of them burst into tears.[180]   Withal there was a dignity about him which the ablest and the bravest men would have been the last to trench upon.

---

[178] In early times it was common to designate a planter according to the number of hogsheads of tobacco he made annually.

[179] *Carrington Memoranda.*

[180] I have received from Robert Grayson Carter, Esq., a reminiscence of Colonel Grayson, taken from the lips of the lady mentioned in the text, who was living last December (1857) in Lewis county, Kentucky, at the age of ninety-three.   Her faculties were all nearly entire.   Her memory was perfect, and she described Colonel Grayson as if she had seen him the day before.   She says that in 1784 his hair was slightly gray, though originally very black ; that he was a very large man; that "he had a bright and intelligent black eye, and that he was altogether the handsomest man she ever laid her eyes upon "; that he used frequently to stay at her house on his way to his mills at Opequon, and that he said he was so pleased to find at her house a bed so much better than any he could get at the mills.   She thought him in 1784 between fifty and sixty ; that he was universally beloved, and that her brother, Captain William Helm, thought " that there was no such man

We have spoken of his mode of debate; and it is fit that we should say something of his manner of speaking. It should seem improbable that a man of good address, of rare reasoning powers, and of undaunted spirit, should be destitute of the ordinary qualities of an orator, unless he had some impediment in his speech, or lost all self-possession the moment he stood upon his feet. Such was not the case with Grayson. It was his self-possession, acquired partly by his speeches in the English clubs and at the bar, partly by his early essays in the House of Burgesses,[181] but mainly by his service in the Congress of the Confederation, which, as it was a small body, and consisted of the first men of the Union, exacted from those who addressed it a severity of manner as well as of matter, and a degree of preparation and research rarely exhibited in popular assemblies, and which was one of the best schools of our early statesmen,[182] and

---

as Colonel Grayson for every faculty and virtue that could adorn a human being." She says that "he was remarkably temperate in his diet—took for breakfast coffee, butter and toast; for dinner, a slice of mutton or a piece of chicken, with vegetables, and no dessert; and that he would take a cup of tea afterwards, but never ate supper." She says that "his portly form and dignified appearance filled her with such reverence that but for his agreeable and bland manners she would have felt restraint in his presence, but that she was entirely relieved by the affectionate manner in which he spoke and acted." Mr. Carter rode through a storm to secure the information of this venerable lady. I ought to add that the name of the lady is Mrs. Lucy Bragg, and that she further says, that Colonel Grayson always rode to her house in his carriage, attended by his negro man, Punch, who used to rub his master's feet, who reclined on the bed. Grayson had the gout, and ultimately died of it.

[181] Several of my correspondents mention his having been a member of the House of Burgesses; but I cannot find his name in the Journals. This absence of his name on the face of the Journals is not conclusive evidence of his not having been a member, as there is no list of members prefixed to the Journals, and the ayes and noes were not taken until after the formation of the Constitution of the State. The only means of ascertaining the membership of individuals must be found in the annual almanacs, which I do not possess, and know not where to seek.

[182] Mr. Jefferson expressed the opinion that if Mr. Madison had not been a member of a small body like the old Congress, his modesty would have prevented him from engaging in debate.

not a little from his mode of argumentation, which, anticipating
from the first all possible objections to the case in hand, made
him eager to court them from the lips of an adversary ; it was
this self-possession that appeared to the observer not the least
characteristic of his manner.   He had also studied oratory as an
art, at a time when Wedderburne, though in full practice at the
bar, deemed it not unworthy to become a pupil of Sheridan, and
in listening to the eloquence of Dunning, of Townsend, of Burke,
of Mansfield, and of the elder Pitt, he had formed conceptions
of the art which it was the tendency as well as the ambition of
his life to develop and to practice.   His person, as has been said
already, was commanding.   His voice was clear, powerful, and
under perfect control, and had been disciplined with care, and
in sarcastic declamation its tones were said to be terrible; but it
had not the universal compass of Henry's, nor those musical
intonations which made the voice of Innes grateful to the most
wearied ear.   He spoke at times with great animation; but his
stern taste, as well as his peculiar range of argument, in some
measure interdicted much action, in the mechanical sense of the
word.   But it was only when the hour of reflection came that
such thoughts occurred to the hearer, who was borne along,
while the orator was wrapped in his subject, unresistingly by the
ever-abounding, ever-varying and transparent current of his
speech.   Yet it is rather in the highest rank of debaters than in
the highest rank of orators we should place the name of Grayson.

In his present position on the floor, when he rose to make the
only one of his great speeches that have come down to us, he
had an advantage which is necessary to a speaker on a great
occasion, and of which he knew how to avail himself—he well
knew his opponents.   Nicholas, Randolph, Lee, and Marshall
were his juniors in the army, and his juniors in years.   With
two of them he had served in Congress, and he had encountered
them all at the bar.   He began his speech with an apology for
the desultory way in which, from the previous debate, he would
be compelled to treat his subject, and with a declaration of his
confidence in the patriotism and worth of the members of the
General Convention who were members of the House.   He
hoped that what he designed to say might not be misapplied.
He would make no allusions to any gentleman whatever.

He admitted the defects of the Confederation, but he apprehended they could not be removed, because they flowed from the nature of that government and from the fact that particular interests were preferred to the interests of the whole. He contended that the particular disorders of Virginia ought not to be attributed to that source, as they were equally beyond the reach of the Federal Government and of the plan upon the table; that the present condition of Virginia was a vast improvement upon the Colonial system ; that the Judiciary was certainly as rapid as under the royal government, where a case had been thirty-one years on the docket. He then detailed the state of public feeling on the subject of a change in the Federal Government before the meeting of the General Convention, and showed that in Virginia alone was there any dissatisfaction. He then reviewed, with a full knowledge of the subject, the dangers alleged to exist from the hostility of foreign powers and of the neighboring States, showing that they were wholly imaginary. " As for our sister States," he said, " disunion is impossible. The Eastern States hold the fisheries, which are their cornfields, by a hair. They have a dispute with the British government about their rights at this moment. Is not a general and strong government necessary for their interest? If ever nations had any inducements to peace, the Eastern States now have. New York and Pennsylvania are looking anxiously forward to the fur trade. How can they obtain it but by union? How are the little States inclined? They are not likely to disunite. Their weakness will prevent them from quarreling. Little men are seldom fond of quarreling among giants. Is there not a strong inducement to union, while the British are on one side and the Spaniards on the other? Thank heaven, we have a Carthage of our own. But we are told that if we do not embrace the present moment to adopt a system which we believe to be fatal to our liberties, we are lost forever. Is there no difference between productive States and carrying States? If we hold out, will not the tobacco trade enable us to make terms with the carrying States? Is there nothing in a similarity of laws, religion, language and manners? Do not these, and the intercourse and intermarriages between people of the different States invite them in the strongest manner to union?

" But what would I do on the present occasion to remedy the defects of the present Confederation? There are two opinions prevailing in the world ; the one that mankind can only be governed by force ; the other that they are capable of freedom and a good government. Under the supposition that mankind can govern themselves, I would recommend that the present Confederation be amended. Give Congress the regulation of commerce. Infuse new spirit and strength into the State governments ; for when the component parts are strong, it will give energy to the government, although it be otherwise weak. This may be proved by the union at Utrecht. Apportion the public debts in such a manner as to throw the unpopular ones on the back lands. Call only for requisitions for the foreign interest, and aid them by loans. Keep on so until the American character be marked with some certain features. We are yet too young to know what we are fit for. The continual migration of people from Europe, and the settlement of new countries on our western frontiers, are strong arguments against making new experiments now in government. When these things are removed, we can with greater prospect of success devise changes. We ought to consider, as Montesquieu says, whether the construction of a government be suitable to the genius and disposition of the people, as well as a variety of other circumstances.

"But, if this position be not true, and men can only be governed by force, then be as gentle as possible. What then would I do? I would not take the British monarchy for my model. We have not materials for such a government in our country, although I will be bold to say, that it is one of the governments in the world by which liberty and property are best secured. But I would adopt the following government. I would have a president for life, choosing his successor at the same time; a Senate for life, with the powers of the House of Lords, and a triennial House of Representatives. If, sir, *if we are to be consolidated* AT ALL, we ought.to be fully represented, and governed with sufficient energy, according to numbers in both Houses.

"Will this new plan accomplish our purposes? Will the liberty and property of the country be secure under it? It is a government founded on the principles of monarchy with three estates. Is it like the model of Tacitus or Montesquieu? Are there checks on it like the British monarchy? There is an executive fettered in some parts, and as unlimited in others as a Roman Dictator. Look at the executive. Contrary to the opinion of all the best writers, it is blended with the legislative. *We have asked for water, and they have given us a stone.* I am willing to give the government the regulation of trade. It will be serviceable in regulating the trade between the States. But I believe it will not be attended with the advantages generally expected."

He then spoke of the inexpediency of giving up the power of taxation. " As to direct taxation," he said, " give up this, and you give up everything, as it is the highest act of sovereignty. Surrender this inestimable jewel and you throw a pearl away richer than all your tribe." When he had proved that the exercise of this power would result in a conflict between the General and the State Government, in opposition to the opinion expressed by Pendleton, and established his position by examples, and had critically surveyed the construction of the new House of Representatives, which he contended was defective, he concluded: " But my greatest objection is, that in its operation it will be found unequally grievous and oppressive. If it have any efficacy at all, it must be by a faction—a faction of one part of the Union against the other. I think that it has a great natural imbecility within itself—too weak for a consolidated, and too strong for a confederate government. But if it be called into action by a combination of seven States, it will be terrible indeed. We need to be at no loss to determine how this combination will be formed. There is a great difference of circumstances between the States. The interest of the carrying States is strikingly different from that of the productive States. I mean not to give offence to any part of America, but mankind are governed by interest. The carrying States will assuredly unite, and our situation then will be wretched indeed. Our commodities will be transported on their own terms, and every measure will have for its object their particular interest. Let ill-fated Ireland be ever present to our view. We ought to be wise enough to guard against the abuse of such a government. Republics, in fact, oppress more than monarchies. If we advert to the page of history, we will find this disposition too often manifested in republican governments. The Romans in ancient, and the Dutch in modern times, oppressed their provinces in a remarkable degree. I hope that my fears are groundless ; but I believe it as I do my creed, that this Government will operate as a faction of seven States to oppress the rest of the Union. But it may be said that we are represented, and cannot, therefore, be injured—a poor representation it will be. The British would have been glad to take America into the union, like the Scotch, by giving us a small representation. The Irish may be indulged with the same favor by asking for it. Will that lessen our misfortunes? A small representation gives a pretense to injure and destroy. But, sir, the Scotch union is introduced by an honorable gentleman, as an argument in favor of adoption. Would he wish his country to be on the same foundation as Scotland? She has but forty-five members in the House of Commons, and sixteen in the House of Lords. They go up regularly in order to be bribed. The smallness of their number puts it out of their power to carry any measure. And this unhappy nation exhibits, perhaps, the only instance in the world where corruption becomes a virtue. I devoutly pray that this description of Scotland may not be picturesque of the Southern States in three years from this time. The committee being tired, as well as myself, I will take another time to give my opinion more fully on this great and important subject.''[183]

[183] Grayson was born in Prince William county, and died at Dumfries, Va., March 12, 1790. He married Eleanor Smallwood, sister of General and Governor Wm. Smallwood, of Maryland. He left issue: i George W., of Fauquier county, died before 1832 (leaving issue: 1. Frances married Richard H. Foote; 2. George W.; 3, William); ii. Robert H. married —— (and left issue: 1. Wm. P.; 2. Hebe C. married William P. Smith; 3. Ellen S); iii. Hebe Smallwood; iv. Alfred W. died before 1829; married (and left issue: John Breckinridge, Brigadier-General Confederate States Army, from Kentucky); v. William J., statesman, born at Beaufort, S. C., Nov., 1788, died in Newberne, N. C., October 4, 1863. was graduated at the College of South Carolina in 1809, and bred to the legal profession. Entering on the practice of law at Beaufort he became a Commissioner of Equity of South Carolina, a member of the State Legislature in 1813, and Senator in 1831. He opposed the Tariff Act of 1831, but was not disposed to push the collision to the extreme of civil war. He served in Congress from December 3, 1833, to March 3, 1837, and in 1841 was appointed Collector of Customs at Charleston, S. C. In 1843 he retired to his plantation. During the secession agitation of 1850 he published a letter to Governor Seabrook deprecating disunion, and pointing out the evils that would follow. He was a frequent contributor to the *Southern Review*, and also published " The Hireling and Slave," a poem (Charleston, S. C, 1854); ''Chicora, and

Monroe, seconded by Henry, moved that the committee should rise, that Grayson should have an opportunity of continuing his argument next day ; and the House adjourned. Its session had been protracted. The heat had been intense, but it was a day which posterity will recall with pride ; for in its course Madison, Mason, Lee, and Grayson made such speeches as have been rarely heard in a single day in any deliberative assembly.

On Thursday, the twelfth of June, as soon as the House went into committee, Wythe in the chair, and the first and second sections of the Constitution still nominally the order of the day, Grayson resumed his speech. His first few sentences told that he felt a greater freedom than even the most adroit debaters are apt to feel in addressing an august assembly for the first time, which had been listening to a succession of able men, and which was destined to unmake as well as make reputations.[184]

" I asserted yesterday," he said, " that there were two opinions in the world—the one that mankind were capable of governing themselves, the other that it required actual force to govern them. On the principle that the first position was true, and which is consonant to the rights of humanity, the House will recollect that it was my opinion to amend the present Confederation, and to infuse a new portion of health and strength into the State Governments, to apportion the public debts in such a

---

other Poems"; "The Country," a poem ; "The Life of James L. Pettigru," (New York, 1866), and is supposed to have been the author of a narrative poem entitled "Marion." Colonel William Grayson, by his will, emancipated all negroes owned by him who were born after the Declaration of Independence. The executors of his will were: Benj. Orr Grayson, Robert Hanson Harrison, and it was witnessed by Spence Grayson. Benjamin Orr Grayson married Miss Bronaugh. He was the second of Armistead Thomson Mason in the fatal duel of the latter with his cousin, John Mason McCarty.—ED.

[184] This fear of the House, if I may so call it, was plainly perceptible in the manner of those who came forth early in the debate on the basis of representation in the Convention of 1829–30. There was a tremulousness even in Randolph in his first speech. Other men of real ability absolutely failed in that debate ; but, as the fear of the House wore off, and the debate passed from the basis question into a more limited range, the number and the freedom of the speakers were quite as great as was desirable, and the same result to a certain extent will presently appear in this body.

manner as to throw the unpopular ones on the back lands, to divide the rest of the domestic debt among the different States, and to call for requisitions only for the interest of the foreign debt. If, contrary to this maxim, force is necessary to govern men, I then did propose as an alternative, not a monarchy like that of Great Britain, but a milder government; one which, under the idea of a general corruption of manners and the consequent necessity of force, should be as gentle as possible. I showed, in as strong a manner as I could, some of the principal defects in the Constitution. *The greatest defect is the opposition of the component parts to the interest of the whole.* For let gentlemen ascribe its defects to as many causes as their imaginations may suggest, this is the principal and radical one. I urged that to remedy the evils which must result from this new government, a more equal representation in the legislature, and proper checks against abuse, were indispensably necessary. I do not pretend to propose for your adoption the plan of government which I mentioned as an alternative to a monarchy, in case mankind were incapable of governing themselves. I only meant that if it were once established that force was necessary to govern men, that such a plan would be more eligible for a free people than the introduction of crowned heads and nobles. Having premised thus much to obviate misconstruction, I shall proceed to the clause before us with this observation, that I prefer a complete consolidation to a partial one, but a Federal Government to either.''

He proceeded to discuss the sections under consideration, and declared that the State which gives up the power of taxation has nothing more to give. " The people of that State,'' he said, " which suffer any but their own immediate government to interfere with the sovereign right of taxation are gone forever. Giving the right of taxation is giving the right to increase the miseries of the people. Is it not a political absurdity to suppose that there can be two concurrent legislatures, each possessing the supreme power of direct taxation? If two powers come in contact, must not the one prevail over the other? Must it not strike every man's mind that two unlimited, co-equal, co-ordinate authorities over the same objects cannot exist together? But we are told that there is one instance of co-existent powers in cases of petty corporations as well here as in other parts of the world.''

He examined this example, and showed that it was wholly inapplicable to two powers possessing each an unlimited right of taxation. He then turned to the case of Scotland, which had been brought up by the friends of the Constitution as a case in point, and showed that it also was inapplicable, as the limit of taxation was fixed in the articles of union, which provide that when England pays four shillings on the pound, Scotland only pays forty-five thousand pounds sterling. He referred to the minor jurisdictions in England, the stannary courts and others, and showed that they had no application whatever to the case of two supreme legislatures in a single country. After showing that the judicious exercise of such a power, according to the received maxims of representation, was impracticable, he placed his opponents in the dilemma, either of being compelled to withhold this power from the Federal Government, or of surrendering the first maxims of representation, that those who lay the taxes should bear their proportion in paying them. A tax that might with propriety be laid and collected with ease in Delaware, would be highly improper in Virginia. The taxes cannot be uniform through the States without being oppressive to some. If they be not uniform, some of the members will lay taxes, in the payment of which they will bear no proportion. The members of Delaware may assist in laying taxes on our slaves; but do they return to Virginia?

Following closely in the track of Madison's speech, delivered the day before, he thus replied to the argument derived from our probable position as a neutral power, which had been argued so ably by that gentleman : " We are then told," he said, " of the armed neutrality of the Empress of Russia, the opposition to it by Great Britain, and the acquiescence of other powers. We are told that, in order to become the carriers of contending nations, it will be necessary to be formidable at sea—that we must have a fleet in case of a war between Great Britain and France. I think that the powers which formed that treaty will be able to support it. But, if we were certain that this would not be the case, still I think that the profits that would arise from such a transient commerce would not compensate for the expense of rendering ourselves formidable at sea, or the dangers that would probably result from the attempt. To have a fleet in the present limited population of America is, in my opinion, impracticable and inexpedient.   Is America in a situation to have a fleet?   I take it to be a rule founded on common sense that manufacturers, as well as sailors, proceed from a redundancy of inhabitants.   Our numbers, compared to our territory, are very small indeed.   I think, therefore, that all attempts to have a fleet, till our western lands are fully settled, are nugatory and vain.   How will you induce your people to go to sea?   Is it not more agreeable to follow agriculture than to encounter the dangers and the hardships of the ocean?   The same reason will apply, in a great degree, to manufacturers.   Both are the result of necessity.   It would, besides, be dangerous to have a fleet in our present weak, dispersed, and defenceless situation.   The powers of Europe, which have West India possessions, would be alarmed at any extraordinary maritime exertions; and, knowing the danger of our arriving at manhood, would crush us in our infancy.   In my opinion, the great objects most necessary to be promoted and attended to in America are agriculture and population.   First, take care that you are sufficiently strong by land to guard against European partitions.   Secure your own house before you attack that of another people.   I think that the sailors, who could be prevailed upon to go to sea, would be a real loss to the community.   Neglect of agriculture and loss of labor would be the certain consequence of such an irregular policy.   I hope that, when these objections are thoroughly considered, all ideas of having a fleet in our infant situation will be given over.   When the American character is better known, and the Government established on permanent principles—when we shall be sufficiently populous, and our situation secure—then come forward with a fleet; not with a small one, but with one sufficient to meet any of the maritime powers."[185]

[185] These early opinions on the subject of a navy have much interest in connection with the controversies that were soon to be waged on that topic.   Adam Stephen was the first of our politicians to predict glory from the establishment of a navy.   In a letter to R. H. Lee, dated February 3, 1775, he says: "We only want a navy to give law to the world, and we have it in our power to get it."   John Adams is usually considered the father of the navy; but in his letters he insists that "the navy is the child of Jefferson."   The resolutions of 1799 gave it a blast, which was followed by the action of Mr. Jefferson. When one of our prominent politicians, near the close of the last cen-

He next adverted to an opinion of Madison on the revenue likely to flow from imposts, and as this passage shows the views held by two of the first political economists in the Convention on the amount of revenue to be expected from the customs, we will give it in full : "The honorable gentleman (Madison)," he said, "has told us that the impost will be less productive hereafter, on account of the increase of population. I shall not controvert this principle. When all the lands are settled and we have manufactures sufficient, this may be the case ; but I believe that for a very long time this cannot possibly happen. In islands and thickly-settled countries, where they have manufactures, the principle will hold good, but will not apply in any degree to our country. I apprehend that among us, as the people in the lower country find themselves straightened, they will remove to the frontiers, which will, for a considerable period, prevent the lower country from being very populous, or having recourse to manufactures. I cannot, therefore, but conclude that the amount of imposts will continue to increase, at least for a great many years."[186]

He next came to the relief of Henry and Mason in sustaining the inferences which they had drawn from Holland, and went into an explanation of the state of parties in that country—the party of the Prince of Orange and the Louvestein faction—England taking the side of one and France of the other; and main-

---

tury, was charged with having said that the union ought to be dissolved, he denied that he made the remark, except with the qualification that "in the contingency of the Federal Government building *three* seventyfours." Though now long dead, he lived to read the bulletins of Hull, Decatur, Stewart, Perry, McDonough, and their gallant compatriots.

[186] It is not uninstructive to recur to the opinions held by our early statesmen on the rate of duties to be laid upon imports. If the States had assented to the plan of vesting in the old Confederation the right to levy five per cent. upon imports (which Virginia assented to), in all human probability the Federal Constitution would not have been called into existence. In the course of his present speech Grayson expressed the opinion that two and a-half per cent. would put more money into the treasury than five, as the high rate would encourage smuggling. As late as 1792, Pendleton, in his letter on a Federal tariff, thought that *five per cent.* was as high as the Federal Government ought to go. It is very plain that in framing a government the wisest men sometimes see but a very little way ahead.

tained that the difficulties of the Dutch were produced by that unnatural contest, and were not the result of the particular construction of their federal alliance. As for the slowness with which our own requisitions were paid, will any patriot blame a non-compliance during the war, when our ports were blockaded, when all means of getting money were destroyed, when our country was overrun by the enemy, when almost every article which the farmer could raise was seized to sustain the armies in the field? And since the war the flourishing States have very fairly complied with requisitions. Others have delayed to pay from inability to make the payment. Massachusetts attempted to correct the nature of things by extracting from the people more than they were able to part with; and what was the result? A revolution that shook that State to its centre; a revolution from which she was rescued by that abhorred and contemned system which gentlemen are anxious to supersede; for it was a vote of Congress for fifteen hundred men, which, aided by the executors of the State, put down all opposition, and restored the public tranquility.

He adverted to an argument which Pendleton had urged as a means of relief against maladministration in the Federal Government: "We are told," he said, "that Conventions gave and Conventions can take away. This observation does not appear to me to be well-founded. *It is not so easy to dissolve a government like that upon the table.* Its dissolution may be prevented by a trifling minority of the people of America. The consent of so many States is necessary to obtain amendments, that I fear they will with great difficulty be obtained." He scanned the clause of the Constitution which sets apart the ten miles square. "I would not deny," he said, "the propriety of vesting the Government with exclusive jurisdiction over this territory, were it properly guarded. Perhaps I am mistaken; but it occurs to me that Congress may give exclusive privileges to merchants residing in the ten miles square, and that the same exclusive power of legislation will enable them to grant similar privileges to merchants within the strongholds of the State. Such results are not without precedent. Else, whence have issued the Hanse Towns, Cinque Ports, and other places in Europe, which have peculiar privileges in commerce as well as in other matters? I do not offer this sentiment as an opinion, but a conjecture; and in this doubtful agitation of mind on a point of such infinite magnitude, I only ask for information from the framers of the Constitution whose superior opportunities must have furnished them with more ample lights on the subject than I am possessed of."[187] He discussed the question of the relative safety of the right of navigating the Mississippi under the old and the new system ; and maintained that under the Confederation nine States were necessary to cede that right away, but that under the new five States only were required for the purpose, as ten members were two-thirds of a quorum in the Senate, and five States send ten members.[188] "In my opinion," he said, "the power of making treaties by which the territorial rights of the States may be essentially affected, ought to be guarded against every possibility of abuse; and the precarious situation to which those rights will be exposed is one reason with me, among a number of others, for voting against the adoption of this Constitution."[189]

Tradition has represented this speech as one of the most argumentative, most eloquent, and most effective delivered during the session ; and from the meagre skeleton of it that has come down to us, we can easily see that it deserved the highest praise. It is said that it gave a new impulse to the opposition, and its influence may be clearly traced in the subsequent discussions.

As soon as Grayson took his seat, Pendleton, who, when the House was in committee, always sat near the chair, caught the eye of Wythe, and, placed upon his crutches, proceeded to deliver the most elaborate of all the speeches which he made upon the floor.[190]

---

[187] In his vaticinations he came very near embracing the case of the *Cohens* v. *the State of Virginia*, WHEATON, Vol. —.

[188] The opposition of New England to the acquisition of Louisiana is an instance within the range of his fears.

[189] I may say here that I do not refer to the page in *Robertson's Debates*, partly because the book, which has been out of print for thirty years, may be reprinted ere long in a different form, when my references would lead astray; but mainly because I record each day's session and the order of the speakers on the floor. *Elliot's Debates* are also out of print, and their paging does not correspond with *Robertson's*. If there had been a new edition of the debates, I would have cited the page for the convenience of the student.

[190] It was interesting to behold the eagerness of the members on both sides of the House in their endeavors to assist Pendleton in his efforts

He began by brushing away the driftwood which had been floating on the stream of debate ; and which defiled the face of the waters.   The venerable speaker had not relished the laugh which Henry had raised by ridiculing his scheme of calling a Convention to withdraw the powers of a Government, the president of which, at the head of a well-equipped and devoted army, was marching against the people of a State which had no arms in its possession, and he followed Henry in the course of his speech.   He regretted that such expressions as those which likened the people to a HERD had been used, and he wished the gentleman (Henry) had felt himself at liberty to let it pass. " We are assembled by the people," he said, " to contemplate in the calm lights of mild philosophy what government is best calculated to promote their happiness and secure their liberty. We should not criticize harshly the expressions which may escape in the effusions of honest zeal.   On the subject of government the worthy member (Henry) and myself differ on the threshold.   I think government necessary to protect liberty. He supposes the American spirit all-sufficient for the purpose. Do Montesquieu, Locke, and Sidney agree with the gentleman ? They have presented us with no such idea.   They denounce cruel and excessive punishments, but they recommend that the ligaments of government should be firmer and the execution of the laws more strict in a republic than in a monarchy.   Was I not then correct in my inference that such a government and liberty were friends and allies, and that their common enemy was faction, turbulence and violence ?   A republican government is the nursery of science.   It turns the bent of it to eloquence as a qualification for the representative character, which is, as it ought to be, the road to our public offices.   I differ from the gentleman in another respect.   He professes himself an advocate for the *middle* and *lower* classes of men.   I profess to be a friend to the *equal* liberty of *all* men from the palace to the cottage, without any other distinction than between *good* and *bad* men."   He then referred to an expression which Mason had quoted from a friend of the Constitution.   " Why introduce

---

to rise.   He took a seat near the chair for the convenience of ascending and descending from it at the beginning and at the end of each day's session.

such an expression as *well-born?* None such are to be found in the paper on your table. I consider every man well-born who comes into the world with an intelligent mind, and with all his parts perfect. Whether a man is great or small, he is equally dear to me. I wish for a regular government for the protection of the honest and industrious planter and farmer. I am old enough to have seen great changes in society. I have often known those who commenced life without any other stock than industry and economy attain to opulence and wealth. This could only happen in a regular government. The true principle of republicanism, and the greatest security of liberty, is regular government. What become of the passions of men when they enter society? Do they leave them? No; they bring them with them, and their passions will overturn your government without an adequate check." He recurred to the use of the word "illumined" by Henry, and charged him with inconsistency in its use. "The gentleman has made a distinction between the *illumined* and the *ignorant*. I have heard elsewhere with pleasure the worthy gentleman expatiate on the advantages of learning, among other things as friendly to liberty. I have seen in our code of laws the *public* purse applied to cherish *private* seminaries. This is not strictly just; but with me the end sanctified the means, and I was satisfied.[191] But did we thus encourage learning to set up those who attained its benefits as butts of invidious distinction? Surely, the worthy member on reflection will disavow the idea. Am I still suspected of a want of attachment to my fellow-citizens, whom the gentleman calls peasants and cottagers? Let me rescue them from the ignominy to which he consigns them. He classes them with the Swiss, who are born and sold as mercenaries to the highest bidder; with the people of the Netherlands, who do not possess that distinguished badge of freedom, the right of suffrage; and with the British, who have to a small extent the right of suffrage, but who sell it for a mess of pottage. Are these people to be compared to our worthy planters and farmers who draw food

---

[191] This is a hit at Henry, but I know not to what it refers, unless to Hampden-Sidney, of which Henry was one of the trustees, or to Quesnay, the builder of the first Richmond academy, whom Henry befriended.

and raiment, and even wealth, from the inexhaustible stores which a bountiful Creator has placed beneath their feet?"

He maintained that the happiness and safety of the people were the objects of the plan under consideration, and they were, therefore, regarded by it as the source of power. But, as the people cannot act in a body, they must act through their representatives; and he showed that a representative government was the only true and safe mode of administering the affairs of a people; that, if the Confederation had rested on a popular basis, we should have found that peace and happiness which we are now in quest of. In the State Constitution you commit the sword to the executive and the purse to the legislature, and everything else without a limitation. In both cases the representative principle is preserved, and you are safe. Legislatures may sometimes do wrong. They have done wrong. Here his voice fell to a low tone, and then became inaudible. His physical suffering had for a moment repressed the faculties of his fine intellect. It was a scene that appealed to the sensibilities of all present. It was the first time that voice, which for the third of a century had been the delight of friends and terror of foes, ever faltered in debate. When he rallied, he was understood to say that his brethren of the judiciary felt great uneasiness in their minds to violate the Constitution by such a law.[192] They had prevented the operation of some unconstitutional acts. Still, preserve the representative principle in your government, and you are safe. He said he had made his remarks as introductory to the consideration of the paper on the table. "I conceive," he said, "that in those respects, where our State Constitution has not been disapproved of, objections will not apply against that on your table. In forming our State Constitution we looked only to our local circumstances; but in forming the plan under consideration we must look to our connection with the neighboring States.

---

[192] He had just mentioned the case of Philips when he ceased to be heard. If in continuation he referred to that case, which I hardly think is probable, it is one of the most singular instances on record of individuals imagining feelings which they never felt; for it is unquestionable that Philips, in company with four or five others, was indicted for highway robbery and condemned, after a fair trial, by the ordinary laws of the land, and not by attainder.

We have seen the advantages and blessings of the union.   God grant we may never see the disadvantages of disunion !''

On the subject of direct taxation, he said that ''if it was necessary for our interests to form an union, then it was necessary to cede adequate powers to attain the end in view.   We must delegate the powers appropriate to the end.   And to whom do we delegate those powers ?   To our own representatives.   Why should we fear more from our representatives there than from our representatives here ?   But a gentleman (Monroe) has said that the power of direct taxation is unnecessary, because the back lands and the impost will be sufficient to answer all Federal purposes.   What, then, are we disputing about ?   Does the gentleman think that Congress will lay direct taxes if other funds are sufficient ?   It will remain a harmless power on paper, and do no injury.   If it should be necessary, will gentlemen run the risk of the union by withholding it ?''   When he had rescued the subject of requisitions and taxation from the misrepresentations which he alleged had been made in the committee, re-established his position respecting the probable harmony of the two judiciary systems, and showed that it was the interest of the General Government to strengthen the government of the States, he discussed the Mississippi question, then passed to the judiciary, and ended with an expression of his opinion, which he sustained by arguments in favor of subsequent amendments.

There was a short intermission while the friends of Pendleton were aiding him to resume his seat, and were congratulating him on his speech.   It was remarked that some of his opponents cordially greeted the old man eloquent, and that others gave a silent pressure of the hand, which spoke not less sensibly than words.   In fact, his speech, apart from the speaker, was a really fine effort.   The rebukes which he dealt to his opponents were galling, his points were well-made, the turning of the argument of Monroe against his own party was adroit, and the beautiful exposition of the theory of a popular representative system in averting misrule and in preserving the public liberty in the long run intact, and of the defects of the Confederation as resulting from the absence of this principle in that instrument, was ingenious and happy.   But when we add to the intrinsic worth of the speech the picture of the venerable old man, in whose person the infirmity of an irreparable accident was added to the infirmi-

ties of age, his high authority, which imparted to every word
that he uttered an almost judicial dignity, and his still higher
spirit beneath which his physical powers sank, the occasion must
have excited uncommon interest. Still there were parts of his
speech which evinced that the old debater had not forgot his
ways. His evident misrepresentation of the argument of Henry
in more than one instance, his ungenerous reflection upon that
individual for his liberality in lending a helping hand to our
infant literary institutions, and, perhaps, his imagined sorrow at
an event that never occurred, indicated that personal feelings
had mingled with political, and that the man was not wholly lost
in the sage.

Madison rose to reply to Grayson. As Grayson had propounded a dilemma for the reflection of the friends of the
Constitution, Madison was resolved to return the compliment.
The dilemma of Grayson was that, on their own admission, the
advocates of the new plan must either admit the impracticability
of laying uniform taxes throughout the States, or surrender the
great principle on which the doctrine of representation rests,
that those who lay the taxes should pay them. "The honorable
gentleman over the way," said Madison, "set forth that by
giving up the power of taxation we should give up everything,
and still insists on requisitions being made on the States; and
that then, if they be not complied with, Congress shall lay direct
taxes by way of penalty. Let us consider the dilemma which
arises from this doctrine. Either requisitions will be efficacious,
or they will not. If they will be efficacious, then I say, sir, we
give up everything as much as by direct taxation. The same
amount will be paid by the people as by direct taxes. But if
they be not efficacious, where is the advantage of this plan? In
what respect will it relieve us from the inconveniencies which we
have experienced from requisitions? The power of laying direct
taxes by the General Government is supposed by the honorable
gentleman to be chimerical and impracticable. What is the consequence of the alternative he proposes? We are to rely upon
this power to be ultimately used as a penalty to compel the
States to comply. If it be chimerical and impracticable in the
first instance, it will be equally so when it will be exercised as a
penalty. The dilemma of Madison has not the force of the
dilemma propounded by Grayson. Both of its horns have a

rottenness visible on its surface.   He assumes a position which he was bound to prove, and which is incapable of proof, that the amount called for by requisition and the amount to be raised by direct taxes levied by the Federal Government could be collected with the same convenience and economy from the citizens of Virginia.   In collecting, the amount of a requisition selected its own objects and availed itself of a well-established machinery for the purpose, merely adding a certain *per centum* to the annual taxes ; while the General Government would be compelled to maintain a staff of officers for carrying into effect a contingency which may happen this year, but which may not happen in the next seven.   There was also another consideration in favor of the States in the case of requisitions.   The Congress, well knowing the difficulty and delicacy, as well as the uncertainty and cost, of collecting a given amount by direct taxation over a region of wild country as vast as the whole of Europe, would be inclined, in order to avoid an unpleasant alternative, to exact as little in the first instance by requisition as would satisfy the public exigencies.   It was the difficulty of the remedy that induced Grayson to propose it as a penalty, and a penalty it would be to the States to the extent of the difference between the two modes of collection.   Nor was the other horn of the dilemma more formidable.   It is true that the collection of the direct taxes might be equally difficult, whether as an original measure or as a penalty ; but the argument of Mason was *ad hominem*, and applied to Madison and to all those who contended that direct taxes could be easily collected by the Federal Government.

Madison replied to the arguments urged by Grayson against the policy of creating a navy in prospect of the uncertain and ephemeral profits to be derived from a neutral trade.   " The gentleman has supposed," he said, "that my argument with respect to a future war between Great Britain and France was fallacious.   The other nations of Europe have acceded to that neutrality, while Great Britain opposed it.   We need not suspect in case of such a war that we should be suffered to participate of the profitable emoluments of the carrying trade, unless we were in a respectable situation.   Recollect the last war.   Was there ever a war in which the British nation stood opposed to so many nations?   All the belligerent nations of Europe, with nearly one-half the British empire, were united against it.   Yet that nation, though defeated and humbled beyond any previous example, stood out against this. From her firmness and spirit in such desperate circumstances, we may divine what her future conduct may be. I did not contend that it was necessary for the United States to establish a navy for that sole purpose, but instanced it as one reason out of several for rendering ourselves respectable. I am no friend to naval or land armaments in time of peace ; but if they be necessary, the calamity must be submitted to. Weakness will invite insults. A respectable government will not only entitle us to a participation of the advantages which are enjoyed by other nations, but will be a security against attacks and insults. It is to avoid the calamity of being obliged to have large armaments that we should establish this government. The best way to avoid danger is to be in a capacity to withstand it."

As a specimen of fair debating, we annex the reply of Madison to the arguments of Grayson in relation to the probable increase of the revenue from imports : " The imports, we are told, will not diminish, because the emigrations to the westward will prevent the increase of population. The gentleman has reasoned on this subject justly to a certain degree. I admit that the imports will increase till population becomes so great as to compel us to recur to manufactures. The period cannot be very far distant when the unsettled parts of America will be inhabited. At the expiration of twenty-five years hence, I conceive that in every part of the United States there will be as great a population as there is now in the settled parts. We see already that in the most populous parts of the union, and where there is but a medium, manufactures are beginning to be established. Where this is the case, the amount of importations will begin to diminish. Although the imports may even increase during the term of twenty-five years, yet, when we are preparing a government for perpetuity, we ought to found it on permanent principles and not on those of a temporary nature." He next reviewed the Mississippi question, and the explanations of Grayson respecting Holland ; and examined the distinction made by Grayson between the carrying and the producing States, showing that the majority of the States would probably be non-carrying, and would unite with Virginia in opposing them when necessary. In the course of his speech he answered the inquiry, " How came the New England States to object to the cession of the navigation of the Mississippi, when the Southern States were willing to part with it? What was the cause of the Northern States being the champions of this right, when the Southern States were disposed to surrender it? The preservation of this right will be for the general interest of the Union. The Western country will be settled from the North as well as from the South, and its prosperity will add to the strength and security of the union."

Henry followed Madison and observed that, however painful it was to be making objections, he was compelled to make some observations. He said that the dangers with which we have been menaced have been proved to be imaginary; but the dangers from the new Constitution were real. Our dearest rights would be left in the hands of those whose interest it would be to infringe them. He reviewed Mr. Jefferson's letter, which had been read by Pendleton, and insisted that according to that letter four States ought to reject the Constitution. Where are the four States to come from if Virginia approves the new plan? Let Virginia instantly reject that instrument, and all amendments necessary to secure the liberties of the people will certainly be adopted. But how can you obtain amendments when Massachusetts, the great Northern State, Pennsylvania, the great Middle State, and Virginia, the great Southern State shall have ratified the Constitution? He examined the doctrine that all powers not expressly granted are reserved, and showed that henceforth our dearest rights would rest on construction and implication. Did this process satisfy our British ancestors? Look at Magna Charta, at the Bill of Rights, and at the Declaration of Rights, which prescribed on what terms William of Orange should reign. " The gentleman (Randolph) has told us his object is union. I admit that the reality of union, and not the name, is the object which most merits the attention of every friend of his country. He told you that you should hear many *sounding words* from our side of the House. We have heard the word *union* from *him*. I have heard no word so often pronounced in this House as he did this. I admit that the American union is dear to every man. I admit that every man who has three grains of information must know and think that union is the best of all things. *But we must not mis-*

take the ends for the means. If he can show that the rights of the union are secure, we will consent. It has been sufficiently demonstrated that they are not secured. It sounds mighty prettily to curse paper money and honestly pay debts. But look to the situation of America, and you will find that there are thousands and thousands of contracts, whereof equity forbids an exact liberal performance. Pass that government, and you will be bound hand and foot. There was an immense quantity of depreciated paper money in circulation at the conclusion of the war. This money is in the hands of individuals to this day. The holders of this money may call for the nominal value, if this government be adopted. This State may be compelled to pay her proportion of that currency pound for pound. Pass this government, and you will be carried to the Federal court (if I understand that paper right), and you will be compelled to pay shilling for shilling. A State may be sued in the Federal court, by the paper on your table.''

He reverted to the frequently cited case of Scotland, contending that the Scotch, like a sensible people, had secured their rights in the articles of union. He said that, if this new scheme would establish credit, it might be well enough ; but if we are ever to be in a state of preparation for war on such airy and imaginable grounds as the possibility of danger, your government must be military and dangerous to liberty. '' But we are to become formidable,'' he said, and have a strong government to protect us from the British nation. Will that paper on your table prevent the attacks of the British navy, or enable us to raise a fleet equal to the British fleet? The British have the strongest fleet in Europe, and can strike everywhere. It is the utmost folly to conceive that that paper can have such an operation. It will be no less so to attempt to raise a powerful fleet. He urged the advantage of requisitions, in preference of direct taxation by the Federal Government, on the ground that ·''the whole wisdom of the science of government with respect to taxation consisted in selecting that mode of collection which will best accommodate the convenience of the people. When you come to tax a great country, you will find *ten* men too few to settle the manner of collection.[193] One capital advantage

---

[193] The number of representatives to which Virginia would be entitled in the first Congress was ten.

which will result from the proposed alternative will be this: that there will be a necessary communication between your ten members of Congress and your one hundred and seventy representatives here.   We might also remonstrate, if by mistake or design the sum asked for is too large.   But, above all, the people would pay the taxes cheerfully.   If it be supposed that this would occasion a waste of time and an injury to public credit, which would only happen when requisitions were not complied with, the delay would be compensated by the payment of interest, which, with the addition of the credit of the State to that of the general government, would in a great measure obviate that objection.''   He repelled the idea that responsibility was secured by direct taxation, maintaining his denial by arguments drawn from the construction of the House of Representatives, and that the State governments would exercise more influence than the general government, contending that the larger salaries and the multiplicity of Federal offices would cast the balance against the State.   ,He recurred to the argument of Pendleton on the nature of representative government, and sought to prove that the principle was only nominally adopted in the new scheme, enforcing his views by a reference to the inequality of representation in the Senate.   Rulers are the servants of the people—the people are their masters.   Is this the spirit of the new scheme?   It is the spirit of our State Constitution.   That gentleman (Pendleton) helped to form that government; and all the applause which it justly deserves go to the condemnation of this new plan.   The gentleman has spoken of the errors and failures of our State government.   " I do not justify,'' he said, " what merits censure, but *I shall not degrade my country*.   The gentleman did our judiciary an honor in saying that they had the firmness to counteract the Legislature in some cases.   Will your Federal judiciary imitate the example?   Where are your landmarks in this government?   I will be bold to say that you cannot find any in it.   I take it as the highest encomium on Virginia that the acts of the Legislature, if unconstitutional, are liable to be opposed by the judiciary.''[194]   He proceeded to show that the two execu-

---

[194] It is remarkable that Henry rarely replied to any personal remark made against him in debate.   In this instance he could easily have retorted on Pendleton the censure which that gentleman cast upon him for helping private literary institutions, but he passed the matter over.

tives and the two judiciaries must necessarily interfere with each other, and that of the State must go down in the collision. The citizen would be oppressed by the Federal collector, and dragged into some distant Federal court, unless there was a Federal court in each county, which he hoped would not be the case.

Madison rose to reply to Henry. He made his usual apology for departing from the order of the day, but was compelled to follow gentlemen on the other side, who had taken the greatest latitude in their remarks. He argued that, if there be that terror in direct taxation, which would compel the States to comply with requisitions to avoid the Federal legislature, and if, as gentlemen say, this State will always have it in her power to make her collections speedily and fully, the people will be compelled to pay the same amount as quickly and as punctually as if raised by the Federal Government. "It has been amply proved," he said, "that the general government can lay taxes as conveniently to the people as the State governments, by imitating the State systems of taxation. If the general government has not the power of collecting its own revenues in the first instance, it will be still dependent on the State governments in some measure; and the exercise of this power after refusal will be inevitably productive of injustice and confusion, if partial compliances be made before it is driven to assume it. Thus, without relieving the people in the smallest degree, the alternative proposed will impair the efficacy of the government, and will perpetually endanger the tranquility of the union." He next combatted with great force the charge of the insecurity of religious freedom under the new system. "Is a bill of rights," he said, "a security for religion? Would the bill of rights in this State exempt the people from paying for the support of one particular sect, if such sect were exclusively established by law?[195] If there were a majority of one sect, the bill of rights would be a poor protection for liberty. Happily for the States they enjoy the utmost freedom of religion. This freedom arises from that multiplicity of sects which pervade America, and which is the best and only security for religious liberty in any society. For where

---

[195] Since the delivery of this speech, the bill of rights has been decided to be a part of the Constitution of the State, and the question has lost its force. Edmund Randolph declared in this debate that it was not a part of the Constitution.

there is such a variety of sects, there cannot be a majority of any one sect to oppress and persecute the rest. Fortunately for this Commonwealth, the majority of the people are decidedly against any exclusive establishment. I think it is so in the other States. There is not a shadow of right in the general government to intermeddle with religion. Its least interference with it would be a most flagrant usurpation. I can appeal to my uniform conduct on this subject, that I have warmly supported religious freedom.[196] It is better that this security should be depended upon from the general government, than from one particular State. A particular State might concur in one religious project. But the United States abound in such a variety of sects, that it is a strong security against religious persecution, and is sufficient to authorize a conclusion that no one sect will ever be able to outnumber or depress the rest." He animadverted on the introduction of Mr. Jefferson's opinions in debate, and sought by an appeal to the pride of the House, couched in terms as sarcastic as his strict sense of propriety allowed him to indulge, to impair the force of Henry's arguments drawn from the contents of the letter of that statesman. "Is it come to this, then," he inquired, "that we are not to follow our own reason? Is it proper to introduce the names of individuals not within these walls? Are we, who, in the honorable gentleman's opinion, are not to be governed by an *erring world*, now to submit to the opinion of a gentleman on the other side of the Atlantic?" He then most adroitly quoted the authority which he had so explicitly condemned as out of place in that hall. "I am in some measure acquainted with his opinions on the question immediately before the House. I will venture to say that this clause is not objected to by Mr. Jefferson. He approves of it because it enables the government to carry on its own operations." He declined to follow the gentleman through all his desultory objections, but would recur to a few points. He rarely fails to contradict the arguments of those on his own side of the question. He complains that the numbers of the Federal Government will add to

---

[196] This is as near an approach to his own personal acts as Mr. Madison ever made. He drew the memorial in favor of religious freedom, which is one of the finest State papers in our language. Had his modesty been less, many a letter and State paper in our historical literature, now passing under the name of another, would be known to be his.

the public expense a weight too formidable to be borne, while he and other gentlemen on the same side object that the number of representatives is too small. He inveighs against the government because such transactions as require secresy may be kept private ; yet forgets that that very part of the Constitution is borrowed from the Confederation—the very system which the gentleman advocates. He seeks to obviate the force of my observations with respect to concurrent collections of taxes under different authorities, and says there is no interference between parochial and general taxes because they irradiate from the same centre. Do not the concurrent collections under the State and general government, to use the gentleman's own term, all irradiate from the people at large? The people is the common superior. The sense of the people at large is to be the predominant spring of their actions. This is a sufficient security against interference. He observed that he would reply to other arguments offered by the gentleman in their proper places.

The House then adjourned.

On Friday morning, the thirteenth day of June, the people began to assemble at an early hour in the new Academy. The seats set apart for spectators were soon filled, and an eager crowd had collected about the windows and beset the approaches to the hall. At the first stroke of the bell which announced the hour of ten every member was in his place. It was observed that the voice of Waugh, as he read the collect for the day, had a tone of more than usual solemnity. For it was generally known that the subject of the navigation of the Mississippi—a subject which enlisted the passions equally of the rich and the poor, and was the absorbing topic of the age in the South—would that day be discussed in a most imposing form ; and it was thought not improbable that under the daring lead of Henry the opponents of the Constitution, who had suddenly sprung this mine under the feet of its friends, might seek to carry their point by an immediate vote on the ratification of that instrument. George Nicholas was the first to rise. He was friendly to the Constitution, and doubtless desired its success ; but he was deeply connected with Kentucky, whither he was soon to remove, and he was indisposed from motives of present as well as future policy to thwart the wishes of the delegation from the district. He urged the Convention either to proceed according to their original determination of discussing the Constitution clause by clause, or to rescind that order, and discuss that paper at large. Henry opposed the policy of proceeding clause by clause, and thought that the mode of discussion should be at large. He observed that there was one question which had taken up much time, and he wished before leaving that subject that the transactions of Congress relative to the navigation of the Mississippi should be communicated to the Convention, in order that the members might draw their conclusions from the best source. With this view he hoped that those gentlemen who had been then in Congress, and the present members of Congress in Convention, could communicate what they knew on the subject. He declared that he did not wish to hurt the feelings of the gentlemen who had been in Congress, or to reflect on any private character; but that for the information of the Convention, he was desirous of having the most authentic account, and a faithful statement of facts. Nicholas assented to the proposition of Henry. Madison, who had at the commencement of the session written his fears to Washington that the topic of the Mississippi might jeopard the success of the Constitution, felt indignant at the snare which he believed Henry had spread for his destruction, and seemed not indisposed, contrary to his usual habit, to construe the action of that individual into a personal reflection upon himself. He rose and declared that, if Henry thought that *he* had given an incorrect account of the transactions relative to the Mississippi, he would on a thorough and complete investigation find himself mistaken ; that it had always been his opinion that the policy which had for its object the relinquishment of that river was unwise, and that the mode of conducting it was still more exceptionable. He added that he had no objection to have every light on the subject that could tend to elucidate it.

The House then resolved itself into a Committee of the Whole, "more particularly for the purpose of receiving information concerning the transactions of Congress relative to the Mississippi." Wythe took the chair, and, on motion, the acts and resolutions of the Assembly relative to the Mississippi were read.

We now proceed to record a scene which our fathers were wont to rehearse to their sons in subdued tones, as if the crisis were imminent, which nearly involved the fate of the Federal Constitution, and which, even at this day, when viewed through the mirage of seventy summers, appears one of the most intensely interesting and thrilling scenes in our history. We are to record the spectacle of a people, in their highest sovereign capacity, holding an inquest into the conduct of their representatives on an occasion of vital importance to their own welfare and to the welfare of their posterity. It will have been seen that the navigation of the Mississippi had often been alluded to in debate, and had been discussed at some length on both sides of the House. At the present day, if we look to the West, we will see many young, populous, and prosperous republics, which feel a more direct interest in that river than we can possibly feel; for while we can only regard it mainly in a national view, they regard it as the source of daily personal convenience and profit as well as in its national aspect; but it was far otherwise with our fathers. They cherished the right to navigate that river as the apple of their eye. It was with a just pride that they looked to the extended limits of the State. Often has the young Virginian, when visiting the picturesque seats on the Thames, told to wondering Englishmen how the eastern frontier of the great Commonwealth from which he came rested on the Atlantic, and how the western, instead of being traced, as now, by an imaginary line running through obscure forests and over hills and creeks,[197] was bounded by that majestic stream, whose many waters, springing from the recesses of far distant and inaccessible mountains, whose base the foot of civilized man had never approached, and in their course of thousands of miles through an illimitable region, into which the fearless La Salle had not ventured to launch his canoe, nor the saintly Hennepin to hold up the cross of his Heavenly Master, gathering tributes from streams vaster than their own, flowed past its entire extent in their triumphal progress to the sea. The present Commonwealth of Kentucky, then a district of Virginia, was divided into six counties, which, like the other counties of the State, sent a delegation of two members each to the present Convention. To the prosperity, nay, almost

---

[197] The word "creek" is an instance of the truth with which the origin of a people may be traced in their use of words. It is properly applicable to salt water œstuaries only, and its use in connection with water-courses a thousand miles distant from tide, shows that the ancestral stock came from the seaboard, and, perhaps, from an island, where the word necessarily abounds more than on the mainland.

to the very existence of that territory, which was soon to become a State, the navigation of the Mississippi was indispensable ; and it was now believed that the twelve members from the district held the fate of the Constitution in their hands. If they voted for that instrument in a body, its ratification was certain ; and if they gave an united vote against it, its rejection was deemed almost certain. There were other contingent interests connected with the subject which were of grave moment. The emigrants to the district were principally Virginians, the sons and daughters, and, in some cases, the fathers and mothers, of those whom they left behind in their quest of the cheap and fertile lands of the west. There was another tie which bound the people of Virginia to the new land of promise, even stronger than that of consanguinity. They lived by agriculture ; and the wide area of land, shelving gradually from the Blue Ridge to the ocean, had been for nearly two centuries in cultivation, and had long ceased to retain the virtues of the virgin soil. While such was the case, with some exceptions, generally, it was especially so in the country not far above tide and nearly all below it, a region of country which embraced much of the active capital of the State. Large speculations had already taken place in western lands, and more than one prominent member of the Convention was casting his eyes to Kentucky as the future home of himself and of his posterity. But all these flattering hopes would be instantly blasted with the loss of the navigation of the Mississippi. The poor man might indeed build his cabin in the district, and rear his family on the products of his farm and from the chase ; but capital there could find no employment unless the proceeds of labor could be made to mingle with the commerce of the world. It had been well known that the cession of that river to Spain had been recently under discussion, and had received the countenance of the Secretary of Foreign Affairs, who, it was said, was acting in friendly union with Guardoqui, the Spanish minister. Rumors only reached the public ear ; for, as the proceedings of Congress were secret, no reliable intelligence on the subject was generally known. An alarm faintly to be expressed by words seized the people generally, irrespective of their place of residence. The Kentuckians were maddened almost to desperation. And it was plain that Kentucky would not only refuse to be a party to a treaty of cession, but to acknowledge its obligation.

Fortunately, several of the members of Congress were also members of the Convention, and from them the true state of the case might be ascertained. What enhanced the interest of the present occasion was the belief that the " six easternmost States " had seemed to acquiesce in the suggestion of Mr. Jay, the Secretary of Foreign Affairs, of a cession of the river to Spain for five and twenty years ; and that, under the new system, as had been shown by Grayson, it was possible that as ten members might constitute a quorum of the Senate competent to make a treaty, and as those ten were returned by five States, the five New England States might seize the lucky moment, and accomplish the ruin of the West. The subject was also regarded with peculiar emotions by the Convention as a body. The friends of the Constitution viewed the whole affair as a plot deliberately designed for their overthrow, and although they felt the deepest indignation, and knew that, though they might lose everything, they could not possibly gain a single advantage, they were compelled from policy to assent to this public exposition. Quite different were the feelings of the opponents of the new scheme. They regarded that scheme as fraught with untold evils to the country, and were ready to avail themselves of all legitimate means to prevent its adoption. The navigation of the great river of the West had hung by a hair, and the safety of that invaluable right alone was of sufficient importance to make or to unmake constitutions. They also believed that not only was this great right insecure, but that all the other great rights which society was formed to protect were in peril from the proposed scheme of government. That the scene might not lack the proper complement in a solemn public inquisition, Henry acted as Attorney for the Commonwealth, and the zeal, the tact, and the keenness which he displayed in his self-assumed office, made him no unmeaning figure in that exciting drama.

The members of the Convention who had been in Congress during the Mississippi affair were Henry Lee and Madison, who were friendly to the Constitution, and Grayson and Monroe, who were opposed to it. It is probable that Madison, who was an expert parliamentarian, had arranged that Lee should first address the committee, reserving for himself the closing of the discussion. Lee accordingly took the floor.

Of the appearance of this brilliant soldier as he then was, in the prime of manhood, we have already spoken. Now there was an evident confusion in his manner. He disliked the subject, he disliked the purposes for which it had been introduced, and he disliked himself; for he had written to Washington when the subject was before Congress, intimating plainly that he was not indisposed to cede the river to Spain for a term of years.[198] He said a few words only, but strongly asserted that it was the determined resolution of Congress not to give up that river, and that they earnestly wished to adopt the best possible plan of securing it. The testimony of Lee was strictly true, but it was the testimony of a tactician, not of a statesman. It was true that Congress did not intend to surrender the right of navigating the Mississippi, and that they wished to secure it in what they deemed the best possible manner, but it was also true that the assent of only three States was wanting to vote the surrender of the navigation for the term of twenty-five years—a period at the expiration of which half the present population of the globe would be in their graves.

Monroe, who was two years younger than Lee, having just entered his thirtieth year, and who well deserved the compliment of honest and brave which Mr. Jefferson had paid him, was called upon to speak. He said he had heretofore preserved silence on the subject, and, although he acknowledged his duty to obey the wishes of the General Assembly, that body had relieved him, at his request, from the necessity of making any disclosure. The right of the Convention was even paramount to that of the Assembly; but he wished it had not been exercised by going into committee for that purpose. He objected to the partial representations which had been made in debate as likely to lead into error. The policy of Virginia in respect of the navigation of the Mississippi had always been the same. It is true that at a severe crisis she had agreed to surrender the navigation; but it was at a time when the Southern States were overrun and in possession of the enemy. Georgia and South Carolina were prostrate. North Carolina made but a feeble resistance. Virginia was then greatly harassed by the enemy in force in the heart of the country, and by impressments for her own defence and for the defence of other States. The finances of the Union

---

[198] *Sparks' Washington Correspondence*, IV, 137.

were totally exhausted, and France, our ally, was anxious for peace. The object of the cession was to unite Spain in the war with all her forces, and thus bring the contest to a happy and speedy conclusion. Congress had learned from our minister at the Spanish court that our Western settlements were viewed with jealousy by Spain. All inferior objects must yield to the safety of society itself. Congress passed an act authorizing the cession, and our minister at the court of Spain was authorized to relinquish this invaluable right to that power on the condition already stated. But what was the issue of this proposition? Was any treaty made with Spain that obtained an acknowledgment of our independence, although she was then at war with England, and such acknowledgment would have cost her nothing? Was a loan of money accomplished? In short, does it appear that Spain herself thought it an object of any importance? So soon as the war was ended, this resolution was rescinded. The power to make such a treaty was revoked. So that this system of policy was departed from only for a short time, for the most important object that can be conceived, and resumed again as soon as it possibly could be.

After the peace, continued Monroe, Congress appointed three commissioners to make commercial treaties with foreign powers, Spain inclusive; so that an arrangement for a treaty with Spain had been already taken. While these powers were in force, a representative from Spain arrived, who was authorized to treat with the United States on the interfering claims of the two nations respecting the Mississippi, and the boundaries and other concerns in which they were respectively interested. A similar commission was given to the honorable the Secretary of Foreign Affairs on the part of the United States, with these *ultimata :* That he enter into no treaty, compact, or convention whatever, with the said representative of Spain which did not stipulate our right to the navigation of the Mississippi, and the boundaries as established in our treaty with Great Britain. Thus the late negotiation commenced under the most flattering auspices. Was it not presumable that she intended, from various circumstances, to make a merit of her concession to our wishes? But what was the issue of this negotiation? Eight or ten months elapsed without any communication of its progress to Congress, when a letter was received from the Secretary, stating that difficulties had arisen in his negotiation with the representative of Spain, which, in his opinion, should be so managed as that even their existence should remain a secret for the present, and proposing that a committee be appointed with full power to direct and instruct him in every case relative to the proposed treaty. As the only *ultimata* in his instructions respected the Mississippi and the boundaries, it readily occurred that these occasioned the difficulties alluded to, and were those which he wished to remove. And for many reasons, said Monroe, this appeared to me an extraordinary proposition. By the Articles of Confederation, nine States are necessary to enter into treaties. The instruction is the foundation of the treaty; for if it is formed agreeably thereto, good faith requires that it be ratified. The instructions under which our commercial treaties have been made were carried by nine States. Those under which the Secretary now acted were passed by nine States. The proposition then would be, that the powers, which, under the Constitution, nine States only were competent to exercise, should be transferred to a committee, and that the object of the transfer was to disengage the Secretary from the *ultimata* in his existing instructions. In this light the subject was taken up, and on these principles discussed. The Secretary, Mr. Jay, summoned before Congress to explain the difficulties mentioned in his letter, presented the project of a treaty of commerce containing, as *he* supposed, advantageous commercial stipulations in our favor, in consideration of which we were to contract to forbear the use of the navigation of the Mississippi for the term of twenty-five or thirty years; and he earnestly advised the adoption of it by Congress. The subject now took a decided form. All ambiguity was at an end. We were surprised that he had taken up the subject of commerce at all. We were still more surprised that it should form the principal object of the project, and that a partial or temporary sacrifice of the very interest, for the advancement of which the negotiation was set on foot, should be the consideration to be given for it. The Secretary urged that it was necessary to stand well with Spain; that the commercial project was highly beneficial; that a stipulation to forbear the use, contained an acknowledgment on the part of Spain of our right; that we were in no condition to take the river, and therefore gave nothing for it; and for other reasons. We differed with the Secretary almost in every respect.

We wished to stand well with Spain, but wished to accomplish that end on equal terms.   We considered the stipulation to forbear the use as a species of barter unbecoming the magnanimity and candor of a nation, and as setting a precedent which might be applied to the Potomac, the Hudson, or the Chesapeake. We thought that there was a material distinction between a stipulation to forbear the use, and an inability to open the river.   The first would be considered by the inhabitants of the Western country as an act of hostility ; the last might be justified by our weakness.   And with respect to the commercial part of the project, we really thought it an ill-advised one on its own merits solely.   The subject was referred to a Committee of the Whole. The delegates from the seven easternmost States voted that the *ultimata* in the instructions of the Secretary should be repealed ; which was reported to the House, and entered on the Journal by the Secretary of Congress, as affirming the fact that the question was carried.   Upon this entry a constitutional question arose to this effect: nine States being necessary, according to the Articles of Confederation, to give an instruction, and seven having repealed a part of an instruction so given for the formation of a treaty with a foreign power, so as to alter its import and authorize, under the remaining part thereof, the formation of a treaty on principles altogether different from what the original instruction contemplated, can such remaining part be considered as in force and constitutionally obligatory?   We pressed on Congress for a decision on this point often, but we pressed in vain.   Notwithstanding this, I understood, said Monroe, that it was the intention of the Secretary to proceed and conclude a treaty in conformity with his project with the Spanish minister.   At this stage I left Congress.   "I thought it my duty," he said, "to use every exertion in Congress for the interest of the Southern States.   With many of those gentlemen to whom I always considered it my particular misfortune to be opposed, I am now in habits of correspondence and friendship ; and I am concerned for the necessity which has given birth to this relation.   Whether the delegates of those States spoke the language of their constituents ; whether it may be considered as the permanent interest of those States to depress the growth and increasing population of the Western country, are points which I cannot pretend to determine."   He concluded with the expression of the opinion that the interest of the Western country would not be as secure under the proposed Constitution as under the Confederation; because under the latter system the Mississippi could not be relinquished without the consent of nine States ; whereas by the former a majority of seven States could yield it. His own opinion was that it would be given up by a majority of the senators present in the Senate, with the president, which would put it in the power of less than seven States to surrender it; that the Northern States were inclined to yield it; that it was their interest to prevent an augmentation of Southern influence and power ; and that, as mankind in general, and States in particular, were governed by interest, the Northern States would not fail of availing themselves of the opportunity afforded by the Constitution of relinquishing that river in order to depress the Western country, and prevent the Southern interest from preponderating.

Now, little did Monroe reflect, as that august assembly was eagerly watching every word that fell from his lips, how vain in respect of the future is the wisdom of the wise, and how rarely the vaticinations of politicians, founded on the most subtle processes of logical deduction, are fulfilled! How little did he dream that in a few short years Spain should, in an agony of terror, cede her dearly cherished province of Louisiana with all its appendages to France ; that in less than fourteen years from the time when he was speaking, not only the right of navigating the Mississippi should be acquired by the United States, but the exclusive title to the river itself; and not only the exclusive title to the river itself, but the exclusive title to the superb realm drained by its waters ; that the beneficent treaty which was to accomplish such results, which was to settle so many dangerous disputes, and which was destined to confer upon untold generations the choicest blessings of heaven, should be mainly negotiated by himself, and should be ratified by a constitutional majority of that Senate which he now viewed with such stern distrust; that, before the expiration of the term stipulated by Mr. Jay, he should preside in the Federal Government, and that he should, in a heedless moment, in a time of profound peace, and when surrounded by a Southern cabinet,[199]

---

[199] Mr. Monroe's cabinet consisted of Mr. Adams of Massachusetts ; Mr. Crawford, of Georgia ; Mr. Calhoun, of South Carolina ; Mr.

virtually cede to Spain a vast and fertile dominion of the South, which a succeeding generation, at the sacrifice of thousands of valuable lives and of more millions than made up the debt of the Revolution, should recover; but not until an infant then puling in the nurse's arms in an humble homestead in Orange (General Zachary Taylor) had won a series of dazzling victories on the soil of the enemy, and not until another Virginia boy, then running barefoot on a farm in Dinwiddie (General Winfield Scott), had landed, from the decks of ships which had already won distinction in contests with the ships of the greatest naval power of the globe, his brilliant battalions on the hostile shore, and, marking his encampments by battles, and his battles by victories, should close his campaign by unfurling in the proud capital of the enemy, above those gorgeous structures from which the once terrible lions of Spain had for two centuries bade defiance to the world, the standard of his country.

The speech of Monroe was well received. It made upon the House a strong impression, which was heightened by the modesty of his demeanor, by the sincerity which was reflected from every feature of his honest face, and by the minute knowledge which he exhibited of a historical transaction of surpassing interest to the South. But if the impression was felt by the members generally, it was felt most keenly by those who were anxious about the sales of their crops and for the prosperity of their families. The members from the West were furious. They had just learned for the first time the imminent hazard to which their most valued privilege had been exposed,[200] and they did not conceal their indignation. And that indignation was neither unbecoming nor uncalled for. That a Secretary of State, instructed strictly to negotiate a treaty for the security of an object of vital importance to the South and West, should lose sight of that object altogether

---

Thompson, of New York; and Mr. Wirt, of Virginia, as attorney-general; including Mr. Monroe himself, it was a strong Southern administration.

[200] In 1788 information traveled slowly. In fact, the intelligence divulged by Monroe, in compliance with the wishes of the Convention, could have been known but to few. Humphrey Marshall saw the numbers of *The Federalist* for the first time in the hands of George Nicholas, whom he fell in with on his way from Kentucky to attend the present Convention.—*Butler's History of Kentucky*, 167.

and propose a treaty relating to an object of lesser importance, which was beyond his powers, and which, insignificant and value-less in itself, could only be obtained by a sacrifice of the invalua-ble rights which he was expressly instructed to secure, and that such a project should be sanctioned by seven Eastern States in direct contravention of the Articles of Confederation, might well arouse the astonishment and anger of the West. Nor was the time of danger past. The treaty may have been already made, and might then be on its way to Spain.

The alarm thus raised soon extended to the new Constitution. For it was plain that the seven States which had so recently voted to cede the right of navigating the Mississippi, and which might be supposed to retain their opinions unchanged, would certainly constitute a majority of the new Senate if every member was in his seat, and might at some unexpected moment and in a thin house, accomplish by a vote of two-thirds of a quorum their decided purpose. Such was the excitement in the Convention that men whose opinions were entitled to respect declared after-wards that, if the final vote on the Constitution had then been pressed, that instrument would have been lost by a majority fully as large as that which ultimately adopted it.

Grayson rose next to give his testimony in the case. In age, in eloquence, and in breadth of statesmanship, he stood nearly in the same relation to Monroe, to Lee, and to Madison, that in a body which sat forty years later in this city Watkins Leigh and Chapman Johnson stood to Dromgoole, to Goode, to Mason of Southampton, to Mason of Frederick, to Miller of Botetourt, and to Moore of Rockbridge. He said that, like Monroe, he felt a delicacy in disclosing what had occurred in secret session ; but he declared that he had protested against the injunction of secrecy on a great constitutional question. He coincided in the statement just made, and said that Spain claimed not only the absolute and exclusive navigation of the Mississippi, but one-half of the State of Georgia and one-half of the district of Kentucky ; and that this was the reason of the limitation imposed on the Secretary relative to the boundaries recognized in our treaty with Great Britain. He said that the Southern States were opposed to a surrender of the Mississippi ; that the Northern States were once opposed to give it up, but that was when they were apprehensive about their fisheries, on which their very existence depended, and regarding the Mississippi as a counter-poise to the fisheries, they apprehended that, if the Mississippi were given up, the fisheries might also be relinquished ; that the fisheries were now secure, and the result was that the seven easternmost States had resolved to release Mr. Jay from the fetters which had been imposed upon him by the constitutional majority of nine States ; that this determination had been communicated to Mr. Jay for his guidance in forming a treaty with the Spanish minister ; that this instruction violated the express injunction of the Constitution, which required nine States to make a treaty. Adhere to the limitations imposed upon Mr. Jay, and Georgia was safe, Kentucky was safe, the Mississippi was safe, the Con-stitution was safe ; depart from them, and the most precious rights and privileges of the South are at his mercy. He said that, as the instructions to Mr. Jay were the foundation and sub-stance of the treaty, any compact which that gentleman might make with the Spanish minister would, if not ratified by Congress, give Spain just cause of war ; so that we would be involved in the dilemma of violating the Constitution by a compliance with it, or, in case of a non-compliance, of incurring the risks of war with that power. The South also contended that it had no right to dismember the empire, or relinquish to a foreign power the exclusive navigation of our rivers. He said that Maryland had coincided with the North. He again reverted to the reluctance which the Eastern States had at one time evinced toward surren-dering the Mississippi, and said that, when their apprehensions were removed, the natural instinct of interest revived, and they became solicitous of securing a superiority of influence in the national councils. Their language, he said, was this : " *Let us prevent any new States from rising in the Western world, or they will outvote us. We will lose our importance, and become as nothing in the scale of nations. If we do not prevent it, our countrymen will remove to those places instead of going to sea, and we will receive no particular tribute or advantage from them.*"[201] When he had expressed his opinions at length, he said that whether this great interest would be safe under the new Constitution he left it to others to determine. It certainly was not safe under the present, though more so than under the one proposed for their adoption.

---

[201] The language and the italics of the quotation are Grayson's.

When Grayson ended, Henry rose to request Monroe to discover the rest of the project, and to inform the House what Spain
was to do on her part as as an equivalent for the cession of the
Mississippi.   Monroe replied that the equivalent was the advantages of commercial intercourse ; but that Spain conceded nothing
more in fact than was granted to other nations trading with her.
When Monroe expressed this opinion, it is said that an expression
of astonishment was visible on the faces of the members.

It was at this culminating point of the discussion that Madison, then in his thirty-seventh year, and in the full possession of
those admirable powers of debate, which, unused and unobserved for more than the third of a century before his death, have
been almost forgotten in the contemplation of the subsequent
titles that he acquired to the grateful remembrance of his country, was called to the floor.   He could not well have been placed
in a more unpleasant predicament.   It was impossible to defend,
directly and unequivocally, the action of Congress.   No speaker
who would rise and approve the deliberate instruction of seven
Eastern States to dismember the half of Georgia and the half of
Kentucky, and to cede with the territory of those States the
absolute and exclusive navigation of the Mississippi, without an
equivalent, to a foreign power, could expect for an instant the
favorable ear of a Southern assembly.   Yet some defence was
required at his hands.   The new Constitution was in imminent
jeopardy.   It is evident from his remarks which have come down
to us, that he was much discomposed.   He could neither conceal
the whole truth nor tell the whole truth without inflicting equal
injury upon the cause which he had so much at heart.   If he
concealed any part of the truth, there were Grayson and Monroe
to refresh his memory ; if he told the whole truth, he would
sustain by his own authority the truth of as palpable an outrage
as was ever aimed at the liberties of a free people.   But it is on
such occasions that the man of genius appears in strong contrast
with the mere man of words, however dexterously he may use
them in common emergencies.   What disarranged him the more
was the belief and certain knowledge that the whole scene had
been conjured up by Henry to effect the ruin of the new Constitution, and it was with emotions bordering on disgust that he
found himself compelled to contribute his share to the entertainment.   As, in the early part of the day, he was disposed to inter-

pret the conduct of Henry in seeking a full disclosure of the subject as, in some measure, personal to himself, so he now reflected upon the action of the House in a way that might have led to a call to order. He said it was extremely disagreeable to him to enter into a discussion which was foreign to the deliberations of the House, and which would sully the reputation of our public councils. He admitted the facts as stated by the gentlemen who had preceded him, but he differed about the principles involved in them. He declared that he never approved the cession ; that neither the Confederation nor the proposed Constitution gave a right to surrender the Mississippi ; that such a surrender was repugnant to the laws of nations; paid a glowing compliment to the virtues and talents of Mr. Jay ; and demonstrated that, whatever may have been the opinions of their representatives at a particular time on the subject, it was the permanent interest of the Northern States, which were the carriers of our produce, to sustain the navigation of the Mississippi; that it would be unwise to argue that, as the South had at one time assented to the cession and changed its opinion, the North might not do the same ; and spread such an ingenious net-work of argument and opinion over the glaring facts of the case as in some degree to conceal its deformity. He ended by saying that there were circumstances within his knowledge which rendered it certain that no effort would be made hereafter unfavorable to the navigation of the Mississippi. His speech, even in its present form, is an exquisite specimen of the tact and skill with which an eminent statesman, wielding the while with extraordinary judgment the weapons of a debater, may appear to walk steadily over ground that was quaking beneath him.

As soon as Madison took his seat Grayson appeared on the floor. He instantly reverted to the considerations which Madison did not think proper to disclose to the House, stated by way of supposition what they were, and sought by a detail of facts and by general reasoning to demonstrate that no reliance could be placed upon them. He followed Madison step by step, and assailed his reasoning in a speech which, by its statesmanlike views of domestic policy, by the fervor of its declamation, and by the force of its logic, was one of the most fascinating exhibitions of the day. Madison, as if disinclined to protract the discussion, made no reply.

Henry then spoke. A more appropriate time for the display of his peculiar powers could not be desired. The occasion, the theme, the immeasurable issues which might be swayed by the deliberations of a single day, threw such an inspiration over his genius that he seemed to be wrapt into a higher sphere, and his lips appeared to glow as if touched with the coals from the altar. The leading facts of a great question of national policy were before him, and it was his duty to press them upon the hearts of his audience. He began by throwing the responsibility of the discussion on Madison, who had gone at large into the subject, and, following for a time his train of argument, threw himself on his own inexhaustible resources. Elderly men, who had heard his most eloquent speeches, and who pronounced his speech on this occasion one of the most eloquent of all, delighted to recall the lineaments of two pictures which he drew with a master's hand. One described the great valley of the Mississippi as stretching from the Alleghanies to the nameless mountains of the distant West, as teeming with a mighty population, cultivated farms, thriving villages, towns, cities, colleges, and churches, filling the vision in every direction—the Mississippi covered with ships laden with foreign and domestic wealth— the West the strength, the pride, and the flower of the Confederacy. Such would be the valley of the West with a free navigation of the Mississippi, and under a Federal system. The other picture was a reverse of the scene, and presented a prospect of unalloyed calamity. The Mississippi no longer alive with ships—its unburdened waters flowing idly to the sea—no villages, no towns, no cities, no schools, no churches, no cultivated plains ; the original solitude of the forest unbroken, save here and there by the rude hut of the outlaw ; capital flying from a land where it would turn to dross. Such would be the West with the loss of the Mississippi, and under a consolidated government to be controlled by those who had no interest in its welfare. The reported speech is more argumentative than eloquent ; but it is plain that the reporter rarely was able to do more than record the main points made by the speaker.

At the close of the speech there was a pause in the House. No Federalist seemed willing to engage in the discussion. It is said that Pendleton, who was in the body of the House, his right hand clenching his crutch, sat silent and amazed. He felt that moment more keenly the spell of Henry's genius than when, in the House of Burgesses in 1765, he heard him defy the king, or when, in the Convention of 1775, he heard him exclaim "Give me liberty, or give me death."

It was at this fearful moment that there rose to address the House one of those remarkable men of whom the Revolution was prolific, and who had nearly changed the fortunes of the hour. He appeared to be about the middle stature, thick and broad ; and though only in his thirty-fifth year, his head was so bald as to suggest the impression that in some fierce Indian foray he had forfeited his scalp. In his features and in his demeanor there was nothing imposing. His voice was the voice of a man accustomed to address popular assemblies, but was to be noted neither for its power nor its sweetness. His influence lay in another direction. He had mingled freely with all classes of society, and was as familiar with the camp and the court-green as if his feet had never pressed the carpets of "Westover," or his lips had never been moistened with the mellow wine from the vaults of "Brandon" or of "Shirley." He was one of that brilliant group of soldier-statesmen who had caught their inspiration and their love of country from the lips of Wythe. At the bar, to the front rank of which he had risen, his tact and knowledge of mankind availed himself as much, if not more, than his learning, which he had drawn mainly from Blackstone, whose commentaries had already superceded the elder writers of the law, and had been for the past eighteen years in the hands of every educated Virginian. He entered the House of Delegates in early life, and soon became one of the leaders of the body. He was utterly fearless. He shrunk from no duty, and in the midst of a civil war he sought to subject to an impeachment a statesman who was the second Governor of Virginia, and whose name now stands, and will stand forever, second only to that of Washington. He bore a name illustrious in the annals of the Colony and of the Commonwealth ; but George Nicholas had a genius of his own which needed no hereditary endorsement, and was ample enough to sustain him in any sphere, military or civil, which might suit his fancy. Soon after the separation of Kentucky from Virginia he emigrated to the new Commonwealth, where he succeeded in attaining the same elevated position which he held at home, and blended his name inseparably with the early history of that State.

His influence in his native State and in the State of his adoption is felt to this day. He possessed great tact in the management of public bodies, and had already participated with great ability in the debates of the body. He saw at a glance that the fate of the Constitution might depend upon the results of that day's session. He well knew that if the Kentucky delegation voted against the Constitution, and was joined by a single county on the Western waters, the fate of that instrument was sealed. He instantly decided on his plan of attack. He saw that all explanations and apologies were idle. He determined, instead of resting on the defensive, to push into the ranks of the enemy, and make a desperate effort to retrieve the fortunes of the day. He said that the statements which he had heard that day had filled him with astonishment A great, an inestimable right, the right of navigating the Mississippi, which was necessary, which was indispensable to the development of the resources of that fertile region and to the prosperity of the South, had nearly been sacrificed. It was in this strain that he continued until he had disarmed suspicion and had gained the sympathy of a majority of the House, when, turning suddenly to Henry, he exclaimed, By whom was this fearful act contemplated? By the gentleman's favorite Confederation. Would gentlemen dare to say that this was an argument which should induce the West to uphold a system of government which might consummate the odious and abominable policy which it had already set in train? It was by this mode of argument that he sought to quiet the fears of the members from the West, and his argument produced a sensible effect upon the House which Edmund Randolph sought to deepen ; but while Corbin, who followed Randolph on the same side, was speaking, a storm arose, which rendered speaking impossible, and the House adjourned. The result of this day's discussion—a discussion which, whether we consider the intense interest of the subject which called it forth, the various talents which were exhibited in its course, and the splendid prize held up to the successful combatants, was one of the most interesting in our history—was, that of the fourteen members from Kentucky, ten voted against the ratification of the Federal Constitution.

On the morning of Saturday, the fourteenth of June, a painful rumor reached the House. Pendleton had fallen suddenly ill the night before, and was unable to take his seat. The House proceeded to the election of a vice-president, which resulted in the choice of John Tyler,[202] who was to preside during the inability of Pendleton. He was one of the staunchest opponents of the new Constitution; but that his appointment might lack no mark of honor, and might show conspicuously to future times the courtesy of a body, which, though agitated by the strongest passions, disdained to look to the opinions of an individual, but regarded only his fitness for the office which he would be called upon to fill, the vote was unanimous. Nor could that exalted honor have been conferred on a purer statesman, or on one more competent in all respects to discharge its duties. The history of the vice-president well deserves to be studied by posterity. His paternal ancestor of the same name, a youth of seventeen, had come over in 1637, had settled in Bruton parish, the official records of which attest, until near the close of the seventeenth century, his zeal in the cause of the Church, and had founded a numerous family, some of the most distinguished members of which still reside within a short range of the ancient seat of their race. It has been said that he could trace his descent from those brave outlaws of Sherwood Forest, who were wont to sally forth and levy upon their generation certain rude extemporaneous assessments, which were respected more from the summary mode in which they were exacted than from their consonance with the laws of the realm.

John Tyler, who had just received from his associates so signal a mark of their respect, was born in the year 1748 in the county of James City, where he grew up to manhood. His mother was of French extraction, and he mingled in his veins the blood of the Anglo-Saxon with the blood of the Huguenot, a mixture not unfriendly to freedom, to genius, to eloquence, and to philosophy.[203] From his nearness to Williamsburg,

---

[202] The Journal of the Convention not only does not contain the name of the mover and seconder, but omits all notice of the election. The "Debates" mention the appointment, but not the name of the member who moved it. It was probably Patrick Henry, who was particularly fond of Tyler, and had nominated him to the speakership of the House of Delegates on more than one occasion, if I mistake not. The ancestor of John Tyler was believed to be the famous *Wat Tyler*, of the times of Richard II.

[203] The mother of John Tyler of the text was a daughter of Dr. Contesse of Williamsburg.

whither his father, who was Marshal of the Colony, and himself frequently repaired, he had an opportunity of observing the incidents of the time.   He could remember Fauquier as well as Botetourt and Dunmore; had seen their stately progresses through the Colony, and at the age of seventeen had heard the speech of Henry on his resolutions against the Stamp Act. From that hour began his opposition to a kingly government, which continued unfalteringly till the day of his death.   He attended William and Mary College, and studied law in the office of Robert Carter Nicholas, from whose character he copied several traits which were afterwards conspicuous in his own. When Dunmore purloined the powder from the magazine at Williamsburg, Tyler, with young Harrison, a son of Benjamin of "Berkeley," enrolled a number of gallant young men, and marched at their head to the capital, where Henry, at the head of his Hanover company, had just arrrived.   On the establishment of the Constitution in 1776, he was appointed by the Convention to the office of Commissioner of Admiralty, the duties of which he discharged throughout the war;[204] and when the first elections for the Senate under the new Constitution were held, he was a candidate, and published an address to the people which is still extant, and which is worthy of note as the first communication addressed to the voters of Virginia that ever appeared in print.[205] He soon after entered the House of Delegates, and in 1782, and again in 1783, he was elected Speaker, having been nominated by Henry.   In 1789 he was elected a judge of the general court, and discharged for twenty years that laborious and responsible office.   In 1808 he was elected Governor, but, as his health suffered from his residence in Richmond, he accepted, near the end of his second term, the office of judge of the Federal district court.   This appointment had in his eyes a peculiar significancy.   It was as a judge of Admiralty, entering on the office the very day the first Constitution of Virginia took effect, and five years before the Articles of Confederation were adopted, that he began his public career; and it was in the discharge of the

---

[204] The *Virginia Gazette* of July 5, 1776, announced the appointment of John Tyler, James Hubard, and Joseph Prentis, as Commissioners of Admiralty.

[205] *Virginia Gazette*, July 26, 1776.   Tyler lost his election.

duties of, practically, the same office under the Federal Constitution that now in his old age he was destined to end it. He resided at "Greenway," his estate on the banks of the James; and it not unfrequently happened that prize cases not admitting of delay were brought by the parties for adjudication to his house ; and on one bright morning of the summer of 1812, in the shade of a wide-spreading willow that grew in his yard, and in the presence of the Marshal of the United States and of the mate and some of the crew, he adjudicated the first prize case that occurred in the war of 1812, that of the ship Sir Simon Clarke. The case was clear and was soon decided, and the parties, having declined a cordial invitation to dine with the judge, went their way. When he returned to his family, his first words were "That proud nation which has so long made war upon our commerce, will soon come to know that the war is no longer altogether on one side." But his time was now come. On the sixth day of February, 1813, in the sixty-fifth year of his age, he breathed his last, and was buried at "Greenway" by the side of his wife, who had died some years before.[206] The ruling passion of the patriot who had witnessed the sufferings endured in the Revolution, was strong to the last. During his last illness his mind dwelt upon the war then raging with Great Britain, which he regarded as the second war of independence with our ancient foe ; and but a short time before his death he raised his head from his pillow and said, "I could have wished to live to see again that haughty nation humbled before America; but it is decreed otherwise, *et nunc dimittas, Domine !* "

But the chief distinction of this worthy patriot was derived from his career in the House of Delegates. Throughout that protracted and perilous period, reaching from the Declaration of Independence to the adoption of the present Federal Constitution, he was foremost in meeting the difficult and perplexing questions of the times, and by his intrepidity, by his knowledge of affairs, by his sound judgment, by a ready and robust eloquence, sustained in the public councils the cause of his country. Indeed, it is to his great honor that, in the decision of the numerous and delicate questions which arose during the war and subsequently, and which created acrimonious and lasting divi-

---

[206] Mrs. Tyler was Mary Armistead, of the county of York.

sions in the State, he embraced those views of finance, of public credit, of domestic and foreign policy, which those who now regard them at the distance of seventy years would pronounce to be the wisest and the best. It was in the session of 1786, however, that he performed an act which, if the other deeds of his long and patriotic course were forgotten, would stamp immortality upon his name. He offered, in the House of Delegates, and sustained by his eloquence, that ever memorable resolution convoking the Convention at Annapolis, which ultimately led to the assembling of the General Convention that formed the present Federal Constitution.

There were points of connection between John Tyler and the venerable statesman who was his colleague from Charles City in the Convention, that attracted the attention of our fathers, and are not without interest in our own age. Benjamin Harrison was born in Charles City; had sprung from a wealthy family in the Colony; had extensive connections which were then deemed almost essential to the success of a rising politician, and had been a leading member of the House of Burgesses when Tyler was a boy. Tyler was born in the neighboring county of James City; had in early manhood settled in Charles City; had engaged in the practice of the law, and had by his open and honorable conduct acquired the esteem of the people. He was regularly returned to the House of Delegates, and had been frequently elected Speaker. Harrison, who had held a seat in the House of Burgesses for near thirty years, was often elected by the Assembly to a seat in Congress, and was compelled, in pursuance of an Act passed in 1777, to vacate his seat in the House of Delegates during his term of service in Congress.[207] At the expiration of his term in Congress he was always a candidate for a seat in the House of Delegates, and, from his position as one of the oldest members of the House of Burgesses as well as of Congress, and as Governor of the Commonwealth, his valuable services, and his reputation as a presiding officer, was usually elected Speaker of that body. Thus insensibly there grew up, rather among the neighbors of these gentlemen than between

---

[207] Until the passage of this Act the members of Assembly, when elected to Congress, always retained their seats, and when Congress was not in session attended to their duties in the Assembly.

themselves, a kind of rivalry, as it was known that, on the election of both to the House of Delegates, a contest would occur between them for the chair.   The result was that on one occasion Harrison ousted Tyler from the chair which he had held at the previous session, and on another Tyler returned the compliment by ousting Harrision from his seat in the House, who, however, resolved not to be outdone, crossed over to the county of Surry, and was immediately returned from that county to the House.   There was one ground held in common by these worthy patriots, and which justly entitled them to the public esteem— their unwavering patriotism in times of trial.   Harrison, by long and arduous service in Congress as well as in our State councils, and Tyler, by his equally efficient service in the House of Delegates, conferred lasting benefits upon their country.   Harrison, as chairman of the Committee of the Whole, had reported to Congress the resolution which dissolved the connection between the Colonies and Great Britain, and the Declaration of Independence; Tyler, as we have before observed, offered, and succeeded in carrying through the House of Delegates, the resolution which may be said to have laid the foundation of the present Federal Constitution.   And, as if the connection between them should be continued and refreshed in the memory of succeeding times, each had a son who, under that Constitution which their fathers had united in opposing with all their eloquence on the floor of the present Convention, became the Chief Magistrate of the Union.

Tyler belonged to that class of statesmen who honestly believed that the government of Virginia was, in respect both of domestic and foreign policy, the safest and the best for the people of Virginia.   Hence he was one of the most open and most fearless opponents of the new scheme.   He had loved Virginia when she was the free dominion of a constitutional king ; but he loved her with redoubled affection when she became, partly by his own efforts, an independent Commonwealth.   Like Henry, he deemed the word *country* applicable only to the land of his birth.[208] That the slightest tax should be levied upon the people by any

---

[208] Henry always used the word "country" only in connection with Virginia.   See the Debates *passim*, and his letter to R. H. Lee in the "Henry Papers," quoted in the discourse of the Virginia Convention of 1776, page 141, note.

other authority than that of the General Assembly ; that a collector appointed by any other power should stalk among the homesteads of Virginia and gather a tribute which was not to find its way into her exchequer ; that Virginia ships, as they passed his door bound on a foreign voyage, should carry any other flag than that which in a day of doubt and dread he had seen when it was first hoisted above the Capitol at Williamsburg ; that under any conceivable complication of affairs Virginia should be required in a time of profound peace to surrender without limitation or qualification to a foreign government the power of the purse and the power of the sword, presented to his mind an idea so revolting to his sense of honor that he was more disposed to denounce it as a scheme of treason than to approve it as a dictate of patriotism.   Yet no man living cherished with greater devotion the union of the States.   By the union of the States he well knew that the common liberty had been secured, and that by the union it would best be preserved ; but it was an union of sovereign States bound by a few simple and general powers adequate to the conduct of foreign affairs that he desired and deemed ample enough to attain the end in view.   It was a simple league or confederation, competent for a few general purposes, that found favor in his eyes.   He deemed Virginia fully able to manage her own affairs, and he shrunk from a plan of government which, under the guise of transacting her foreign affairs more economically than she could transact them herself, was endowed with an authority as great, in his opinion, as that of the king and Parliament of Great Britain, whose yoke had been but lately overthrown, and paramount to the laws of the States.   And he opposed the new scheme with the greater boldness, because in common with others he had honestly sought to amend the Articles of Confederation on some points in which they had been found defective, and had taken an active interest in calling the General Convention which had, in his opinion, so far transcended its legitimate office.   The severe simplicity of his manners and the purity of his life, which recalled the image of Andrew Marvel or of Pym, his long and distinguished career in the House of Delegates, his unblemished honor as a public man, lent an additional force to his opposition.

But it is as Tyler was when, in his fortieth year, and before he had been called to that bench on which he sat for twenty years, he was elected vice-president of the Convention, that we wish to present him to the view.   There was a gravity in his demeanor that became the presiding officer of such an assembly.   His stature was broad and full, and was nearly six feet in height.   A large head, which had been bald from his early life ; a large, calm blue eye overcast by a massive forehead ; a nose as prominent as the beak of an eagle, a firmly set mouth and chin, imparted at first sight to his aspect an air of sternness, which was softened by a benignant smile and by the courtesy of his manner.   He was scrupulously neat in his person, and was dressed in a suit of homespun ; for he lived at a time when it was the pride of the Virginia wife to array her husband throughout in the fabrics of her own loom.   He had long been familiar with the duties of the chair.   In fact, he had presided oftener in deliberative bodies than—with the exception of Harrison—any member of the House. On taking his seat a motion was made to go into committee, and his first act was to call Wythe to the chair.[209]

Corbin, with the remark that the subject of the Mississippi had been sufficiently discussed, moved that the committee proceed to the discussion clause by clause.   Grayson thought that the discussion of the day before ought to be renewed.   The question of the Mississippi was, practically, whether one part of the continent should rule the other.   Alexander White, then a promising young lawyer from Frederick, and known to our own times as a venerable judge of the general court, expressed the opinion that the discussion of that topic might be postponed until the treaty-making power came up in course, and seconded the motion of Corbin ; which was agreed to.

The third section of the first article was then read.   Tyler hoped that when amendments were brought forward, the members ought to be at liberty to take a general view of the whole Constitution.   He thought that the power of trying impeach-ments, added to that of making treaties, was something enor-mous, and rendered the Senate too dangerous.   Madison answered that it was not possible to form any system to which objections could not be made ; that the junction of these powers

---

[209] A portrait of Judge Tyler, taken mainly from memory, some years after his death, is at Sherwood Forest, the residence of his son, the ex-President.   An obituary from the pen of Judge Roane may be seen in the *Richmond Enquirer* of the 8th or 9th of February, 1813.

might in some degree be objectionable, but that it could not be amended. He agreed with Tyler that when amendments were brought on, a collective view of the whole system might be taken.

The fourth and fifth sections of the same article were read, and were briefly discussed by Monroe, Madison, and Randolph. The sixth section was read, when Henry addressed the committee, and was followed by Madison, Nicholas, Tyler, and Grayson, and by Mason and Grayson in reply. The seventh section was discussed by Grayson and Madison.

When the eighth section was read, Charles Clay, of Bedford, took the floor. The position and the patriotism of Clay, who was one of the three clergymen holding seats in the Convention, and who clung to his native country through a long and perilous war, maintaining her cause by his fluent and fearless eloquence, which is said to have been not unlike that of his illustrious kinsman who recently descended to the grave amid the tears of his country,[210] merit the remembrance of posterity. He was born and educated in the Colony, was ordained by the Bishop of London in 1769, and was immediately installed as rector of St. Anne's parish, in the county of Albemarle. Some of his sermons yet extant in manuscript have been pronounced by a severe judge to be sound, energetic, and evangelical beyond the character of the times. During the Revolution, instead of flying his native land, he never lost an occasion of exhorting his countrymen to prosecute the war with vigor; and on a fast day in 1777, he preached at Charlottesville before a company of minute-men a sermon which reminds us of that preached on a similar occasion seventeen years before by Samuel Davies, and which displays a chivalric spirit of patriotism. "Cursed be he," he said, "who keepeth back his sword from blood in this war." He protested against apathy and backwardness in such a cause; denounced "those who would rather bow their necks in the most abject slavery than face a man in arms," and implored the people that as the cause of liberty was the cause of God, they should plead the cause of their country before the Lord with their blood. He frequently addressed the British prisoners taken at Saratoga, who were cantoned in Albemarle. Removing in 1784 from Albemarle

---

[210] Bishop Meade thinks that Charles was probably an own cousin of Henry Clay.

to Bedford, he resided there during the rest of his life. He was a large and handsome man, cordial in his manners, fond of society, and a most entertaining and instructive companion. He was an intimate friend of Jefferson, who owned an estate in Bedford which he visited; and then these venerable patriots in their declining years discoursed of men and things that had long passed away. Clay was the first to depart, having died in 1824 near his eightieth year, and in the midst of his descendants, and having survived most of his present associates.[211] His peculiar temper was seen in his will. He selected a spot for his grave, and ordered a mound of stones to be raised over it; and this monument, now covered with turf, resembles in its full proportions one of those ancient burrows which were formerly to be seen in the low-grounds of some of our mountain streams.[212]

The political principles of Clay were as fixed as his religious. The right of taxation he regarded as the greatest of all rights; and he thought that a people who assented to a surrender of that right without limitations clearly and unequivocally expressed, might possibly retain their freedom, but that freedom would no longer be a privilege, but an accident or a concession. Taxation, he said, could only be exercised judiciously and safely by agents responsible to those who paid the taxes; and, as this result was, in his opinion, impracticable under the new scheme, he thought that, in adopting that scheme, we virtually relinquished the great object attained by the Revolution. He was probably born in Hanover, and in early life may have heard Samuel Davies, whose noble sermons on Braddock's Defeat, on Religion and Patriotism, the Constituents of a Good Soldier, and on the Curse

---

[211] At the death of Clay in 1824, the members of the Convention then living, were Madison, Marshall, Monroe, and John Stuart of Greenbrier, Archibald Stuart of Augusta, White of Frederick, Johnson of Isle of Wight.

[212] For particulars concerning Clay consult Bishop Meade's valuable work on the *Old Churches, &c., of Virginia*, II, 49. The mound is described by the Bishop as being twenty feet in diameter, twelve feet high, and neatly turfed. I suppose Clay to have been five and twenty at his ordination, which would make him eighty at his death. I am indebted to Clay at second-hand through my friend, John Henry of " Red Hill," for some interesting incidents of the present Convention, which are introduced in their proper place.

of Cowardice, found a counterpart in the animated and daring appeals of Clay.   Nor is the merit of Clay less, if it be not greater, than that of Davies.   Davies was a dissenter.   He had felt the power of the established Church, and had wrestled with success against the authority claimed for her by her zealous but imprudent defenders.   He had no respect for the doctrines of passive obedience.   He had no respect for kings unless they were wise and good men.   He was also a Calvinist.   He belonged to a sect which had no scruples about drawing the sword in defence of civil and religious liberty.   In fact, the religion of the Sage of Geneva was nearly as militant as the religion of the Prophet of Mecca.   Of the more than three hundred years which had elapsed since John Calvin had, in the midst of a scene of unrivaled natural beauty, promulgated to the world the tenets of his stern faith, more than two-thirds of the whole had been spent by their votaries in contests with principalities and powers, and with various fortune.   Sometimes they were crushed to the earth beneath the heel of the oppressor.   Then they rose in their terrible strength, and struck the head of the oppressor from the block.   To revert to times which have no indirect relation to our own, Calvinism had nearly overturned the government of James the First.   It brought his successor to the scaffold, and, in the person of one of its truant votaries, seized on the supreme power of the State, and made the name of England a terror to Europe.   Then it sank down, and in its coverts scowled at the storm which overwhelmed it, and with it the common morality and the common decency in one seemingly irretrievable ruin. Then it reared its head once more, grappled with another Stuart, drove him into exile, and placed upon the British throne one of its truest and ablest defenders.   It shook the throne of Louis the Fourteenth, and filled Europe with victories, the glory of which became a national inheritance.   It crossed raging seas, and in the New World, amid ice and snow, on a rock-bound coast, moored its frail vessels, felled forests, smote the Indian with the edge of the sword, reared flourishing republics which vexed the most distant seas with their keels, inscribed the names of more than one of its votaries on the American Declaration of Independence, and ended one great cycle of its destiny.   Then it fell asleep in its strongholds, until Geneva and Edinburgh and Boston, forgetting its three-fold tongue, began to utter each a language of its own. Of this fierce sect, then in its vigor, Davies was a staunch and most eloquent adherent. Yet, though his spirit was ever equal to any emergency, he had only exhorted his countrymen to take the field against the public enemies—and those enemies, the French and the Indians, between whom and the Anglo-Saxon race there was a natural, an inveterate, and an irreconcilable hostility. Clay, as an individual, if not as a patriot, went a step beyond. He belonged to another and a very different family of Christians. He was a priest of the Established Church. He was a member of that splendid hierarchy whose highest representative was the first peer of the British realm, whose bishops sat with equal honor side by side with the hereditary legislators of Britain, and whose supreme head on earth was the king. One of the purest bishops of that Church had laid upon him his consecrating hand, and had by a solemn ordination set him apart for her service. He was thus bound to the king, not only by those tender ties of veneration and love which bound our fathers to the House of Hanover as the great political bulwark of Protestant Christianity, but by those no less formidable ties which bound a priest to his ecclesiastical superior. But the intrepid spirit of Clay did not hesitate for an instant to sunder all political and religious connection with a king who sought to enslave Virginia. He stood on a platform too elevated for most of his clerical brethren ; and when the cloud of war had burst, and the sun of a new day had risen, and men could look quietly around them, it was seen that he stood almost alone.[213] He was in his forty-fourth year, and, although fluent and undaunted in debate, he wisely resigned the office of discussion to the able men whose whole lives had been spent in political affairs, and rarely rose unless to make some pertinent inquiry ; and, as it was observed by a learned jurist, that Dirlton's Doubts were more certain than the certainties of other people, so it was remarked that Clay's questions had often the effect of an argument enforced by a regular speech. He now rose to inquire why Congress was to have power to provide for calling forth the militia to put the laws of the Union into execution.

---

[213] Bishop Meade states that of the ninety-one clergymen at the beginning of the war, not more than twenty-eight appeared at its close. Among the clerical representatives of the Established Church in the field were Colonel Thurston and Major-General Mecklenburg.

Madison explained and defended the clause, and was followed by Mason, who denounced it as not sufficiently guarded, in an able harangue, which called forth an elaborate reply from Madison. Clay was not satisfied with the explanations of Madison. "Our militia," he said, "might be dragged from their homes and marched to the Mississippi." He feared that the execution of the laws by other than the civil authority would lead ultimately to the establishment of a purely military system. Madison rejoined, and was followed by Henry, who exhorted the opponents of the new scheme to make a firm stand. "We have parted," he said, "with the purse, and now we are required to part with the sword." Henry spoke for an hour, and was followed by Nicholas and Madison in long and able speeches. Henry replied, and was followed by Madison and Randolph. Mason rejoined at length, and was followed by Lee, who threw with much dexterity several pointed shafts at Henry. Clay rose evidently under strong excitement. He said that, as it was insinuated by a gentleman (Randolph) that he was not under the influence of common sense in making his objection to the clause in debate, his error might result from his deficiency in that respect ; but that gentleman was as much deficient in common decency as he was in common sense. He proceeded to state the grounds of his objection, and showed that in his estimation the remarks of the gentleman were far from satisfactory. Madison rejoined to Clay, and passing to the arguments of Henry, spoke with great force in refuting them. Clay asked Madison to point out the instances in which opposition to the laws did not come within the idea of an insurrection. Madison replied that a riot did not come within the legal definition of an insurrection. After a long and animated session the committee rose, and the House adjourned.

On Monday, the sixteenth day of June, Pendleton appeared and resumed the chair. The House went into committee, Wythe in the chair, the eighth section of the first article still under consideration. Henry rose and reviewed the previous sections, and was followed in detail by Madison. Mason then spoke, and was followed by Madison and Corbin. Marshall replied to a speech delivered the day before by Grayson, who rejoined. Henry rose in reply, and Madison rejoined. Mason replied to Madison, and was answered by Nicholas. A prolonged debate ensued, in which Grayson, Nicholas, Mason, Madison, Lee, Pendleton, and

Henry took part. The day closed with a passage between Nicholas and Mason, Nicholas affirming that the Virginia Bill of Rights did not provide against torture, and Mason proving to the conviction of Nicholas that it did. The House then adjourned.[214]

On Tuesday, the seventeenth day of June, a subject to which recent developments in the South have added a present interest, came up for consideration. As soon as the House went into committee, Wythe in the chair, the first clause of the ninth section of the first article was read. That clause is in these words: "The migration or importation of such persons as any of the States now existing shall think proper to admit, shall not be prohibited by the Congress prior to the year one thousand eight hundred and eight; but a tax or duty may be imposed on such importation not exceeding ten dollars for each person."

Mason rose and denounced it as a fatal section, which has created more dangers than any other. "This clause," he said, "allows the importation of slaves for twenty years. Under the royal government this evil was looked upon as a great oppression, and many attempts were made to prevent it; but the interest of the African merchants prevented its prohibition. No sooner did the Revolution take place than it was thought of. It was one of the great causes of our separation from Great Britain. Its exclusion has been a principal object of this State, and most of the States of the Union. The augmentation of slaves weakens the States; and such a trade is diabolical in itself and disgraceful to mankind. Yet by this Constitution it is continued for twenty years. As much as I value the union of all the States, I would not admit the Southern States into the Union unless they agreed to the discontinuance of this disgraceful trade. And though this infamous traffic be continued, we have no security for the property of that kind which we have already. I have ever looked upon this clause as a most disgraceful thing to America.

---

[214] It is remarkable that the Virginia Declaration of Rights was always spoken of in debate, even by Mason, who drafted it, as the Bill of Rights—a name appropriate to the British Bill of Rights, which was first the Petition of Right, and was then enacted into a law; but altogether inapplicable to our Declaration, which had never been a bill, and was superior to all bills. It is true that the Declaration of Rights was read three times in the Convention which adopted it; but so was the Constitution, which nobody would call a bill.

I cannot express my detestation of it. Yet they have not secured us the property of the slaves we have already. So that 'they have done what they ought not to have done, and have left undone what they ought to have done.' "

Madison made answer that he should conceive this clause impolitic, if it were one of those things which could be excluded without encountering great evils. The Southern States would not have entered the union without the temporary permission of that trade. And if they were excluded from the union, the consequences might be dreadful to them and to us. We are not in a worse situation than before. That traffic is prohibited by our laws, and we may continue the prohibition. Under the Articles of Confederation it might be continued forever. But by this clause an end may be put to it in twenty years. There is, therefore, an amelioration of our circumstances. A tax may be laid in the mean time ; but it is limited, otherwise Congress might lay such a tax as would amount to a prohibition. "From the mode of representation and taxation," continued Madison, "Congress cannot lay such a tax on slaves as will amount to manumission. Another clause secures us that property which we now possess. At present, if any slave elopes to any of those States, he becomes emancipated by their laws. For the laws of the States are uncharitable to one another in this respect. But in this Constitution 'no person held to service or labor in one State under the laws thereof, escaping into another, shall, in consequence of any law or regulation therein, be discharged from any such service or labor ; but shall be delivered up on claim of the party to whom such service or labor may be due.' This clause was expressly inserted to enable owners of slaves to reclaim them. No power is given to the general government to interpose with respect to the property in slaves now held by the States." "I need not," he said in concluding, "expatiate on this subject. Great as the evil of this clause is, a dismemberment of the union would be worse. If those Southern States should disunite from the other States for not indulging them in the temporary use of this traffic, they might solicit and obtain aid from foreign powers."

Tyler warmly enlarged on the impolicy, iniquity, and disgracefulness of this wicked traffic. He thought the reasons urged by gentlemen in support of it were ill-founded and inconclusive. It was one cause of the complaints against British tyranny that this trade was permitted. His earnest desire was that it should be handed down to posterity that he had opposed this wicked clause. He also contended that as, according to the admission of Madison, Congress would have had power to abolish the traffic but for the restriction, and as no express power so to do was contained in the Constitution, then it followed that the discretion of Congress was its rule of authority, and that the necessity of a bill of rights was indispensable. Madison rejoined, and was followed by Henry, who enforced at length the argument advanced by Tyler, and urged in eloquent terms the absolute necessity of a bill of rights. He denied that Madison had shown the security of our slave property. The argument of Madison, he said, was no more than this—*that a runaway negro could be taken up in Maryland or in New York.* This could not prevent Congress from interfering with that kind of property by laying a grievous and enormous tax upon it, so as to compel owners to emancipate their slaves rather than pay the tax. He feared that this property would be lost to this country. Nicholas replied to Henry with peculiar tact, showing the inconsistency of those who with one and the same breath blamed the Constitution for allowing the introduction of slaves for a limited period, and for not protecting the very interest which it allowed to increase for twenty years. He urged that it was better to have this clause and union, than disunion without it. He also contended that the ratio of taxation was fixed by the Constitution; and that as the people were now reduced to beggary by the taxes on negroes, so by the adoption of the Constitution which exempts two-fifths, the taxes would rather be lightened than rendered more oppressive. He intimated an inconsistency in the arguments urged by gentlemen here and those offered in the House of Delegates at a previous period.

The second, third, and fourth clauses of the ninth section were now read.[215] Mason said that the restriction in the fourth clause of the capitation tax was nominal and deceptive. It only meant that the *quantum* to be raised of each State should be in proportion to their numbers in the manner directed in the Consti-

---

[215] Concerning the writ of *habeas corpus*, bills of attainder, and *ex post facto* laws, and the capitation and direct tax.

tution. But the general government was not precluded from laying the proportion of any particular State on any one species of property. They might lay the whole tax on slaves, and annihilate that species of property. The security was extended only to runaway slaves. Madison replied that the Southern States in the Convention were satisfied with the protection accorded by the Constitution; that every member of that body desired an equality of taxation, which uniformity could not secure; that some confidence must be placed in human discretion, or civil society could not exist; and that five States were permanently interested in the security of slave property, and other States in a greater or less degree.

The fifth and sixth clauses of the ninth section were read.[216] Mason thought the expression "from time to time" was loose. It might refer to triennial or septennial periods. Lee objected to such remarks as trivial. He wished gentlemen would confine themselves to an investigation of the principal parts of the Constitution, as the Assembly was about to meet the coming week. Mason begged to be allowed to use the mode of arguing to which he had been accustomed. However desirous he was of pleasing that worthy gentleman, his duty would give way to that pleasure. Nicholas, Corbin, and Madison replied to Mason, who still insisted on the vagueness of the words "from time to time," and said that in the Articles of Confederation a monthly publication was required.

The seventh clause of the ninth section, which prohibits titles of nobility from being granted by the United States, or the public officers accepting presents from foreign powers without the consent of Congress, was now read. Henry said he considered himself at liberty to review all the clauses of the ninth section of the first article. He said that this seventh section was a sort of bill of rights to the Constitution, and, by comparing it in detail with the Virginia Bill of Rights, argued that it was wholly inefficient. He concluded by saying that if gentlemen thought that this section would secure their liberties, then he and his friend (Mason) had spoken in vain. Randolph followed in an

---

[216] No tax or duty to be laid on articles exported from any State, or preference shown by any regulation; no moneys to be drawn from the treasury but by appropriations, and a regular statement published from time to time, &c.

elaborate review of the ninth section, and in reply to Henry. On the *sweeping clause* he thus spoke: " The rhetoric of the gentleman has highly colored the dangers of giving the general government an indefinite power of providing for the general welfare. I contend that no such power is given. They have power 'to lay and collect taxes, duties, imposts, and excises, to pay the debts and provide for the common defence and general welfare of the United States.' Is this an independent, separate, substantial power to provide for the general welfare ? No, sir. They can lay and collect taxes—for what ? To pay the debts and provide for the general welfare. Were not this the case, the following part of the clause would be absurd. It would have been treason against common language. Take it altogether, and let me ask if the plain interpretation be not this : a power to lay and collect taxes, etc., in order to provide for the general welfare and pay debts."

In his remarks upon the clause which forbids public officers from receiving presents from foreign powers, he observed that " an accident which actually happened operated in producing that restriction. A box was presented to our ambassador by the king of our allies. It was thought proper, in order to exclude corruption and foreign influence, to prohibit any one in office from receiving or holding any emoluments from foreign States. I believe that if at that moment, when we were in harmony with the king of France, we had supposed that he was corrupting our ambassador, it might have disturbed that confidence and diminished that mutual friendship which contributed to carry us through the war."[217]

In reply to an objection of Henry that the trial by jury was unsafe, he showed that it was secured in criminal cases, and that in civil cases, as there was then great contrariety in the practices of the different States on this subject, the matter was wisely

---

[217] Dr. Franklin is the person alluded to by Randolph. In the winter of 1856, in Philadelphia, under the roof of a venerable granddaughter of Dr. Franklin, I saw the beautiful portrait of Louis XVI, snuff-box size, presented by that king to the doctor. As the portrait is exactly such as is contained in the snuff-boxes presented by crowned heads, one of which I have seen, it is probable this portrait of Louis was originally attached to the box in question, which has in the lapse of years been lost or given away by Franklin.

referred to legislation; and in reply to another objection of that gentleman, that the common law was not established by the Constitution, he argued that "the wisdom of the Convention was displayed by its omission, because the common law ought not to be immutably fixed. It is established, not in our own Bill of Rights or in our State Constitution, but by the Legislature, and can therefore be changed as circumstances require. If it had been established by the new Constitution, it would be in many respects destructive to republican principles. It would have revived the writ for burning heretics, and involved other absurdities equally enormous. But it is not excluded. It may be established by the Legislature with such modifications as the public convenience and interests may hereafter prescribe."

Henry lamented that he could not see with that perspicuity which other gentlemen were blessed with.

The first clause of the tenth section, which prevents a State from entering into any treaty or alliance with a foreign power, or granting letters of marque or reprisal, or coining money, or making anything but gold and silver a tender in payment of debts, or passing any bill of attainder, *ex post facto* law, or any law impairing the obligation of contracts, or of laying, without the consent of Congress, any imposts or duties on imports or exports, except what might be absolutely necessary for executing its inspection laws, etc., etc., was read. Henry regarded with concern these restrictions on the States. They may be good in themselves; but he feared the States would be compelled by them to pay their share of the Continental money shilling for shilling. There had been great speculations in Continental money. He had been informed that some States had collected vast quantities of that money, which they should be able to recover in its nominal value of the other States. Madison admitted that there might be some speculation on the subject, and believed that the old Continental money had been settled in a very disproportionate manner. But the first clause of the sixth article settled this matter. That clause provided that all debts and engagements entered into before the adoption of the Constitution shall be as valid as under the Confederation. He affirmed that it was meant there should be no change with respect to claims by this political alteration. The validity of claims ought not to diminish by the adoption of the Constitution. It could not increase the demands on the public. Mason said that there had been enormous speculations in Continental money, in the hope of recovering shilling for shilling. The clause was well enough as far as it went. The money had depreciated a thousand for one. The old Congress could settle this matter. The hands of Congress were now tied. Under the new scheme we must pay it shilling for shilling, or at least one for forty. Madison made answer that the question as to who were the holders of the money was immaterial; it could not be affected by the Constitution, which made all claims as valid as they were before, *and not more so.* Henry replied that he saw clearly that we would be compelled to pay shilling for shilling. No *ex post facto* law could be passed by Congress or by the States, and there could be no relief. He instanced the case of relief by the Assembly from the payment of British debts. The State could be sued in the Federal court. Barrels of paper money had been hoarded at the North. There could be no relief. Judgment will be given against you, and the people will be ruined. Nicholas said that Virginia could make no law affecting the value of Continental money. So the case will stand hereafter as it does now. He denied that Congress could be sued by speculators. Congress may be plaintiff, but not defendant in her own courts. Randolph urged the restriction concerning *ex post facto* laws had no relation to the case at all; that the term was technical, and applied only to criminal cases. He said that the British debts, which were held contrary to treaty, ought to be paid. The payment might press the country, but we should retrench our extravagance and folly. He denied that private benefit affected his views, as, unless reduced very low indeed, he should never feel the benefit of the payment. Madison rose to quiet the fears which had been raised by Henry. Strike out the clause altogether, he said, and the case would stand just as it does now. As for the ruin threatened by the payment of debts, the original amount was only one hundred millions, of which some had been destroyed. But before it was destroyed, the share of Virginia was only twenty-six millions, which, at forty for one, amounted to five hundred thousand dollars only. Mason was still of his former opinion. Had three words been added after the words *ex post facto*, confining those words to crimes, then the position of those debts would be the same hereafter as now. Randolph replied that *ex post facto* laws applied exclusively to criminal cases ; that such was the meaning of the words in interpreting treaties, and it was so understood by all civilians.

The next clause of the section concerning the inspection laws was read, and was discussed by Mason, Nicholas, and Madison.

The first clause of the first section of the second article, which provides that the executive power shall be vested in a President of the United States of America, who shall hold his office during the term of four years, and, together with the Vice-President, chosen for the same term, be elected as follows, was then read. Mason said that there was not a more important article in the Constitution than this.   The great fundamental principle of republicanism is here sapped.   The President is elected without rotation.   It is said that you may remove him by a new election, but is there a single instance of a great man not being re-elected? Our governor is obliged to return after a given period to a private station.   Your President is in office for life.   The great powers of Europe will not allow you to change him.   The people of Poland have a right to displace their king ; but will Russia and Prussia allow them ?   He may receive a pension from European powers.   One of those powers, since the Revolution, offered emoluments to persons holding offices under our government.   I should be contented that he might be elected for eight years.   As it now stands, he may be elected for life.   Your government will be an elective monarchy.   The gentleman (Randolph), my colleague in the late Convention, says not a word about those parts of the Constitution which he denounced.   He will excuse me for repeating his own arguments against this dangerous clause.''   Randolph thought that he had mentioned his objections with freedom and candour ; but he believed that the Constitution, in the present state of affairs, ought to be adopted as it stands.   He had changed his opinion on this clause, believing that the hope of a re-election would stimulate the incumbent to direct his attention to his country instead of his own private gains.   The President was excluded from receiving emoluments from foreign powers.   It was impossible to guard better against corruption.

Mason said that the Vice-President was not only an unnecessary but a dangerous officer ; that the State from which he comes may have two votes when the others have but one ; that he blended in his person executive and legislative functions ; that though he could not foresee in the distance of time the consequences of such an appointment, he feared he would become a tool in overturning the liberties of his country. He objected that as the Vice-President was to succeed the President in certain contingencies, and as there was no provision for a fresh election of a President, it would be the interest of the Vice President to postpone or prevent an election. Perhaps, he said, he might be mistaken. Madison replied that there were some peculiar advantages incident to this office, that he would probably come from one of the larger States, and his vote so far would be favorable ; that he approved the fact that he would be the choice of the people at large, as it was better to confer this power on a person so elected than on a senator elected by a single State ; that he also approved of the power which authorized Congress to provide against the death of the President and the Vice-President, and he saw that such an event would rarely occur, and that this power, which was well-guarded, kept the government in motion. The House then adjourned.

On Wednesday, the eighteenth of June, the House went into committee, Wythe in the chair, the first section of the second article still under consideration. Monroe addressed the committee at some length, contending that our circumspection in politics should be commensurate with the extent of the powers granted ; that the President ought to act under the strongest impulses of rewards and punishments, the strongest incentives to human actions; that there were two ways of securing this point—dependence on the people for his appointment and continuation in office, and responsibility in an equal degree to all the States, and trial by dispassionate judges. He proceeded to show in detail that these objects were not secured by the section under discussion, and declared that the person first elected might continue in office for life. He argued that the United States might become the arbiter between foreign powers ; that vast territories belonging to foreign powers adjoined our own, and that the continuance of an individual in office might be important to their purposes, and that corruption would ensue. He opposed the office of Vice-President as unnecessary, and as justly amenable to the objections urged by Mason. Grayson followed, and in an argument of uncommon ingenuity opposed the clause. He said that if we adverted to the democratic, aristocratical, or executive branch of this new government, we would find their powers perpetually varying and fluctuating throughout the whole; that the democratic branch could be well constructed but for this defect; that the executive branch was still worse in this respect than the democratic; that the President was to be elected by a majority of electors, but that the principle was changed in the absence of that majority, when the election was to be decided by States. He pointed out the probability of the interference of foreign powers, and instanced in detail the case of Sweden; and adverted to the motives which might govern France and England in seeking to influence the election of President. He sought to demonstrate the want of responsibility in the President; and showed by an elaborate calculation that he might be elected by seventeen votes out of the whole number of one hundred and thirty-nine. Mason followed in corroboration of the views of Grayson. He said that it had been wittily remarked that the Constitution married the President and the Senate; and he believed that the usual results of marriage would follow— *they would be always helping one another.* There could be no true responsibility in such a case. He referred to the trial of Milo at Rome, when the court was bristling with the myrmidons of the executive. Your President, he said, might surround the Senate with thirty thousand armed men.

Madison rose and encountered the opposition with more than his usual tact. He did not object to some of the opinions which had been advanced in detail; that the mode of electing the President created much difficulty in the general Convention; that gentlemen who opposed the mode prescribed by the Constitution had suggested no mode of their own; that it was the result of a compromise between the large and the small States, the large States having the opportunity of deciding the election in the first instance, and the small States in the last; that the gentleman last up erred in saying that there must be a majority of the *whole* number of electors appointed; and that a majority of votes, equal to a majority of the electors appointed, will be sufficient. Mason replied and Madison rejoined.

The first clause of the second section of the second article, which provides "that the President shall be commander-in-chief of the army and navy of the United States, and of the militia of

the several States, when called into the actual service of the
United States," &c., was read. Mason did not object to the
President's being the official head of the army and navy, but
thought that he ought to be prohibited from commanding in
person without the consent of Congress. He reminded the committee of what Washington could have done, if to his great abilities and popularity he had added the ambition of the mere
soldier. He did not disapprove of the President's consulting
the executive officers, but he denounced the absence of a regular
and responsible council. He thought the President ought not
to have an unrestricted liberty of pardoning, as he might pardon
crimes perpetrated by his own advisement ; and he should be
expressly debarred from granting pardons before conviction.
" It may happen," he said, " at some future day, he may destroy
the republic and establish a monarchy." Lee observed that it
did not follow that the President would command in person. He
thought the pardoning power wisely lodged in the President.
The experience of New York was in favor of the plan. Mason
observed that he did not mean that the President was of necessity
to command in person, but that he might do so when he pleased,
and that if he were an ambitious man, he might make a dangerous use of his position. Nicholas reminded the committee
that the army and navy were to be raised, not by the President,
but by Congress. The arrangement was the same in our State
government, where the governor commanded in chief. As to
possible danger, any commander might pervert what was intended
for the public safety. The President went out every four years.
Any other commander might have a longer term of office.
Mason denied that there was a resemblance between the President and the governor. The latter had very few powers, went
out every year, and had no command over the navy. He was
comparatively harmless. The danger of the President consisted
in the union of vast civil, military, and naval powers in a single
person, without proper responsibility and control. The public
liberty had been destroyed by military commanders only. Madison, adverting to Mason's objections to the pardoning power
being given to the President, said it would be extremely improper
to vest that power in the House of Representatives. Such was
the fact in Massachusetts, and it was found in the case of the late
insurgents that the House at one session was for universal ven-

geance, and at another for general mercy. He said one great security from the malfeasance of the President consisted in the power of impeaching and of suspending him when suspected. Mason replied that the seeming inconsistency of the Massachusetts House of Representatives was sound policy. It was wise to punish pending the rebellion, and to pardon when it was past. Madison rejoined that it so happened that both sessions of that House had been held after the rebellion was over.

The second clause of the second section of the second article, which empowers the President by and with the advice and consent of the Senate to make treaties, provided two-thirds of the Senators present concur, to nominate and, by and with the advice and consent of the Senate, to appoint ambassadors, other public ministers and consuls, judges of the Supreme Court, and all other officers of the United States, with certain restrictions, was read. Mason thought this a most dangerous clause. Five States could make a treaty. Now nine States were necessary. His principal fear, however, was not that five, but that seven States, a bare majority, would make treaties to bind the Union. Nicholas answered that we were on a more safe footing in this Constitution than under the Confederation. The possibility of five States forming a treaty was founded on the absence of the Senators from the other States. The absence would be reciprocal. It may be safely presumed that in important cases there would be a full attendance, and then nine States would be necessary. He thought the approbation of the President, who was elected by all the States, was an additional security. Mason differed widely from the gentleman. He conceived that the contiguity of some States and the remoteness of others would present that reciprocity to which Nicholas alluded. Some States were near; others were nine hundred miles off. Suppose a partial treaty made by the President. He has a right to convene the Senate. Is it presumable that he would call or wait for distant States whose interests were to be affected by the treaty? Nicholas asked if it was probable that the President, who was elected by the people of all the States, would sacrifice the interest of the eight larger States to accommodate the five smallest? Lee compared the non-attendance of the Senators to that in our own Legislature, which consisted of one hundred and seventy members, of whom eighty-six were a majority sufficient to form a House; and of that House forty-four would make a majority. He asked if all our laws were bad because forty-four members could pass them? Madison wondered that gentlemen could think that foreign nations would be willing to accept a treaty made by collusion. The President would instantly be impeached and be convicted, as a majority of the States so injured would try the impeachment. Henry begged the committee to consider the condition the country would be in if two-thirds of a quorum could alienate territorial rights and our most valuable commercial advantages. The treaty-making power of this new scheme exceeded that of any other nation of the earth. Gentlemen were going on in a fatal career, but he hoped they would stop before they concede this power unguarded and unaltered. Madison said that, instead of being alarmed, he had no doubt that the Constitution would increase rather than decrease our territorial and commercial rights, as it would augment the strength and respectability of the country. If treaties are to have *any* efficacy at all they must be the law of the land. He denied that the country could be dismembered by a treaty in time of peace. The king of England could make a treaty of peace, but he could not dismember the empire or alienate any part of it. The king of France even had no such right. The right to make a treaty does not invoke the right of dismembering the Union. Henry asked how the power of the king of Englard would stand in respect to dismembering the empire if treaties were the supreme law of the land? He would confess his error if the gentleman would prove that the power of the king and that of the Congress, as to making treaties, were similar. Madison conceived that as far as the king of England had a constitutional right of making a treaty, such a treaty was binding. He did not say that his power was unlimited. One exception was that he could not dismember the empire.

Grayson rose and made a brilliant and characteristic speech. After pointing out the difference of what was called the laws of nations in various countries and its different operations, he expressed his alarm at the clause under discussion. He recurred to the dangers to which the right of navigating the Mississippi would be exposed, by surrendering the power of alienating it to the very States which had sought to attain their object by overleaping the existing Constitution. He declared that such was his repugnance to the alienation of a right so dear to the South, so important to its expansion and prosperity, that, if the new scheme contained no other defect, he would object to it on this ground alone.

Nicholas, if with less elegance, with equal vigor of logic, replied to Grayson. He criticised with severity his views respecting the laws of nations ; represented his arguments derived from the risk of losing the navigation of the Mississippi as a renewal of the scuffle for Kentucky votes, and argued the power of the king of England and of the Congress in respect of the nature of treaties was the same. In each country it was equally without limit. In each it was, and must ever be, the supreme law of the land. If gentlemen can show that the king can go so far, I will show them the same limitation here. If, as the gentleman says, the weight of power ought to be with the South because we have more people here, then these people, who elect the President, will elect a man who will attend to their interests. This is a sufficient check.

Henry instanced the case of the Russian ambassador in Queen Anne's time, to show that there was in England a limit to the treaty-making power. The emperor demanded that the man who had arrested his ambassador should be given up to him to be put to death. Queen Anne wrote with her own hand a letter to the emperor, in which she declared that it was beyond her power to surrender a British subject to a foreign power. We are in contact, he said, with Great Britain and with Spain. It is easy to define your rights now. Hereafter, when your citizens are charged with violating a treaty, will they have a fair trial? Will the laws of Virginia protect them in a Federal court? He denied that the same checks existed in the new scheme as existed in England. Can the king violate Magna Charta or the Bill of Rights by a treaty? Even the king of France calls on his parliament to aid him in the making of treaties. When Henry VI made a treaty with Sigismund, king of Poland, he submitted it to parliament. Here we have only the President and the Senate.

Randolph availed himself of the concession of Henry, that if the treaty-making power were put on as good footing here as in England, he would consent to the power, because there the king had a limit to his power ; and showed the restraints placed upon the President and Senate. Would they seek to overturn the

very government of which they were the creatures? He defied
any one to show how the treaty power could be limited. As for
dismembering a State, the Constitution expressly declares that
nothing contained therein shall prejudice any claims of the
United States or of any particular State. The House then adjourned.

On Wednesday, the eighteenth of June, the House went into
committee, Wythe in the chair, and the second clause of the
second section of the second article still under consideration.
Grayson took the floor. He adverted to the imminent risk of
losing the Mississippi by the adoption of the clause in debate ;
showed that the words of the Constitution quoted by Randolph
as a protection to the territorial rights of the States applied exclusively to the titles held by the different States to the back
lands ; and replied to the arguments of Nicholas in refutation of
his views of the nature of the law of nations. He laid it down
as a principle that a nation, like an individual, can renounce any
particular right, and, to show that the Mississippi might be given
up, he mentioned the case of the Scheldt which was surrendered
by the treaty of Munster. Nicholas made an elaborate argument to prove that there was no limit to the treaty-making
power in England, and quoted directly in point the authority of
Blackstone, who adds that the ministers who advised a bad
treaty could be punished by impeachment. Here we can im-
peach the President himself. In each country the treaty is the
supreme law of the land ; but under the new Constitution only
such treaties are binding as are made under the authority of the
United States, which authority is bounded by that instrument.
He argued that the case of the Russian ambassador did not apply. It had no relation to a treaty. It was an offence against
the law of nations, and Great Britain immediately passed an act
which punished such offences in future committed within her
own limits.

Corbin then rose, and in a capital speech, in which he exhibited
great perspicacity in anticipating the real action of the Federal
Government, supported the Constitution. He enforced some of
the arguments urged by Nicholas, and in order to prove that a
treaty was the supreme law in England, he said he would confirm it by a circumstance fresh in the memory of every body.
When our treaty of peace was made by England, Parliament

disapproved of it, and the ministry was turned out; but the treaty was good. The great distinction in our favor was that while in England the minister only was responsible, here the President in person was responsible. Treaties must not be binding at all—that is, we must have no treaties—or they must be binding altogether, or the country would be involved in perpetual war with foreign powers, and lose all the advantages of commercial intercourse. He drew a distinction between common and commercial treaties. By the first, if territory was dismembered, the people of Kentucky, for instance, would be justified by the laws of nations in resisting the treaty; by the last, the House of Representatives would act, because of the necessity of the passage of laws adapted to the state of the case. He said that the treaty-making power was amply guarded. If we are told that five States can make a treaty, we answer that three States can prevent it from being made. If the whole twenty-eight members are present, and, as men are apt to attend to their interests, it is fair to presume that they will be, then it will require nineteen to make a treaty, which is one member more than the nine States required by the Confederation. Henry said that the gentleman had fallen, unconsciously he knew, into an error when he said that the treaty of peace was binding on the nation though disapproved by Parliament. Did not an act pass acknowledging the independence of America? No cession of territory is binding in England without the authority of an act of Parliament. Will it be so here? They will tell you that they are omnipotent on this point.

Madison then pronounced an admirable disquisition on the treaty-making power. He showed that this power was exactly the same under the Confederation and under the Constitution; that the exercise of this power must always be consistent with the object which it was delegated to attain; that, as this power could only be exercised with foreign nations, its objects must be external; that, as it is impossible to foresee all our relations with other nations, so it would be imprudent to limit our capacity of action in regard to them; that, in transactions with foreign countries, it is fair to presume that we would prefer our own interests and honor to theirs, and not wantonly sacrifice the rights of our people; and the minister who negotiates the treaty, who is indeed our President, is liable to be punished in person for malfeasance. He said the case of the Russian ambassador was not applicable to the subject any more than other quotations made by the gentleman (Henry). Corbin admitted that an act of Parliament did pass acknowledging the independence of America, but said that there was nothing about the fisheries in that act, yet that part of the treaty relating to them was binding.[218]

We now approach a theme which, in itself considered, possessed an importance in the eyes of our fathers that language would vainly attempt to measure, which was discussed with a fullness of learning, with a keenness of logic, and with a glow of eloquence that it might well elicit, and which, though technical, and seen through a vista of seventy years, cannot fail to strike a responsive chord in the breasts of every true son and daughter of our noble Commonwealth. But, added to its own intrinsic dignity, it now received an additional interest derived from the state of the contest between the friends and the opponents of the Constitution. It was to be the last battle-ground of the parties into which the Convention was in nearly equal proportions divided, and from which the members were to pass to the final vote.

In reviewing the discussions of the Convention we should not forget that the experience of seventy years, derived from a minute observation of the workings of a political system, will place a child apparently on the same level with a giant, and the merest tyro in politics with a Somers or a Mason ; and we should especially remember that time was an element in the calculations of our ancestors ; that seventy years bears to the life of a nation no greater proportion than a single year bears to the life of an individual, and that the fears and gloomy predictions uttered by the opponents of the Constitution have, by the vigilance and caution which they inspired, operated in a material degree in preventing their own fulfillment. As no two complicated political systems which were identical in all their relations and circumstances ever did or can exist, the wisest statesmen in predicting their opera-

---

[218] Corbin was probably present in the House of Commons when the treaty was under discussion. The lovers of Fox must always deplore his unprincipled and factious opposition to the treaty, and the iniquitous coalition with Lord North, which succeeded in turning out Lord Shelburne for his approval of the treaty. To this day that coalition stands alone in its deformity and in the contempt and scorn of mankind.

tion can only judge from the general experience of the past. Hence arguments and analogies, hopes and fears, which seem chimerical now, might have had great weight with men who were quite as wise and as bold as those who have succeeded them, and who were more intimately acquainted with the difficulties of their age than it was possible for their successors to be. Another great element which pervaded the reasonings both of the friends and enemies of the new scheme consisted in the belief that, as the State governments, even when they drew a revenue from imposts, relied mainly for their support on direct taxation, such would also be the case with the Federal Government. The immense revenue which has flowed from the customs and from the sales of western lands into the Federal treasury, was not fore-seen in its full extent by either of the great parties. It is true that both looked to a revenue from the customs ; but while the ablest statesmen on either side agreed that the revenue from cus-toms would increase for a limited period, the friends of the new system contended that the period when the increase from that source would determine, was not very remote.[219]   But the states-man who would have ventured to predict that in half a century the customs of a single year would equal the amount of the entire debt of the Revolution, would have been derided as a vain theo-rist, or a wild babbler who sought to mislead other minds by the absurd creations of his own. The low rate of duties which the principal friends of the Constitution fixed upon as the standard for the customs, indicates what was anticipated from that source.[220] And the result was that both parties looked to direct taxation as the source from which the income of the new government would accrue. Their arguments were based on this supposition; and it can hardly be doubted that, if direct taxation had been the prin-

---

[219] See a previous debate between Grayson, Madison, and Corbin. Grayson argued that the period of decline would be very remote; Madison, that the highest point would be reached in less time than that specified by Grayson, when the duties would begin to decline. Corbin showed by arithmetical calculations that the revenue from the customs would immediately become a handsome source of revenue.

[220] Pendleton, as late as 1792, thought five per cent. high enough ; and Grayson thought that two and a half per cent. would, by preventing smuggling, put more money into the treasury. Grayson, *supra*, and Pendleton's letter on the tariff.

cipal source of the Federal revenue, and the rate of expenditure under the Constitution had been the same, the most dismal vaticinations would have been verified, and the union would scarcely have survived a quarter of a century. And it may be safely affirmed that the calamities predicted by our fathers have been averted, and the union preserved safe to our times, not so much in consequence of the provisions of the Constitution, as of the source from which the principal revenue has accrued.

But the prospect which was presented in the year 1788 was widely different. The unlimited power of direct taxation was to be ceded to the new government, and the Congress was to be empowered to pass such laws as might be deemed necessary to carry it into effect. And what increased the general anxiety was, that those laws were to be enforced by tribunals appointed by the Federal authority, responsible to that authority, and wholly beyond the reach of the government of the State. The citizen who had heretofore looked with confidence to his own General Assembly for protection, now, when the land was to be overrun with Federal judges, Federal sheriffs, Federal constables, and Federal jails, and when he needed that protection most, would look in vain.

From these apprehensions, however, it was possible to escape. The citizen who had satisfied the full demands of the Federal sheriff, and who was so fortunate as not to owe a dollar, might be safe. The dangers which beset that epoch were peculiar to a people who had just passed through a revolution of eight years, and are not likely to occur again; but they then presented an aspect so fearful as to fill the most dispassionate statesman with alarm. These dangers were such that no effort of an individual could elude them, and which threatened whole communities with ruin. Extensive grants of land, made under the royal government, had been confiscated by the State, and in the lapse of twelve years had been purchased and settled by active, industrious, and brave men, who had encountered the terrors of the wilderness, had driven back the savage, had cleared farms, and had built homes for their families. Every foot of these lands were now in jeopardy. Every farmer in the Northern Neck was liable to be dragged into a Federal court, to be evicted from his home, and to be cast with his wife and children on the world. Every farmer of the valley of Virginia, from the summit of the

Blue Ridge to the summit of the Alleghany, was in equal peril. The claims of the Indiana Company, if established by the Federal court, would involve thousands of poor, honest, but high-spirited men, who had fought gallantly during the war, in total ruin. Federal decisions involving such results could only be enforced by the bayonet, and civil war, deplorable as it must ever be, was one only of the evils that might flow from a resort to arms. The Commonwealth might be cut in twain. There might arise in the West a new, enterprising, and warlike State, which, sustained by the valor and skill of the soldiers who had been trained in the Indian wars and in the Revolution, and who had made, or might make, Kentucky their home, and upheld by the willing aid of England in the North and of Spain in the South, would not only bid defiance to the laws of the Federal Government, but might succeed in confining the boundaries of the States to the eastern slopes of the Blue Ridge. Wise statesmen, who saw the extent of the public peril, cautiously withheld any open expression of their opinions, but sought in private to contravene the dreaded calamity as far as was within their power. The intensity of a great crisis is not always to be estimated by the causes which produced it; and fearful as was, in the opinion of many, the surrender of the purse and the sword, the surrender of the right of trial involving men's lives and lands seemed more fearful still.

Another topic which created no little anxiety in the minds of those who were now to discuss the judiciary department of the new system was the payment of the British debts. The payment of these debts, estimated at several millions of dollars,[221] and deemed by many judicious persons a harsh measure in itself, might prove a fruitful source of annoyance to the people. These debts had been confiscated by the State, had been paid in whole or in part into the public treasury, and were claimed by foreigners. The debtors might then be brought into a Federal court held hundreds of miles from their homes, and forced to pay those debts a second time, and in coin. As these debts were

---

[221] I have never been able to make up my mind as to the true amount of the British debts. Some estimate it at ten millions. If this estimate was made on the value of a paper currency before that currency began to decline rapidly, it may be not far from the mark. I am disposed to think that three millions of dollars in coin would cover the amount.

owed by Eastern men, the subject of the new judiciary had a relation to them in this respect alone as delicate and as personal as to the people of the West.

None saw the difficulties of the crisis more distinctly than the friends of the Constitution, or could have adopted a safer line of policy. The judiciary department of the new system must be introduced to the committee by one of their number, and under the most favorable auspices. Its virtues should be carefully and deliberately set forth, its defects even pointed out, and the mode of amending those defects prescribed; and this office must devolve on an individual who to eminent skill as a debater, as a lawyer, and as a judge, should add the authority of high character and great services. In a body of which Pendleton was a member there could be no hesitation in the choice of the proper person. His years, his weakness, the frail tenure which seemed to hold him to life, would impart to his opinions on a subject peculiarly his own the weight of a parting benediction. Accordingly, as soon as the first and second sections of the third article were read,[222] though showing in his face the effects of re-

---

[222] "SEC. I. The judicial power of the United States shall be vested in one supreme court, and in such inferior courts as Congress may from time to time ordain and establish. The judges, both of the supreme and inferior courts, shall hold their offices during good behavior, and shall at stated times receive for their services a compensation, which shall not be diminished during their continuance in office.

"SEC. II. The judicial power shall extend to all cases, in law and equity, arising under this Constitution, the laws of the United States, and treaties made, or which shall be made under their authority, to all cases affecting ambassadors, other public ministers and consuls; to all cases of admiralty and maritime jurisdiction; to controversies to which the United States shall be a party; to controversies between two or more States, between a State and the citizens of another State, between citizens of different States, between citizens of the same State claiming lands under grants of different States, and between a State, or the citizens thereof, and foreign States, citizens or subjects.

"In all cases affecting ambassadors, other public ministers and consuls, and those in which a State shall be a party, the supreme court shall have original jurisdiction. In all the other cases before mentioned, the supreme court shall have appellate jurisdiction, both as to law and fact, with such exceptions, and under such regulations as the Congress shall make.

"The trial of all crimes, except in cases of impeachment, shall be by

cent illness, this venerable man was assisted to his crutches, and forthwith addressed the Chair.   Nor did he ever deliver, in the vigor of health and in the height of his fame, a more ingenious or a more conclusive speech.   He had studied the subject with the strictest attention, had analyzed with inimitable tact the various powers ceded to the judiciary, had scanned the defects of the system as he had scanned its perfections, and delivered a speech which, even in the meagre shreds that have come down to us, displays the attributes of a consummate debater in admirable juxtaposition with those of an accomplished judge.   He began by saying that, in a former review of the Constitution at large, he had mentioned the necessity of making the judiciary an essential part of the government; that it was necessary to arrest the executive arm, to prevent arbitrary punishments, to guard the innocent, to punish the guilty, to protect honesty and industry, and to punish violence and fraud.   Conceding, then, that a judiciary was necessary, it must also be conceded that it must be co-extensive with the legislative power, and extend to all parts of the society intended to be governed.   It must be so arranged that there shall be some court which will be the central point of its operations ; and for the plain reason that all the business cannot be done at the central point, there must be inferior courts to carry it on.   The first clause contains an arrangement of the courts—one supreme, and such inferior as Congress may ordain and establish.   This is highly proper.   Congress will be the judge of the public convenience, and may change and vary the inferior courts as experience shall dictate.   It would therefore have been not only improper, but exceedingly inconvenient to fix the arrangement in the Constitution itself, instead of leaving it to be changed according to circumstances.   He then expressed an opinion, which was confirmed in the same debate by Madison, and which may seem strange in our times, that the first experiment would probably be to appoint the State courts to have the inferior Federal jurisdiction, as such a plan would give general satisfaction and promote economy.   But even this eligible mode experience may furnish powerful reasons for changing,

---

jury ; and such trial shall be held in the State where the said crimes shall have been committed ; but when not committed within any State, the trial shall be at such place or places as the Congress may by law direct."

and Congress very properly possesses the power to alter the arrangement. He said this clause also secures the independence
of the judges, both as to tenure of office and pay of salary ; and
he wished it had extended to increase as well as diminution.
When he had enumerated and dwelt upon the subject of the
jurisdiction of the supreme court, he concluded that the necessity
and propriety of Federal jurisdiction in such general cases would
be obvious to all. He adverted to the second clause of the section
which settles the original jurisdiction of the supreme court, and
confines it to ambassadors, ministers, and consuls, and to cases
in which a State shall be a party. And here he sought to an-
ticipate an objection which he knew would be urged by his opponents, by showing that, though the original jurisdiction was
limited to the objects mentioned, yet Congress may go farther
and exclude its original jurisdiction by limiting, for obvious and
beneficial purposes, the cases in which it shall be exercised.
Yet the Legislature cannot extend its original jurisdiction. He
then dwelt on the appellate jurisdiction of the court. He said
that it was necessary, in all free systems, to allow appeals under
certain circumstances, in order to prevent injustice by correcting
the erroneous decisions of inferior tribunals, and to introduce
uniformity in decisions.   This appellate jurisdiction was manifestly proper, and could not have been objected to, if the Constitution had not unfortunately contained the words, "both as to
law and fact."   He sincerely wished these words had been buried
in oblivion ; if they were, the strongest objection against the
section would have been removed. He would give his free ana
candid sentiments on the subject.   "We find," he said, "these
words followed by others, which remove a great deal of doubt :
' *With such exceptions and under such regulations as Congress
shall make.*' So that Congress may make such regulations as
the public convenience may require."

   " Let us consider the appellate jurisdiction, if these words had
been left out. The general jurisdiction must embrace decrees in
chancery and admiralty, and judgments in courts of common
law, in the ordinary practice of this appellate jurisdiction.
When there is an appeal from the inferior court to the court of
chancery, the appellate jurisdiction goes to law and fact, because
the whole testimony appears in the record.   The court proceeds
to consider the circumstances of both law and fact blended

together, and then decrees according to equity. This must be unexceptionable to everybody. How is it in appeals from the admiralty? That court, except in some cases, proceeds as a court of chancery. In some cases they have trials by jury. But in most cases they proceed as in chancery. They consider all the circumstances, and determine as well what the fact as what the law is. When this goes to the superior court, it is determined in the same way. Appeals from the common law courts involve the consideration of facts by the superior court, when there is a special verdict. They consider the fact and the law together, and decide accordingly. But they cannot introduce new testimony. When a jury proceeds to try a cause in an inferior court, a question may arise on the competency of a witness, or some other testimony. The inferior court decides that question. They either admit or reject that evidence. The party intending to object states the matter in a bill of exceptions. The jury then proceeds to try the cause according to the judgment of the inferior court; and, on appeal, the superior court determines upon the judgment of the inferior court. They do not touch the testimony. If they determine that the evidence was either improperly admitted or rejected, they set aside the judgment, and send back the cause to be tried again by a jury in the same court. These are the only cases in appeal from inferior courts of common law where the superior court can even consider facts incidentally. I feel the danger, he said, as much as any gentleman in this committee, of carrying a party to the Federal court to have a trial there. But it appears to me that it will not be the case if that be the practice I have now stated; and that that is the practice must be admitted. The appeals may be limited to a certain sum. You cannot prevent appeals without great inconvenience. But Congress can prevent that dreadful oppression which would enable many men to have a trial in the Federal court, which is ruinous. Congress may make regulations which will render appeals as to law and fact proper and perfectly inoffensive. If I thought that there was a possibility of danger I would be alarmed; but when I consider who Congress are, I cannot conceive that they will subject the citizens to oppressions of that dangerous kind." When he had arrived at that point of his argument when the trial by jury, and

that trial to be held in the State where the offence was committed,
was considered, his voice failed, and he resumed his seat.

Mason then spoke. He had cherished the hope, he said, that
the warmest friends of the Constitution would have pointed out
the important defects of the judiciary; and, as it was not in his
line, he would have held his peace, if he were not convinced that
it was so constructed as to destroy the dearest rights of the community. Having read the first section, he inquired, what is there
left to the State courts? What remains? There is no limitation.
The inferior courts are to be as numerous as Congress may think
proper. All the laws of the United States are paramount to the
laws and the Constitution of Virginia. "The judicial power
shall extend to all cases in law and equity arising under this
Constitution." What objects will not be comprehended by this
provision? Such laws may be framed as will include every
object of private property. When we consider the nature and
the operation of these courts, we must conclude that they will
destroy the State governments. As to my own opinion, he said,
I most religiously and conscientiously believe that it was the
intention to weaken the State governments, to make them contemptible, and then to destroy them. But, whatever may have
been the intention, I think that it will destroy the State governments. There are many gentlemen in the United States who
think it right that we should have one great consolidated government, and that it was better to bring it about slowly and imper-
ceptibly than all at once. This is no reflection on any man, for
I mean none. I know from my own knowledge that there are
many worthy gentlemen of this opinion. (Here Madison inter-
rupted Mason, and demanded an unequivocal explanation. As
those insinuations might create a belief that every member of
the late Federal Convention was of that opinion, he wished him to
tell to whom he alluded.) Mason replied: "I shall never refuse
to explain myself. It is notorious this is a prevailing principle.
It was at least the opinion of many gentlemen in Convention,
many in the United States. I do not know what explanation
the honorable gentleman asks. I can say with great truth that
the honorable gentleman, in private conversation with me, expressed himself against it. Neither did I ever hear any of the
delegates from this State advocate it." Madison declared him-

self satisfied with this, unless the committee thought themselves entitled to ask a further explanation.[223]

Mason continued : " I have heard that opinion advocated by gentlemen for whose abilities, judgment, and knowledge I have the highest reverence and respect.   I say that the general description of the judiciary involves the most extensive jurisdiction.   Its cognizance in all cases arising under that system, and the laws of Congress, may be said to be unlimited.   In the next place it extends to treaties made, or which shall be made, under their authority.   This is one of the powers that ought to be given them.   I also admit that they ought to have judicial cognizance in all cases affecting ambassadors, public ministers, and consuls, as well as in cases of maritime jurisdiction.   The next power of the judiciary is also necessary, under some restrictions.   Though the decision of controversies to which the United States shall be a party, may at first view seem proper, it may, without restraint, be extended to a dangerously oppressive length.   The next, with respect to disputes between two or more States, is right.   I cannot see the propriety of the next power, in disputes between a State and the citizens of another State.   As to controversies between citizens of different States, their power is improper and inadmissible.   In disputes between citizens of the same State claiming lands under the grants of different States, the power is proper.   It is the only case in which the Federal judiciary ought to have appellate cognizance of disputes between private citizens.   The last clause was still more improper.   To give them cognizance between a State and the citizens thereof is utterly inconsistent with reason and sound policy."   Here Nicholas rose and informed Mason that his interpretation was not warranted by the words.   Mason replied that if he recollected rightly, the propriety of the power as explained by him had been contended for ; but that, as his memory had never been good, and was now much impaired from his age, he would not insist on that interpretation.   He then proceeded : "Give me

---

[223] Madison manifested great sensitiveness during the speech of Mason, and it is not to be disguised that he did touch doctrines in the Convention which would have led the way to the plan denounced by Mason; for he is reported by Yates to have said that the States were never sovereign, and were petty corporations. See *Yates' Reports,* and the letter of Madison, published in the collection of McGuire.

leave," he said, "to advert to the operation of this judicial power. Its jurisdiction in the first case will extend to all cases affecting revenue, excise and custom-house officers. It will take in of course what others do to them, and what is done by them to others. In what predicament will our citizens then be? If any of the Federal officers should be guilty of the greatest oppressions, or behave with the most insolent and wanton brutality to a man's wife or daughter, where is this man to get relief? His case will be decided by Federal judges. Even supposing the poor man may be able to obtain judgment in the inferior court for the greatest injury, what justice can he get on appeal? Can he go four or five hundred miles? Can he stand the expense attending it? On this occasion they are to judge of fact as well as law. He must bring his witnesses where he is not known, where a new evidence may be brought against him, of which he never heard before, and which he cannot contradict."

The honorable gentleman who presides, he said, has told us that the supreme court of appeals must embrace every object of maritime, chancery, and common law controversy. In the two first the indiscriminate appellate jurisdiction as to fact must be generally granted; because otherwise it would exclude appeals in those cases. But why not discriminate as to matters of fact in common law controversies? The honorable gentleman has allowed that it was dangerous, but hopes regulations will be made to suit the convenience of the people. But mere hope is not a sufficient security. I have said that it appears to me (though I am no lawyer) to be very dangerous. Give me leave to lay before the committee an amendment which I think convenient, easy, and proper. (Here Mason proposed an alteration nearly the same as the first part of the Fourteenth Amendment recommended by the Convention, which see in the Appendix.).

The jurisdiction of the Federal courts extends to controversies between citizens of different States. Can we not trust our State courts with the decision of these? If I have a controversy with a man in Maryland—if a man in Maryland has my bond for a hundred pounds—are not the State courts competent to try it? Why carry me a thousand miles from home—from my family and business—where it may perhaps be impossible for me to prove that I have paid it? I may have a witness who saw me pay the money; and I must carry him a thousand miles or be

compelled to pay the money again.   "What effect," he inquired,
"will this power have between British creditors and the citizens
of this State?   This is a ground on which I shall speak with confidence.   Everyone who heard me speak on the subject knows
that I always spoke for the payment of the British debts.   I wish
every honest debt to be paid.   Though I would wish to pay the
British creditor, yet I would not put it in his power to gratify
private malice, to our injury.   Every British creditor can bring
his debtors to the Federal court.   There are a thousand instances where debts have been paid, and yet by this appellate
cognizance be paid again.   'To controversies between a State
and the citizens of another State.'   How will their jurisdiction
in this case do?   Let the gentleman look to the westward.   Claims
respecting those lands, every liquidated account, or other claim
against this State, will be tried before the Federal court.   Is not
this disgraceful?   Is the State of Virginia to be brought to the
bar of justice like a delinquent individual?   Is the sovereignty
of the State to be arraigned like a culprit, or a private offender?
Will the States undergo this mortification?   I think this power
perfectly unnecessary.   What is to be done if a judgment be
obtained against a State?   Will you issue a *fieri facias?*   It
would be ludicrous to say that you would put the State's body
in jail.   How is the judgment then to be enforced?   A power
which cannot be executed ought not to be granted."

"Let us consider," said Mason, "the operation of the last
subject of its cognizance—controversies between a State, or the
citizens thereof, and foreign States, citizens, or subjects.   There
is a confusion in this case.   This much, however, may be raised
out of it—that a suit will be brought against Virginia.   She may
be sued by a foreign State.   What reciprocity is there in it?   In
a suit between Virginia and a foreign State, is the foreign State
to be bound by the decision?   Is there a similar privilege given
to us in foreign States?   How will the decision be enforced?
Only by the *ultima ratio regum.*   A dispute between a foreign
citizen or subject and a Virginian, cannot be tried in our own
courts, but must be decided in the Federal conrts.   Cannot we
trust the State courts with a dispute between a Frenchman,
or an Englishman, and a citizen ; or with disputes between
two Frenchmen?   This is digraceful.   It will annihilate your
State judiciary.   It will prostrate your Legislature.   Thus, sir,"

he said, "it appeared to me that the greater part of the powers
are unnecessary, dangerous, tending inevitably to impair and
ultimately to destroy the State judiciaries, and by the same principle, the legislation of the State governments. After mentioning
the original jurisdiction of the supreme court, it gives it appellate
jurisdiction in all the other cases mentioned, both as to law and
fact, indiscriminately, and without limitation. Why not remove
the cause of fear and danger ? But it is said that the regulations
of Congress will remove it. I say that, in my opinion, those
regulations will have a contrary effect, and will utterly annihilate
your State courts. Who are the court ? The *judges*. It is a
familiar distinction. We frequently speak of a court in contra-
distinction to a jury. The judges on the bench are to be judges
of fact and law. Now give me leave to ask : Are not juries
excluded entirely? This great palladium of national safety,
which is secured by our own State governments, will be taken
from us in the Federal courts ; or, if it be reserved, it will be but
in name, and not in substance. This sacred right ought to be
secured."

He then adverted to some of the probable effects of the decisions of Federal courts. "I dread," he said, "the ruin that
will be brought upon thirty thousand of our people with respect
to disputed lands. I am personally endangered as an inhabitant
of the Northern Neck. The people of that section will be compelled by the operation of this power to pay the quit-rents of
their lands. Whatever other gentlemen may think, I consider
this a most serious alarm. It will little avail a man to make a
profession of his candor. It is to his character and reputation they
will appeal. To these I wish gentlemen to appeal for an interpretation of my motives and views. Lord Fairfax's title was
clear and undisputed. After the Revolution we taxed his lands as
private property. After his death an Act of Assembly was made
(in 1782) to sequester the quit-rents due at his death in the hands
of his debtors. Next year an act was made restoring them to
the executor of the proprietor. Subsequent to this the treaty of
peace was made, by which it was agreed that there should be no
further confiscations. But after this an Act of Assembly passed
confiscating this whole property. As Lord Fairfax's title was
indisputably good, and as treaties are to be the supreme law of
the land, will not his representatives be able to recover all in the

Federal court? How will gentlemen like to pay an additional tax on the lands in the Northern Neck? This the operation of this system will compel them to do. They are now subject to the same taxes other citizens are, and if the quit-rents be recovered in the Federal court they will be doubly taxed. This may be called an assertion; but were I going to my grave I would appeal to Heaven that I think it true. How will a poor man get relief when dispossessed unjustly? Is he to go to the Federal court eight hundred miles off? He might as well give up his claim.''

'' Look,'' said Mason, '' to that great tract of country between the Blue Ridge and the Alleghany mountains. Every foot of it will be claimed, and probably recovered in the Federal court from their present possessors, by foreign companies which have a title to them. These lands have been sold to a great number of people. Many settled on them on terms which were advertised. How will this be in respect of *ex post facto* laws? We have not only confirmed the title of those who made the contracts, but those who did not, by a law in 1779, on their paying the original price. Much was paid in a depreciated value, and much not paid at all. Look now to the Indiana Company. The great Indiana purchase, which was made to the westward, will by this new judicial power be made a cause of dispute. The possessors may be ejected from those lands. That company paid a consideration of ten thousand pounds to the Crown before the lands were taken up. That company may now come in and show that they have paid the money, and have a full right to the land. Three or four counties are settled on those lands, and have long enjoyed them peacefully. All these claims before those courts, if successful, will introduce a scene of distress and confusion almost without a parallel. The gloomy pictures which Virgil has painted of a desolated country and an ejected people will be seen in our own land; and from hundreds of honest and thrifty men reduced to ruin and misery, and driven with their families from their homes, we will hear the mournful ditty of the poet :

Nos patriam fugimus—et dulcia linquimus arva.

Mason concluded by offering an amendment which would prevent such direful results as he feared would happen, in these words : '' That the judiciary power shall extend to no case where the cause of action shall have originated before the ratification of this Constitution, except in suits for debts due to the United States, disputes between States about their territory, and disputes between persons claiming lands under the grants of different States." In these cases there is an obvious necessity for giving the court a retrospective power. "I have laid before you," he said, "my ideas on the subject, and expressed my fears, which I most conscientiously believe to be well-founded."

It was now past the usual hour of adjournment, but late as it was, Madison rose to break the effect of Mason's speech. He said that he did not wonder that Mason, who believed the judiciary system so fatal to the liberties of the country, should have opposed it with so much warmth ; but as he believed his fears were groundless, he would endeavor to refute his objections wherein they appeared to him ill-founded. He confessed that there were defects in the judiciary—that it might have been better expressed ; but that truth obliged him to put a fair interpretation upon the words of the Constitution ; and as it was late, he could not then enter fully on the subject. He hoped, however, that gentleman would see that the dangers pointed out by Mason did not necessarily follow. The House then adjourned.

On Friday, the twentieth of June, the House went into committee, Wythe in the chair, and the first and second sections of the third article still under consideration.

Madison rose to reply to Mason. There was an evident interest shown to hear the speech of Madison, who, like Mason, was not a lawyer, on a topic which was beyond the usual sphere of a politician, and which had been argued with such eminent ability by Mason the day before. When Madison had detailed at some length the difficulties inseparable from the task of forming a Federal compact between different States whose interests and opinions were apparently diverse, and had referred to the executive department of the Constitution, and especially the judiciary in the way of illustration, he discussed the question of the judiciary under two heads ; the first, whether the subjects of its cognizance be proper subjects for Federal jurisdiction, and next, whether the provisions respecting it will be consistent with safety and propriety, will answer the purposes intended, and suit local circumstances. Under the first head he discussed the powers of the judiciary. As to its jurisdiction in controversies

between a State and the citizens of another State, its only operation would be that if a State wished to bring suit against an individual, it must be brought in the Federal court. *It is not in the
power of individuals to call any State into court.* As to its cognizance of disputes between citizens of different States, perhaps
this authority ought to have been left to the State courts. He
thought that the result would be rather salutary than otherwise.
As to disputes between foreign States and one of our States,
should such a case ever arise, it could only come on by consent
of parties. It might avert difficulties with foreign powers.
Ought a single State have it in its power to involve the union at
any time in war?

Under the second head, he said, suppose the subjects of jurisdiction had only been enumerated, and full power given to Congress to establish courts, would there have been any valid objection? But the present arrangement was better and more
restrictive. As to the objections against the appellate cognizance
of fact as well as law, he mainly relied on the arguments and
authority of Pendleton, which were conclusive with him. Congress may make a regulation to prevent such appeals entirely.
He argued that in so far as the judicial power extended to controversies between citizens of different States, it was beneficial to
the commercial States, and proportionally to Virginia. He believed that the Legislature would accommodate the judicial power
to the necessities of the people, and instead of making the
supreme court stationary, will fix it in different parts of the
Continent, as was done with the admiralty courts under the Confederation. It would also be in the power of Congress to vest
the judicial power in the inferior and superior courts of the
States. Gentlemen argued that the Legislature would do all
the ill that was possible. Distrust to a certain extent was wise ;
he did not lean to over-confidence himself ; but without some
measure of confidence government was impossible. Without
confidence no theoretical checks, no form of government could
render us secure. It was objected that the jurisdiction of the
Federal courts would annihilate the State courts ; but, though
there then were from peculiar circumstances many cases between
citizens of different States, it might never occur again, and he
affirmed that hereafter ninety-nine cases out of a hundred would
remain with the State courts. As to vexatious appeals, they can

be remedied by Congress. If the State courts were on a good footing, what would induce men to take such trouble? And if this provision should have the effect of establishing universal justice, and accelerating it in America, it would be a most fortunate result for debtors. Confidence would take the place of distrust, and the circulation of confidence was better than the circulation of money. No political system can directly pay the debts of individuals. Industry and economy are the only resources of those who owe money. But by the establishment of confidence the value of property will be raised, capital will go in quest of labor, and all will share in the general prosperity. Madison concluded by saying that he would not enter into those considerations which Mason added, but hoped some other gentleman would undertake to answer him.[224]

Henry rose to reply to Pendleton and Madison. He said that he had already expressed painful sensations at the surrender of our great rights, and was again driven to the mournful recollection. The purse is gone—the sword is gone—and here is the only thing of any importance that remains with us! He contended that the powers in the section under discussion were either impracticable, or, if reducible to practice, dangerous in the extreme. He deplored the idea suggested by Pendleton and sanctioned by Madison, that "our State judges would be contented to be Federal judges and State judges too." "If we are to be deprived of that class of men, and if they are to combine against us with the Federal Government, *we are gone!* I regard the Virginia judiciary as one of the best barriers against the strides of power. So few are the barriers against the encroachments and usurpations of Congress, that when I see this last barrier, the independency of the judges impaired, I am persuaded that I see the prostration of all of our rights. In what a situation will your judges be when they are sworn to preserve the Constitution of the State and that of the Federal Government? If there should be a concurrent dispute between the two governments, which shall prevail? My only comfort, he said, was the independence of the judges. If by this system we lose it, we must sit down quietly and be

---

[224] In relation to British debts, the Fairfax grants, the Indiana Company, &c.

oppressed.   He discussed at length the appellate jurisdiction of
the courts, and contended that, if the arguments of the gentlemen were just, and that Congress would make such a judiciary
as it pleased, then Congress can alter and amend the Constitution.   And if the Constitution is to be altered, on whom ought
that duty to devolve?   On the members of Congress, or on those
who are now entrusted with the office of securing the public
rights on a firm and certain foundation beyond the reach of contingencies?   He reverted to the remark of Madison that there
were great difficulties in framing a Constitution.   "I acknowledge it," he said ; "but I have seen difficulties conquered which
were as unconquerable as this.   We are told that trial by jury is
a technical term.   Do we not know its meaning?   I see one
thing in this Constitution—I made the remark before—that
everything with respect to privileges is so involved in darkness,
it makes me suspicious, not of those gentlemen who formed it,
but of its operation in its present form.   Trial by jury is secured
in criminal cases, it is said; I would rather it had been left out
altogether than have it so vaguely and equivocally provided for.
He endorsed the reasoning of Mason about the incarcerating of
a State, begged to know how money was to be paid if the State
was cast, and denounced the folly of investing the judiciary with
a power that could not be enforced.   He contended that the provisions of the clause in debate would operate as a retrospective
law, which was odious in civil cases as *ex post facto* were in
criminal, and that citizens would be subject to a tribunal unknown
at the time the contracts were made.   He contested the assertion
of Madison that, in controversies between a State and the citizens of other States, a State could not be brought into court.
The gentleman asserts that the State can only be plaintiff; but
that paper says Virginia may be defendant as well as plaintiff.
If gentlemen construe that paper so loosely now, what will they
do when our rights and liberties are in their power?   He declared that this judiciary presented the first instance ever known
among civilized men of the establishment of a tribunal to try
disputes between the aggregate society and foreign powers.   He
then discoursed at length upon the trial by jury, quoting Blackstone's remarks upon it, and its virtual sacrifice under the new
scheme ; and asked: "Shall Americans give up that which
nothing could induce the English people to relinquish?   The

idea is abhorrent to my mind.   There was a time when we would
have spurned at it.   This gives me comfort that as long as I live
my neighbors will protect me.   Old as I am, it is probable I may
yet have the appellation of rebel.   I trust I shall see congressional oppression crushed in embryo.   As this government
stands, I despise and abhor it.   Gentlemen demand it, though it
takes away the trial by jury in civil cases, and does worse than
take it away in criminal cases.   It is gone, unless you preserve
it now.   I shall add no more but that I hope that gentlemen will
recollect what they are about to do, and consider that they are
about to give up this last and best privilege.''

Pendleton replied to Mason and Henry.   He said that if there
had been any person in the audience who had never read the
Constitution and had heard what has just been said, he would be
surprised to learn that trial by jury was not excluded in civil
cases, and was expressly provided in criminal cases.   He had
not heard that kind of argument in favor of the Constitution.   It
is insisted that the right of challenging has not been secured ;
but when the Constitution says that the trial shall be by jury,
does it not also say that every incident shall go along with it?
The honorable gentleman (Mason) was mistaken yesterday in
his reasoning on the propriety of a jury from the vicinage.   He
supposed that a jury from the vicinage was had from this
view—that they should be acquainted with the character of the
person accused.   I thought, said Pendleton, that it was with
another view—that the jury might have some personal knowledge of the fact and acquaintance with the witnesses who will
come from the neighborhood.[225]   The same gentleman objected

___

[225] Pendleton sought to make mirth with those gentlemen of the law
in the Convention who thought that none but lawyers can understand
legal questions.   The fact is that Mason was clearly right, and Pendleton clearly wrong.   Mason did not contend that a jury from the vicinage was the sole benefit accruing from jury trial, but that it was an
important one, as it assuredly is, which a criminal, carried a thousand
miles from his home, would lose.   As Pendleton wholly excludes from
his view this great benefit, it is he that errs, and not Mason.   The history of trial by jury proves incontestibly that one of its most precious
privileges was that the criminal should be tried by his *peers* (*pares*)—
that is, by men living in the same region, placed under the same circumstances, and liable to be punished for the same crimes, upon the
testimony of the same men.   When it is considered that it was mainly

to the unlimited power of appointing inferior courts. Why limit the power? Ought there not to be a court in every State? Ought there not to be more than one, should the convenience of the people hereafter require it? Look at our own legislation. What would have been the condition of our Western counties, and of Kentucky in particular, if our Legislature had not possessed this power? We established a general court in that district, but we did not lose sight of making every part of our territory subject to one supreme tribunal. Appeals lay from that court to the court of appeals here. And what was the result? There has not been a single appeal. He also objected to the clause which provides that cases under the Constitution and the laws made in pursuance thereof, should be tried in the Federal court. Ought such matters to be tried in the State courts? But he says that Congress will make bad laws. Is not this carrying suspicion to an extreme that tends to prove that there should be no Legislature or judiciary at all? But we are alarmed with the idea that this is a consolidated government. It is so, say gentlemen, in the other two great departments, and it must be so in the judiciary. I never considered it, said Pendleton, to be a consolidated government as to involve the interests of all America. Of the two objects of judicial cognizance, one is general and national, and the other local. The former is given to the general judiciary, and the latter left to the local tribunals. They act in co-operation to secure our liberty. For the sake of economy the appointment of these courts might be in the State courts. I rely on an honest interpretation from independent judges. An honest man would not serve otherwise, because it would be to serve a dishonest purpose. To give execution to proper laws is their peculiar province. There is no inconsistency, impropriety, or danger in giving the State judges the Federal cognizance. Every gentleman who beholds my situation, my infirmity, and various other considerations, will hardly suppose that I carry my view to an accumulation of power. Ever since I had any power, I was more anxious to discharge my duty than to increase my power.

---

introduced to prevent oppression by the government and by superior lords, the vicinage of his triers is an important consideration to the culprit, whose character will then, and only then, have its proper weight in his favor.

Pendleton then argued that the impossibility of calling a sovereign State to the tribunal of another sovereign State, showed the propriety and necessity of vesting the Federal court with the decision of controversies to which a State shall be a party. But the principal objection of the gentleman (Mason) was, that jurisdiction was given the Federal court in disputes between citizens of different States. I think, said Pendleton, that in general those decisions might be left to the State tribunals, especially as citizens of one State are declared citizens of all. But cases may arise in which this jurisdiction would be proper, as in the case of Rhode Island, where a citizen of another State would be compelled to accept payment of one-third or less of his money. Ought he not to be able to carry his claim to a court where such unworthy principles do not prevail? He denied that there was any force in the case put by Mason of the malicious assignment of a bond to a citizen of a neighboring State, Maryland for instance. The creditor cannot carry the debtor to Maryland. He must sue in the local Federal court; the creditor cannot appeal. He gets a judgment. The defendant only can appeal, and gains a privilege instead of an injury. As to the amendment proposed by the gentleman, I attended to it, said Pendleton, and it gave force to my opinion, that it is better to leave the subject to be amended by the legislation of Congress. The honorable gentleman (Henry) argued to-day that it was placing too much confidence in agents and rulers. Will the representatives of any twelve States sacrifice their own interest and that of their citizens to answer no purpose? But suppose we should be deceived; have we no security? So great was the spirit of America that it was found sufficient to oppose the greatest power in the world. Will not that spirit protect us against any danger from our own representatives? As it was late, he said he would add no more.

Pendleton was followed by a young man of thirty years who resided in Richmond, who had already taken a prominent part in debate, whose arguments, enforced with logical precision, were delivered with modesty and were heard with profound respect, and whose fame, then in its early dawn, was destined in the course of a third of a century, during which he held the office of chief-justice of that court which he was now required to defend, to attain its greatest lustre. His opinions, as well from the ability with which they were maintained as from his subsequent career,

have a living interest even in our own times. He had deliberately prepared himself to reply to the arguments of Mason,
and followed that gentleman step by step. He said it was argued
that the Federal courts will not determine the causes which may
come before them with the same fairness and impartiality with
which other courts decide. What are the reasons of this supposition? Do gentlemen draw them from the manner in which
the judges are chosen, or the tenure of their office? What is it
that makes us trust our judges? Their independence in office
and their manner of appointment. Are not the judges of the
Federal court chosen with as much wisdom as the judges of the
State governments? Are they not equally, if not more independent? If there be as much wisdom and knowledge in the
United States as in a single State, shall we conclude that that
wisdom and knowledge will not be equally exercised in the selection of judges? What are the subjects of Federal jurisdiction?
Let us examine each of them with the supposition that the same
impartiality will be observed in those courts as in other courts,
and then see if any mischief will arise from them.

With respect to their cognizance in all cases arising under the
Constitution and the laws of the United States, the gentleman
(Mason) observes that the laws of the United States being paramount to the laws of the particular States, there is no case but
what this will extend to. Has the government of the United
States power to make laws on every subject? Does he understand it so? Can they make laws affecting the mode of transferring property, or contracts, or claims between citizens of the
same State? Can they go beyond their delegated powers? If
they did exceed those powers, their acts would be considered by
the judges beyond their jurisdiction and declared void. But,
says the gentleman, the judiciary will annihilate the State courts.
Does not every gentleman here know that the causes in our
courts are more numerous than they can decide according to
their present construction? Are there any words in this Constitution which excludes the courts of the States from those cases
which they now possess? Will any gentleman believe it? Are
not controversies respecting lands claimed under the grants of
different States the only controversies between citizens of the
same State which the Federal judiciary can take cognizance of?
The State courts will not lose the jurisdiction of the causes

which they now decide. They have a concurrence of jurisdiction with the Federal courts in those cases in which the latter have cognizance. How disgraceful is it, says the honorable gentleman, that the State courts cannot be trusted? Does the Constitution take away their jurisdiction? Is it not necessary that Federal courts should have cognizance of cases arising under the Constitution and laws of the United States? What is the purpose of a judiciary but to execute the laws in a peaceable, orderly manner, without shedding blood, or availing yourself of force? To what quarter will you look for protection from an infringement of the Constitution, if you will not give the power to the judiciary? The honorable gentleman objects to it because the officers of government will be screened from merited punishment by the Federal authority. The Federal sheriff, he says, will go into a poor man's house and beat him or abuse his family, and the Federal court will protect him. Is it necessary that officers should commit a trespass on the property or persons of those with whom they are to transact business? The injured man would trust to a tribunal in his neighborhood, and he would get ample redress. There is no clause in the Constitution which bars the individual injured from seeking redress in the State courts. He says that there is no instance of appeals as to fact in common law cases. The contrary is well known to be the case in this State. With respect to mills, roads, and other cases, appeals lie from the inferior to the superior courts as to fact as well as law. Is it a clear case that there can be no case in common law in which an appeal as to fact would be necessary and proper? If an appeal in matters of fact could not be carried to the superior court, then it would result that such cases could not be tried before the inferior courts for fear of injurious and partial decisions.

Where, says Marshall, is the necessity of discriminating between the three cases of chancery, admiralty, and common law? Why not leave it to Congress? Is it necessary for them wantonly to infringe your rights? Have you anything to apprehend, when they can in no case abuse their power without rendering themselves hateful to the people at large? Where power may be trusted, and there is no motive to abuse it, it seems to me to be as well to leave it undetermined as to fix it in the Constitution. With respect to disputes between a State and the citizens of another State, its jurisdiction has been decried with unusual vehemence. I hope, he said, *that no gentleman will think that a State will be called at the bar of the Federal court.* Is there no such case at present? Are there not many cases in which the Legislature of Virginia is a party, and yet the State is not sued? It is not rational to suppose that the sovereign power shall be dragged before a court. The intent is to enable States to recover claims of individuals residing in other States. I contend this construction is warranted by the words. I see a difficulty in making a State a defendant, which does not prevent its being plaintiff. As to controversies between the citizens of one State and the citizens of another State, I should not use my own judgment were I to contend that it was necessary in all cases to bring such suits in a Federal court; but cases may happen when it would be proper. It is asked, in the court of which State will the suit be instituted? In the court of the State wherein the defendant resides, and it will be determined by the laws of the State in which the contract was made. As to controversies between a State and a foreign State, the previous consent of the parties is necessary ; and therefore, as the Federal court will decide, each party will acquiesce. The exclusion of trial by jury in this case, the gentleman (Mason) urged would prostrate our rights. Does the word court only mean the judges? Does not the determination of a jury necessarily lead to the judgment of the court? Is there anything here that gives the judges exclusive jurisdiction of matters of fact? What is the object of a jury trial? To inform the courts of the facts. When a court has cognizance of facts, does it not follow that they can make enquiry by a jury? But it seems the right of challenging the jurors is not secured in this Constitution. Is this done in our own Constitution or by any provision of the English government? Is it done by their Magna Charter or by their Bill of Rights? This privilege is founded on their laws. If we are secure in Virginia without mentioning it in our laws, why should not this security be found in the Federal court? As to the quit-rents in the Northern Neck, has he not acknowledged that there was no complete title? Was he not satisfied that the right of the legal representative of the proprietor did not exist at the time he mentioned? If so, it cannot exist now. A law passed in 1782, which settles this subject. He says that poor men may be harassed by the representative of Lord Fairfax. If he has no right this cannot be done. If he has this right and comes to Virginia, what laws will this claim be determined by? By the laws of Virginia. By what tribunals will the claim be determined? By our own tribunals. After replying to some incidental objections which had been urged by Mason and Henry, Marshall concluded his speech, and was followed in a few words by Randolph, when the committee rose, and the House adjourned.

On Saturday, the twenty-first of June, the House resolved itself into a committee, Wythe in the chair, the first and second sections of the third articles still under consideration. Grayson rose and reviewed the structure and the jurisdiction of the Federal judiciary at great length, and denounced its defects in a splendid oration, and was followed by Randolph at equal length in reply. At the close of Randolph's speech the House adjourned.

On Monday, the twenty-third of June, the House again went into committee, Harrison in the chair, and the same sections still under consideration. Nicholas rose to suggest that the committee now pass on to the next clause of the Constitution, but he was opposed by Henry, who made a handsome acknowledgment of the fairness and ability of Marshall, and replied to some of his arguments. He was succeeded by a member far advanced in life, who had not as yet spoken in the committee, and who was not only held in high repute by his contemporaries, but deserves the favorable regard of posterity. For nearly the third of a century last past he had been engaged in the military service of his country. He was one of the oldest and most prominent military men in the Commonwealth. In the Indian wars from 1755 to nearly the beginning of the Revolution he had borne a conspicuous part, and was often in command of the Virginia troops raised for the defence of the frontier. His large stature and great muscular strength, added to his experience in war, made him the terror of the Indians. On one occasion he was sent to South Carolina with the Virginia companies to aid in beating back the Indians. As early as 1756, when Washington went to Boston to consult General Shirley on a point of military etiquette, Colonel Adam Stephen was left in command of the military forces of the colony until his return. In 1763 the Governor of

Virginia, when Stephen was in command of a levy of five hundred men to defend the frontiers against the Indians, spoke highly of his military capacity and courage. In 1776 he commanded the Fourth battalion of Virginia troops at Portsmouth, when he was appointed a brigadier-general in the army of the United States. On retiring from his command in Portsmouth, a valedictory letter was addressed to him by his officers, who speak of him as the polite gentleman and the accomplished soldier; and in his answer he mentioned the fact that "the present was his twelfth campaign."[226] In February, 1777, he was elected a major-general by Congress. In the battle of Brandywine he distinguished himself by his valor, as on other important occasions. He had probably been a member of the House of Burgesses, and was returned from Berkeley to the March Convention of 1775, when he sustained the resolutions of Henry for putting the Colony into military array. In the following July he was also returned to the Convention, but from some informality in the return he lost his seat.[227] A warm admirer of the Federal.Con-

[226] *Virginia Gazette*, September 20, 1776.

[227] Journal of the Convention of July, 1775, page 7. Irving, in his *Life of Washington*, has several allusions to Stephen, but the best source of information is *Sparks's Writings of Washington*, which the reader may consult by referring to the name of Stephen in the index in the last volume. In the years 1775 and 1776, of the *American Archives*, are letters of Stephen. A letter of his heretofore quoted may be found in the *Life of R. H. Lee*, by his grandson.

Stephen died in August, 1791, in Berkeley county, and lies buried on the estate owned by the Hon. Charles J. Faulkner; a rude stone marks the spot. He has left descendants, all of whom occupy respectable and honorable positions in the communities in which they reside. *Letter of the Hon. C. J. Faulkner to Francis B. Jones, Esq., dated May 19, 1856.* I am indebted to Mr. Jones for his great courtesy in assisting me in my inquiries concerning Stephen and other persons belonging to the history of the Valley of Virginia. It is believed that Stephen was born in what is now Berkeley county, though I think it questionable. He lived in Martinsburg in his latter days. The cause of his losing his seat in the Convention of 1775 was, that two districts of the county did not know that an election was to be held when Stephen was elected, and that Stephen, who was on election day parading the militia, marched at their head to the polls, and was elected by their votes. See *Kercheval's History of the Valley*, pages 244, 245; also, *Burke's History of Virginia*, IV, 91; and *Marshall's Life of Washington*, revised edition, I, 157, 158.

stitution, and as fearless on the floor as in the field, he now rose to give utterance to his feelings. Indeed, his speech is rather a fierce personal attack upon Henry than a defense of the judiciary, which was the topic in debate, or of the Constitution at large."

"The gentleman," says Stephen, "means to frighten us by his bugbears and hobgoblins—his sale of lands to pay taxes—Indian purchases, and other horrors, that I think I know as much about as he does. I have traveled through the greater part of the Indian countries; I know them well. I can mention a variety of resources by which the people may be enabled to pay their taxes." (He then went into a description of the Mississippi and its waters, Cook's river, the Indian tribes residing in that country, and the variety of articles which might be obtained to advantage by trading with those people.) "I know, he said, of several rich mines of gold and silver in the western country. And will the gentleman tell me that these precious metals will not pay taxes? If the gentleman does not like this government, let him go and live among the Indians. I know of several nations that live very happy; and I can furnish him with a vocabulary of their language."

Nicholas rose to answer some arguments which had fallen from the gentlemen on the other side. He denied that the English judges were more independent than the judges of the Federal judiciary. May not a variety of pensions be granted to the judges with a view to influence their decisions? May they not be removed by a vote of both Houses of Parliament? We are told that quit-rents are to be sued for. To satisfy gentlemen, I beg leave to refer them to an Act of Assembly, passed in the year 1782, before the peace, which absolutely abolishes the quit-rents, and discharges the holders of lands in the Northern Neck from any claim of that kind. As to the claims of certain companies which purchased lands of the Indians, they were determined prior to the opening of the land office by the Virginia Assembly; and it is not to be supposed that they will be again disposed to renew their claim. But, said Nicholas, there are gentlemen who have come by large possessions that it is not easily to account for. Here Henry interfered, and hoped the gentleman meant nothing personal. Nicholas answered: "I mean what I say, sir." He then alluded to the Blue Laws of Massachusétts, of which he said he had never heard till yesterday, and said he thought those laws should have as little weight in the present discussion as an argument which he had heard out of doors, to the effect that as New England men wore black stockings and plush breeches, there could be no union with them.   He said the ground had been so much traveled over, he thought it unnecessary to trouble the committee any farther on the subject.

Henry rose and said that if the gentleman means personal insinuations, or wishes to wound my private reputation, I think this an improper place to do so.   If, on the other hand, he means to go on in the discussion of the subject, he ought not to apply arguments which might tend to obstruct the discussion.   As to land matters, I can tell how I came by what I have ; but I think that gentleman (Nicholas) has no right to make that inquiry of me.   I mean not to offend any one—I have not the most distant idea of injuring any gentleman.   My object was to obtain information.   If I have offended in private life, or wounded the feelings of any man, I did not intend it.   I hold what I hold in a right and just manner.   I beg pardon for having obtruded thus far.   Nicholas then observed that he meant no personality in what he said, nor did he mean any resentment.   If such conduct meets the contempt of that gentleman, I can only assure him, said Nicholas, it meets with an equal degree of contempt from me.

The President hoped gentlemen would not be personal, and that they would proceed to investigate the subject in a calm and peaceable manner.   Nicholas again rose and said that he did not mean the honorable gentleman (Henry), but he meant those who had taken up large tracts of land in the western country.   The reason he could not explain himself before was that he thought some observations had dropped from the honorable gentleman as ought not to have come from one gentleman to another.[228]

---

[228] Nicholas was the brother-in-law of Randolph, and was, it is believed, deeply interested in western lands, and in fact removed to Kentucky in a short time after the adjournment of the Convention.   The account of the quarrel, as reported in the debates, I have given, but there does not seem to be any excuse for the prompt refusal of Nicholas to make an explanation.   The explanation may, perhaps, be found in the high state of excitement which prevailed as the final voting was coming on ; in the tone in which Henry made his inquiry, and not a little, perhaps, in the feeling with which Henry was regarded by the

An animated conversation in respect of the powers of the judiciary now sprang up between Monroe, Madison, Grayson, Henry and Mason, when the sections under consideration were passed over, and the first section of the fourth article was read.[229]

Mason observed that how far Congress shall declare the degree of faith to which public records were entitled to was proper, he could not clearly see. Madison answered that the clause was absolutely necessary, and that he had not employed a thought on the subject.

The second section of the fourth article was then read.[230] Mason said that on a former occasion gentlemen were pleased to make some observations on the security of property coming within this section. It was then said, and he now said, that there is no security, nor have gentlemen convinced him that there was.[231]

---

leading friends of the Constitution, who laid the whole burden of opposition at his door. There were repeated attempts to wound his feelings, but he treated most of them with silence.

[229] "Full faith and credit shall be given in each State to the public acts, records and judicial proceedings of every other State. And the Congress may, by general laws, prescribe the manner in which such acts, records and proceedings shall be passed, and the effect thereof."

[230] "The citizens of each State shall be entitled to all privileges and immunities of citizens in the several States."

"A person charged in any State with treason, felony, or other crime, who shall flee from justice and be found in another State shall, on demand of the executive authority of the State from which he fled, be delivered up, to be removed to the State having jurisdiction of the crime."

"No person held to service or labour in one State, under the laws thereof, escaping into another shall, in consequence of any law or regulation therein, be discharged from such service or labour, but shall be delivered up, on claim of the party to whom such service or labour may be due."

[231] More than sixty years after this remark was made by Mason, one of his grandsons in the Senate of the United States drew up an act to carry this clause of the Constitution into effect.

If it had been objected to the first clause of this section, that a Southern gentleman could not travel with his servants through another State without having them forcibly taken from him, or in *transitu* to some other State, the friends of the Constitution would have answered that from their own experience no such result would ever follow.

The third section of the fourth article was then read.[232] Grayson said that it appeared to him that there never can be a Southern State admitted into the union. There are seven States who are a majority, and whose interest it is to prevent it. The balance being actually on their side, they will have the regulation of commerce and the Federal ten miles square whenever they please. It is not to be supposed then, that they will admit any Southern State into the union so as to lose that majority. Madison thought this part of the plan more favorable to the Southern States than the present Confederation, as there was a greater chance of new States being admitted.[233] Mason glanced at different parts of the Constitution, and argued that the adoption of a system so replete with defects could not but be productive of the most alarming consequences. He dreaded popular resistance to its operation. He expressed in emphatic terms the dreadful effects which must ensue should the people resist, and concluded by observing that he trusted gentlemen would pause before they decided a question which involved such awful consequences. Lee declared that he was so overcome by what Mason had said that he could not suppress his feelings. He revered that gentlemen, and never thought he should hear from him sentiments so injurious to the country, so opposed to the dignity of the House, and so well calculated to bring on the horrors which the gentleman deprecated. Such speeches within those walls would lead the unthinking and the vicious to overt acts. God of Heaven, said Lee, avert that fearful doom ; but should the madness of some and the vice of others risk that awful appeal, he trusted that the friends of the Constitution would

---

[232] "SEC. III. New States may be admitted by the Congress into this union; but no new State shall be formed or erected within the jurisdiction of any other State ; nor any State be formed by the junction of two or more States without the consent of the Legislatures of the States concerned, as well as of Congress."

"The Congress shall have power to dispose of and make all needful rules and regulations respecting the territory or other property belonging to the United States; and nothing in this Constitution shall be so construed as to prejudice any claims of the United States, or of any particular State.

[233] Under the Confederation, the assent of all the States was necessary to the admission of a new State.

encounter with alacrity and resignation every difficulty and danger in defence of the public liberty.

The remainder of the Constitution was then read, and we only
know, in the absence of any reported debate, that the part referring to amendments to the Constitution was animadverted
upon by its opponents.   The committee then rose, and the House
adjourned.

On Tuesday, the twenty-fourth of June, the members began
to assemble in the hall at an early hour, and all appeared conscious that the crisis was at hand.   That day or the next the final
vote would be cast ; and the grave question, which had so long
engaged their serious attention, and on the decision of which, in
the estimation of both parties, depended the fate of the country,
would be irrevocably settled.   The same policy which had induced the friends of the Constitution to select Pendleton to open
the debate on the judiciary, impelled them to select Wythe as
the proper person to bring forward the resolution of ratification.
As soon as the House was called to order, a motion was made
that it should resolve itself into committee, and adopted.   Pendleton, who was privy to the plans of his friends, beckoned
Thomas Mathews to the chair.   Of this gentleman, who, born
in one of the British West India islands, had emigrated in early
life to Norfolk, which borough he represented for many years in
the General Assembly; who opposed with zeal those measures
of the British Parliament that led to the Revolution, and served
faithfully during the war (attaining the rank of lieutenant-colonel); who was long Speaker of the House of Delegates; whose
fine person, whose courteous manners, and whose lively wit
made him popular even with men who were apt to frown on those
lighter foibles which were quite as conspicuous in our earlier as
in our later statesmen, and whose name, conferred upon an eastern county created during his speakership, is fresh in our own
times, we have not leisure to speak at large.   Like most of the
military men of the Revolution, he approved the Constitution,
and faithfully executed the will of a town which celebrated the
inauguration of that instrument with one of the most brilliant
exhibitions in her history.[234]   Wythe instantly rose to address

---

[234] The historical student will see the name of Thomas Mathews, as
Speaker of the House of Delegates, certifying the ratification of the

the chair.   There was need of haste; for Henry had prepared
a series of amendments which he desired the House to adopt,
and thus postpone the final vote on the Constitution for an indefinite period.   He looked pale and fatigued ; and so great was
his agitation that he had uttered several sentences before he was
distinctly heard by those who sat near him.   When he was heard,
he was recapitulating the history of the Colonies previous to the
war, their resistance to the oppressions of Great Britain, and the
glorious conclusion of that arduous conflict.   To perpetuate the
blessings of freedom, he contended that the union of the States
should be indissoluble.   He expatiated on the defects of the
Confederation.   He pointed out the impossibility of securing
liberty without society, the impracticability of acting personally,
and the inevitable necessity of delegating power to agents.   He
recurred to the system under consideration.   He admitted its
imperfection, and the propriety of some amendments.   But, he
said, it had virtues which could not be denied by its opponents.
He thought that experience was the best guide, and that most of
the improvements that had been made in the science of government, were the result of experience.   He appealed to the advocates for amendments to say whether, if they were indulged with
any alterations they pleased, there might not be still a necessity
of alteration?   He then proceeded to the consideration of the
question of previous or subsequent amendments.   He argued
that, from the dangers of the crisis, it would be safer to adopt
the Constitution as it is, and that it would be easy to obtain all
needful amendments afterwards.   He then proposed a form of
ratification, which was handed to the clerk and read to the
committee. [235]

Well might Wythe evince unusual emotion in presenting his
scheme.   Henry rose in a fierce humor strangely mixed with
grief and shame.   Whether he felt discomfitted by having been

---

first amendment of the series proposed by Congress to the consideration of the States. [He was Grand Master of the Grand Lodge of Ma-
sons of Virginia from October 28, 1790, to October 28, 1793.—Ed.] John
Pride, another member of the Convention, was at that date (December
15, 1791,) Speaker of the Senate of Virginia ; and Humphrey Brooke,
another member, was clerk of the Senate at the time.

[235] See the form as it was adopted the following day.

forestalled by Wythe in offering his own scheme, which had been prepared with great care, to the committee, or was moved by the terms of Wythe's proposition, or was influenced by the sense of the imminent danger of losing the great battle which he had been waging in behalf of what he deemed the common liberty, there was something in his manner and in the subdued tones of his voice that foretold a fearful explosion. In the beginning of his speech he pitched his passion to a low key. He thought the proposal of ratification premature, and that the importance of the subject required the most mature deliberation. He dissented from the scheme of Wythe, because it admitted that the new system was capitally defective; for immediately after the proposed ratification comes the declaration that the paper before you is not intended to violate any of the three great rights—liberty of the press, liberty of religion, and the trial by jury. What is the inference when you enumerate the rights which you are to enjoy? That those not enumerated are relinquished. He then discanted on the omission of general warrants, so fatal in a vast country where no judge within a thousand miles can be found to issue a writ of *habeas corpus*, and where an innocent man might rot in jail before he could be delivered by process of law; the dangers of standing armies in times of peace, and ten or eleven other things equally important, all of which are omitted in the scheme of Wythe. Is it the language of the Bill of Rights that these things only are valuable? Is it the language of men going into a new government? After pressing with great force the inconsistency and futility of a ratification with subsequent amendments, he exhorted gentlemen to think seriously before they ratified the Constitution and persuaded themselves that they will succeed in making a feeble effort to obtain amendments. With respect to that part of Wythe's proposal which states that every power not granted remains with the people, it must be *previous* to adoption, or it will involve this country in inevitable destruction. To talk of it as a thing subsequent, not as one of your inalienable rights, is leaving it to the casual opinion of the Congress who shall take up the consideration of that matter. They will not reason with you about the effect of this Constitution. They will not take the opinion of this committee concerning its operation. *They will construe it as they please.* If you place it subsequently, let me ask the consequences? Among ten thousand implied powers which they may assume, they may, if we be engaged in war, liberate every one of your slaves if they please. And this must and will be done by men, a majority of whom have not a common interest with you.

It has been repeatedly said here that the great object of a national government is national defence. All the means in the possession of the people must be given to the government which is entrusted with the public defence. In this State there are two hundred and thirty-six thousand blacks, but there are few or none in the Northern States. And yet, if the Northern States shall be of opinion that our numbers are numberless, they may call forth every national resource May Congress not say that every black man must fight? Did we not see a little of this last war? We were not so hard pushed as to make emancipation general, but Acts of Assembly passed that every slave who would go to the army should be free. Another thing will contribute to bring this thing about. Slavery is detested; we feel its fatal effects; we deplore it with all the pity of humanity. Let all these considerations, at some future period, press with full force upon the minds of Congress. They will search that paper and see if they have the power of manumission. And have they not, sir? said Henry. Have they not the power to provide for the general defence and welfare? May they not think that these call for the abolition of slavery? May they not pronounce all slaves free, and will they not be warranted by that power? This is no ambiguous implication or logical deduction. That paper speaks to the point. They have the power in clear, unequivocal terms, and will clearly and certainly exercise it. The majority of Congress is to the North, and the slaves are to the South. In this situation I see great jeopardy to the property of the people of Virginia, and their peace and tranquility gone away. Dwelling on this topic for some time, he recurred to the subject of subsequent amendments, and denounced the novelty as well as the absurdity of such a proposition. He said he was distressed when he heard the expression from the lips of Wythe. It is a new thought altogether. It is opposed to every idea of fortitude and manliness in the States or in anybody else. Evils admitted in order to be removed subsequently, and tyranny submitted to, in order to be excluded by a subsequent alteration, are things totally new to me. "But I am sure," he said, "that the gentleman meant nothing but to amuse the committee. I know his candor. His proposal is an idea dreadful to me. I ask, does experience warrant such a thing from the beginning of the world to the present day? Do you enter into a compact of govern-ment first, and afterwards settle the terms of the government? It is admitted by everyone that this is a compact. Although the Confederation be lost, it is a constitutional compact, or something of that nature. I confess I never heard of such an idea before. It is most abhorrent to my mind. You endanger the tranquility of your country. You stab its repose, if you accept this gov-ernment unaltered. How are you to allay animosities? For such there are, great and fatal. He flatters me, and tells me that I can reconcile the people to it. Sir, their sentiments are as firm and steady as they are patriotic. Were I to ask them to apos-tatize from their ancient religion, they would despise me. They are not to be shaken in their opinions with respect to the pro-priety of preserving their rights. You can never persuade them that it is necessary to relinquish them. Were I to attempt to persuade them to abandon their patriotic sentiments, I should look on myself as the most infamous of men. I believe it to be a fact that the great body of the yeomanry are in decided oppo-sition to that paper on your table. I may say with confidence that for nineteen counties adjacent to each other, nine-tenths of the people are conscientiously opposed to it. I have not hunted popularity by trying to injure this government. Though public fame may say so, it was not owing to me that this flame of oppo-sition has been kindled and spread. These men will never part with their political opinions. Subsequent amendments will not do for men of this cast. You may amuse them by proposing amendments, but they will never like your government."

He invoked the committee to look to the real sentiments of the people even in the adopting States. "Look," he said, "at Penn-sylvania and Massachusetts. There was a majority of only nine-teen in Massachusetts. We are told that only ten thousand were represented in Pennsylvania, although seventy thousand were entitled to be represented. Is not this a serious thing? Is it not worth while to turn your eyes from subsequent amendments to the situation of your country? Can you have a lasting union in these circumstances? It will be in vain to expect it. But if you agree to previous amendments, you shall have union firm and solid. I cannot conclude without saying that I shall have nothing to do with the Constitution, if subsequent amendments be determined upon. I say I conceive it my duty, if this government is adopted before it is amended, to go home. I shall act as my duty requires. Every other gentleman will do the same. Previous amendments are, in my opinion, necessary to procure peace and tranquility. I fear, if they be not agreed to, every movement and operation of government will cease; and how long that baneful thing, *civil discord*, will stay from this country, God only knows. When men are free from constraint, how long will you suspend their fury? The interval between this and bloodshed is but a moment. The licentious and the wicked of the community will seize with avidity everything you hold. In this unhappy situation, what is to be done? It surpasses my stock of wisdom. If you will, in the language of freemen, stipulate that there are certain rights which no man under heaven can take from you, you shall have me going along with you ; not otherwise.''

He then informed the committee that he had a resolution prepared to refer a Declaration of Rights, with certain amendments to the most exceptionable parts of the Constitution, to the other States of the confederacy, for their consideration previous to its ratification. The clerk read the resolution, the Declaration of Rights, and the amendments, which were nearly the same as those ultimately proposed by the Convention [236] When the clerk had read the resolution and amendments, Henry resumed his remarks, and by considerations drawn from our domestic and foreign affairs, enforced the necessity of the adoption of previous amendments.

Randolph replied to Henry. He declared that he anticipated this awful period, but he confessed that it had not become less awful by familiarity with it. Could he believe that all was tranquil as was stated by the gentleman, that no storm was ready to burst, and that previous amendments were possible, he would concur with the gentleman ; for nothing but the fear of inevitable destruction compelled him to approve the Constitution. " But," says Randolph, ''what have I heard to-day? I sympathized most warmly with what other gentlemen said yesterday, that,

---

[236] See them in the Appendix.

let the contest be what it may, the minority should submit to the majority. With satisfaction and joy I heard what *he* then said—that he would submit, and that there should be peace, if his power could procure it. What a sad reverse to-day! Are we not told by way of counterpart to language that did him honor, that he would secede? I hope he will pardon and correct me if I mis-recite him ; but, if not corrected, my interpretation is that secession by him will be the consequence of adoption without previous amendments." (Here Henry rose and denied having said anything of secession ; but he had said he would have no hand in subsequent amendments ; that he would remain and vote, and afterwards he would have no business here). "I see," continued Randolph, "that I am not mistaken. The honorable gentleman says he will remain and vote, but after that he has no business here, and that he will go home. I beg to make a few remarks about secession. If there be in this house members who have in contemplation to secede from the majority, let me conjure them by all the ties of honor, and of duty, to consider what they are about to do. Some of them have more property than I have, and all of them are equal to me in personal rights. Such an idea of refusing to submit to the decision of the majority is destructive of every republican principle. It will kindle a civil war, and reduce everything to anarchy, uncertainty and confusion. To avoid a calamity so lamentable, I would submit to the Constitution, if it contained greater evils than it does. What are they to say to their constituents when they go home ? ' *We come to tell you that liberty is in danger, and though the majority are in favor of it, you ought not to submit.*' Can any man consider, without shuddering with horror, the awful consequences of such desperate conduct ? I conjure all to consider the consequences to themselves as well as to others. They themselves will be overwhelmed in the general disorder."

When Randolph closed his eloquent and patriotic invocation to the members, he considered the scheme proposed by Wythe, and showed by a minute examination of its words that it secured all other rights as well as the liberty of speech, and of the press, and trial by jury. He answered the reasoning of Henry in respect of the abolition of slavery by Congress. He said he hoped that none here, who, considering the subject in the calm light of philosophy, will advance an objection dishonorable to Virginia; that at the moment they are securing the rights of their citizens, an objection is started that there is a spark of hope that those unfortunate men now held in bondage, may, by the operation of the general government, be made free. But he denied that any power in the case was granted to the general government, and defied any man to point out the grant. He examined the clause in relation to the importation of persons prior to 1808, and proved that no such power could be drawn from that source, and he instanced the extradition of persons held to labor as a recognition of the right of property in slaves, and of the co-operation of the government to sustain that right. He recited his former exposition of the general welfare clause, and proved incontestibly that no other construction than his own could be placed upon it. He then reviewed all the articles in the schedule presented by Henry, and expressed his opinions respecting them in detail, concluding with a manly and pathetic appeal to the members not to reject the Constitution and sunder Virginia from her sister States, for the Confederation was now no more, but to encounter the risk of obtaining subsequent amendments, and preserve the Federal union.

Mason rose to correct a remark made by Randolph in respect of the right of regulating commerce and navigation contained in the Constitution, and made a most interesting disclosure. Randolph had said that the right of regulation as it now stands was a *sine qua non* of the Constitution. Mason said he differed from him. It never was and, in his opinion, never would be. " I will give you," he said, " to the best of my recollection, the history of that affair. This business was discussed at Philadelphia for four months, during which time the subject of commerce and navigation was often under consideration ; and I assert that eight States out of twelve, for more than three months, voted for requiring two-thirds of the members present in each House to pass commercial and navigation laws. True it is that it was afterwards carried by a majority as it now stands. If I am right, there was a great majority for requiring two-thirds of the States in this business, till a compromise took place between the Northern and the Southern States, the Northern States agreeing to the temporary importation of slaves, and the Southern States conceding in return that navigation and commercial laws should be on the footing on which they now stand. These are my reasons for saying that this was not a *sine qua non* of their concurrence. The Newfoundland fisheries will require that kind of security which we are now in want of. The Eastern States, therefore, agreed at length that treaties should require the consent of two-thirds of the members present in the Senate."

Now, for the first time, John Dawson, who was the brother-in-law of Monroe, as well as his colleague from Spotsylvania, who was frequently a member of the House of Delegates, and was subsequently, for a long period, a member of the House of Representatives, and whose elegant address and sumptuous apparel were throughout life in strong contrast with his hatred of a splendid government, and with the stern severity of his republican principles, addressed the committee. He reviewed the Constitution at large and spoke for an hour with much earnestness in opposition to the Constitution, declaring at the close of his speech "that liberty was a sacred deposit which he would never part with, and that the cup of slavery, which would be pressed to the lips of the people by the adoption of the Constitution, was equally unwelcome to him, whether administered by a Turk, a Briton, or an American." [237]

Grayson followed in a rapid review of those parts of the new system which he considered radically defective, urged the indispensable necessity of previous amendments, and pointed out with unerring sagacity the ultimate destruction of the commercial and manufacturing interests of the Southern States which must result from the adoption of the Constitution. He concluded by saying that but for one great character so many men could not be found to support such a system. "We have one ray of hope," he said. "We do not fear while he lives. But we can expect only his *fame* to be immortal. We wish to know who, besides him, can concentrate the confidence and affections of all America?"

---

[237] Years after Dawson was in his grave, and half a century after the date of the Convention, a friend described him to me as having red hair, most *recherche* in his dress, and wearing fair top boots. His attention to his dress gave him a sobriquet, which is long since forgotten and which I shall not revive. He was amiable in his deportment. He was sent to France on an important occasion with despatches. Henry was very fond of him.

[The sobriquet was "Beau," as is still quite generally recollected. Dawson died in Washington, D. C., March 30, 1814, aged fifty-two years.—ED.]

Madison then rose, and in an argument of extreme beauty and force, addressed alike to the pride, the interests, and the honor of the House, demonstrated the necessity of adopting the Constitution, with a firm reliance on the justice and magnanimity of our sister States. He spoke of the admiration with which the world regarded the United States for the readiness and ability with which, in a time of revolution, they had formed their governments on the soundest principles of public policy. But why this wonder and applause? Because the work was of such magnitude, and was liable to be frustrated by so many accidents. How much more admiration will the example of our country inspire should we be able peaceably, freely, and satisfactorily to establish a general government when there is such a diversity of opinions and interests, and when our councils are not cemented and stimulated by a sense of imminent danger? He spoke of the difficulty and delicacy of forming a system of government for thirteen States unequal in territory and population, and possessing various views and interests, and the necessity of a spirit of compromise. He then reverted to the clashing opinions of the opponents of the Constitution. Some of them thought that it contained too much State influence;[238] others that it was consolidated. Some thought that the equality of the States in the Senate was a defect ; others regarded it as a virtue. He discussed the scheme of ratification proposed by Wythe, and urged that it was not only not liable to the objections offered by Henry, but was fully adequate to secure all the great rights supposed to be imperiled by the Constitution. He followed mainly in the track of Henry's arguments, and dwelt upon the danger apprehended by that gentleman to the slave property of the South. "Let me ask," says Madison, "if even Congress should attempt anything of the kind, would it not be an usurpation of power?" There is no power to warrant it in that paper. If there be, I know it not. But why should it be done? The honorable gentleman says for the general welfare ; it will infuse strength into our system. Can any member of this committee suppose that it will increase our strength? Can any one believe that the American

---

[238] Madison must have alluded to the views of persons in the General Convention, and beyond the limits of Virginia ; for certainly no such opinion was expressed in the present Convention, unless he descended so far as to allude to the hypothetical argument of Grayson.

councils will come into a measure which will strip them of their property, discourage and alienate the affections of five-thirteenths of the Union? Why was nothing of this sort aimed at before? I believe such an idea never entered into an American breast; nor do I believe it ever will, unless it will enter into the heads of those gentlemen who substitute unsupported suspicions for reasons. He concluded by observing that such of Henry's amendments as were not objectionable might be recommended for adoption in the mode prescribed by the Constitution; not that those amendments were necessary, but because they can produce no possible danger, and may promote a spirit of peace. "But I never can consent," he said, "to previous amendments; because they are pregnant with dreadful dangers."

Henry replied to the objections of Randolph to his schedule of amendments, and to the arguments of Madison. When he had performed this office in detail, he concluded his speech in a strain of lofty and pathetic eloquence. "The gentleman (Madison) has told you of the numerous blessings which he imagines will result to us and the world in general from the adoption of this system. I see the awful immensity of the dangers with which it is pregnant. I see it—I feel it. I see *beings* of a higher order anxious concerning our decision. When I look beyond the horizon that binds human eyes, and see the final consummation of all human things, and see those intelligent beings which inhabit the ethereal mansions, reviewing the political decisions and revolutions which in the progress of time will happen in America, and the consequent happiness or misery of mankind, I am led to believe that much of the account on one side or the other will depend on what we now decide. Our own happiness alone is not affected by the event. All nations are interested in the determination. We have it in our power to secure the happiness of one-half of the human race. Its adoption may involve the misery of the other hemispheres." Here we are told "that a storm suddenly rose. It grew dark. The doors came to with a rebound like a peal of musketry. The windows rattled; the huge wooden structure rocked; the rain fell from the eaves in torrents, which were dashed against the glass; the thunder roared; and the lightning, casting its fitful glare across the anxious faces of the members, recalled to the mind those terrific pictures which the imaginations of Dante and Milton have drawn of those angelic spirits that, shorn of their celestial brightness, had met in council to war with the hosts of Heaven." In the height of the confusion Henry stood unappalled, and, in the language of a member present, "rising on the wings of the tempest, he seized upon the artillery of Heaven, and directed its fiercest thunders against the heads of his adversaries." The scene, we are told, became insupportable, and the members rushed from their seats into the body of the House.[239]

While the members were moving about the House, and were preparing to depart, a gleam of sunshine penetrated the hall, and in a few moments every vestige of the tempest was lost in a glorious noon-day of June. The House resumed its session ; when Nicholas proposed that the question should be put at eleven o'clock next day. Clay objected. Ronald also opposed the motion, and wished amendments should be prepared by a committee before the question was taken. Nicholas contended that the language of the proposed ratification would secure all that was desired, as it declared that all the powers vested in the Constitution were derived from the people, and might be resumed by them whensoever they should be perverted to their injury and oppression, and that every power not granted remained at their will. For, said Nicholas, these expressions will become a part of the contract. If thirteen individuals are about to make a contract, and one agrees to it, but at the same time declares that he understands its meaning, signification and intent to be what the words of the contract plainly and obviously denote ; that it is not to be construed as to impose any supplementary condition upon him ; and that he is to be exonerated from it whensoever any such imposition shall be attempted—I ask, said Nicholas, whether in this case these conditions on which he assented to it, would not be binding on the other twelve ? In like manner, these conditions will be binding on Congress.

Ronald replied that unless he saw amendments, either previous or subsequent, introduced to secure the liberties of his constituents, he must vote, though much against his inclination, against the Constitution.

---

[239] Judge Archibald Stuart, of Augusta, then a young man, and a member of the Convention, and a friend of the Constitution, has described this scene with great animation in a letter to Wirt. *Life of Henry*, 313.

Madison conceived that what defects there might be in the Constitution might be removed in the mode prescribed by itself. He thought a solemn declaration of our essential rights unnecessary and dangerous ; unnecessary, because it was evident that the general government had no power but what was given it, and the delegation alone warranted the exercise of power; dangerous, because an enumeration, which is not complete, is not safe. Such an enumeration could not be made within any compass of time as would be equal to a general negation such as was proposed in the form presented by Wythe. He renewed his declaration that he would assent to any subsequent amendments that were not dangerous.

The committee then rose, and the House adjourned, to meet next day at ten o'clock.

On Wednesday morning the twenty-fifth day of June, before the bell had announced the hour of ten, every member was in his seat, and an eager and anxious crowd filled the hall. It was known that the final vote would be cast in the course of the day, and it was generally believed that the Constitution would be ratified ; but by what majority, was a question of doubt and apprehension to its warmest friends. The manœuver of Henry, which had at a single blow struck from the list of its friends nearly the whole of the Kentucky delegation, was freshly remembered ; some such dexterous and daring movement might affect the votes of four or five members who had hitherto been friendly, and the loss of five votes would turn the scale and destroy the new system. And it was inferred from the fierce tone of Henry in the debate of the previous day, that, if the Constitution were carried, he might, on the announcement of the vote, rise from his seat, protest against the action of a small majority on so vital a question, and, at the head of the minority, withdraw from the Convention. The secession of so large a number of the most able and most popular men in the Commonwealth would in every aspect be fatal to the Constitution. The result must follow either that the friends of the new system would be compelled to reconsider the vote of ratification, and accept the schedule of previous amendments proposed by Henry, or remain firm and uphold their decision by an appeal to arms. Either alternative was most unwelcome, and fraught with extreme peril. To rescind the vote of ratification at a time when nine States had adopted the new system and would proceed to organize the Federal Government in pursuance of its provisions,[240] and to surrender the fruits of a victory so dearly earned, involved not only a deep sense of humiliation in the minds of the majority, but a complete frustration of all their plans and all their hopes. In many respects the delay would be fatal. It was plain that Washington could not have been chosen the head of a government of which Virginia was not a component part, and the danger likely to arise from the selection of any other individual to carry the new system into effect was imminent. There was another danger, which, though it might not so keenly affect the sensibilities of the majority, was yet appalling. As the new President would certainly be a Northern man, and probably the Vice-President also, and as, in the organization of the new system, some measures not agreeable to the taste or to the feelings of its opponents might be adopted, hostility to the Constitution, already great, might gain strength, and a confederacy, consisting of Virginia, Kentucky, and North Carolina in the first instance, and embracing ultimately South Carolina and Georgia, would be called into existence. Such were the difficulties to be apprehended from the first alternative. But alarming and perilous as the first alternative decidedly was, the second was still more formidable. If the majority resolved to sustain their vote by a resort to arms, to what quarter would they look for help? Not to the General Assembly, which was shortly to meet ; for that body, as the fact proved, was opposed to the new scheme, and, glad of an opportunity of overthrowing it, would have upheld its opponents. Nor could they look for support to the people ; for, as was generally believed at the time, two-thirds of the people at least regarded the new scheme with apprehension and dislike.[241] The only resource of the friends of

---

[240] Henry stated in debate this day that " we are told that nine States have adopted it "; and it is probable that Madison had heard from New Hampshire that that State would certainly adopt the Constitution, which it had actually done on the 21st, three days before ; but the fact could not have been known in Richmond on the 25th. Indeed, Harrison did not allude to the act of New Hampshire in his speech delivered during the morning, when he spoke of the course of that State respecting amendments.

[241] Judge Marshall states that, "in some of the adopting States it is scarcely to be doubted that a majority of the people were in the opposition "; and he doubtless had reference to Virginia, the State he knew

the Constitution would have been to appeal to the new government, and bring about a war between the non-slaveholding and the slaveholding States ; the result of which, whether prosperous or adverse to the arms of the new government, would equally destroy all hopes of a friendly union of the States.

On the other hand, the opponents of the Constitution were in a dangerous mood. They believed that instrument at best, with the aid of all the amendments which were likely to be adopted, to be fatal to the public liberty ; and they thought that they had gone to the farthest verge of concession in assenting to its ratification with the hope of subsequent amendments. But it now seemed that they were not to obtain even the boon of subsequent amendments. The liberal promises which had been dealt out were all a sham. Strange rumors were indeed abroad. It was first mentioned in whispers, and was then currently reported that, as soon as the Constitution was ratified, its leading friends would, under various pretexts, quit the city and leave the question of future amendments to its fate, with a deliberate design to prevent their incorporation into the new system. To incur a defeat on the question of the ratification of the Constitution was a source of the deepest mortification to its opponents; but to be tricked into the bargain was past bearing. They would not submit at one and the same time to a loss of liberty and to a flagrant outrage. The session of the Assembly was at hand. That body must be looked to to save the country. It might refuse to recognize the new system ; might refuse to pass the necessary laws for carrying it into effect, and might refuse to order an election of representatives, or an election of senators, until the proposed amendments were made a part of the Constitution. In the meantime, it might appoint commissioners to ascertain the terms of a union with North Carolina, which State was determined to reject the Constitution,[242] and might hold the militia in readiness for contin-

---

best. He also confirms the remark of Grayson, "that had the influence of character been removed, the intrinsic merits of the instrument would not have secured its adoption." *Life of Washington*, II, 127. I quote the second edition of the work, which is in every possible respect superior to the first. Had the work appeared originally as it now is, the fame of the author would have been greatly enhanced.

[242] North Carolina rejected the Constitution by a majority of one hundred. The vote stood one hundred and eighty-four to eighty-four.

gencies. Never, at any period in the history of the Colony or of the Commonwealth, did a deliberative assembly meet in such painful circumstances of doubt and alarm as on this memorable morning.

The House immediately went into committee, Pendleton calling Mathews to the chair. Nicholas was the first to break silence. He said that he did not wish to enter into further debate, that delay could only serve the cause of those who wished to destroy the Constitution, and that, should the Constitution be ratified, amendments might be adopted recommending Congress to alter that instrument in the mode prescribed by itself. He warmly repelled the charge that the friends of the Constitution meditated a flight after its adoption, and defied the author of the charge to establish its truth. He declared his own wish for amendments; thought the amendments secured in the form proposed by Wythe were satisfactory, but was willing to agree to others which would not destroy the spirit of the Constitution. He moved that the clerk read the form of ratification proposed by Wythe, that the question might be put upon it. The clerk read the form, and also read, at the suggestion of Tyler, the bill of rights and the amendments proposed by Henry.

The urgency of the crisis brought Harrison to the floor. This venerable man had in all the great conjunctures of a quarter of a century then past acted an honorable part. He was a member of that celebrated committee which, in 1764, had drawn the memorials to the king, the lords, and the commons of England. He was an old member of high standing in the House of Burgesses in 1765, when Henry offered his resolutions against the Stamp Act. In all the early Conventions he had strenuously upheld the rights of the Colony and the dignity of the new Commonwealth. In Congress he had been during the war at the head of the most important military committees; had been deputed on emergencies to the headquarters of the army, and had presided in the Committee of the Whole when the resolution of independence and the Declaration of Independence had

---

The Convention began its session on the 21st of June and, of course, was sitting when the vote of Virginia was taken.—*Wheeler's History of North Carolina*, page 60. It was not until the 21st of November of the following year that the Federal Constitution was adopted.

been approved, and when the Articles of Confederation had been prepared by Congress. He rarely spoke at great length, and his speeches were adapted rather to a council of men charged with responsible duties to be instantly performed than to popular bodies; but his great experience as a statesman, and his practical sense, expressed in a short harangue, had often more influence than the well-reasoned speeches of ordinary orators. He now rose to utter his solemn protest against the ratification of the Constitution. He denounced the policy of trusting to future amendments. When the Constitution was once ratified it was beyond our reach. Even future amendments might be evaded by the flight of its friends; and if adopted by the House, what was the hope of their ultimate success? The small States, he said, refused to come into the Union without extravagant concessions: and can it be supposed that those States, whose interest and importance are so greatly enhanced under the Constitution as it stands, will consent to an alteration that will diminish their influence? Never! Let us act now, he said, with that fortitude which animated us in our resistance to Great Britain. He entered into a minute analysis of the views of the different States in respect of amendments, and drew the conclusion that seven States were anxious to obtain them. Can it be doubted that, if these seven States make amendments a condition of their accession, they will be discarded from the union? Let us, then, not be persuaded into the opinion that, if we reject the Constitution, we will be cast adrift and abandoned. He had no such idea. He was attached to the union. A vast majority of the people were attached to it. But he thought he saw a desire to make a great and powerful government. Look at the recent settlement of the country, and its present population and wealth, and who can fail to perceive that such a scheme was premature and impossible. National greatness ought not to be forced. Like the formation of great rivers, it should be gradual and progressive. Gentlemen tell us that we must look to the Northern States for help in danger. Did they relieve us during the Revolution? They left us to be buffeted by the British. But for the fortunate aid of France we should have been ruined. He concluded by an appeal to Heaven that he cherished the union; but he deemed the adoption of the Constitution without previous amendments to be unwarrantable, precipitate, and dangerously impolitic.

Madison spoke with something more than his usual courtesy. He would not have risen, he said, but for the remarks which had fallen from Harrison. He protested against the unkind suspicions of withdrawal which had been raised against the friends of the Constitution on the subject of amendments, and argued from Harrison's statements that, if seven States desired amendments, the accession of Virginia would secure the success of the common object. It was easy to obtain amendments hereafter ; but, if we called upon the States to rescind what they had done, to confess that they have done wrong, and to consider the subject anew, it would produce delays and dangers which he shuddered to contemplate. Let us not hesitate in our choice, and he declared that there was not a friend of the Constitution that would not concur in procuring amendments.

Monroe followed Madison, and contended that previous amendments alone were worth anything. Would the small States refuse to grant them, and make enemies of the large and powerful States ? He did not think that the Federal Government would immediately infringe the rights of the people, but he thought that the operation of the government would be oppressive in process of time. He pronounced the argument of Madison, derived from the impracticability of obtaining previous amendments, fallacious, and a specious evasion. The Constitution is admitted to be defective. Did ever men meet with so loose and uncurbed a commission as the General Convention ? And can it be supposed that subsequent reflection on the plan which they put forth may not make it more efficient and complete ? As to the amendments presented to the committee, they are acknowledged to be harmless ; but their previous acceptance will secure our rights. He hoped that gentlemen would concur in them.

The friends of the Constitution well knew that Henry would address some parting words to the House, and had foreseen the necessity of presenting the new system in its most favorable light when the question was about to be taken. The choice of an individual to perform that delicate office was made with their usual tact. Second to Henry, and second to Henry alone, in action, in a varied and splendid eloquence, and in all those faculties that enable men to move popular assemblies, stood confessedly a young man, then entering his thirty-fourth year, whose name, becoming extinct in the early part of the present century by the sudden and untimely death of its representative while engaged in the naval service of his country in a distant sea, was widely known and honored in his generation, but which, rarely mentioned in the political controversies of the day, has almost slipped from the memory of men.   On the field of battle, at the bar, and in the House of Delegates he held a distinguished rank among his compeers ; but, owing to his attendance on the courts then sitting as the Attorney-General of the Commonwealth, he did not appear often in the House, and had not opened his lips in debate.   Of that brilliant group of soldier-statesmen, who drew their inspiration from the counsels of Wythe, and whose virtues shed renown not only on Virginia, but on the Union at large, none more eminently merits the grateful and affectionate regard of succeeding times than James Innes.   Like Henry, he was the son of a Scotchman—the Rev. Robert Innes, who was a graduate of Oxford; who had come over to this country some years before the birth of James, on the recommendation of the Bishop of London, and who became the rector of the parish of Drysdale, in the county of Caroline.   His classical training James received from his father, who intended him, the youngest of three sons, for the Church, and who bequeathed to him his library.   In 1771 he entered William and Mary College, and in a class consisting of Blands, Boushes, Diggeses, Fitzhughs, Madisons, Maurys, Pages, Randolphs, Rootes, Stiths, and Wormleys, he was singled out as the most eminent for skill in declamation, for fluent elocution, and for elegant composition. George Nicholas, Bishop Madison, St. George Tucker, then a clever youth, who had come over from Bermuda to attend college, and who magnanimously took the side of his foster-home in the approaching war, and Beverley Randolph, were his friends and associates.[243]   He had exhausted his slender patrimony in paying his college bills, and accepted the office of usher, under Johnson, in the school of humanity.   At the beginning of the troubles he rallied a band of students, and secured some stores which were about to be secreted by Dunmore ; and, as a reward of his patriotism, was dismissed by the faculty, which as yet re-

---

[243] See the class of 1771 in the general catalogue of William and Mary.

mained faithful to the Crown.[244] In February, 1776, he was elected captain of an artillery company, and marched to Hampton to repress the incursions of the enemy.[245] In November, 1776, he was appointed lieutenant-colonel of one of the six battalions of infantry to be raised on the Continental establishment; and joining the Northern army, he became one of the aids of Washington, and shared in the glory of Trenton, Princeton, Brandywine, Germantown, and Monmouth.[246] His regiment having dwindled, from the casualties of war, beneath the dignity of a lieutenant-colonel's command, he resigned his commission, and returned to Virginia. In October, 1778, he was appointed by the Assembly one of the commissioners of the navy.[247] In 1780 he entered the House of Delegates as a member from James City, where he made his first essay as a debater. At the solicitation of Washington he raised a regiment for home defence, and was present with his command at the siege of York. He then devoted himself to the profession of law, and attained a high rank at the bar. His popular manners, his classical taste, and his captivating eloquence soon attracted public attention, and he was elected the successor of Edmund Randolph in the office of Attorney-General. In the faculty of addressing popular

---

[244] Letter of Miss Lucy H. Randolph, September 24, 1855. Miss Randolph is a granddaughter of Colonel Innes. I trust that she will see that, wherein I have not adopted her statements, I have record evidence beyond dispute to sustain me.

[245] *Virginia Gazette* of that date. For his appointment as lieutenant-colonel, see Journal of the House of Delegates, November 13, 1776, page 54. George Nicholas was appointed major at the same time; also Holt Richeson. For the settlement of the father of Innes in Drysdale parish, see Bishop Meade's *Old Churches*, I, 414.

[246] *Burk's Virginia*, IV, 234.

[247] Journal of the House of Delegates, October 21, 1778, page 22. It has been stated that Colonel Innes was at the battle of Monmouth. An anecdote, told of Innes in connection with that battle, has been long current in Virginia, for the truth of which I do not avouch. It seems that he at once comprehended the reason of Lee's retreat, and being asked why he did not communicate his impressions to Washington when that gentleman overhauled Lee in rough terms, he said that at that moment he would as soon have addressed the forked lightning. Innes was born in 1754. His mother was Miss Catharine Richards, of Caroline.

bodies, of all his contemporaries he approached, in the general estimation, nearest to Patrick Henry. There were those, who, fascinated by the graces of his manner, by his overwhelming action, by the majestic tones of his voice, and by his flowing periods, thought him more eloquent than Henry. We know that the most distinguished living Virginian, who had heard both speakers, has pronounced Innes the most classical, the most elegant, and the most eloquent orator to whom he ever listened.[248] Born in Caroline, the residence of Pendleton, and the pupil of Wythe, he possessed the confidence of those illustrious men, who watched with affectionate attachment the development of his genius, who witnessed his finest displays, and who, in their extreme old age, deplored his untimely death.

His physical qualities marked him among his fellows as distinctively as his intellectual. His height exceeded six feet. His stature was so vast as to arrest attention in the street. He was believed to be the largest man in the State. He could not ride an ordinary horse, or sit in a common chair, and usually read or meditated in his bed or on the floor. On court days he never left his chamber till the court was about to sit, studying all his cases in a recumbent posture. It is believed that he was led to adopt this habit not so much from his great weight as from a weakness induced by exposure during the war. In speaking, when he was in full blast, and when the tones of his voice were sounding through the hall, the vastness of his stature is said to have imparted dignity to his manner. His voice, which was of unbounded power and of great compass, was finely modulated; and in this respect he excelled all his compeers with the exception of Henry. From his size, from the occasional vehemence of his action, and from a key to which he sometimes pitched his voice, he is said to have recalled to the recollections of those who had

---

[248] Such is the opinion of Governor Tazewell, who, when a young man, was accustomed to hear Innes. I once asked Governor Tazewell what he thought of Innes as a lawer. "Innes, sir, was no lawyer (that is, he was not as profound a lawyer as Wythe, or Pendleton, or Thomson Mason, who were eminent when Innes was born); but he was the most elegant *belles-lettres* scholar and the most eloquent orator I ever heard." It must be remembered that Innes, at the time of his death, in 1798, had not completed his forty-fourth year, and that Wythe and Pendleton attained to nearly double his years.

heard Fox the image of that great debater. A miniature by Peale, still in the possession of his descendants, has preserved his features to posterity. He is represented in the dress of a colonel in the Continental line ; and we gather from that capacious and intellectual brow, shaded by the fresh auburn hair of youth, those expressive blue eyes, that aquiline nose, some notion of that fine caste of features and that expression which were so much admired by our fathers. His address was in the highest degree imposing and courteous ; and in the social circle, as in debate or at the bar, his classical taste, and an inexhaustible fund of humor, of wit, of accurate and varied learning, kindly and generously dispensed, won the regard and excited the admiration of all.

From the day when a youth he entered the family of Washington to the day of his death, Innes shared the confidence of his chief.[249] He was dispatched by him on a secret mission to Kentucky at a dangerous crisis, and was tendered the office of Attorney-General of the United States, which the state of his health and the condition of his family compelled him to decline. Had he accepted that appointment, and had his life been protracted to the age of his colleagues and associates—of Madison, of Monroe, of Marshall, and of Stuart, of Augusta—his history, instead of being made up of meagre shreds collected from old newspapers, from the scattering entries in parliamentary journals, from moth-eaten and half-decayed manuscripts, from the testimony of a few solitary survivors of a great era, and from the fond but hesitating accents of descendants in the third and fourth generation, might have been yet living on a thousand tongues, and his name have been, in connection with the names of the friends and co-equals of his youth, one of the cherished household words of that country whose infancy had been protected by his valor, and whose glory had been enhanced by the almost unrivaled splendor of his genius, and by the undivided homage of his heart.[250]

---

[249] Innes died the year before Washington.

[250] It is proper to say that I have frequently conversed during the past thirty years with those who knew James Innes from his youth upward, and that my impressions of his character have been drawn from various other sources than those already cited.

Unfortunately for the reputation of Innes, no fair specimen of his eloquence remains. We are told that, like Henry,[251] he rarely spoke above an hour ; and that, as he prepared himself with the utmost deliberation, he presented a masterly outline of his subject, dwelling mainly upon the great points of his case ; that he embellished his arguments with the purest diction and with the aptest illustrations, and that he delivered the whole with a power of oratory that neither prejudice nor passion could effectually resist.

Such was the man whom the friends of the Constitution had chosen to make the last impression upon the House in its favor. The occasion was not wholly congenial to his taste. Nor was it altogether favorable to his fame as a statesman. If he discussed the new system in detail he would injure the cause of its friends who were eager for the question, and he would promote the ends of its enemies who were anxious for delay and would rejoice to re-open the debate. And if he passed lightly over his subject he would suffer in a comparison with his colleagues who had, after months of study, debated at length every department of the new government. In the brief notes of his speech which have come down to us, this vacillation of purpose is plainly visible.[252] He

---

[251] Henry spoke in the present Convention several times for more than two hours, and on one occasion more than three, and at the bar in important cases he has spoken over three hours, and in the British debt cause for three entire days ; but in the House of Delegates he rarely spoke over half an hour. One part of his policy was to provoke replies, which furnished him with fresh matter.

[252] Innes adhered to the Federal party during the administration of Adams, and would have been sent envoy to France in place of Judge Marshall, had not a friend informed the President that he would be unable from the condition of his family to accept the appointment. He accepted, however, the office of Commissioner under Jay's treaty, in the latter part of 1797, and was discharging its duties in Philadelphia at the time of his death, on the second of August, 1798. He was buried in Christ Church burial ground in that city, not far from the grave of Franklin. A plain marble slab marks the spot. It once stood on columns, but from the filling up of the yard some years ago, is now level with the ground.

Henry Tazewell, one of his early friends and classmates, was buried within three feet of his grave. Innes died of a dropsy of the abdomen. The following epitaph from the pen of his classmate, Judge St. George Tucker, now legible in some of its parts only, was inscribed upon the

began by saying that his silence had not proceeded from neutrality or supineness, but from public duties which could not be
postponed.   The question, he said, was one of the gravest that
ever agitated the councils of America.   "When I see," he said,
"in this House, divided in opinion, several of those brave officers whom I have seen so gallantly fighting and bleeding for
their country, the question is doubly interesting to me.   I
thought that it would be the last of human events that I should
be on a different side from them on this awful occasion."

He said that he was consoled by the reflection that difference
of opinion had a happy consequence, inasmuch as it evoked dis-

---

tombstone of Innes : "To the memory of James Innes, of Virginia, formerly Attorney-General of that State.   A sublime genius, improved
by a cultivated education, united with pre-eminent dignity of character
and greatness of soul, early attracted the notice and obtained the confidence of his native country, to whose service he devoted those conspicuous talents, to describe which would require the energy of his
own nervous eloquence.   His domestic and social virtues equally endeared him to his family and friends, as his patriotism and talents to
his country.   He died in Philadelphia August the second, 1798, whilst
invested with the important trust of one of the commissioners for carrying into effect the treaty between Great Britain and the United
States."   This beautiful tribute to the memory of Innes has one great
defect—the absence of the date of his birth.   As the inscription is now
nearly washed out by the rains of sixty years, it may not be amiss to
say that the grave is directly in front of the seventh column of the
brick wall (on Fifth) from Arch, about a foot from the wall.   I am indebted to my friend, Townsend Ward, Esq., of Philadelphia, for his aid
in deciphering the inscription, an accurate copy of which I afterwards
received from another quarter.   My impression is that Innes was a
grand-nephew of Colonel James Innes, who at the date of his birth was
a military character in the Colony.—Writings of Washington, XII,
Index.

[Colonel James Innes, who commanded a regiment from North Carolina in the French and Indian wars, was a native of Scotland, and a citizen of New Hanover county, North Carolina.   He had served in 1740,
it is believed, as a captain in the unsuccessful expedition against Carthagena, commanded by Colonel William Gooch, subsequently knighted
and Lieutenant-Governor of Virginia.   He was doubtless a familiar of
Governor Dinwiddie in Scotland, as the latter constantly addressed
him as "Dear James."   See Dinwiddie Papers, Virginia Historical
Collection, Vols. III, IV.   The editor can adduce nothing in confirma-
tion of the supposition of Mr. Grigsby as to his relationship to Colonel
James Innes of the text.]

cussion, and was a friend to truth. He came hither under the persuasion that the felicity of our country required that we should accept this government, that he was, nevertheless, open to conviction, but that all that he had heard confirmed him in the belief that its adoption was necessary for our national honor, our happiness, and our safety. He then discussed the policy in respect of amendments, and contended that previous amendments were beyond the power of the Convention. Adopt this system with previous amendments, and you transcend your commission from the people, who have a right to be consulted upon them. They have seen the Constitution, and have sent us hither to accept or reject it. And have we more latitude upon the subject? He alluded to the distrust and jealousy of our Northern brethren which was abroad. Did we distrust them in 1775? If we had distrusted them, we would not have seen that unanimous resistance which had enabled us to triumph through our enemies. It was not a Virginian, or a Carolinian, or a Pennsylvanian, but the glorious name of an American, that was then beloved and confided in. Did we then believe that, in the event of success, we should be armed against each other? Had I believed then what we are told now, he said, that our Northern brethren were destitute of that noble spirit of philanthropy which cherishes paternal affections, unites friends, enables men to achieve the most gallant exploits, and renders them formidable to foreign powers, I would have submitted to British tyranny rather than to Northern tyranny. When he had reviewed at length the arguments founded on the dissimilar interests of the States, and on the condition of our foreign relations, he said that "we are told that we need not be afraid of Great Britain. Will that great, that warlike, that vindictive nation lose the desire of avenging her losses and her disgraces? Will she passively overlook flagrant violations of the treaty? Will she lose the desire of retrieving those laurels that are buried in America? Should I transfuse into the breast of a Briton that love of country which so strongly predominates in my own, he would say, *while I have a guinea, I shall give it to recover lost America.*" He then treated with stern disdain the insinuation that we should check our maritime strength on account of fears apprehended from foreign powers. To promote their glory, he said, we must become wretched and contemptible. It may be said that the ancient nations which deserved and acquired glory lost their liberty. But have not mean and cowardly nations, Indians and Cannibals, lost their liberty likewise? And who would not rather be a Roman than one of those creatures that hardly deserves to be incorporated among the human species? I deem this subject, he said, as important as the Revolution which severed us from the British empire. It is now to be determined whether America has gained by that change which has been thought so glorious; whether those hecatombs of American heroes, whose blood was so freely shed at the shrine of liberty, fell in vain, or whether we shall establish such a government as shall render America respectable and happy! It is my wish, he said, to see her not only possessed of civil and political liberty at home, but to be formidable, to be terrible, to be dignified in war, and not dependent upon the corrupt and ambitious powers of Europe for tranquility, security, or safety. I ask, said Innes, if the most petty of those princes, even the Dey of Algiers, were to make war upon us, we should not be reduced to the greatest distress? Is it not in the power of any maritime nation to seize our ships and destroy our commerce with impunity? We are told, he said, that the New Englanders are to take our trade from us, and make us hewers of wood and drawers of water, and in the next moment to emancipate our slaves. They tell you that the admission of the importation of slaves for twenty years shows that their policy is to keep us weak: and yet the next moment they tell you that they intend to set them free! If it be their object to corrupt and enervate us, will they emancipate our slaves? Thus they complain and argue against the system in contradictory principles. The Constitution is to turn the world *topsy-turvy* to make it suit their purposes. He looked to the alleged dangers to religious freedom from the Constitution, and argued that they were imaginary and absurd. With respect to previous amendments, he contended that it was discourteous to request the other States, which, after months of deliberation, had ratified the new system, to undo all that they have done at our bidding. Those States will say: " *The Constitution has been laid before you, and if you do not like it, consider the consequences. We are as free, sister Virginia, and as independent as you are. We do not like to be dictated to by you.*" But, say gentlemen, we can afterwards come into the union. I tell you, he said, that those States are not of such pliant, yielding stuff as to revoke a solemn decision to gratify your capricious wishes. He concluded with an animated appeal to the members to accept the Constitution. Unless we look for a perfect Constitution, he said, we ought to take this. From India to the Pole you will seek a perfect Constitution in vain. It may have defects, but he doubted whether any better system can be obtained at this time. Let us try it. Experience is the best test. The new system will bear equally upon all, and all will be equally anxious to amend it. I regard, he said, the members of Congress as my fellow-citizens, and rely upon their integrity. Their responsibility is as great as can well be expected. We elect them, and we can remove them at our pleasure. In fine, the question is, whether we shall accept or reject this Constitution? With respect to previous amendments, they are equal to rejection. They are abhorrent to my mind. I consider them the greatest of evils. I think myself bound to vote against every measure which I believe to me a total rejection, than which nothing within my conception can be more imprudent, destructive, and calamitous.

The sensation produced by the speech of Innes was profound. The loose report of it which has come down to us presents some of the main points on which he dwelt, and enables us to form a vague opinion of the mode in which he blended severe argument with the loftiest declamation ; but it affords only a faint likeness of the original, and conveys no idea of the prodigious impression which the speech made at the time. And what that impression was we know from conclusive authority. Old men have been heard to say that, exalted by the dignity of his theme and conscious that the issue was to be instantly decided, he spoke like one inspired. The tones of tender affection when he spoke of our Northern brethren, who had fought side by side with us in battle and had achieved with us the common liberty ; of fierce disdain when he described his opponents as lowering the flag of his country to ingratiate the petty princes of Europe ; of apprehension when he portrayed the terrible power of England and her thirst for vengeance; of unutterable scorn when he repelled the charge that Northern men would make hewers of wood and drawers of water of the people of the South ; and of passionate patriotism when he conjured the House not to throw away the fruits of the Revolution by rejecting the proposed system, but in

a spirit of fraternal love to ratify it without amendment; his atti-
tudes and his gestures, as he moved his gigantic stature to and
fro, and the unbroken and overflowing torrent of his speech, were
long remembered. His friends were liberal in their congratulations, and declared that he had surpassed himself—that he had
surpassed any speaker whom they had ever heard. But the
expectations of friends are sometimes easily satisfied. There is,
however, one witness whose testimony is beyond cavil. Henry
could hardly find words to express the admiration with which
the eloquence of Innes had inspired him. It was grand. It was
magnificent. It was fit to shake the human mind.[253]

Statesmen of real genius, of pure morals, and of sincere patriotism, though pitted by heated and hating partisans against each
other, rarely undervalue one another. In the breasts of such
men detraction, envy and jealousy, which corrode the temper of
meaner spirits, find no durable abiding-place. Innes appreciated
the magnanimity of Henry; and when, in the early part of the
following year, the character of his great rival was traduced in a
series of articles by an anonymous writer in a Richmond paper,
and when, from the political complexion of those articles and
from the research, pungency and point with which they were
written, public opinion had fixed their authorship on Innes, he
wrote to Henry to contradict the rumor, and to assure him of his
highest admiration and esteem.[254]

Tyler followed Innes. He was many years younger than his
colleague, Harrison, who had spoken in the early part of the day.
Indeed, when Harrison, in the debate on Henry's resolutions
against the Stamp Act, was a leading member of the House of
Burgesses, Tyler, then a boy of sixteen, was looking on from the

---

[253] See the speech of Henry, to be noticed in this day's debate. The
only instance that occurs to me of an opponent extolling, at a time of
intense excitement, in such exalted terms, the speech of a rival whom
he followed in debate and whom he sought to overthrow, was in the
debate in the House of Commons on the peace of 1803, when Fox,
rising after Pitt, said of his speech that "the orators of antiquity would
have admired—probably would have envied it."

[254] I allude to the letters of "Decius," the first of which appeared in
the *Richmond Independent Chronicle* of the 7th of January, 1789. Of
these letters I may say something in the sequel. The letter of Innes is
in the Henry papers at "Red Hill."

gallery. But, from his long and exclusive devotion to the interests of the Commonwealth, he had gained an ascendancy in the public councils which was possessed by few of his contemporaries, and which caused him to be singled out as a fit person to bring forward the resolution inviting the meeting at Annapolis. He was also a ready, forcible, and, not unfrequently, an eloquent speaker, and was generally followed as a leader by the delegates from the tide-water counties. It was doubtless with a view of rousing the fears of some of the smaller counties on the seaboard, which had shown a disposition to sustain the new system, that he now spoke, not only more at length than he had yet done, but with a force and a freedom unlooked for by his opponents.

He said that he was inclined to have voted silently on the question about to be put; but, as he wished to record his opposition for the eyes of posterity, he felt bound to declare the principles on which he opposed the Constitution. His objections in the first instance were founded on general principles; but when upon a closer examination he saw the terms of the Constitution expressed in so indefinite a manner as to call forth contradictory constructions from those who approved it, he could find no peace in his mind. If able gentlemen who advocate this system cannot agree in construing it, could he be blamed for denouncing its ambiguity? The gentleman (Innes) has brought us to a degrading condition. We have no right to propose amendments. He should have expected such language after the Constitution was adopted; but he heard it with astonishment now. The gentleman objected to previous amendments because the people did not know them. Did they know their subsequent amendments? (Here Innes rose and made a distinction between the two classes of amendments. The people would see those that were subsequent, and, if they disliked them, might protest against them.) Tyler continued: Those subsequent amendments, he said, I have seen, and, although they hold out something that we wish, they are radically deficient. What do they say about direct taxation? about the judiciary? The new system contains many dangerous articles. Shall we be told by the gentleman that we shall be attacked by the Algerians, and that disunion shall take place, unless we adopt it? Such language I did not expect here. Little did I think that matters would have come to this when we separated from the mother country. There, every

man is amenable to punishment.   There is far less responsibility
in that system.   British tyranny would have been more tolerable.
Under the Articles of Confederation every man was at least secure in his person and in his property.   Liberty was then in its
zenith.   Human nature will always be the same.   Men never
were nor ever will be satisfied with their happiness.   When once
we begin these radical changes, where shall we find a place of
rest?   He contended that, if the new system were put into operation unamended, the people would not bear it; that two omnipotent agents exercising the right of taxation without restraint,
could not co exist; that a revolt or the destruction of the State
governments would follow; that as long as climate produces its
effects upon men, men would differ from each other in their
tastes, their interests, and affections; and that a consolidated
system could only be sustained under a military despotism.   He
discussed in detail the policy of amendments, and concluded that
the public mind would not be satisfied until the great questions
at issue should be settled by another Convention.   He reviewed
the chances of interference by foreign powers, and argued that
as it was their interest to be at peace with us, they would obey
the dictates of interest.   He deprecated the idea of a great and
powerful government.   Self defence in the present age and condition of the country was all that we ought to look for.   He said
he sought invariably to oppose oppression.   His course through
the Revolution would justify him.   He held now a paltry office,
away with it.[255]   It had no influence upon his conduct.   He was
no lover of disunion.   He wished Congress to possess the right
of regulating trade, as he thought that a partial and ever-varying
system of regulation by the individual States would not suffice,
and he had proposed to vest that right in the general government; but since this new government had grown out of his

---

[255] Tyler was appointed one of the Commissioners of Admiralty in
July, 1776, by the Convention, and performed the duties of his office
under a State appointment until 1781, when the Articles of Confederation took effect, and when his appointment as Judge of Admiralty was
renewed by the Federal government.   By the ninth of those articles
the general government received the power " of establishing rules for
deciding in all cases what captures on land or water shall be legal, and
in what manner prizes taken by land or by the naval forces of the
United States shall be divided or appropriated."

scheme to effect a desirable object, he lamented that he had put
his hand to it.   It never entered his head that we should quit
liberty and throw ourselves into the hands of a great and energetic government.   But, if we are to surrender liberty, we surely
ought to know the terms of the surrender.   The new system,
however, as construed by its own friends, does not accord us that
poor privilege.   He said he was not prone to jealousy ; that he
would trust his life to the members of this House, but he could
not trust the Constitution as it stood.   Its unlimited power of
taxation, the supremacy of the laws of the union, and of treaties, were, in his opinion, exceedingly dangerous.   There was no
responsibility.   Who would punish the President?   If we turn
out our own ten representatives, what can we do with the remaining fifty-five?   The wisdom of Great Britain gave each
colony its separate legislature, a separate judiciary, and the exclusive right to tax the people.   When that country infringed our
rights, we declared war.   This system violates all those precious
rights.   In 1781 the Assembly were compelled by the difficulties
of the times to provide by law that forty members should constitute a quorum.   That measure has been harshly blamed by
gentlemen ; but if we could not trust forty then, are we to be
blamed for not trusting to *ten* now ?   After denouncing the impolicy and the folly of altering or amending a contract when it
was signed and sealed, he concluded by saying that his heart
was full—that he could never feel peace again till he saw the defects of the new system removed.   Our only consolation, he said,
is the virtue of the present age.   It is possible that the friends
of this system, when they see their country divided, will reconcile
the people by the introduction of such amendments as shall be
deemed necessary.   Were it not for this hope he would despair.
He should say no more, but that he wished his name to be seen
in the yeas and nays, and that it may be known hereafter that his
opposition to this new system arose from a full persuasion and
conviction of its being dangerous to the liberties of his country.

The fierce and uncompromising assault of Tyler called up
Adam Stephen.   Stephen had risen some days before for the
purpose of rebuking Henry for the course which he had pursued
in debate, but had not gone fully into a discussion of the new
scheme.   Nor did he now proceed to examine that system in
detail, but in a highly figurative strain of eloquence advocated

its ratification without previous amendments. The country, he said, was in an unhappy condition, and that the members had been sent here to accept or reject the new system. That was their sole duty. Still he would concede future amendments, and he felt assured that such amendments would at an early day be engrafted on the Constitution. He praised the Constitution as embodying in just proportions the virtues of the three different kinds of government. Let gentlemen remember that we now have no Federal government at all. It is gone. It has been asked where is the genius of America? He would answer that it was that genius which convoked the Federal Convention, and which sent us here to decide upon the merits of the system framed by that body. What has now become of that genius? that beneficent genius which convoked the Federal Convention? "Yonder she is," he said, "in mournful attire, her hair dishevelled, distressed with grief and sorrow, supplicating our assistance against gorgons, fiends, and hydras, which are ready to devour her and carry desolation throughout her country. She bewails the decay of trade and the neglect of agriculture—her farmers discouraged, her ship carpenters, blacksmiths, and all other tradesmen unemployed. She casts her eyes on these, and deplores her inability to relieve them. She sees and laments that the profits of her commerce go to foreign States. She further bewails that all she can raise by taxation is inadequate to her necessities. She sees religion die by her side, public faith prostituted, and private confidence lost between man and man. Are the hearts of her citizens so steeled to compassion that they will not go to her relief?" He closed his remarks by holding up the magnanimity of Massachusetts in ratifying the Constitution in a spirit of union, and by declaring that the question was whether Virginia should be one of the United States or not.

Stephen was succeeded by a member who had not yet participated in debate, but who, as a representative of the Valley, was listened to with profound respect. Zachariah Johnston came from Augusta, a county which had been distinguished by the valor of its sons in the Indian wars, especially at the battle of Point Pleasant,[256] and in the Revolution; which had hailed the

---

[256] One of the Augusta companies that marched to Point Pleasant reminded one of Frederick the Second's tall regiment. We are told

conduct of the Virginia members of the Congress of 1774 in a patriotic letter still extant, and which had urged the Convention of May, 1776, before that body had dissolved the allegiance of the Colony to the crown, to establish an independent government, and to form an alliance of the States.[257]   The position of the Valley helped to give a cast to the politics of its inhabitants. Its waters ran to the east and sought the Atlantic through the Chesapeake.   Its rich lands were thinly settled.   The emigration, which had since the war been winding its way to Kentucky, passed through its breadth, and not only left none behind, but was taking off some of its citizens.   The people of the Valley

---

by Dr. Foote "that the company excited admiration for the height of the men and their uniformity of stature.   In the bar-room of Sampson Mathews a mark was made upon the walls, which remained until the tavern was consumed by fire about seventy years after the measurement of the company was made   The greater part of the men were six feet two inches in their stockings, and only two were but six feet."— *Foote's Sketches of Virginia*, second series, 162.

[Sampson Mathews was a brother of Colonel George Mathews of the Revolution, subsequently Governor of Georgia, etc., and the brothers, prior to the Revolution, were merchants and partners under the firm name of Sampson and George Mathews.—ED.]

[257] The address of the freeholders of Augusta, dated February 22, 1775, to Thomas Lewis and Samuel McDowell, and the letter to the delegates in Congress are now well known, and may be found in the *American Archives* compiled by Mr. Force, but it is a mistake to suppose that my allusion in the discourse on the Convention of 1776, in the sketch of Thomas Lewis, to a memorial of Augusta had any reference to these papers.   They are honorable to the people of Augusta, but they did not refer to independence.   The memorial to which I allude in the text was presented by Thomas Lewis in the Convention of May, 1776, and distinctly pointed to the establishment of an independent State government and a Federal union.   (See Journal, page 11.)   The only paper which can stand near this, and a noble paper it is, is the instructions forwarded by the freeholders of Buckingham to Charles Patteson and John Cabell, then delegates in the same Convention.   These instructions were drawn before the resolution of the Convention instructing the delegates in Congress to declare independence had reached Buckingham, and require the delegates from that county to form an independent government.   These instructions were printed in the *Virginia Gazette* of June 14, 1776, though written certainly before the middle of the previous month.   The paper should be printed and framed and hung from every wall in Buckingham.

were, therefore, more disposed to look to the East than to the West, and no appeal founded on the probable loss of the navigation of the Mississippi had any effect upon them. In fact, the stoppage of the navigation of that stream was more likely to prove a benefit than an injury to them. It would check emigration. It would not only keep their own people at home, but it would probably collect the emigrants from the East within the borders of the Valley. On the other hand, the dangers which the people of the Valley had most to apprehend, were from the Indians, who might not molest their own firesides, but who, if they made an inroad on the frontiers, must be repelled mainly by their arms. Hence a strong and energetic government, which might bring at any moment the military resources of the Union to bear upon the Indians, had in itself nothing unpleasing in the sight of the Valley people. And when we recall the subsequent Indian campaigns, during which two well-equipped armies of the Federal government, officered by brave and skillful men, were surprised and slain, it should appear that their fears were not wholly groundless.

Only one member from the Valley had spoken; but Stephen was an old soldier, and was apt to view political questions more in the spirit of a soldier than of a statesman. Thomas Lewis was a man of large experience in civil affairs; but it was now believed that he would support the Constitution.[258] It was plain that the opponents of that paper regarded the Valley delegation with alarm. It was mainly composed of men who had seen hard military service, and were devoted to Washington; and a large proportion of such men were in favor of a scheme of government which their chief had assisted in framing; which bore his august name on its face; which was recommended to the Congress of the Confederation in an eloquent letter from his pen, and the adoption of which it was well known that he had used all the just influence of his character to secure.[259] Nor were the

[258] In the discourse on the Virginia Convention of 1776, trusting to the researches of others instead of consulting the records for myself, I inadvertently represented Lewis as voting against the ratification of the Constitution. He voted in favor of it.

[259] Washington enclosed copies of the Constitution to many prominent men throughout the Union. See the form of his letter to them,

tender ties which bound the soldier to Washington severed by the peace. The society of the Cincinnati had been called into existence; its diplomas, admirably printed, for the times, on parchment, were seen neatly framed, and were to be seen in the rude cabins of the frontier as well as in the costlier dwellings of the East; and of that influential body he was the head. Stuart, of Greenbriar, who had behaved with gallantry at Point Pleasant, and who has handed down in his *Memoir* a description of the battle, lived on the other side of the mountain; but by marriage, by association, and by similarity of interest, was induced to sustain the policy of the Valley people. Stuart, of Augusta, had left William and Mary College to engage in the war, and, fighting gallantly at Guilford, had seen his commander, who was his own father,[260] fall from his horse, pierced with many wounds, and dragged off the field by the enemy, to be incarcerated in a prison-hulk on the seaboard. Darke, as well as his colleague, Stephen, *fortemque Gyan fortemque Cloanthum,* the opponents of the Constitution knew regarded that instrument with affection. Moore, of Rockbridge, who had seen arduous service in the Northern army, and was present when the flag of St. George was lowered on the field of Saratoga, had received instructions to oppose the new system; but it was believed that he would disobey them.[261] Gabriel Jones was not a soldier, but an able lawyer; but his shrewdness in business; his vast wealth, made up of lands and cash; his hatred of paper money, and the eccentric cast of his character, would insensibly lead him to approve an energetic and hard-money government.

In this state of apprehension respecting the opinions of the

---

and the manly answers of Harrison and Henry, in the *Writings of Washington.* Index to the volumes in the XII Volume, Articles, Harrison and Henry.

[260] [Major Alexander Stuart, whose sword, presented by his grandson, Hon. Alex. H. H. Stuart, is among the relics of the Virginia Historical Society.—ED.]

[261] He did disobey them; but, though warmly opposed by the celebrated William Graham [founder of Liberty Academy, now Washington and Lee University], he was returned from Rockbridge at the next election of the House of Delegates by a large majority. General Moore was not present at the battle of Point Pleasant, as is represented by Dr. Foote, and in *Howe's Virginia.*

members from the Valley, the words of Johnston were closely watched. Of the sentiments held by others, however, he said nothing, but in a few sentences removed all doubt about his own. After presenting some remarks appropriately introduced respecting the nature and value of government, and offering a deserved compliment to Pendleton, he discussed, concisely and clearly the legislative department, and pointed out its fine adaptation, in his opinion, to attain the end in view. He approved the provisions touching the militia, which, as the father of a large family, he regarded with caution ; saw no danger to religious freedom, or fear from direct taxation, and defended the irregularities of the new system by an illustration drawn from the number of fighting men in the county of Augusta and in the county of Warwick, and argued that the representation in the House of Representatives was more equal and more just than in our own House of Delegates. He saw full responsibility in the houses of Congress. Men would not be wicked for nothing, and when they became wicked we would turn them out. When the members of Congress knew that their own children would be taxed, there was sufficient responsibility. He animadverted sternly on the amendments brought forward by the opponents of the new scheme. They had left out the most precious article in the bill of rights. They feared, he said, that emancipation would be brought about. That had begun since the Revolution ; and, do what you will, it will come round. If slavery, he said, were totally abolished, it would do much good. He now looked forward to that happy day when discord and dissension shall cease. Division was a dreadful thing. The Constitution, he admitted, might have defects ; but where do the annals of the world show us a perfect constitution ? He closed his remarks by a novel and well-drawn parallel between the condition of the British people, who, when they had overthrown monarchy, were unable to govern themselves, and had in despair called Charles the Second to the throne, and the condition of our own country, warning the members of the fate which might overtake them, if, by rejecting the Constitution, they became involved in disunion and anarchy.[262]

Henry rose to utter his last words. We are told, he said, of the difficulty of obtaining previous amendments. I contend that

---

[262] This speech is quite able, and is well reported by Robertson.

they may be as easily obtained as subsequent amendments. We are told that *nine* States have adopted this Constitution. If so, when the government gets in motion, have they not the right to consider our amendments as well as if we had adopted first? If we remonstrate, may they not consider our amendments? I fear subsequent amendments, he said, will make our condition worse. They will make us ridiculous. I speak in plain direct language. It is extorted from me. I say, if the right of obtaining amendments is not secured, then our rights are not secured. The proposition of subsequent amendments is only to lull our apprehensions. He dwelt upon the surrender of the right of direct taxation. Taxes and excises are to be laid on us. The people are to be oppressed. The State Legislature is to be prostrated. The power of making treaties is also passed over. Our country may be dismembered. He might enumerate many other great rights that are omitted in the amendments. I am astonished, he said, at what my worthy friend (Innes) said—that we have no right of proposing previous amendments. That honorable gentleman is endowed with great eloquence—eloquence splendid, magnificent, and sufficient to shake the human mind. He has brought the whole force of America against this State. He has shown our weakness in comparison with foreign powers. His reasoning has no effect upon me. He cannot shake my political faith. He admits our power over subsequent amendments, though not over previous ones. If we have the right to depart from the letter of our commission in one instance, we have in the other. We shall absolutely escape danger in the one case, but not in the other. If members are serious in wishing amendments, why do they not join us in a manly, firm, and resolute manner to procure them? "I beg pardon of this House," he said, "for having taken up more time than came to my share, and I thank them for the patience and polite attention with which I have been heard. If I shall be in the minority, I shall have those painful sensations which arise from a conviction of being overpowered in a good cause. Yet I will be a peaceable citizen. My head, my hand, and my heart shall be ready to retrieve the loss of liberty, and remove the defects of that system, in a constitutional way. I wish not to go to violence, but will await with hopes that the spirit which predominated in the Revolution is not yet gone, nor the cause of those who are attached to the

Revolution yet lost. I shall therefore patiently wait in expectation of seeing that government changed so as to be compatible with the safety, liberty, and happiness of the people."

Randolph ended that long and brilliant debate in a touching valedictory. One parting word, he said, he humbly supplicated. The suffrage which he should give in favor of the Constitution will be ascribed by malice to motives unknown to his breast. "But, although for every other act of my life," he said, "I shall seek refuge in the mercy of God, for this I request his justice only. Lest, however, some future annalist, in the spirit of party vengeance, deign to mention my name, let him recite these truths : that I went to the Federal Convention with the strongest affection for the union ; that I acted there in full conformity with this affection ; that I refused to subscribe because I had, as I still have, objections to the Constitution, and wished a free enquiry into its merits ; and that the accession of eight States reduced our deliberations to the single question of union or no union."

The President now resumed the chair, and Mathews reported that the committee had, according to order, again had the Constitution under consideration, and had gone through the same, and come to several resolutions thereupon, which he read in his place, and afterwards delivered in at the clerk's table, where they were again read, and are as followeth :

" WHEREAS, The powers granted under the proposed Constitution are the gift of the people, and every power not granted thereby remains with them and at their will ; no right therefore, of any denomination can be cancelled, abridged, restrained or modified by the Congress, by the Senate or House of Representatives acting in any capacity, by the President, or any department or officer of the United States, except in those instances in which power is given by the Constitution for those purposes ; and among other essential rights, liberty of conscience and of the press cannot be cancelled, abridged, restrained, or modified by any authority of the United States ;

" AND WHEREAS, Any imperfections which may exist in the said Constitution ought rather to be examined in the mode prescribed therein for obtaining amendments, than by a delay, with a hope of obtaining previous amendments, to bring the union into danger ;

" *Resolved*, That it is the opinion of this committee that the said Constitution be ratified.

" But in order to relieve the apprehensions of those who may be solicitous for amendments,

" *Resolved*, That it is the opinion of this committee, that whatsoever amendments may be deemed necessary, be recommended to the consideration of Congress, which shall first assemble under the said Constitution, to be acted upon according to the mode prescribed in the fifth article thereof."

The first resolution proposing a ratification of the Constitution having been read a second time, a motion was made to amend it by substituting in lieu of the resolution and its preamble the following :

" *Resolved*, That previous to the ratification of the new Constitution of government recommended by the late Federal Convention, a declaration of rights asserting and securing from encroachment the great principles of civil and religious liberty, and the unalienable rights of the people, together with amendments to the most exceptionable parts of the said Constitution of government, ought to be referred by this Convention to the other States in the American confederacy for their consideration."

The vote on this amendment, which involved the question of previous or subsequent amendments, was taken without debate, and resulted in its rejection by a majority of *eight* votes.[263]

---

[263] The ayes and noes, which were ordered for the first time in a Virginia convention, on motion of Henry seconded by Bland, were 80 to 88, as follows :

AYES: Edmund Custis, John Pride, Edmund Booker, William Cabell, Samuel Jordan Cabell, John Trigg, Charles Clay, Henry Lee, of Bourbon, the Hon. John Jones, Binns Jones, Charles Patteson, David Bell, Robert Alexander, Edmund Winston, Thomas Read, Benjamin Harrison, the Hon. John Tyler, David Patteson, Stephen Pankey, junior, Joseph Michaux, Thomas H. Drew, French Strother, Joel Early, Joseph Jones, William Watkins, Meriwether Smith, James Upshaw, John Fowler, Samuel Richardson, Joseph Haden, John Early, Thomas Arthur, John Guerrant, William Sampson, Isaac Coles, George Carrington, Parke Goodall, John Carter Littlepage, Thomas Cooper, John Mann, Thomas Roane, Holt Richeson, Benjamin Temple, Stevens Thompson Mason, William White, Jonathan Patteson, Christopher Robinson, John Logan, Henry Pawling, John Miller, Green Clay, Samuel Hopkins, Richard Kennon, Thomas Allen, Alexander Robertson, John Evans, Walter Crockett, Abraham Trigg, Matthew Walton, John Steele, Ro-

The main question was then put, that the Convention agree with the committee on the said first resolution—the resolution of ratification—and was carried in a house of one hundred and sixty-eight members by *ten* votes.[264]

bert Williams, John Wilson, of Pottsylvania, Thomas Turpin, Patrick Henry, Robert Lawson, Edmund Ruffin, Theodrick Bland, William Grayson, Cuthbert Bullitt, Thomas Carter, Henry Dickenson, James Monroe, John Dawson, George Mason, Andrew Buchanan, John Howell Briggs, Thomas Edmunds, the Hon. Richard Cary, Samuel Edmonson, and James Montgomery—80.

NOES: The Hon. Edmund Pendleton, president, George Parker, George Nicholas, Wilson Nicholas, Zachariah Johnston, Archibald Stuart, William Darke, Adam Stephen, Martin McFerran, William Fleming, James Taylor, of Caroline, the Hon. Paul Carrington, Miles King, Worlick Westwood, David Stuart, Charles Simms, Humphrey Marshall, Martin Pickett, Humphrey Brooke, John S. Woodcock, Alexander White, Warner Lewis, Thomas Smith, George Clendenin, John Stuart, William Mason, Daniel Fisher, Andrew Woodrow, Ralph Humphreys, George Jackson, John Prunty, Isaac Vanmeter, Abel Seymour, His Excellency Governor Randolph, John Marshall, Nathaniel Burwell, Robert Andrews, James Johnson, Robert Breckenridge, Rice Bullock, William Fleet, Burdet Ashton, William Thornton, James Gordon, of Lancaster, Henry Towles, Levin Powell, Wm. O. Callis, Ralph Wormley, junior, Francis Corbin, William McClerry, Wills Riddick, Solomon Shepherd, William Clayton, Burwell Bassett, James Webb, James Taylor, of Norfolk, John Stringer, Littleton Eyre, Walter Jones, Thomas Gaskins, Archibald Wood, Ebenezer Zane, James Madison, James Gordon, of Orange, William Ronald, Anthony Walke, Thomas Walke, Benj. Wilson, John Wilson, of Randolph, Walker Tomlin, William Peachy, William McKee, Andrew Moore, Thomas Lewis, Gabriel Jones, Jacob Rinker, John Williams, Benj. Blunt, Samuel Kello, John Hartwell Cocke, John Allen, Cole Digges, Henry Lee, of Westmoreland, Bushrod Washington, the Hon. John Blair, the Hon. George Wythe, James Innes, and Thomas Mathews—88.

[264] The ayes and noes, ordered on motion of George Mason, seconded by Henry, were ayes 89, noes 79, as follows:

AYES: The Hon. Edmund Pendleton, president, George Parker, George Nicholas, Wilson Nicholas, Zach. Johnston, A. Stuart, W. Darke, A. Stephen, M. McFerran, W. Fleming, Jas. Taylor, of Caroline. the Hon. P. Carrington, D. Patteson, M. King, W. Westwood, D. Stuart, C. Simms, H. Marshall, M. Pickett, H. Brooke, J. S. Woodcock, A. White, W. Lewis, T. Smith, G. Clendenin, J. Stuart, W. Mason, D. Fisher, A. Woodrow, R. Humphreys, G. Jackson, John Prunty, I. Vanmeter, A. Seymour, His Excellency Governor Randolph, J. Marshall, N. Burwell, R. Andrews, J. Johnson, R. Breckenridge, Rice Bullock, W. Fleet, B.

When the vote was announced from the chair, and when it appeared that the long and arduous contest had been at last decided in favor of the new system, there was no show of triumph or exultation on the part of its friends. A great victory had been achieved by them; but it was impossible to say that the Constitution was yet safe. It was carried by a meagre majority; and it was carried, it was believed by those who had the control of the Assembly, in plain opposition to the wishes of the people; the Legislature might yet interpose obstacles to the organization of the government, and might virtually annul, for some time at least, the ratification which had been so dearly won. The vote which we shall soon record, attests in the strongest manner the desire for conciliation which governed the conduct of the friends of the Constitution.

The second resolution having been amended by striking out the preamble, was then agreed to by a silent vote.[265]

Ashton, W. Thornton, J. Gordon, of Lancaster, H. Towles, L. Powell, W. O. Callis, R. Wormeley, junior, F. Corbin, Wil. McClerry, W. Riddick, S. Shepherd, W. Clayton, B. Bassett, J. Webb, J. Taylor, of Norfolk, J. Stringer, L. Eyre, W. Jones, T. Gaskins, A. Woods, E. Zane, James Madison, J. Gordon, of Orange, W. Ronald, A. Walke, T. Walke, B. Wilson, J. Wilson, of Randolph, W. Tomlin, W. Peachy, W. McKee, A. Moore, T. Lewis, G. Jones, J Rinker, J. Williams, B. Blunt, S. Kello, J. H. Cocke, J. Allen, C. Digges, H. Lee, of Westmoreland, B Washington, the Hon. J. Blair, the Hon. G. Wythe, J. Innes, and T. Mathews—89.

NOES: E Custis, J. Pride, E. Booker, W. Cabell, S. J. Cabell, J. Trigg, C. Clay, H. Lee, of Bourbon, the Hon. J. Jones, B. Jones, C. Patteson, D. Bell, R. Alexander, E. Winston, T. Read, B. Harrison, the Hon. J. Tyler, S. Pankey, Jr., J. Michaux, T. H. Drew, F. Strother, Joel Early, J. Jones, W. Watkins, M. Smith, J. Upshaw, J. Fowler, S. Richardson, J. Haden, John Early, T. Arthur, J. Guerrant, W. Sampson, I. Coles, G. Carrington, P. Goodall, J. C. Littlepage, T. Cooper, J. Mann, T. Roane, H. Richeson, B. Temple, S. T. Mason, W. White, Jona. Patteson, C. Robertson, J. Logan, H. Pawling, J. Miller, G. Clay, S. Hopkins, R. Kennon, T. Allen, A. Robertson, J. Evans, W. Crockett, A. Trigg, M. Walton, J. Steele, R. Williams, John Wilson, of Pottsylvania, F. Turpin, P. Henry, R. Lawson, E. Ruffin, T. Bland, W. Grayson, C. Bullitt, T. Carter, H. Dickenson, James Monroe, J. Dawson, Geo. Mason, A. Buchanan, J. H. Briggs, T. Edmunds, the Hon. Richard Cary, S. Edmonson, and James Montgomery—79.

[265] The vote on striking out the first resolution, and inserting the amendment in its stead, was the test vote, and was lost by eight votes. A change, therefore, of four of the votes of the majority would have

A committee was then appointed to prepare and report a form of ratification, and Randolph, George Nicholas, Madison, Marshall, and Corbin were placed upon it.[266] A committee was also appointed " to prepare and report such amendments as shall by them be deemed necessary to be recommended in pursuance of the second resolution," and consisted of Wythe, Harrison, Mathews, Henry, Randolph, George Mason, Nicholas, Grayson, Madison, Tyler, Marshall, Monroe, Ronald, Bland, Meriwether Smith, Paul Carrington, Innes, Hopkins, John Blair, and Simms.

Randolph immediately reported a form of ratification, which was read and agreed to without debate ; and is as follows :

" We, the Delegates of the People of Virginia, duly elected in pursuance of a recommendation from the General Assembly, and now met in Convention, having fully and freely investigated and discussed the proceedings of the Federal Convention, and being prepared, as well as the most mature deliberation hath enabled us, to decide thereon, Do, in the name and in the behalf of the People of Virginia, declare and make known, that the powers granted under the Constitution being derived from the People

---

made a tie, and a single additional vote would have settled the fate of the Constitution for that time. Had Moore and McKee obeyed their instructions, and had Stuart, of Augusta, remained at home at the time of the Botetourt election, instead of using his influence effectually on the ground in favor of the Constitution, and of causing the Botetourt candidates to pledge themselves to sustain that system ; and had Paul Carrington voted with his colleague, Read, in favor of it, those five votes would have been forthcoming. That some of the delegates voted in opposition to the wishes of their constituents was well known at the time.

[266] This was an able committee, but a grave objection exists against it that it did not contain the name of an opponent of the Constitution. I am reminded by the names of Madison and Marshall of the fact that those two gentlemen were appointed to a similar committee in a similar body forty years afterwards. On the adjournment of that body, I walked home to our lodgings in the Eagle Tavern with the president, the late Philip Pendleton Barbour, and by the way asked him if he had been in the chair at a joint session of the Senate and House of Representatives, could he have selected such a committee, when he answered without hesitation, " No, nor from the Union at large." That committee consisted of Madison, Marshall, Tazewell, Doddridge, Leigh, Johnson, and Cooke ; one from the tidewater country, two from above tide, two from the Valley, and one from the extreme west.

of the United States, may be resumed by them whensoever the same shall be perverted to their injury or oppression, and that every power not granted thereby remains with them, and at their will ; that therefore, no right of any denomination can be cancelled, abridged, restrained, or modified by the Congress, by the Senate or House of Representatives acting in any capacity, by the President, or any department, or officer of the United States, except in those instances in which power is given by the Constitution for those purposes ; and that among other essential rights, the liberty of conscience and of the press cannot be cancelled, abridged, restrained, or modified, by any authority of the United States.

"With these impressions, with a solemn appeal to the searcher of hearts for the purity of our intentions, and under the conviction that whatsoever imperfections may exist in the Constitution, ought rather to be examined in the mode prescribed therein, than to bring the Union into danger by a delay, with a hope of obtaining amendments previous to the ratification:

"We, the said Delegates, in the name and in behalf of the People of Virginia, do, by these presents, assent to, and ratify the Constitution, recommended on the seventeenth day of September, one thousand seven hundred and eighty-seven, by the Federal Convention for the government of the United States, hereby announcing to all those whom it may concern, that the said Constitution is binding upon the said People, according to an authentic copy hereto annexed, in the words following:"[267]

(See the Constitution in the Appendix.)

The Convention then ordered two fair copies of the form of ratification and of the Constitution to be engrossed forthwith, and adjourned to the next day at twelve o'clock.

---

[267] The form of ratification has been usually attributed to the pen of Madison; but I am compelled to give up this opinion, which was common thirty years ago. It is but an enlargement of the preamble offered by Wythe, and doubtless from internal evidence written by him. That preamble is not such as in my opinion Madison or Randolph would have drawn, and is very properly amended in a vital part in the form of ratification. As Randolph was chairman of the committee which reported the form, and was a critical writer, and as the form was mainly an enlargement of the preamble presented by Wythe, the safer conjecture is that its merit belongs jointly to Randolph and Wythe.

On Thursday, the twenty-sixth day of June, at twelve o'clock, the Convention met, and, one copy only of the form of ratification having as yet been transcribed, it was read by the clerk, was signed by the president on behalf of the Convention, and was ordered "to be transmitted by the president to the United States in Congress assembled."[268] As the Committee on Amendments had not yet completed its schedule, the House, after making certain allowances to its officers for services rendered during the session, adjourned until the next day at ten o'clock.[269]

On Friday, the twenty-seventh day of June, the Convention met for the last time. The session, which had lasted during twenty-five eventful days, was to close with the adjournment of that day. Nor was the public anxiety less intense than at an earlier stage of the proceedings. The hall of the Academy was crowded. Several of the members of the select committee, who happened to be late, could with difficulty force their way to their seats. It was certain that, unless the proposed amendments were acceptable to the minority, the worst results were yet to be apprehended. The members of that minority, who, in a house of one hundred and seventy members, were only ten less than the majority, and who, in all those qualities necessary for the guidance of men in a great crisis, were certainly not inferior to their opponents, might proceed to organize, and to digest a plan of operations, the effect of which would certainly be, in the first instance, to prevent all participation by Virginia in setting up the new government, and might ultimately end in the organization of a Southern confederacy.[270] Fortunately the friends of the

---

[268] That is, to the Congress of the Confederation, which held its sittings in New York, and "which determined on the 13th of September, 1788, under the resolutions of the General Convention, that the Constitution had been established, and that it should go into operation on the first Wednesday of March (the fourth), 1789."

[269] The president was allowed forty shillings per day, Virginia currency, for his pay; the secretary, forty pounds in full; the chaplain, thirty pounds; the sergeant, twenty-four pounds; each door-keeper, fifteen pounds.

[270] It is proper to remind the reader, what has been said before, that our greatest statesmen, to their dying day, believed that they had been *trapped* in calling the general Federal Convention, and that they distrusted "the military gentlemen," as George Mason called them, into

Constitution saw the full extent of the conjuncture, and determined, by a manly patriotism, and by a spirit of concession as rare as it was honorable, to avert the impending danger.

When Pendleton took the chair the clerk proceeded to read the second engrossed copy of the form of ratification, which was signed by the president. It was then ordered that the form should be deposited in the archives of the General Assembly. Wythe now rose and presented the amendments proposed by the select committee to be made to the Constitution in the mode prescribed by that instrument. Those amendments consisted of a Declaration of Rights, in twenty articles nearly similar to those prefixed to the Constitution of the State, and a series of amendments proper, also in twenty articles, to be added to the body of the Federal Constitution. The report of the committee ended in these words: "And the Convention do, in the name and behalf of the people of this Commonwealth, enjoin it upon their representatives in Congress to exert all their influence, and use all reasonable and legal methods to obtain a ratification of the foregoing alterations and provisions in the manner provided by the fifth article of the said Constitution; and in all congressional laws to be passed in the meantime, to conform to the spirit of these amendments as far as the said Constitution will admit."

The Declaration of Rights was then adopted without a division. The amendments proper were read, and a motion was made to amend them by striking out the third article in these words: "When Congress shall lay direct taxes or excises, they shall immediately inform the executive power of each State, of the quota of such State according to the census herein directed, which is proposed to be thereby raised; and if the Legislature of any State shall pass a law which shall be effectual for raising such quota at the time required by Congress, the taxes and excises laid by Congress shall not be collected in such State."

---

whose hands they feared the new government would be committed. All had unlimited confidence in the integrity of Washington; but they had known him, as yet, as a silent member by their sides in the House of Burgesses, as an Indian fighter, and as the great commander of the armies during the Revolution, but never as a statesman. But, however eminent he might be in every respect, he must lean mainly on the friends of the Constitution, who were the greatest soldiers of their day. Grayson expressed the general opinion when he said: "We have no fear of tyranny *while he lives*."

This amendment, which it was proposed to strike out, was, in the estimation of the opponents of the Constitution, the most important of all.   It struck at the root of the new Federal polity. Of that polity the distinguishing characteristic was that it was complete in itself and by itself in effectuating all measures within its scope; especially, that it was free to lay and collect taxes of its own authority and at its own discretion.   This was deemed a cardinal virtue by its friends, and a cardinal vice by its opponents. To strike this feature from the Constitution was substantially to fall back upon requisitions.   What passed in the select committee is not known, and, unless it may be gleaned from stray letters written at the time, which may hereafter be cast up, will remain a secret ; but it can hardly be doubted that the adoption of this amendment by the committee was made by Henry and Mason an indispensable preliminary of a peaceful adjustment. But it must also be sanctioned by the House ; otherwise its adoption by the committee would be too palpable a farce to impose on two such statesmen.   Accordingly, the motion to strike it out failed by twenty votes.   Pendleton was the most prominent opponent who gave way.   He was followed by Paul Carrington.   The gallant and patriotic Fleming, who carried to his grave a troublesome wound which he received in the thickest of the fight at Point Pleasant, followed the example of Carrington.   Eight other members magnanimously followed Fleming, and ten votes taken from one scale and added to the other make up the decisive number.   Thus, by the most decisive vote given during the session the Convention solemnly pledged itself to amend the power of direct taxation, and virtually to fall back upon requisitions.[271]

---

[271] The ayes and noes were called by Nicholas, seconded by Harrison, and were ayes, 65 ; noes, 85, as follows :

AYES: G. Parker, G. Nicholas, W. Nicholas, Z. Johnston, A. Stuart, W. Dark, A. Stephen, M. McFerran, James Taylor, of Caroline, D. Stuart, C. Simms, H. Marshall, M. Pickett, H. Brooke, J. S. Woodcock, A. White, W. Lewis, T. Smith, John Stuart, D. Fisher, A. Woodrow, G. Jackson, J. Prunty, A. Seymour, His Excellency Governor Randolph, John Marshall, N. Burwell, R. Andrews, James Johnson (who was the latest survivor of the Convention, died at his residence in Isle of Wight county on the 16th day of August, 1845, aged ninety-nine years), R. Bullock, B. Ashton, W. Thornton, H. Towles, L. Powell, W. O. Callis, R. Wormeley, Francis Corbin, W. McClerry, James Webb, James Taylor, of Norfolk, J. Stringer, L. Eyre, W. Jones, T. Gaskins,

The main question on concurring in the amendments proposed by the committee was then put, and decided in the affirmative without a division. The secretary was ordered to engross the amendments on parchment, to be signed by the president, and to transmit the same, with the ratification of the Federal Constitution, to the United States in Congress assembled. A fair engrossed copy of the form of ratification, with the proposed amendments, was ordered to be signed by the president, and to be forwarded to the executive of each State in the Union. It was further ordered that the proceedings of the body be recorded in a well-bound book, and, when signed by the president and secretary, to be deposited in the archives of the Council of State. The printer was ordered to transmit fifty copies of the form of ratification, with the amendments, to each county in the State. Some accounts of the printer and of the carpenters, who had fitted up the hall of the Academy, were referred to the auditor for settlement, and the business of the Convention was done.

A. Woods, James Madison, J. Gordon, of Orange, W. Ronald, T. Walke, Anthony Walke, Benjamin Wilson, John Wilson, of Randolph, W. Peachey, Andrew Moore, T. Lewis, G. Jones, J. Rinker, J. Williams, Benjamin Blunt, S. Kello, J. Allen, Cole Digges, B. Washington, the Hon. George Wythe, and Thomas Mathews—65.

Noes: The Hon. Edmund Pendleton, president, E. Custis, J. Pride, William Cabell, S. J. Cabell, J. Trigg, C. Clay, William Fleming, Henry Lee, of Bourbon, John Jones, B. Jones, C. Patteson, D. Bell, R. Alexander, E. Winston, Thomas Read, the Hon. Paul Carrington, Benjamin Harrison, the Hon. John Tyler, D. Patteson, S. Pankey, junior, Joseph Michaux, French Strother, Joseph Jones, Miles King, J. Haden, John Early, T. Arthur, J. Guerrant, W. Sampson, Isaac Coles, George Carrington, Parke Goodall, John C. Littlepage, Thomas Cooper, W. Fleet, Thomas Roane, Holt Richeson, B. Temple, James Gordon, of Lancaster, Stevens Thompson Mason, W. White, Jona. Patteson, J. Logan, H. Pawling, John Miller, Green Clay, S. Hopkins, R. Kennon, Thomas Allen, A. Robertson, Walter Crockett, Abraham Trigg, Solomon Shepherd, W. Clayton, Burwell Bassett, M. Walton, John Steele, R. Williams, John Wilson, of Pittsylvania, T. Turpin, Patrick Henry, Edmund Ruffin, Theodoric Bland, William Grayson, C. Bullitt, W. Tomlin, W. McKee, Thomas Carter, H. Dickenson, James Monroe, J. Dawson, George Mason, A. Buchanan, John Hartwell Cocke, J. H. Briggs, Thomas Edmunds, the Hon. Richard Cary, S. Edmonson, and J. Montgomery—85.

This list of names deserves to be well studied.

And now the last scene was at hand.   Some member, whose name has not come down to us, offered a resolution expressive of the sense entertained by the Convention of the dignity, the impartiality, and the ability displayed by Pendleton in the chair. It was received with unanimous assent.   A motion to adjourn *sine die* was then made and carried.   Then that old man, who had hitherto kept his seat when putting a question to the House, was seen to rise slowly from the chair ; and while he was adjusting himself on his crutches, the members on the farthest benches crept quietly into the body of the hall.   They were unwilling to lose any of the last words of an eminent man whose name had been honored by their fathers and by their grandfathers ; whose skill in debate was unrivalled, and who was about to close, on a solemn occasion aptly designed for such an event, a parliamentary career the longest and most brilliant in our annals.   His first words were almost inaudible to those nearest him.   He said "he felt grateful to the House for the mark of respect which they had just shown him.   He was conscious that his infirmities had prevented him from discharging the duties of the chair satisfactory to himself, and he therefore regarded the expression of the good will of his associates with the more grateful and the more tender sensibility.   He knew that he was now uttering the last words that he should ever address to the representatives of the people. His own days were nearly spent, and whatever might be the success or failure of the new government, he would hardly live to see it.   But his whole heart was with his country.   She had overlooked his failings and had honored him far beyond his deserts, and every new mark of her esteem had been to him a fresh memorial of his duty to serve her faithfully.   The present scene would recall to others, as it did to him, a similar one which occurred twelve years ago.   The Convention had then declared independence, and the members who had cheerfully incurred the risks of a war with a powerful nation, were about to depart to sustain their country by their counsels and by their valor.   He saw some of those members before him.   A kind Providence had blessed them beyond their hopes.   They had gained their liberty, and their country was placed among the nations of the earth.   They had acquired a territory nearly as large as the continent of Europe.   That territory connected them with two great warlike and maritime nations, whose power was formidable and whose friendship was at least doubtful. The defects of the Confederation were generally admitted, and the Constitution, which has been ratified by us, is designed to take its place. This Convention was called to consider it.

"Heretofore our Conventions had met in the midst of a raging war. Now all was peace. There was no enemy within our borders to intimidate or annoy us. The Constitution was in some important respects defective. The numerous amendments proposed by the Convention were designed to point out those defects, and to remove them. The members had performed their duty with the strictest fidelity, and he was pleased to see so many young, eloquent, and patriotic men ready to take the places of those who must soon disappear. He beseeched gentlemen who had acquitted themselves with a reputation that would not be lost to posterity, to forget the heats of discussion, and remember that each had only done what he deemed to be his duty to his country. Let us make allowances for the workings of a new system. It is the Constitution of our country. If our hopes should be disappointed, and should the government turn out badly, the remedy was in our own hands. Virginia gave, and Virginia would take away. But all radical changes in governments should be made with caution and deliberation. We could know the present, but the future was full of uncertainties. The best government was not perfect, and even in a government that has serious defects, the people might enjoy, by a prudent and temperate administration, a large share of happiness and prosperity. But it was his solemn conviction that a close and firm union was essential to the safety, the independence, and the happiness of all the States, and with his latest breath he would conjure his countrymen to keep this cardinal object steadily in view. We are brothers ; we are Virginians. Our common object is the good of our country. Let us breathe peace and hope to the people. Let our rivalry be who can serve his country with the greatest zeal ; and the future would be fortunate and glorious. His last prayer should be for his country, that Providence might guide and guard her for years and ages to come. If ever a nation had cause for thankfulness to Heaven, that nation was ours. As for himself, if any unpleasant incident had occurred in debate between him and any member, he hoped it would be forgotten and forgiven ; and he tendered to all the tribute of his most grateful and affectionate respect.

One duty alone remained to be performed, and he now pronounced the adjournment of the Convention without day."

While Pendleton was speaking, we are told that the House was in tears. Members who had mixed in the fierce *mêlée*, and who had uttered the wildest imprecations on the Constitution, as they listened to his calm, monitory voice, could not restrain their emotions. Old men, who had heard his parting benediction twelve years before to the Convention which declared independence, and called to mind his manly presence and the clear silver tones of a voice now tremulous and faint from infirmity and age, bowed their heads between their hands and wept freely. But in the midst of weeping the deep blue eye of Pendleton was undimmed. When he concluded his speech he descended from the chair, and, taking his seat on one of the nearest benches, he bade adieu to the members individually, who crowded around him to press a parting salutation. The warmest opponents were seen to exchange parting regards with each other. For it was a peculiar and noble characteristic of our fathers, when the contest was decided, to forgive and forget personal collisions, and to unite heart and hand in the common cause. On the breaking up of the House many members ordered their horses, and were before sunset some miles on their way homeward; and before the close of another day all had disappeared ; and there was no object to remind the citizen of Richmond, as at nightfall through deserted streets he sought his home, that the members of one of the most illustrious assemblies that ever met on the American continent had finished their deliberations, had discharged the high trust confided to them by their country, and had again mingled with the mass of the people.

APPENDIX.

As a specimen of the complaints about the state of trade in 1785, I annex, with some comments upon it, an extract from a letter of Mr. Madison, dated Orange C. H., July 7, 1785, and addressed to R. H. Lee, which may be seen in Mr. Rives' *History of the Life and Times of Madison*, Vol. II, 47, note:

"What makes the British monopoly the more mortifying is the abuse which they make of it. Not only the private planters, who have resumed the practice of shipping their own tobacco, but many of the merchants, particularly the natives of the country, who have no connections with Great Britain, have received accounts of sales this season which carry the most visible and shameful frauds in every article. In every point of view, indeed, the trade of the country is in a most deplorable condition.

"A comparison of current prices here with those in the Northern States, either at this time or at any time since the peace, will show that the loss direct on our produce, and indirect on our imports, is not less than fifty per cent. Till very lately the price of one staple has been down at 32s. and 33s. on James river, at 28s. on Rappahannock river tobacco. During the same period the former was selling in Philadelphia, and I suppose in other Northern ports, at 44s. of this currency, and the latter in proportion, though it cannot be denied that tobacco in the Northern ports is intrinsically worth less than it is here, being at the same distance from the ultimate market, and burthened with the freight from this to the other States. The price of merchandise here is, at least, as much above, as that of tobacco is below, the Northern standard."

The British monopoly spoken of in the letter was nothing more or less than that England, having more ships than any other nation, sent more of them to Virginia than any other nation did. Had France, or Spain, or Holland, or any other country, been fortunate enough to own more ships than its neighbor, the same ground of complaint would have existed; or had all the foreign shipping that entered our ports been equally divided among foreign powers, the ground of complaint would have been the same. The ship-carpenters, and the merchants who owned home-built ships, were dissatisfied at the state of things, and called for relief. And supposing, for the sake of argument, it would have been expedient to burden foreign vessels with taxes, the Assembly of Virginia had full authority to administer the proposed relief, which was done at the session following the date of the letter by the passage of an act imposing a tax on British shipping. And if it be alleged that, if Virginia imposed a tax, Maryland would admit the vessel taxed duty-free, it is conclusive to say that Virginia, with the assent of Congress, which followed as a matter of course, could form any agreement she pleased with Maryland, and did take efficient measures for so doing at the session of 1785. Thus far all that is complained of by Mr. Madison could be accomplished by an ordinary Act of Assembly, and required no change in the organic law.

The next ground of complaint is, that the foreign commission merchants made fraudulent returns to the planter; a very bad thing indeed, and justified a change of agents; but surely such a change could be made without overturning the government of the Confederation. Indeed, the Philadelphians, as it appears from the last sentence of the letter, did find honest agents abroad, we may suppose, if it be true, as alleged, that they sold their imported articles so much lower than they could be sold on James river. What the Northern merchant could do under the existing Confederation, we could do as well.

The second paragraph, which relates to current prices of tobacco in Philadelphia and in the Virginia waters, will strike every man of business as representing an abnormal state of trade, which is frequently seen under every system of laws. The obvious explanation is, *that Philadelphia was not a tobacco market*, and that what little tobacco she had was mainly designed to make up the complement of assorted cargoes, and would naturally command under such circumstances a higher price than the article was selling for several hundred miles off. If the Philadelphia market had been stable at the prices named in the letter, and if the Virginia planter lost fifty per cent. of his crop and of his return purchases by sending it to England, it is plain that the whole tobacco crop of Virginia would have been at the foot of Market-street wharf in that city in less than six weeks from the time when the intelligence reached James river ; for vessels were abundant, according to the letter itself. The saving in time, in freight, and in foreign purchases, would have put the Northern market ahead of all the world. Such inequalities, then, could have been remedied by a little management and common sense alone, without any change in the Federal alliances of Virginia.

But the great value of this letter, which has been selected from the files of Mr. Madison to show the desperate condition of affairs under the government of the Confederation, and to justify that statesman in his policy of depriving his native State of the invaluable right of regulating her own trade, consists in affording an unconscious, but not the less remarkable, proof of the commercial prosperity of Virginia at the time in question. Let it be remembered that the treaty with Great Britain, that ended the war of the Revolution, was not signed at Paris till the 3d day of September, 1783, and was not ratified by Congress until the 14th day of January, 1784 ; and that this letter of Mr. Madison was written in July, 1785 ; and that, besides the large trade and commerce of Norfolk, which we know from other sources, it represents the planters shipping from their own estates their abundant agricultural products in the ships of a single nation which were so numerous as to monopolize the trade and fix what rates they pleased ; and that all this trade and commerce was the growth of less than eighteen months, and we have before us, under all the circumstances of the case, a picture of prosperity almost without a parallel. And this picture is heightened by the purport of three petitions, which are given on the same pages which contain the above letter. These petitions come from Norfolk, Portsmouth and Suffolk. That from Norfolk is in the following words : "That the prohibition laid by Great Britain on the trade to the West Indies, and the almost total monopoly of the other branches of trade by *foreigners*, has produced great distress and much injury to the trade of the Commonwealth ; that the rapid decrease of American bottoms, the total stop to ship-building and to the nursery of American seamen occasioned thereby, threaten the most alarming consequences unless timely avoided by the wisdom of the Legislature."

The object of this petition, which comes from the ship-carpenters and the merchants who built vessels, is the laying of a tax on the ships of all countries trading to our ports to favor their own private gain, which, so far as that private gain is the public gain, and no farther, is commendable ; and in asking for a tax on foreign tonnage, they sought what the Assembly could grant most effectually if it pleased, and was granted at the said session of 1785, no change in the Federal system being necessary for such a purpose. As for the prohibition on the West India trade, which only means that Great Britain would not allow our vessels, any more than the vessels of other nations, to engage in what she regards as her coasting trade, the petition, whether presented in 1785 or 1826, would have been beyond the power of any nation under any possible form of government to have granted. Great Britain determined to be the carrier of the productions of her Colonies in her own bottoms ; but—and this is one of the bright signs of those times—all those productions were brought to our ports by her vessels, which received in return the products of our own industry, and the result was a most profitable business that greatly enhanced our prosperity. The complaint of the Norfolk merchants was that, in addition to the gains resulting from such a commerce, they could not secure the profits of the carrying trade. They sucked the orange dry, and muttered that the producer of the orange kept the rind to himself.

The petitioners further urged as a grievance that, besides their inability to substitute their own vessels for the vessels owned by the West Indians who brought their valuable cargoes to Norfolk, and took back our produce in return, "there was an almost total monopoly of other branches of trade by *foreigners.*" The history of the case is this : Norfolk had been reduced to ashes at the beginning of the war, and the whole population sent into the interior. It was so effectually destroyed by the British and by our own people that it was a boast that in that once flourishing town a shed could not be found to shelter a cow. Let it be remembered that among the merchants and traders of the town before it was burned, comparatively few were native Virginians, who regarded mercantile employments with dislike. As soon as the war was over, hundreds of enterprising business men of every class and of every country flocked to the town, and in a short time restored it to a degree of prosperity which it had never known before. These men from abroad brought with them a capital in money as well as skill, and the business naturally fell into their hands. They became good citizens, married good Virginia wives, and the blood of one who came to Virginia from Scotland in 1783, and helped to build up the prosperity of that era, flows in the veins of him who traces these lines. I only wish we had the same ground of complaint now that the Norfolk petitioners had then.

The Norfolk petition further urges some relief against "the decrease of American bottoms." Then the business men of that day had a choice between home and foreign bottoms, and preferred the foreign. Now, according to the received laws of free trade, for which the South has ever been such an advocate, that preference was just; as to place the home bottoms on a level with the foreign, by legislation, would be to pay the home ship-owner a bounty not only equal to the difference in the charge of freight, but to the costs of collection. But, whatever we may think of the doctrines of free trade, the Assembly was competent to apply the remedy, and no organic change was needed on this account. And let it be kept in mind that, as Norfolk was a wilderness, destitute of people, capital, and skill at the close of the war, the men, the capital, and the skill which built these home-made vessels, which were said to be diminishing, were all the result of a space of time not exceeding eighteen months.

The Portsmouth memorial, quoted by Mr. Rives, is as follows: The petitioners affirm that "the present deplorable state of trade, occasioned by the restrictions and policy of the British acts of navigation, has caused great and general distress, and threatens total ruin and decay to the several branches of commerce;" and we add from the Journal of the House of Delegates (October session of 1785, page 24,) the mode of relief desired by the petitioners, which is "that certain restrictive acts may be imposed on the British trade, or other more adequate and effectual measures adopted for relief therein." Here we have the remedy proposed by the petitioners, which is to tax foreign tonnage to such a degree as either to drive it from our ports or to enable them to build ships to compete with it. And Suffolk adds "that even the coasting trade and inland navigation had fallen into the hands of foreigners." What we would call attention to is the fact that these petitioners fully believed that the Assembly possessed the power, as it assuredly did, to grant the relief desired, and professed no wish for a change in our federal system. As to a business view of the matter, when we recall the fact that, on the declaration of peace, we had hardly a canoe to launch on the waters of the Elizabeth, and not a solitary dollar in specie, and that our merchants had accumulated so early a moneyed capital which inspired them with the hopes of driving all foreign bottoms from our waters—and all this in the space of eighteen months—we see in all these memorials from our seaports, not the proofs of a decreasing trade, as some would have us believe, but the most infallible indications of commercial success.

Of all the men of his times, Mr. Madison possessed that caste of intellect best adapted for the discussions of commerce and political economy. But his sphere of personal observation was very limited. He never visited Petersburg, I believe; and, as well as I could learn from his writings, from the recollections of his intimate friends, and from conversations which I have had with him from time to time about Norfolk, he never visited our seaport in the interval between 1783 and 1788, if ever. He lived far beyond the scent of salt water in Orange, which was then as distant from Norfolk, if we measure distance by the time of ordinary travel, as Quebec or New Orleans is now. The only breath of sea air he probably ever drew was in crossing from the Jersey shore to New York to take his seat in Congress. He served but a single session in our Assembly, the October session of 1776, when he was twenty-five, and the next deliberative body of which he was a member was Congress, in which he remained the constitutional term of three years, and to which he was returned as soon as he was eligible. He was thus led to regard the Union as his patriotic stand-point—and a glorious stand-point it was—and not the State of Virginia, one more glorious still; and his occasional appearances in the Assembly, in which he rendered invaluable service to his country, but in which on federal topics he was almost powerless, did not conquer his central prepossessions. But in or out of Congress, a truer patriot never lived.

CONSTITUTION.

WE the people of the United States, in order to form a more perfect Union, establish Justice, insure domestic Tranquility, provide for the common defence, promote the general Welfare, and secure the Blessings of Liberty to ourselves and our Posterity, do ordain and establish this CONSTITUTION for the United States of America.

ARTICLE I.

SECTION I. All legislative Powers herein granted shall be vested in a Congress of the United States, which shall consist of a Senate and House of Representatives.

SECTION II. 1. The House of Representatives shall be composed of members chosen every second Year by the People of the several States, and the Electors in each State shall have the Qualifications requisite for Electors of the most numerous Branch of the State Legislature.

2. No person shall be a representative who shall not have attained to the Age of twenty five Years, and been seven Years a Citizen of the United States, and who shall not, when elected, be an Inhabitant of that State in which he shall be chosen.

3. Representatives and direct Taxes shall be apportioned among the several States which may be included within this Union, according to their respective Numbers, which shall be determined by adding to the whole Number of free Persons, including those bound to Service for a Term of Years, and excluding Indians not taxed, three-fifths of all other Persons. The actual Enumeration shall be made within three Years after the first Meeting of the Congress of the United States, and within every subsequent Term of ten Years, in such Manner as they shall by Law direct. The Number of Representatives shall not exceed one for every thirty Thousand, but each State shall have at Least one Representative; and until such enumeration shall be made, the State of New Hampshire shall be entitled to chuse three, Massachusetts eight, Rhode-Island and Providence Plantations one, Connecticut five, New-York six, New Jersey four, Pennsylvania eight, Delaware one, Maryland six, Virginia ten, North Carolina five, South Carolina five, and Georgia three.

4. When vacancies happen in the Representation from any State, the Executive Authority thereof shall issue Writs of Election to fill such Vacancies.

5. The House of Representatives shall chuse their Speaker and other Officers; and shall have the sole Power of Impeachment.

SECTION III. 1. The Senate of the United States shall be composed of two Senators from each State, chosen by the Legislature thereof, for six Years: and each Senator shall have one Vote.

2. Immediately after they shall be assembled in Consequence of the first Election, they shall be divided as equally as may be into three Classes. The seats of the Senators of the first Class shall be vacated at the Expiration of the second Year, of the second Class at the Expiration of the fourth Year, and of the third Class at the Expiration of the sixth Year, so that one-third may be chosen every second Year; and if Vacancies happen by Resignation, or otherwise, during the Recess of the Legislature of any State, the Executive thereof may make temporary Appointments until the next Meeting of the Legislature, which shall then fill such Vacancies.

3. No person shall be a Senator who shall not have attained to the Age of thirty Years, and been nine Years a Citizen of the United States, and who shall not, when elected, be an Inhabitant of that State for which he shall be chosen.

4. The Vice President of the United States shall be President of the Senate, but shall have no Vote, unless they be equally divided.

5. The Senate shall chuse their other Officers, and also a President pro tempore, in the Absence of the Vice President, or when he shall exercise the Office of President of the United States.

6. The Senate shall have the sole Power to try all Impeachments. When sitting for that Purpose, they shall be on Oath or Affirmation. When the President of the United States is tried, the Chief Justice shall preside: And no Person shall be convicted without the Concurrence of two-thirds of the Members present.

7. Judgment in Cases of Impeachment shall not extend further than to removal from Office, and Disqualification to hold and enjoy any Office of honour, Trust or Profit under the United States: but the Party convicted shall nevertheless be liable and subject to Indictment, Trial, Judgment and Punishment, according to law.

SECTION IV. 1. The Times, Places and Manner of holding Elections for Senators and Representatives, shall be prescribed in each State by the Legislature thereof; but the Congress may at any time by Law make or alter such Regulations, except as to the places of chusing Senators.

2. The Congress shall assemble at least once in every Year, and such Meeting shall be on the first Monday in December, unless they shall by Law appoint a different Day.

SECTION V. 1. Each House shall be the Judge of the Elections, Returns and Qualifications of its own Members, and a Majority of each shall constitute a Quorum to do Business; but a smaller Number may adjourn from day to day, and may be authorized to compel the Attendance of Absent Members, in such Manner, and under such Penalties as each House may provide.

2. Each House may determine the Rules of its Proceedings, punish its Members for disorderly Behaviour, and, with the Concurrence of two thirds, expel a Member.

3. Each House shall keep a Journal of its Proceedings, and from time to time publish the same, excepting such Parts as may in their Judgment require Secrecy ; and the Yeas and Nays of the Members of either House on any question shall, at the Desire of one fifth of those Present, be entered on the Journal.

4. Neither House, during the Session of Congress, shall, without the Consent of the other, adjourn for more than three days, nor to any other Place than that in which the two Houses shall be sitting.

SECTION VI. 1. The Senators and Representatives shall receive a compensation for their Services, to be ascertained by Law, and paid out of the Treasury of the United States. They shall in all Cases, except Treason, Felony and Breach of the Peace, be privileged from Arrest during their Attendance at the Session of their respective Houses, and in going to and returning from the same ; and for any Speech or Debate in either House, they shall not be questioned in any other Place.

2. No Senator or Representative shall, during the Time for which he was elected, be appointed to any civil Office under the Authority of the United States, which shall have been created, or the Emoluments whereof shall have been encreased during such time; and no Person holding any Office under the United States, shall be a Member of either House during his Continuance in Office.

SECTION VII. 1. All Bills for raising Revenue shall originate in the House of Representatives ; but the Senate may propose or concur with Amendments as on other Bills.

2. Every Bill which shall have passed the House of Representatives and the Senate, shall, before it become a law, be presented to the President of the United States ; if he approve he shall sign it, but if not he shall return it, with his Objections to that House in which it shall have originated, who shall enter the Objections at large on their Journal, and proceed to reconsider it. If after such Reconsideration two thirds of that House shall agree to pass the Bill, it shall be sent, together with the Objections, to the other House, by which it shall likewise be reconsidered, and if approved by two thirds of that House, it shall become a Law. But in all such Cases the Votes of both Houses shall be determined by Yeas and Nays, and the Names of the Persons voting for and against the Bill shall be entered on the Journal of each House respectively. If any Bill shall not be returned by the President within ten Days (Sundays excepted) after it shall have been presented to him, the Same shall be a law, in like Manner as if he had signed it, unless the Congress by their Adjournment prevent its Return, in which Case it shall not be a Law.

3. Every Order, Resolution, or Vote to which the Concurrence of the

Senate and House of Representatives may be necessary (except on a question of Adjournment) shall be presented to the President of the United States; and before the Same shall take Effect, shall be approved by him, or being disapproved by him, shall be repassed by two thirds of the Senate and House of Representatives, according to the Rules and Limitations prescribed in the Case of a Bill.

SECTION VIII. The Congress shall have Power

1. To lay and collect Taxes, Duties, Imposts and Excises, to pay the Debts and provide for the common Defence and general Welfare of the United States; but all Duties, Imposts and Excises shall be uniform throughout the United States;

2. To borrow Money on the credit of the United States;

3. To regulate Commerce with foreign Nations, and among the several States, and with the Indian Tribes;

4. To establish an uniform Rule of Naturalization, and uniform Laws on the subject of Bankruptcies throughout the United State;

5. To coin Money, regulate the Value thereof, and of foreign Coin, and fix the Standard of Weights and Measures;

6. To provide for the Punishment of counterfeiting the Securities and current Coin of the United States;

7. To establish Post Offices and post Roads;

8. To promote the progress of Science and useful Arts, by securing for limited Times to Authors and Inventors the exclusive Right to their respective Writings and Discoveries;

9. To constitute Tribunals inferior to the supreme Court;

10. To define and punish Piracies and Felonies committed on the high Seas, and Offences against the Law of Nations;

11. To declare War, grant Letters of Marque and Reprisal, and make Rules concerning Captures on Land and Water;

12. To raise and support Armies, but no Appropriation of Money to that Use shall be for a longer Term than two Years;

13. To provide and maintain a Navy;

14. To make Rules for the Government and Regulation of the land and naval forces;

15. To provide for calling forth the Militia to execute the Laws of the Union, suppress Insurrections and repel Invasions;

16. To provide for organizing, arming, and disciplining, the Militia, and for governing such Part of them as may be employed in the Service of the United States, reserving to the States respectively, the Appointment of the Officers, and the Authority of training the Militia according to the Discipline prescribed by Congress;

17. To exercise exclusive Legislation in all Cases whatsoever, over such District (not exceeding ten Miles square) as may, by Cession of particular States, and the Acceptance of Congress, become the Seat of the Government of the United States, and to exercise like Authority over all Places purchased by the Consent of the Legislature of the

State in which the Same shall be, for the Erection of Forts, Magazines, Arsenals, Dock-Yards, and other needful Buildings;—And

18. To make all Laws which shall be necessary and proper for carrying into Execution the foregoing Powers, and all other Powers vested by this Constitution in the Government of the United States, or in any Department or Officer thereof.

SECTION IX. 1. The Migration or Importation of such Persons as any of the States now existing shall think proper to admit, shall not be prohibited by the Congress prior to the Year one thousand eight hundred and eight, but a Tax or Duty may be imposed on such Importation, not exceeding ten dollars for each Person.

2. The Privilege of the Writ of Habeas Corpus shall not be suspended, unless when in Cases of Rebellion or Invasion the public Safety may require it.

3. No Bill of Attainder or ex post facto Law shall be passed.

4. No Capitation or other direct Tax shall be laid, unless in Proportion to the Census or Enumeration herein before directed to be taken.

5. No Tax or Duty shall be laid on Articles exported from any State.

6 No Preference shall be given by any Regulation of Commerce or Revenue to the Ports of one State over those of another: nor shall Vessels bound to, or from, one State, be obliged to enter, clear, or pay Duties in another.

7. No Money shall be drawn from the Treasury, but in Consequence of Appropriations made by Law; and a regular Statement and Account of the Receipts and Expenditures of all public Money shall be published from time to time.

8. No title of Nobility shall be granted by the United States : And no Person holding any Office of Profit or Trust under them, shall without the Consent of the Congress, accept of any present, Emolument, Office, or Title, of any kind whatever, from any King, Prince, or foreign State.

SECTION X. 1. No State shall enter into any Treaty, Alliance, or Confederation; grant Letters of Marque and Reprisal; coin Money; emit Bills of Credit; make any Thing but gold and silver Coin a Tender in Payment of Debts; pass any Bill of Attainder, ex post facto Law, or Law impairing the Obligation of Contracts, or grant any Title of Nobility.

2. No State shall, without the consent of the Congress, lay any Impost or Duties on Imports or Exports, except what may be absolutely necessary for executing it's inspection Laws : and the net Produce of all Duties and Imposts laid by any State on Imports or Exports, shall be for the Use of the Treasury of the United States; and all such Laws shall be subject to the Revision and Controul of the Congress.

3. No State shall, without the Consent of Congress, lay any duty of Tonnage, keep Troops, or Ships of War in time of Peace, enter into any agreement or Compact with another State, or with a foreign Power,

or engage in War, unless actually invaded, or in such imminent Danger as will not admit of Delay.

ARTICLE II.

SECTION I. 1. The executive Power shall be vested in a President of the United States of America. He shall hold his Office during the Term of four Years, and, together with the Vice President, chosen for the same Term, be elected, as follows:

2. Each State shall appoint, in such Manner as the Legislature thereof may direct, a Number of Electors, equal to the whole Number of Senators and Representatives to which the State may be entitled in the Congress: but no Senator or Representative, or Person holding an Office of Trust or Profit under the United States, shall be appointed an elector.

3. The Electors shall meet in their respective States, and vote by Ballot for two Persons, of whom one at least shall not be an Inhabitant of the same State with themselves. And they shall make a list of all the Persons voted for, and of the number of votes for each; which List they shall sign and certify, and transmit sealed to the Seat of the Government of the United States, directed to the President of the Senate. The President of the Senate shall, in the Presence of the Senate and House of Representatives, open all the Certificates, and the Votes shall then be counted. The Person having the greatest number of Votes shall be the President, if such a number be a Majority of the whole Number of Electors appointed; and if there be more than one who have such Majority, and have an equal number of votes, then the House of Representatives shall immediately chuse by Ballot one of them for President; and if no Person have a Majority, then from the five highest on the List the said House shall in like manner chuse the President. But in chusing the President, the Votes shall be taken by States, the Representation from each State having one Vote: A Quorum for this Purpose shall consist of a Member or Members from two-thirds of the States, and a Majority of all the States shall be necessary to a Choice. In every Case, after the Choice of the President, the Person having the greatest Number of Votes of the Electors shall be the Vice President. But if there should remain two or more who have equal Votes, the Senate shall chuse from them by Ballot the Vice President.

4. Congress may determine the Time of Chusing the Electors, and the Day on which they shall give their Votes; which day shall be the same throughout the United States.

5. No Person except a natural born Citizen, or a Citizen of the United States, at the time of the Adoption of this Constitution, shall be eligible to the Office of President; neither shall any Person be eligible to that Office who shall not have attained to the Age of thirty-five Years, and been fourteed Years a Resident within the United States.

6. In Case of the Removal of the President from Office, or of his Death, Resignation, or Inability to Discharge the Powers and Duties of the said Office, the same shall devolve on the Vice President, and the Congress may by Law provide for the Case of Removal, Death, Resignation, or Inability, both of the President and Vice President, declaring what Officer shall then act as President, and such Officer shall act accordingly, until the Disability be removed, or a President shall be elected.

7. The President shall, at stated Times, receive for his Services, a Compensation, which shall neither be increased nor diminished during the Period for which he shall have been elected, and he shall not receive within that Period any other Emolument from the United States, or any of them.

8. Before he enter on the Execution of his Office, he shall take the following Oath or Affirmation:—

"I do solemnly swear (or affirm) that I will faithfully execute the "Office of President of the United States, and will to the best of my "Ability, preserve, protect and defend the Constitution of the United "States."

SECTION II. 1. The President shall be Commander in Chief of the Army and Navy of the United States, and of the Militia of the several States, when called into the actual Service of the United States; he may require the Opinion, in writing, of the principal Officer in each of the executive Departments, upon any Subject relating to the Duties of their respective Offices, and he shall have power to grant Reprieves and Pardons for Offences against the United States, except in Cases of Impeachment.

2. He shall have Power, by and with the Advice and Consent of the Senate, to make Treaties, provided two thirds of the Senators present concur; and he shall nominate, and by and with the Advice and Consent of the Senate, shall appoint Embassadors, other public Ministers and Consuls, Judges of the supreme Court, and all other Officers of the United States, whose Appointments are not herein otherwise provided for, and which shall be established by Law: but the Congress may by Law vest the Appointment of such inferior Officers, as they think proper, in the President alone, in the Courts of Law, or in the Heads of Departments.

3. The President shall have Power to fill up all Vacancies that may happen during the Recess of the Senate, by granting Commissions which shall expire at the End of their next Session.

SECTION III. He shall from time to time give to the Congress Information of the State of the Union, and recommend to their Consideration such Measures as he shall judge necessary and expedient; he may, on extraordinary Occasions, convene both Houses, or either of them, and in Case of Disagreement between them, with Respect to the time of Adjournment, he may adjourn them to such time as he shall think proper : he shall receive Ambassadors and other public Ministers ; he shall take Care that the Laws be faithfully executed, and shall Commission all the Officers of the United States.

SECTION IV. The President, Vice President and all civil Officers of the United States, shall be removed from Office on Impeachment for, and Conviction of, Treason, Bribery, or other high Crimes and Misdemeanors.

ARTICLE III.

SECTION I. The judicial Power of the United States, shall be vested in one supreme Court, and in such inferior Courts as the Congress may from time to time ordain and establish. The Judges, both of the supreme and inferior Courts, shall hold their Offices during good Behavior, and shall, at stated Times, receive for their Services, a Compensation, which shall not be diminished during their Continuance in Office.

SECTION II. 1. The judicial Power shall extend to all Cases, in Law and Equity, arising under this Constitution, the Laws of the United States, and Treaties made, or which shall be made, under their Authority; to all Cases affecting Ambassadors, other public Ministers, and Consuls ; to all Cases of admiralty and maritime Jurisdiction ;—to Controversies to which the United States shall be a Party ;—to Controversies between two or more States ;—between a State and Citizens of another State ;—between Citizens of different States,—between Citizens of the same State claiming Lands under Grants of different States, and between a State, or the Citizens thereof, and foreign States, Citizens or Subjects.

2. In all Cases affecting Ambassadors, other public Ministers and Consuls, and those in which a State shall be a Party, the supreme Court shall have original Jurisdiction. In all the other Cases before mentioned, the supreme Court shall have appellate Jurisdiction, both as to Law and fact, with such Exceptions, and under such Regulations as the Congress shall make.

3. The trial of all Crimes, except in Cases of Impeachment, shall be by Jury ; and such trial shall be held in the State where the said Crimes shall have been committed ; but when not committed within any State, the Trial shall be at such Place or Places as the Congress may by Law have directed.

SECTION III. 1. Treason against the United States, shall consist only in levying War against them, or in adhering to their Enemies, giving them Aid and Comfort. No Person shall be convicted of Treason unless on the Testimony of two Witnesses to the same overt Act, or on Confession in open Court.

2. The Congress shall have Power to declare the Punishment of Treason, but no Attainder of Treason shall work Corruption of Blood, or Forfeiture except during the Life of the Person attainted.

ARTICLE IV.

SECTION I. Full faith and Credit shall be given in each State to the public Acts, Records, and judicial Proceedings of every other State. And the Congress may by general Laws prescribe the Manner in which such Acts, Records and Proceedings shall be proved, and the Effect thereof.

SECTION II. 1. The Citizens of each State shall be entitled to all Privileges and Immunities of Citizens in the several States.

2. A Person charged in any State with Treason, Felony, or other Crime, who shall flee from Justice, and be found in another State, shall on Demand of the executive Authority of the State from which he fled, be delivered up, to be removed to the State having Jurisdiction of the Crime.

3. No Person held to Service or Labour in one State, under the Laws thereof, escaping into another, shall, in Consequence of any Law or Regulation therein, be discharged from such Service or Labour, but shall be delivered up on Claim of the Party to whom such Service or Labour may be due.

SECTION III. 1. New States may be admitted by the Congress into this Union; but no new State shall be formed or erected within the Jurisdiction of any other State; nor any State be formed by the Junction of two or more States, or Parts of States, without the Consent of the Legislatures of the States concerned as well as of the Congress.

2. The Congress shall have Power to dispose of and make all needful Rules and Regulations respecting the Territory or other Property belonging to the United States; and nothing in this Constitution shall be so construed as to Prejudice any Claims of the United States, or of any particular State.

SECTION IV. The United States shall guarantee to every State in this Union a Republican Form of Government, and shall protect each of them against Invasion; and on Application of the Legislature, or of the Executive (when the Legislature cannot be convened) against domestic Violence.

ARTICLE V.

The Congress, whenever two thirds of both Houses shall deem it necessary, shall propose Amendments to this Constitution, or, on the Application of the Legislatures of two thirds of the several States, shall call a Convention for proposing Amendments, which, in either Case, shall be valid to all Intents and Purposes, as Part of this Constitution, when ratified by the Legislatures of three fourths of the several States, or by Conventions in three fourths thereof, as the one or the other Mode of Ratification may be proposed by the Congress: Provided that no Amendment which may be made prior to the Year one

thousand eight hundred and eight shall in any Manner affect the first and fourth Clauses in the Ninth Section of the first Article; and that no State, without its Consent, shall be deprived of its equal Suffrage in the Senate.

ARTICLE VI.

1. All Debts contracted and Engagements entered into, before the Adoption of this Constitution, shall be as valid against the United States under this Constitution, as under the Confederation.

2. This Constitution, and the Laws of the United States which shall be made in Pursuance thereof; and all Treaties made, or which shall be made, under the authority of the United States, shall be the supreme Law of the Land; and the Judges in every State shall be bound thereby, any Thing in the Constitution or Laws of any State to the Contrary notwithstanding.

3. The Senators and Representatives before mentioned, and the Members of the several State Legislatures, and all executive and judicial Officers, both of the United States and of the several States, shall be bound by Oath or Affirmation, to support this Constitution; but no religious test shall ever be required as a Qualification to any Office or public Trust under the United States.

ARTICLE VII.

The Ratification of the Conventions of nine States, shall be sufficient for the Establishment of this Constitution between the States so ratifying the Same.